Third World Approaches to International Law

This book addresses the themes of praxis and the ro... ...ternational lawyers as intellectuals and political actors engaging with questions of justice for Third World peoples. The book brings together 12 contributions from a total of 15 scholars working in the TWAIL (Third World Approaches to International Law) network or tradition. It includes chapters from some of the pioneering Third World jurists who have led this field since the time of decolonization, as well as prominent emerging scholars in the field. Broadly, the TWAIL orientation understands praxis as the relationship between what we say as scholars and what we do – as the inextricability of theory from lived experience. Understood in this way, praxis is central to TWAIL, as TWAIL scholars strive to reconcile international law's promise of justice with the proliferation of injustice in the world it purports to govern. Reconciliation occurs in the realm of praxis and TWAIL scholars engage in a variety of struggles, including those for greater self-awareness, disciplinary upheaval, and institutional resistance and transformation. The rich diversity of contributions in the book engage these themes and questions through the various prisms of international institutional engagement, world trade and investment law, critical comparative law, Palestine solidarity and decolonization, judicial education, revolutionary struggle against imperial sovereignty, Muslim Marxism, Third World intellectual traditions, Global South constitutionalism, and migration.

This book was originally published as a special issue of *Third World Quarterly*.

Usha Natarajan is Assistant Professor of International Law and Associate Director of the Centre for Migration and Refugee Studies at the American University in Cairo, Egypt. Her research is multidisciplinary, utilising Third World and postcolonial approaches to international law to provide an interrelated understanding of the relationship between international law and issues of development, migration, environment, and conflict.

John Reynolds is Lecturer in International Law at the National University of Ireland, Maynooth. His research focuses on the operation of international law in states of emergency and in contexts of conflict, crisis, and coloniality.

Amar Bhatia is an Assistant Professor at Osgoode Hall Law School, York University, Canada. His research focuses on transnational migration in a settler-colonial context and the intersection of immigration law, Aboriginal law, treaty relations, and Indigenous legal traditions.

Sujith Xavier joined the University of Windsor Faculty of Law in January of 2014 as an Assistant Professor. His interests span domestic and international legal theory, international law, Third World Approaches to International Law (TWAIL), as well as the intersections of law and society with an emphasis on race, colonialism and imperialism, gender, and sexuality.

ThirdWorlds

Edited by Shahid Qadir, *University of London, UK*

ThirdWorlds will focus on the political economy, development and cultures of those parts of the world that have experienced the most political, social, and economic upheaval, and which have faced the greatest challenges of the postcolonial world under globalisation: poverty, displacement and diaspora, environmental degradation, human and civil rights abuses, war, hunger, and disease.

ThirdWorlds serves as a signifier of oppositional emerging economies and cultures ranging from Africa, Asia, Latin America, Middle East, and even those 'Souths' within a larger perceived North, such as the U.S. South and Mediterranean Europe. The study of these otherwise disparate and discontinuous areas, known collectively as the Global South, demonstrates that as globalisation pervades the planet, the south, as a synonym for subalterity, also transcends geographical and ideological frontier.

For a complete list of titles in this series, please visit https://www.routledge.com/series/TWQ

Recent titles in the series include:

Corruption in the Aftermath of War
Edited by Jonas Lindberg and Camilla Orjuela

Everyday Energy Politics in Central Asia and the Caucasus
Citizens' Needs, Entitlements and Struggles for Access
Edited by David Gullette and Jeanne Féaux de la Croix

The UN and the Global South, 1945 and 2015
Edited by Thomas G. Weiss and Pallavi Roy

The Green Economy in the Global South
Edited by Stefano Ponte and Daniel Brockington

Food Sovereignty
Convergence and Contradictions, Condition and Challenges
Edited by Eric Holt-Giménez, Alberto Alonso-Fradejas, Todd Holmes and Martha Jane Robbins

The International Politics of Ebola
Edited by Anne Roemer-Mahler and Simon Rushton

Rising Powers and South-South Cooperation
Edited by Kevin Gray and Barry K. Gills

The 'Local Turn' in Peacebuilding
The Liberal Peace Challenged
Edited by Joakim Öjendal, Isabell Schierenbeck and Caroline Hughes

China's Contingencies and Globalization
Edited by Changgang Guo, Liu Debin and Jan Nederveen Pieterse

The Power of Human Rights/The Human Rights of Power
Edited by Louiza Odysseos and Anna Selmeczi

Class Dynamics of Development
Edited by Jonathan Pattenden, Liam Campling, Satoshi Miyamura and Benjamin Selwyn

Fragility, Aid, and State-building
Understanding Diverse Trajectories
Edited by Rachel M. Gisselquist

Third World Approaches to International Law
On Praxis and the Intellectual
Edited by Usha Natarajan, John Reynolds, Amar Bhatia and Sujith Xavier

Aid to Support Fragile States
The Challenge of Chronic State Weakness
Edited by Rachel M. Gisselquist

Third World Approaches to International Law

On Praxis and the Intellectual

Edited by
Usha Natarajan, John Reynolds, Amar Bhatia and Sujith Xavier

Routledge
Taylor & Francis Group
LONDON AND NEW YORK

First published 2018 by Routledge

2 Park Square, Milton Park, Abingdon, Oxfordshire OX14 4RN
52 Vanderbilt Avenue, New York, NY 10017

Routledge is an imprint of the Taylor & Francis Group, an informa business

First issued in paperback 2019

British Library Cataloguing in Publication Data
A catalogue record for this book is available from the British Library

ISBN 13: 978-1-138-04072-4 (hbk)
ISBN 13: 978-0-367-88923-4 (pbk)

Typeset in Myriad Pro
by RefineCatch Limited, Bungay, Suffolk

Publisher's Note
The publisher accepts responsibility for any inconsistencies that may have arisen during the conversion of this book from journal articles to book chapters, namely the possible inclusion of journal terminology.

Disclaimer
Every effort has been made to contact copyright holders for their permission to reprint material in this book. The publishers would be grateful to hear from any copyright holder who is not here acknowledged and will undertake to rectify any errors or omissions in future editions of this book.

Contents

Citation Information

The chapters in this book were originally published in *Third World Quarterly*, volume 37, issue 11 (2016). When citing this material, please use the original page numbering for each article, as follows:

Chapter 1

Foreword: Third World Approaches to International Law (TWAIL) special issue
Richard Falk
Third World Quarterly, volume 37, issue 11 (2016), pp. 1943–1945

Chapter 2

Introduction: TWAIL - on praxis and the intellectual
Usha Natarajan, John Reynolds, Amar Bhatia and Sujith Xavier
Third World Quarterly, volume 37, issue 11 (2016), pp. 1946–1956

Chapter 3

The Third World intellectual in praxis: confrontation, participation, or operation behind enemy lines?
Georges Abi-Saab
Third World Quarterly, volume 37, issue 11 (2016), pp. 1957–1971

Chapter 4

On fighting for global justice: the role of a Third World international lawyer
M. Sornarajah
Third World Quarterly, volume 37, issue 11 (2016), pp. 1972–1989

Chapter 5

Regulation of armed conflict: critical comparativism
Nesrine Badawi
Third World Quarterly, volume 37, issue 11 (2016), pp. 1990–2009

Chapter 6

Decolonisation, dignity and development aid: a judicial education experience in Palestine
Reem Bahdi and Mudar Kassis
Third World Quarterly, volume 37, issue 11 (2016), pp. 2010–2027

Chapter 7
The conjunctural in international law: the revolutionary struggle against semi-peripheral sovereignty in Iraq
Ali Hammoudi
Third World Quarterly, volume 37, issue 11 (2016), pp. 2028–2046

Chapter 8
Mir-Said Sultan-Galiev and the idea of Muslim Marxism: empire, Third World(s) and praxis
Vanja Hamzić
Third World Quarterly, volume 37, issue 11 (2016), pp. 2047–2060

Chapter 9
International lawyers in the aftermath of disasters: inheriting from Radhabinod Pal and Upendra Baxi
Adil Hasan Khan
Third World Quarterly, volume 37, issue 11 (2016), pp. 2061–2079

Chapter 10
The South of Western constitutionalism: a map ahead of a journey
Zoran Oklopcic
Third World Quarterly, volume 37, issue 11 (2016), pp. 2080–2097

Chapter 11
Disrupting civility: amateur intellectuals, international lawyers and TWAIL as praxis
John Reynolds
Third World Quarterly, volume 37, issue 11 (2016), pp. 2098–2118

Chapter 12
Migration, development and security within racialised global capitalism: refusing the balance game
Adrian A. Smith
Third World Quarterly, volume 37, issue 11 (2016), pp. 2119–2138

Notes on Contributors

Georges Abi-Saab is Emeritus Professor of International Law, Graduate Institute of International Studies, Geneva; Honorary Professor, Cairo University Faculty of Law; Member of the Institute of International Law; and winner of the 2013 Hague Prize.

Nesrine Badawi is Assistant Professor of Public and International Law at the American University in Cairo, Egypt.

Reem Bahdi has been a faculty member at Windsor University, Canada, since 2002 and she is currently an Associate Professor in the Faculty of Law.

Amar Bhatia is an Assistant Professor at Osgoode Hall Law School, York University, Toronto, Canada.

Richard Falk is Albert G. Milbank Professor of International Law and Practice, Emeritus at Princeton University, USA.

Ali Hammoudi is a PhD candidate at Osgoode Hall Law School, York University, Toronto, Canada.

Vanja Hamzić is Senior Lecturer in the School of Oriental and African Studies (SOAS), University of London, UK.

Mudar Kassis has been a faculty member at Birzeit University, Palestine, since 1992. He is currently Director of the MA Programme in Democracy and Human Rights, and co-Director of the Windsor-Birzeit Dignity Initiative (an international interdisciplinary research partnership).

Adil Hasan Khan was recently awarded his PhD in International Studies by the Graduate Institute of International and Development Studies (IHEID), Geneva, Switzerland.

Usha Natarajan is Assistant Professor of International Law and Associate Director of the Centre for Migration and Refugee Studies at the American University in Cairo, Egypt.

Zoran Oklopcic teaches at the Department of Law and Legal Studies at Carleton University, Ottawa, Canada.

John Reynolds is Lecturer in International Law at the National University of Ireland, Maynooth.

Adrian A. Smith has taught Law and Political Economy at Carleton University in Ottawa, Canada, since 2011.

M. Sornarajah is CJ Koh Professor at the Faculty of Law, National University of Singapore and Visiting Professor at the Centre for Human Rights, London School of Economics, UK.

Sujith Xavier joined the University of Windsor Faculty of Law in January of 2014 as an Assistant Professor.

Foreword: Third World Approaches to International Law (TWAIL)

Richard Falk

This Special Issue of *Third World Quarterly* consists of a selection of papers initially presented at a 2015 conference under the auspices of TWAIL (Third World Approaches to International Law) at the American University in Cairo, and later revised for publication. TWAIL has been in existence for over 20 years, holding periodic conferences since 1995 and spearheading a self-conscious effort by international jurists from Asia, Africa, and Latin America to rethink international law from the perspective of the Global South. The Cairo gathering has added significance as the first TWAIL conference to be held in a Third World academic environment. Egypt also offered a geographical setting that called dramatic attention to a pattern of regional turbulence that cannot begin to be understood without a keen appreciation of both colonial legacies and post-colonial struggles that together constitute the unfinished agenda of decolonisation.

Contrary to the widespread impression that colonialism ends when national flags fly from governmental buildings, it is a premise of TWAIL that *after* political independence, the most difficult of challenges arise, above all decolonising the mind of both colonisers and colonised. In this sense, international legal studies and praxis is a crucial site of struggle as, by the persistence of Western-oriented international legal regimes, much of the Global South has remained trapped within structures evolved during the colonial era.

In this respect, it is notable that the sub-title given to the TWAIL Cairo Conference was 'On Praxis and the Intellectual'. And the explicit call was to awaken the intellectual (and not just as 'legal scholar'') to her or his role as 'political actor' and 'animator of praxis', specified to involve 'reflection, agitation, and transformative action'.[1] It would be unimaginable for a Western professional association of lawyers to articulate its goals in such language. The prevailing international law claim in the West remains linked to the false consciousness of universalism, as if there is no hegemony or hierarchy in international life that needs to be taken into account when establishing the norms of substance and procedure that comprise international law. Further, the idea that international law scholars and experts should dare to advocate and agitate goes sharply against the grain of Western pretensions of 'professionalism', 'detachment', and 'objectivity'. Even the idea that an international law expert should self-identify as an 'intellectual' is completely alien to the identity claims of professionalism, which projects primarily the role of a law person to be either one of technician of the law or more characteristically to serve the state as apologist and ardent supporter of governmental and private sector elites. It is thus not surprising that the excellent articles published in this issue are notable for their responsiveness to those social forces that are actively resisting Western hegemony, and are doing their best to reframe international law in light of emancipatory and transformative goals whose undisguised primary motive is not to interpret the world but to change it (*pace* Marx).

As someone who has lived and worked in the West as a dissident scholar and political activist, my outlook has become progressively more closely aligned with that of TWAIL, and thus more separated from my mainly conservative academic and governmental colleagues here in the Global North. For me, venturing into the realms of praxis became a moral imperative in the course of my opposition to the Vietnam War during the 1960s and early 1970s. It was not enough to analyse the juridical issues to oppose American interventionism, it was at least as important to speak at rallies and to exhibit solidarity with the Vietnamese struggle against the remnants of French colonialism. So long as my views were confined to academic circles, I was tolerated as a misguided critic; but when I went further, and started acting as an engaged citizen, I crossed a red line that placed me in a domain cordoned off from the mainstream, a condition best called 'political quarantine'. While so quarantined I found myself excluded from realms of 'responsible' debate, and therefore no longer welcome in influential media domains nor invited to testify as an expert before congressional committees.

My exclusion intensified later when I was seen as supportive of the Iranian Revolution and, much more so, when playing a public role as Israeli critic and supporter of the Palestinian struggle for a just and sustainable peace. Such praxis was deemed to have crossed a *substantive* red line that tightened the already restrictive quarantine, adding unpleasant defamatory campaigns, which presented me to the world as a notorious anti-Semite and self-hating Jew. This kind of personal abuse reached its climax during the six years (2008–2014) that I served as United Nations Special Rapporteur for Palestine Human Rights on behalf of the UN Human Rights Council. To bear witness before the world to the ugly truths of the oppressive Israeli occupation of Palestine, and to the resulting Palestinian suffering, was to operate in forbidden territory and suffer adverse consequences. I found, however, that exposing injustice and standing behind my witnessing role was intellectually and personally fulfilling, and so the pressures mounted against me actually deepened my commitments, rather than fulfilling their purpose of intimidation and silence.

I owe this sense of engagement to my friendship and collaborative closeness with a series of extraordinary Third World intellectuals, both among such formative and stalwart TWAIL figures as Mohammed Bedjaoui, Upendra Baxi, B. S. Chimni, Georges Abi-Saab, Christopher Weeramantry, and many others; as well as kindred non-TWAIL intellectual warriors from the Global South including Edward Said, Eqbal Ahmed, Ashis Nandy, Rajni Kothari, and Walden Bello. It is such communities of engaged intellectuals that must forge not only activist networks of solidarity but also give shape to an empowering radical epistemology that liberates international law from its colonial and elitist shackles and validates the transformative and liberationist potential of international law. The essays making up this Special Issue deserve a close reading by all who would embark on this journey, beset as it is by obstacles, yet enlivened by an inspiring alignment with ongoing struggles against injustice and exploitation, and emboldened by its visions of a just, ecologically sustainable, and spiritually enhancing human future that benefits the entire species.

Disclosure statement

No potential conflict of interest was reported by the author.

Note

1. TWAIL Cairo Conference, 'On Praxis and the Intellectual', Call for Papers: http://www.uwindsor.ca/twail2015/

Introduction: TWAIL - on praxis and the intellectual

Usha Natarajan , John Reynolds , Amar Bhatia and Sujith Xavier

ABSTRACT
This Special Issue emerges from the Third World Approaches to International Law (TWAIL) Cairo Conference in 2015 and addresses the conference theme, 'On Praxis and the Intellectual', by focusing on different aspects of the intellectual as a political actor. In introducing this Issue, we provide some background to the TWAIL network, movement, event, and publications; and delineate our own understandings of scholarly praxis as editors and conference organisers. Broadly, we understand praxis as the relationship between what we say as scholars and what we do – as the inextricability of theory from lived experience. Understood in this way, praxis is central to TWAIL, as TWAIL scholars strive to reconcile international law's promise of justice with the proliferation of injustice in the world it purports to govern. Reconciliation occurs in the realm of praxis and TWAIL scholars engage in a variety of struggles, including those for greater self-awareness, disciplinary upheaval, and institutional resistance and transformation.

I. Conspiring in Cairo

Third World Approaches to International Law (TWAIL) is a movement encompassing scholars and practitioners of international law and policy who are concerned with issues related to the Global South. The scholarly agendas associated with TWAIL are diverse, but the general theme of its interventions is to unpack and deconstruct the colonial legacies of international law and engage in efforts to decolonise the lived realities of the peoples of the Global South. The movement coalesced in the 1990s through an alliance of scholars committed to critically investigating the mutually constitutive relationship between international law and the Third World/Global South.[1] For legal projects operating at the margins of the mainstream discipline, the TWAIL network enables solidarity and mutual support through a shared political commitment to advocating for the interests of the Global South. It endeavours to give voice to viewpoints systemically underrepresented or silenced. The group first met at Harvard Law School in 1997 and has grown rapidly since then, with conferences at Osgoode Hall Law School in 2001, Albany Law School in 2007, University of British Colombia in 2008, Université Paris 1 Panthéon-Sorbonne in 2010, and Oregon Law School in 2011. This Special Issue stems from the TWAIL Conference held in Cairo on 21–24 February 2015.[2] The Cairo conference marked a significant, albeit belated, milestone as the first time TWAIL scholars have formally convened in the Global South. The Cairo conference was also the largest gathering of TWAIL scholars to date, with 85 speakers from five continents uniting to reflect on the conference theme, 'On Praxis and the Intellectual'.

Against a backdrop of the ongoing revolutionary struggles, conflicts, and contestations across the Middle East and North Africa, we wanted to focus on the intellectual as a political actor: the animation of praxis, broadly conceived as reflection, agitation, and transformative action. What is the role of the intellectual in political life? What is the relationship between our scholarly endeavours and societal structures; whether preserving the status quo, shaping reform, or advocating for radical change? The theme necessitated self-reflection, as TWAIL has sought to distinguish itself from other critical legal approaches through its political and transformative commitments. Building upon past TWAIL meetings,[3] and with praxis in mind, this conference provided the space for scholars and practitioners to continue to collaborate and conspire on multiple registers.

We were overwhelmed by the quality and volume of submissions received in response to our call for papers. Over four days, 19 panels brought together eminent and emerging scholars from all over the world to address diverse themes including the politics of writing history, subalternity, Indigenous movements, the legacies of the Bandung Conference, the environment, Palestine, international institutions, Islamic law, national and international criminal law, local and global constitutional law, transitional justice, migration and asylum law, pedagogy and legal education, economic governance, and private ordering. The conference led to two follow-up publication workshops and produced four publications[4] beginning with this Special Issue, which commences with Professor Georges Abi-Saab's closing keynote address and Professor Muthucumaraswamy Sornarajah's plenary address, followed by nine articles that built on presentations made at the conference.[5]

In addition to reflecting on the conference theme, the Cairo conference – as with previous TWAIL conferences – was an opportunity for the network to take stock and look to the future. It provided a forum for the TWAIL community to both reconnect and grow. Seeking to deepen and reimagine engagement with underexplored alliances, we wanted to engage with Indigenous movements, environmental issues, and transnational intellectual and political actors in the Middle East and North Africa. We also pursued relationships with potential interdisciplinary allies in cognate fields, focusing on interdisciplinary approaches to population movement. TWAIL conferences have attempted to be opportunities for building useful links between like-minded networks and resources in the global North with those in Africa, Asia, and Latin America in mutually beneficial ways. In reviewing the preparation and correspondence for the conference and workshops, it remains clear that our aspirations for wide inclusion and a sharp focus on praxis were not without their challenges, which included limited funding, visa barriers, political instability and insecurity, long-distance travel, unilingual proceedings, translation costs, and editorial and political differences, among other things. While the final programme and publications reveal some progress along desired lines, they also show that much more remains to be done, reflecting only a partial achievement of our goals as well as the limits of our roles as momentary organisers within an organically evolving scholarly movement. Nonetheless, each successive TWAIL gathering has sought, and will continue to grow, alliances and solidarity between international lawyers and scholars committed to protecting the interests and amplifying the voices of the peoples and movements systematically excluded from, and by, international law. This form of scholarly relationship building serves as the main register for our praxis as conference organisers and editors, though it forms only a small part of the wide spectrum of institutional and social movement praxis that conference participants engage with in their scholarly work and wider lives.

II. Diversities of praxis

The wider theme of praxis was present throughout the four days of the conference. The influence of many formative theorists and exponents of praxis loomed large, from Marx and Gramsci to Arendt and Fanon, but perhaps none more so than Paulo Freire. 'Reflection and action' is a mantra of *Pedagogy of the Oppressed*, where praxis is described as '*reflection* and *action* directed at the structures to be transformed'.[6] The oppressed, writes Freire, 'whose task it is to struggle for their liberation together with those who show true solidarity, must acquire a critical awareness of oppression through the praxis of this struggle'.[7] For international legal scholars, activists, and practitioners whose work is animated by solidarity with oppressed peoples, a critical awareness of international law's role in such oppression is vital if the law is to be a terrain of transformative struggle. Over the course of the conference, we heard varied articulations of this critical awareness, including the idea that 'if you don't do international law, international law will do you', evoking the central TWAIL themes of counter-hegemony and resistance. Also resurfacing was the question of how TWAIL understands its relationship with Critical Legal Studies, a movement strongly influential on TWAIL scholars but sometimes subject to critique for its disconnection from material realities. In the Middle Eastern context, the legacy of Lebanese teacher and intellectual Hassan Hamdan (aka Mahdi Amel) was resonant.[8] Mahdi Amel brought Marxism to the homes, villages, mosques, and tobacco farms of south Lebanon in the 1970s, but constantly emphasised the importance of the colonised Arab world. Rather than importing concepts wholesale, he adapted and innovated in order to situate these philosophies of praxis within their own local realities.

This latter sense is closest to our understanding of praxis as the relationship between what we say and what we do, as the inextricability of theory from lived experience. Understood in this way, praxis is central to TWAIL as TWAIL scholars have argued that – from its foundational precepts to its contemporary discourse, from its disciplines and institutions to its operationalisation and implementation – international law contributes to actualising injustice and misery in the lives of Third World peoples while professing to do the opposite. After making this argument, TWAIL scholars attempt to reconcile what we say as international lawyers with what we do by engaging in a variety of struggles, including those for greater self-awareness, disciplinary upheaval, and institutional resistance and transformation.

The Cairo conference generated multidisciplinary and intersecting debates revolving around this axis of praxis, with many rich and diverse articulations of praxis itself, from the minute and technical and pragmatic, to the grand and theoretical and utopian. Subjects of particular contemporary interest were concerns about environmental justice in an era of climate change and increasing ecological degradation, as well as the not-unrelated issue of population movement - whether regular and irregular labour migration, development-induced or environment-induced displacement, or mass and protracted forced displacement of particular concern in the Arab region. These subjects and others generated conversations about how we theorise the state and the international order, and what kind of alternative sovereignties, non-sovereignty, or post-sovereignty we can imagine – debates destined to continue given the nature of urgent global challenges. The broad spectrum of ideas spanned in Cairo ranged from Indigenous conceptions of spirituality and responsibility, to social movement enactments of radical democracy, to visions of a new international economic anarchy that pluralises our economic thinking and challenges the orthodoxies of the prevailing neoliberal (dis)order.

We also grappled with more immediate praxical questions of if, how, and when to deploy international legal argument, whether as sword, shield, or strategy of rupture. The conference engaged explicitly with three main registers of praxis pertinent to the international law scholar: political engagement with international institutions, scholarly engagement, and pedagogy. On engagement with international institutions, approaches ranged from participation for subversive purposes or transformative purposes, via actively resisting international institutions, to ignoring them altogether. Obiora Okafor's opening keynote address examined praxis beyond, but not necessarily without, the academy, and the limits and possibilities of 'TWAILing' the UN, reflecting on his experiences as the then Vice-Chair, now Chair, of the UN Human Rights Council Advisory Committee.[9] On scholarly engagement, we reflected on praxis as here and now in our scholarship and our intellectual encounters, as well as our constitution of disciplinary expertise, from the politics of publication, citation, syllabus construction, and event organisation, to those of hiring, admissions, and collaboration. The importance of pedagogy as praxis was also highlighted, with emphasis on intergenerational legacies and on teaching international law in ways that allow Third World struggles and perspectives to emerge organically through common sensibilities. Our discussions and panels approached the issue of praxis through, among other things, reflecting on the legacy of the Bandung Conference upon its sixtieth anniversary; addressing TWAIL's own subalterns and biases (including issues of Indigeneity, gender, and caste); focusing on private spheres of ordering and governance; and learning from operations of praxis in Islamic Law; with each pointing in its own way towards what TWAIL praxis may entail.

III. The conference Special Issue

On the back of these rich exchanges, we are delighted to introduce this Special Issue comprised of selected papers from the conference, which we hope goes some way toward representing the wonderful diversity of themes and approaches that we heard in Cairo. The issue opens with the contributions of Georges Abi-Saab and Muthucumaraswamy Sornarajah, whose closing keynote panel in Cairo produced a remarkable conversation between two formative Third World voices in international law. While their remarks in the debate were of relevance to international law more generally, both focused on their experience with international tribunals and dispute resolution, particularly in the field of international investment law. Abi-Saab outlined the possibility of infiltration and operation 'behind enemy lines', with Sornarajah holding that compromise is impossible and we should never concede or move to the middle ground. The keynotes generated discussions that teased out many of the crucial dilemmas of tactics and strategy, resistance and reform, and nuances in between; with areas of disagreement indicating fruitful avenues for ongoing inquiry.

These themes are reflected in their written pieces here. Abi-Saab begins with a 'three act psychodrama' surveying the Third World's ups and downs in international law from formal decolonisation through to the recent economic crisis and contemporary challenges. He then reflects on some of the different tactics available to the Third World intellectual in praxis by looking back on some of his experiences over the last five decades as a judge, arbitrator, teacher, scholar, and member of his national delegation. Sornarajah delineates the techniques used by adherents of neoliberal international law to protect and conserve their interests, and advocates a confrontational response. He identifies a framework of common contemporary concerns around which Third World lawyers could build collectivity and solidarity – concerns that centre on the operations of private power that increasingly fashion international law.

Following these two viewpoints, the issue's first full length article by Nesrine Badawi advocates for a praxis of critical comparativism as a means of better understanding legal paradigms and the biases and blind spots that underlie them. Badawi undertakes a comparison of international humanitarian law with Islamic laws regulating armed conflict, building on contextual and critical interpretations to illustrate the operations of power in both fields. Her analyses of *jihād* overcome the shortcomings of functional comparativism through her consistent refusal to essentialise either Islamic law or international humanitarian law. By not treating international law as the objective benchmark against which other legal systems are measured, Badawi sheds light usefully on how violence is channelled and legitimised through both fields. The article opens much needed space for a plurality of understandings of the potentialities and shortcomings of both Islamic laws of war and international humanitarian law, and at a time when the regulation of armed conflict is of increasing interest across the Middle East and North Africa.

Reem Bahdi and Mudar Kassis assess the prospects for decolonisation in Palestine through the example of a judicial education initiative seeking to promote dignity within a colonial condition overlaid by the paradox of development aid. This article specifically focuses on the authors' experiences organising the Karamah (dignity) initiative aimed at judicial education in the Palestinian justice system. Among other outcomes, the project afforded members of the Palestinian judiciary the opportunity to resist doing the 'dirty work' of occupation and otherwise exacerbating the indignities of everyday life for their fellow Palestinians. In a context of occupation and development aid that simultaneously reinforces and obscures the colonial condition, the authors emphasise the inescapable hurdles of performing praxis (and not just solidarity) on such colonial terrain. In this vein, Bahdi and Kassis' emphasis on judicial dignity and professionalisation-under-occupation serve as interesting counterpoints to Reynolds' contribution pointing to when the expected 'civility' of 'professional intellectuals' contributes to stymieing decolonisation efforts in Palestine.

John Reynolds' article interrogates a spectrum of international lawyers as public intellectuals, from traditional and professional intellectuals to organic and amateur intellectuals, through the lens of solidarity for Palestine. Moving from these larger archetypes to the specific examples of the Salaita and Schabas affairs, this article rehabilitates the notion of partisan, subversive, 'guerrilla' intellectuals operating within international law as a space for social movements. In recounting the repressive use of 'civility' to arrest academic freedom, Reynolds also demonstrates the limits of liberal legality that ruptures when truth is spoken, and tweeted, to power. The article engages with a running concern throughout this conference and Special Issue of how to contend with the threat of cooption, 'mainstreaming', and silencing of the language of struggle and resistance; and the negotiation of such risks through directed outrage and incivility when faced with atrocity in an uncivil world. Ultimately, the article concludes by way of contrast between the different types of intellectuals and the different spaces and tactics of praxis for anticolonial lawyers, both within current solidarity campaigns for Palestine and in contemplation of actual decolonisation that is yet to come.

Ali Hammoudi brings us back to an earlier register of decolonisation in the Middle East context. His piece tells a story of resistance to colonialism, and rejection of international legal instrumentation in the form of the treaty. The 1948 *wathba* in Iraq – mass mobilisation against the revised Anglo–Iraq Treaty – is situated as an episode of 'conjunctural resistance' against the semi-colonial governance that had been constructed by the Mandate system. In refusing to accept this unequal treaty, the Iraqi masses sought a broader liberation from the semi-peripheral sovereignty that had been juridically manufactured under British administration. Hammoudi emphasises the centrality of the Iraqi labour movement to this revolutionary move to subvert the imperialist strains of international law, and the importance of situating it within the broader conjuncture of decolonisation in the international legal order. In doing so, the article challenges what the author sees as the narrowness of certain TWAIL accounts of Third World resistance and calls for more attention to be paid to the structural and conjunctural dynamics of such resistance. This prompts reflection on how we view and study resistance to colonial ordering and international law, and how this in turn may help our analysis of international law's history and contemporary practices in its making and unmaking.

Vanja Hamzić follows this with a compelling account of the early twentieth century life and work of Tatar Muslim and Bolshevik intellectual and revolutionary, Mir-Said Sultan-Galiev. This article draws on Sultan-Galiev's praxis to rehabilitate the idea of Muslim Marxism and to trace the connections between Marxist thought on socio-economic justice and Muslim understandings of belonging, class consciousness and socio-political selfhood. Hamzić traces these syntheses of Muslim and communist lifeworlds in Sultan-Galiev's oeuvre, and situates them especially 'in the Worlds designated as Third'. In the context of Tatar resistance to Russian imperialism, Sultan-Galiev's revival of the *jadīd*ist concealment practice of *satr* – as a strategic means of protecting religious faith and anti-colonial commitments in order to evade censure and political violence – offers a fascinating window into his particular Muslim subjectivity and praxis. With this analysis, Hamzić provides reason for us to reflect upon and rethink accepted contemporary narratives on Muslim social and political consciousness.

Adil Hasan Khan calls for a close attentiveness to our inheritance from previous generations of Third World scholars as a means of understanding how to more ethically respond to 'disastrous times' present and past. He argues that the importance given to legacy is more than just an enduring characteristic of the TWAIL movement, but rather it is an indispensable part of a just and effective praxis in the present. Khan undertakes a sympathetic yet nuanced assessment of the conduct and scholarship of Radhabinod Pal and Upendra Baxi in the wake of two disasters: respectively, the nuclear holocausts in Hiroshima and Nagasaki and fire-bombing of Tokyo, and the massive Bhopal industrial disaster. Through these two studies, Khan illustrates that our framing and contextualising of the past and how we understand its relationship to the present affects among other things our capacity for compassion and responsiveness to suffering. That is to say, through our conduct, international lawyers participate in constructing and producing 'disasters'. In the difficult task of attempting to formulate a responsible, just, and useful disciplinary response from the point of view of those directly engaged in the struggle to survive disastrous times, Khan directs that we would be wise to learn from our ancestry.

Khan's piece is followed by an important contribution from Zoran Oklopcic which examines the field of constitutional studies. This paper addresses a significant gap in reflection and scholarly praxis on constitutionalism from a Third Worldist perspective. Oklopcic sets out by questioning why a Third World approaches to contemporary constitutional studies movement has not emerged in a manner analogous to that of TWAIL in the context of international law and its coloniality. Oklopcic moves, in response, to begin charting the contours of a 'Southern constitutionalism'. While acknowledging TWAIL's own ambiguities and internal frictions, the paper takes inspiration from the sustained impact that TWAIL has had on intellectual production in international legal studies over the past 20 years. In navigating towards this Southern constitutionalism, the paper plots the initial course to be traversed as one of 'constitutional imagination' that begins with locating the South of Western constitutionalism. This 'South' is the critical antithesis to positivist Western constitutional modernity: the liberal comparative constitutionalism that has traditionally overlooked questions of inequality, class, and imperialism; and the methodological and geographic biases that have projected parochial constitutional experiences in the global North as universally representative. Oklopcic sketches an intricate map towards 'ex-centric' approaches to constitutionalism, while at the same time leaving certain grey zones that compel us to think more concretely about what a praxis of TWAILing constitutionalism entails for lawyers, scholars, and theorists of the South.

Adrian Smith closes our Special Issue with a trenchant critique that reflects the multiple registers of praxis even as it challenges disciplinary orthodoxies about migration and speaks to a 'migration gap' in TWAIL scholarship. This article first acknowledges and then demolishes the supposed silos between discourses of development and security in the global governance of migration and specifically temporary labour migration. Rather than being bound to the balancing acts of harmonizing migration with either security or development, Smith outlines how these two discourses mutually constitute the 'unfreedom' of migrant workers and their bodies. Smith emphasises the role of racialised, securitised global capitalism in constructing migrant workers from the Global South as, simultaneously, agents of development and existential threats. Such racialised 'threats' are both mobilised and contained by the logics of development and security that mutually reinforce each other in pursuit of public and private accumulations of capital. However, Smith also notes that every programme seeking to pacify migrant workers and their communities inherently acknowledges ordinary workers' powers to resist. Already working at the intersection of law and political economy, Smith's article serves as an important call to TWAIL and other critical legal scholars to recognise the nexus of racialisation, pacification, and resistance in the supposedly disconnected realms of migration, security, development, and law.

We are grateful to Richard Falk for his support and his Foreword to the Special Issue, which so succinctly captures the essence of the conversations we have hoped to provoke. Praxis and intellectual work in and of the Global South are crucial sites of struggle in the 'ongoing agenda' of decolonisation, as Falk puts it. In a context in which the persistence and proliferation of Western-orientated international legal regimes have contrived to keep much of the Global South trapped within structures evolved during the colonial era, the role of international lawyers is critical to exposing and unravelling those structures. Falk frames his own remarkable praxis of dissident scholarship and political activism (spanning six decades to date, from his formative critiques of the Vietnam War to his trenchant analysis of the ongoing oppression of Palestine) as increasingly aligned to TWAIL and Third World voices over time. In describing how his resolve was redoubled rather than weakened by his ostracism from

Western professional sites of power and knowledge production, Falk impels us to engage in a praxis of the South in pursuit of radical epistemologies that can liberate international law from its colonial and elitist shackles.

IV. The place of praxis, the praxis of place

In organising the Cairo conference, our understanding of praxis as central to TWAIL – a striving to reconcile international law's promise of justice with the proliferation of injustice in the world it purports to govern – was manifest in our desire to gather together in the Third World. At the same time, we do not invoke divides and dichotomies with intent to fetishise the South or to essentialise its location by representing it as being in any way beyond the peripheries of institutional international law.

If gathering in the Global South is noteworthy, it is also of note that the conference was hosted at the American University in Cairo, an institution with American missionary origins and close links to United States and Egyptian state institutions as well as the private sector. Similarly, while most of the Conference participants originate from the South, more than half are based in institutions in the North. For the most part, postcolonial scholars have employed distinctions such as that between North and South, First World and Third World, developed and developing, coloniser and colonised, not so as to reinforce these distinctions but to do just the opposite: to analyse how such distinctions have come about with a view to breaking them down. Since the movement's early days, TWAIL scholars have continuously negotiated the tactical and strategic possibilities and pitfalls of utilising the concept of the Third World. The notion of the Third World, and any meaning attached to holding a TWAIL meeting here, is employed and done with cognisance of: continuously shifting global alliances; increasing inequalities of wealth and power and the maintenance of poverty traps in wealthy states and islands of privilege in poor states; and patterns of subordination and domination that cut across North and South creating, among other things, a transnational capitalist class and a Fourth World of Indigenous peoples and unrecognised nations.[10] As such, we employ the concept not with a view to asserting an essentialised Third World identity but to deconstruct it, so as to allow for a fuller disciplinary engagement with the plural, hybrid, ever-evolving, and contested performance of identity everywhere.

In seeking out such disciplinary engagement, it is equally important to recognise that the contested constructions of identity and law that characterise both the 'Third World' and 'international law' are no less relevant when it comes to our scholarship. For example, not long after the initial gathering of the TWAIL network in 1997, James Gathii published his influential essay on 'International Law and Eurocentricity' in the *European Journal of International Law*.[11] Two decades later, Eurocentricity still reigns within our discipline, exemplified in the same journal's continuing worldview: 'We divide the world into four regions for our statistical purposes: the European Union, the Council of Europe countries outside the EU, the US and Canada, and the rest of the world.'[12] In effect this division 'sees' the world as comprised of the West, places near the West, and the rest. That the rest of the world amounts to 'most of the world'[13] is apparently inconsequential, with three continents in their complexity and diversity collectively reduced to the status of nameless other – a 'none of the above' in the geographical categories of mainstream international law. In fact, it is here in 'most of the world' that TWAIL is not a peripheral eccentricity, but rather a grounded and coherent explanation of the field of international law.

In the longer view, the Third World places of 'most of the world', including cities like Cairo, have led the way in seeking to reshape Eurocentric international law and relations. From the 1919 revolt against colonial rule to the 2011 uprising to overthrow an authoritarian president, Cairo has had significance in the history of Third World peoples' struggles against domination both foreign and domestic. The Arab League was founded in Cairo in 1945 and its first action was to condemn French colonial presence in Syria and Lebanon. In December 1957, Cairo hosted the first major Third World meeting after the Bandung Conference, the Afro-Asian People's Solidarity Conference, where the aftermath of the Suez Crisis provoked a much more partisan stance against the First World than had been the case at Bandung. Cairo also played host to the first Afro-Asian Women's Conference in 1961, the Second Conference of Non-Aligned States in 1964, and various other such meetings, leading Vijay Prashad to recount how, during this period, 'Cairo became the favoured destination for a host of Afro-Asian solidarity meetings'.[14]

In the contemporary context, for those based in this region, the Arab uprisings over the past five years have inevitably provoked a closer examination of the notion of praxis. Intellectuals in Cairo are confronted on a daily basis with what role we play in the events unfolding around us; whether the courage and hopefulness with which revolutionaries confronted the might of the state in Tahrir Square in January and February 2011, or the fearfulness, acquiescence, and despair that followed during the swift counter-revolution that silenced dissent through coercion, torture, and death. While praxis is of relevance to intellectuals everywhere, some places make it harder to remain oblivious to the consequences of our actions and inactions than others. In such difficult times, there is a greater need for solidarity, and the coming together of the largest gathering of TWAIL scholars thus far was a meaningful and appreciated expression of unity. While not without their own gaps, exclusions, and silences, such meetings mean a great deal to those seeking to collectively think through whether and how we can put forward principled and effective responses to the fast-proliferating patterns of contemporary global injustice. We are hopeful that TWAIL scholars will continue to meet in the Third World to think through the conundrums of praxis and accountability inherent to such critical scholarship.

Ultimately, moving towards TWAIL praxis holds out hope of one day speaking of international law without it being a synonym for structural bias. We might even imagine a gathering of establishment international lawyers or institutions telling each other, 'if you don't do TWAIL, TWAIL will do you'. In looking toward such scenarios, we do so with particular attentiveness to the danger of cooption, which looms large for formerly emancipatory language, for scholars and activists, and for supposedly counterhegemonic and anticolonial discourses and practices. In part encapsulated in the debates between our plenary speakers, and wider conversations and challenges at the conference and beyond, these issues will not be resolved anytime soon.

Disclosure statement

No potential conflict of interest was reported by the authors.

Notes

1. The terms Third World, Global South, developing world, and so on, have been extensively problematised and unpacked by TWAIL scholars since the commencement of the movement so we will not repeat this analysis here. See for example, Mickelson, "Rhetoric and Rage"; Rajagopal, "Locating the Third World"; and Chimni, "Third World Approaches to International Law."

2. The authors co-organised the TWAIL Cairo Conference.
3. We built particularly on discussions at the previous TWAIL gathering in Oregon where, through the interrogation of capitalism and the common good, Michael Fakhri had set out to 'provide an opportunity for scholars to continue to strategize and collaborate, thereby pushing TWAIL towards praxis'. See *Call for Papers for the Third World Approaches to International Law (TWAIL): Capitalism and the Common Good*, University of Oregon, 20–22 October 2011.
4. Two publication workshops were held on 6–8 June 2015 at University of Windsor, Canada, and 11–13 September 2015 at Maynooth University, Ireland, to review conference paper drafts. These papers were eventually published in this Special Issue of *Third World Quarterly*, a TWAIL Cairo Symposium in the *Windsor Yearbook of Access to Justice*, a mini-symposium in the *Journal of International Criminal Justice*, as well as an *AJIL Unbound* symposium on TWAIL praxis (all forthcoming 2016).
5. The opening keynote address by Professor Obiora Chinedu Okafor leads a group of 10 papers in the TWAIL Cairo Symposium in the *Windsor Yearbook of Access to Justice*.
6. Freire, *Pedagogy of the Oppressed*, 107 (emphasis in the original).
7. Freire, *Pedagogy of the Oppressed*, 33.
8. Prashad, "The Arab Gramsci."
9. See Note 5.
10. On transnational capitalist class, see Chimni, "Capitalism, Imperialism International Law," and on the Fourth World see Coulthard, "Beyond Recognition."
11. Gathii, "International Law and Eurocentricity."
12. Weiler, "Vital Statistics."
13. Chatterjee, *Politics of the Governed*.
14. For an account of Cairo's role during this period see Prashad, *The Darker Nations*, 51–61.

Bibliography

Chatterjee, P. *The Politics of the Governed: Reflections on Popular Politics in Most of the World*. New York: Columbia University Press, 2004.

Chimni, B. S. "Third World Approaches to International Law: A Manifesto." In *The Third World and International Order: Law, Politics and Globalisation*, edited by A. Anghie, B. S. Chimni, K. Mickelson, and O. Okafor, 47–73. Leiden: Brill, 2004.

Chimni, B. S. "Capitalism, Imperialism and International Law in the Twenty-first Century." *Oregon Review of International Law* 14 (2012): 17–45.

Coulthard, G. "Beyond Recognition: Indigenous Self-determination as Prefigurative Practice." In *Lighting the Eighth Fire: The Liberation, Resurgence, and Protection of Indigenous Nations*, edited by L. Simpson, 187–204. Winnipeg: Arbeiter Ring Press, 2008.

Freire, P. *Pedagogy of the Oppressed, 1970*. Translated by Myra Bergman Ramos. Reprinted, London: Penguin, 1996. Page references are to the 1996 edition.

Gathii, J. "International Law and Eurocentricity." *European Journal of International Law* 9 (1998): 184–211.

Mickelson, K. "Rhetoric and Rage: Third World Voices in International Legal Discourse." *Wisconsin International Law Journal* 16, no. 2 (1998): 353–419.

Prashad, V. *The Darker Nations: A People's History of the Third World*. New York: New Press, 2007.

Prashad, V. "The Arab Gramsci." *Frontline*, 5 March (2014). http://www.frontline.in/world-affairs/the-arab-gramsci/article5739956.ece

Rajagopal, B. "Locating the Third World in Cultural Geography." *Third World Legal Studies* 15, no. 2 (1998–9): 1–20.

Weiler, J. "Vital Statistics." *EJIL: Talk!* 27, no. 1 (2015). http://www.ejiltalk.org/vital-statistics-ejils-assistant-editors-and-with-gratitude-shirley-wayne-vol-27-1/

The Third World intellectual in praxis: confrontation, participation, or operation behind enemy lines?

Georges Abi-Saab

ABSTRACT
In his closing keynote address for the TWAIL Cairo Conference, Professor Georges Abi-Saab engages with the conference theme 'On Praxis and the Intellectual' by considering the diverse roles that can be played by Third World international law intellectuals in trying to transform theory into social practice. He commences with an overview of the Third World's engagement with international law thus far in the form of a 'three act psychodrama'. Following from this, he explores the meanings of the terms 'intellectual' and 'praxis', noting that not all international lawyers are the former, and breaking the latter down into several stages in the spectrum between reflection and action. Professor Abi-Saab concludes with some examples of praxis from personal experience, including as a professor, teacher, and scholar of international law, ghostwriting for the UN Secretary-General, participation in country delegations, and as judge and arbitrator in numerous courts and tribunals. Through these examples he illustrates some of the different tactics available to the Third World intellectual including confrontation, participation, or operation 'behind enemy lines'.

It is with intense pleasure and emotion that I deliver the closing speech in this Conference, organised under the banner of TWAIL – Third World Approaches to International Law. Indeed, my very first piece in a foreign language (my mother tongue being Arabic), published in 1960 while I was a graduate student at Harvard Law School, was entitled 'The Newly Independent States and the Scope of Domestic Jurisdiction'.[1] Thus, the problématique of the position of the Newly Independent States – a category that corresponds roughly to what we now call the Third World – and their attitudes, actual or prospective, to international law, was on my mind since then. I did write a few pieces on that theme at this early period;[2] but then I moved on to other fields and other subjects of international law; only to find myself here, at the end of the journey, speaking on the same subject. However, when I reflect on all that I did in the interim, I realise that I have been grappling all along with the same problématique, under different guises or from different angles. As if one is always haunted or trapped by one's first intellectual inclinations or love, that continue instinctively to structure, in the manner of an ingrained gene, one's perspectives and choices.

I

I have two preliminary remarks. The first is about the acronym TWAIL. I said that I published my first piece in English in 1960. Around that time, in the late 1950s and early 1960s, when I decided, as a young Third World intellectual, to specialise in international law and explore the problems of the newly independent states in that field, I felt like Robinson Crusoe, ship wrecked on a deserted island. There was nothing written on the subject that I could find, even at the Harvard Law Library. However, just after I published my second piece on the subject,[3] I fell with great delight on an article published around the same time by an Indian scholar by the name of R. P. Anand.[4] I immediately wrote to him and we became life-long friends. I also found a published thesis, prepared at Yale Law School by an Indonesian scholar, J. J. G. Syatauw, entitled 'Some Newly Established Asian States and the Development of International Law',[5] with a sizeable chapter on the position of Indonesia during the then recent Law of the Sea Conference that led to the adoption of the four Geneva Conventions of 1958. That was all that I could find at that time.

Now, suddenly, I find that I am retroactively a member of a network; even a first generation member, and a founding father of this network. In fact, as you define TWAIL, it is not only a network, but a 'conspiracy'; in other words, a criminal association. Still, I am glad to be part of it. But I am with two minds about the label TWAIL. If taken literally – Third World Approaches to International Law – then, of course, I am a TWAILer or TWAILian. But if it is taken, as presented or perceived by some, as an off-shoot of the Critical Legal Studies school, I am not. I have to say that I share much of that school's criticisms, particularly the uncovering of the deeply ingrained biases and injustices in the rules and institutions of the international legal system. But I am for constructive criticism. It is the summum of cynicism to criticise the existing rules vehemently, while refusing to propose any alternatives, as do the members of this school. My approach is a little bit like that of the German Constitution. The Bundestag can withdraw confidence in the Federal Chancellor, but only by electing a successor.[6] Otherwise, destructive criticism, as a mere demolition job, leaves us with no law at all, or rather with the law of the jungle.

That concludes the first preliminary point. The second point relates to the title of this presentation. When I received the invitation to address this Conference on its general theme: 'Third World Approaches to International Law: On Praxis and the Intellectual', I thought I was supposed to present the role of the Third World intellectual in formulating a discourse on the praxis of international law from a Third World perspective, or rather a macro-analytical synthesis of this discourse to which I was a tributary. I even prepared an outline that I'll describe very briefly, because it is *not* that of the presentation you will hear today. I thought I would present this discourse as part of the North–South confrontation that takes the form of a psychodrama in three acts, each comprising three scenes, the last of which is still being written.

First Act: the emergence of a new voice and the quest for a new paradigm

Scene 1: contesting the rules

Rejecting the traditional view staunchly held in Western quarters, that a new State is born in a legal universe that binds it, newly independent Third World States started by contesting the universality and legitimacy of the international legal system: a system developed without their participation and used to justify their subjugation; an unjust system, for whilst formally based on sovereign equality and hence reciprocity, in actuality it works in one direction and in favour of one side only; and finally an antiquated system that does not correspond to contemporary conditions and their specific needs. New states claimed the right to pick and choose the rules that apply to them, in a voluntarist attitude reminiscent of that of the early Soviet Union.

Scene 2: renegotiating the rules

Soon, however, both sides found interest, for opposite reasons, to examine and update the rules. This took place primarily in the International Law Commission, leading to its 'prodigious decade' (that extended over 12 years), starting with the adoption of the four Geneva Conventions on the Law of the Sea in 1958; including, *inter alia* the Vienna Convention on Diplomatic Relations (1961) and on Consular Relations (1963); and culminating with the ILC's master piece, the Vienna Convention on the Law of Treaties of 1969, which responded in good measure to the concerns of the Third World.

The development of international law took place also directly within the UN General Assembly, where the Third World has more weight, particularly on subjects of a less technical but more political and controversial nature; all of utmost interest to the Third World. This led to the adoption, usually by consensus or very large majorities, of several momentous resolutions, during roughly the same period, such as the *Declaration on the Granting of Independence to Colonial Countries and Peoples* (GA Res. 1514 XV) in 1960; the *Declaration on Permanent Sovereignty over Natural Resources* (GA Res. 1803 XVII) in 1962; culminating with the fundamental *Declaration on Principles of International Law Concerning Friendly Relations and Cooperation among States in accordance with the Charter of the United Nations* (GA Res. 2526 XXV) in 1970, in the elaboration of which the representatives of the Third World played a significant role.

Scene 3: the tip of the tide; a new international economic order

With the first oil shock (1973–1974), and the apparent shift of the balance of power, starts an era of prevalence of the legal discourse of the Third World, particularly within the UN, leading to the adoption of the momentous *Declaration on the Establishment of a New International Economic Order* (GA Res. 3201 S VI 1974) and the *Charter of Economic Rights and Duties of States* (GA Res. 3281 XXIX 1974); an era of upsurge and apogee of the Third World's influence and role, both in formulating the general discourse and in practice; or so it seemed at the time.

Second Act: the empire strikes back

Scene 1: how the Arabs dissipated their oil power and how the west dissipated the oil crisis

A play within the play in the form of a mini tragicomedy of errors by the former; shrewdly capitalised on by the latter.

Scene 2: debilitating the Third World; the debt crises and their aftermath

The excessive liquidity in the form of petrodollars that inundated the financial markets facilitated indirectly the over-indebtedness of a number of Third World countries, leading in turn to a series of debt crises particularly in Asia and Latin America. These crises provided the opportunity to impose on those countries a severe package of economic, legal, and institutional policies in order to manage their debt, that included structural adjustment, deregulation, privatisation, liberalisation, and so on, which came to be known as the Washington Consensus, and which also led to profound political transformations and newly indoctrinated or docile governing elites, with the 'Chicago Boys' taking over the economic policy of many Third World states.

Scene 3: the end of the Cold War or the 'End of History'? From the new international economic order to the new world order

The Western counteroffensive starts at the turn of the 1980s, with the advent to power of Thatcherism in the UK and Reaganism in the US, with their muscular monetarist economic policies and the dismantlement of the welfare state internally; and their frontal assaults on the positions of the Third World internationally, including the imposition of the Washington Consensus as the new economic orthodoxy, together with strong interventionist tendencies.

The pinnacle of this offensive is reached a decade later, at the turn of the 1990s. The fall of the Berlin Wall in 1989 and the end of the Cold War, with the dislocation of the Eastern bloc and the implosion of the Soviet Union, herald an era declared 'the end of history' (reminiscent of Nirvana, or the attainment of a communist society in Marxist theory), with the apparent total triumph of neoliberalism or 'market democracy'. It marks a dramatic shift from the discourse of the New International Economic Order to that of a New World Order of globalisation and the WTO, under which everybody worships in the temple of the new religion of Marketheism, whose bible is the Washington consensus: 'fiscal responsibility', market liberalisation, and the 'rolling-back' of the state (again, this is paradoxically reminiscent of the Marxist tenet of the 'withering away of the State', at a time when 'real communism' was collapsing).

On the legal-political level, when the Security Council found its voice at the beginning of the 1990s, the General Assembly where the Third World played a significant role lost its own as legal oracle of the international community. There were no prospects of further major normative Declarations; rumours circulated of the demise of the Third World as an entity; and its avatars, the Group of 77 and the Non-Aligned Movement, were reduced to empty shells.

Third Act: the turn of the tide; premises of a new Third World discourse

Scene 1: the awakening of dormant cells

The Kosovo crisis provided the occasion to disprove the above rumours, by the strong reaction of Third World countries within the UN and outside it, in the Non-Aligned Movement Meeting in Havana in 1999, strongly denying the existence in international law of a so-called right of 'humanitarian intervention' outside the UN Charter, and also expressing the same scepticism later regarding the so-called 'Responsibility to Protect' doctrine, and thus confirming their general stance against all forms of intervention under any guise.

Scene 2: the rise of the BRICS

The emergence of the BRICS as rising economic powers demonstrated that globalisation can work both ways if one learns how to use effectively the existing rules despite their bias. Simultaneously, the BRICS criticise the hypocritical and selective use by the Western Powers of these rules, which are of the West's own making; and claim a 'level playing field' in their application; without totally abandoning the objective of readjusting these rules in the longer run to take greater account of the concerns and needs of the Third World.

Scene 3: the swing of the pendulum; the financial crisis of 2008 and its aftermath

This financial crisis and the economic meltdown that ensued (equalling that of 1929) glaringly revealed the fundamental failings, inequities, and inherently speculative nature of financial capitalism. It gave rise to strong calls not only from the Third World, but from Western public opinion and civil society, as well as large sectors of the political spectrum, for, if not a total system change, at least an in-depth restructuring, in order to rein in financial capitalism's abuses and manipulations. Another symptom of the looming crisis of neoliberalism is the strong backlash against investment law and arbitration, particularly the ICSID system, and the strong resistance in Europe against the TAFTA and TTIP projects.

The play continues to unfold, but the writing of the third act is not finished yet.

II

This is not, however, the outline of today's presentation. Indeed, the organisers prevailed on me, in spite of my diffidence, to speak of my personal experience, arguing that it would be more interesting for an audience well-versed in the discourse of the Third World, to hear about a lifelong experience of reflection and engagement in or with practice on the basis of this evolving reflection.

How can one summarise such experience and objectivise its rendering as far as possible? One way is to use it as an illustration of the subtitle of the Conference 'Praxis and the intellectual'. But who is the intellectual envisaged in this sub-title? Given the umbrella title 'Third World Approaches to International Law', she or he is obviously the lawyer or jurist, and more particularly the international lawyer. But can we say that all lawyers are intellectuals? For most lawyers, including Third World lawyers, are mere legal plumbers who mechanically apply law as they studied (or received) it; a far cry from legal architects or social engineers. Do they deserve the qualification 'intellectual'?

We are told that the 'intellectual' of the subtitle is meant to be the 'organic intellectual' of Antonio Gramsci, who considered that, as reasoning beings, 'all men are intellectuals … but not all men have in society the function of intellectuals'.[7] Those who do can be divided, still according to Gramsci, into two categories: the 'traditional intellectuals', by the nature of the function they occupy – involving an intellectual activity in contrast to manual of physical occupations – such as teachers, priests, and administrators, who continue to do the same thing, transmit or apply the knowledge as they received it, from generation to generation; to whom we can add the ordinary lawyer. The second category is the 'organic intellectual', a kind of Schumpeterian entrepreneur who introduces new ideas in society and transforms them into current social practice. Indeed Gramsci gives as examples 'the capitalist entrepreneur … the organisers of a new culture, of a new legal system, etc'.[8] And this tallies perfectly with the Dictionary definition of the other term of the title, 'praxis', as being 'in Marxism, the willed action by which a theory or philosophy becomes practical social activity'.[9]

Returning to my personal experience, it can be described in the light of the above definitions, as a long March seeking – through trial and error and by successive approximations – to approach and apprehend legal reality and to explain it in terms of theory; then trying through diverse types of action – which constitute praxis stricto sensu – to transform this theory into current social activity or practice. This personal journey can thus be analysed by sequencing it into three stages or components:

(1) The first stage consists of the purely intellectual activity of *reflection*, and *conceptualisation and articulation* of the outcome of this reflection. For most of us this has been done through the critical analysis of the structures of international law and how the system developed and its rules were and are applied, used or abused, and to what total effect; a kind of dynamic analysis of international law in action from the perspective of the Third World.[10] But theorising is not enough if we are speaking of 'praxis' and the 'organic intellectual'. It is of course very useful and even a necessary prerequisite for praxis, but it is not itself part of this praxis, which is the action by the organic intellectual to transform theory into social practice, and which is constituted of the following two stages or components.

(2) How to bridge the gap between theory and practice? This involves two stages, the first of which is still purely intellectual or technical. It is *the legal operationalisation of alternative paradigms, theories, and concepts*. As was said earlier, mere criticism is not enough. To be really effective, it has to be accompanied by positive suggestions to repair deficiencies and inequities; not just any general, abstract, and fanciful suggestion, but legally credible proposals. And the more the suggestion is radical, the more it needs proving that it is a workable legal proposition. Thus, the real contribution here takes the form of *legal feasibility studies* of new legal concepts that looked strange at first sight to the mainstream conventional international lawyer, such as 'wars of national liberation',[11] a 'right to development',[12] or the form of *detailed blueprints* of radical new paradigms, such as the 'New International Economic Order'.[13]

(3) Bringing theory to bear on practice. Once the two intellectual components – conceptualisation and the legal operationalisation of concepts – are there, the hardest part remains to be done, which is to transport these concepts from the realm of thought to that of social reality, that is to transform them from legal virtual reality to reality *tout court*. By what means can a Third World intellectual bring his ideas to bear on practice? Either indirectly by dissemination or more directly by approaching or acceding to the decision-making process.

(a) As concerns *dissemination*, here too there are direct and indirect means. The most direct means is teaching. And here, in spite of my deep admiration for Gramsci, I beg to differ with him when he classifies the teacher among the 'traditional intellectuals'. For, apart from my considering teaching as the most intellectually exhilarating and thought-provoking profession; it provides the organic intellectual, if he is sincere, cogent, and persuasive enough, an ideal platform not only to disseminate his ideas, but also to secure the perpetuation of his message; secure that younger generations will go on to continue the work. Personally, my greatest pride is in my students; to see someone like Judge Abdulqawi Yusuf sitting on the International Court of Justice (ICJ) Bench, a leading figure in the progressive wing of the Court, writing on African contributions to international law,[14] bringing a strong African voice in international academic and adjudicative circles; someone like Professor Marcelo Kohen, a leading writer on territorial affairs,[15] and a prominent member of the invisible bar of the ICJ; not only Third World former students but also many others from the North who share the same outlook and bring it into their environment, such as Professor Laurence Boisson de Chazournes. All those former students constitute a large intellectual family, which gives me the greatest pride and constitutes my first and foremost contribution to international law.

Beyond that personalised circle, dissemination is done through writing and publication. It is a diffuse means of influence aiming at raising awareness or what the French call *conscientisation*. This is done in two ways, as mentioned before. First by deconstruction, showing that the existing rules and institutions which look objective, in fact reflect special interests and values and in many cases cover deeply engrained biases and injustices. But deconstruction, to be beneficial, has to be accompanied by reconstruction, by proposals of viable alternatives, as was mentioned before; in order to mobilise relevant public opinion around them, rather than simply against the status quo.

(b) The most direct way, however, to bring theory to bear on practice, is to carry the 'feasibility studies', 'roadmaps', and 'blueprints' – which transform theory into practical and legally workable normative propositions – to the level of *international decision-making*. Given the non-centralised structure of the international legal system, lacking a legislature and a unified judicial system, the development of the law is effected mainly through the accumulation of authoritative decisions, in the form of adoption of normative treaties, decisions of authorised collective organs, of diverse courts and tribunals, including arbitral ones.

This is why I consider it of the essence, if one really wants to transform his ideas, once operationalised, into current social practice, to make every effort to insinuate these ideas into the decision-making process. This can be done either directly, if he finds himself in the decision-maker position, for example as a negotiator or a member of a country's negotiating team of a multilateral normative treaty, or as a judge or arbitrator; or indirectly by situating herself or himself in a position that allows transmission of ideas to the decision-maker, for example by preparing reports for the UN Secretary-General.

On a number of occasions, often by a freak of circumstance, I was offered such positions. I usually ended by accepting, in spite of initial doubts and mental reservations, as I felt duty bound to seize every opportunity to inch things in what I considered the right direction, sometimes in full knowledge that I would be swimming against the tide. I shall describe some of these episodes in the rest of this presentation. But before doing that I would like to clarify a point relating to the above strategy, namely what I mean by the word 'participation', in the title I gave to this presentation 'The Intellectual in Praxis: Confrontation, Participation or Operation behind Enemy Lines?' Participation in the decision-making process in the above-mentioned sense does not mean 'collaboration', even less 'cooptation'. In a war, for example, negotiating or signing an armistice or an exchange of prisoners agreement does not mean that one is 'collaborating' with the enemy. 'Participation' here simply means that if decisions will be taken in any case – decisions that affect our interests or the system in general (a legal system that is applicable to us whether we like it or not) – then it is imperative to take part in the process of decision-making if we can, in order to safeguard and if possible further our interests, and make sure that the decision will not veer the system in the wrong direction.

Such participation does not exclude 'confrontation' if need be. But it brings it into the heart of the process itself. And if the looming result is quite unsatisfactory it does not exclude 'operations behind enemy lines'. After all, 'behind enemy lines' means being within the territory controlled by the enemy. Here these operations entail trying to prevent the adverse decision from being taken or the treaty from being adopted; and if this proves impossible, to expose high and loud what went wrong, and all the legal defects and failings of the outcome, in order to undermine its credibility and legitimacy. This is by far a better, more productive, proactive, and courageous strategy than that of the empty chair, or refusal to engage, invoking doctrinal purity from fear of being accused of collusion with enemy; the soft option of staying away from the battle field in comfort, doing nothing about it other than crying injustice from afar or throwing stones at windows, while leaving the decision to the opposite party and undergoing its consequences.

III

Turning to specific examples of the roles that could be played to bring one's ideas and theories to the level of the decision-making process, I start with that of ghost writer to the Secretary-General of the United Nations. I was teaching in a special course at Harvard in the summer of 1969 when I received a phone call from the Director of the UN Human Rights Division in New York inviting me to visit him. When we met he said: 'the General Assembly has asked us to do a study on "respect of human rights in armed conflict" and we don't have the personnel to do it'. I was not particularly versed in the law of armed conflict, but he insisted that as a reputed professor I should be able to do it, and that two assistants would be provided to help me. Where does the Third World come into it? After the two UN human rights Covenants were adopted in 1966, the first International Human Rights Conference was held in Tehran 1968 to chart the road ahead. The UN had kept completely out of the laws of war because, at the establishment of the International Law Commission, the UN had asked Professor Hersch Lauterpacht to do a study on subjects suitable for codification and progressive development. In this study he said the UN should keep out of the laws of war, one of the reasons being that the treatment of the subject might be seen as an admission that the UN had failed in its principal mission of maintaining peace and security; and since then the UN had kept away from the subject.

A series of disastrous wars, particularly for civilian populations, had just taken place or were still going on throughout the Third World: the 1967 war in the Middle East; the Rann of Kutch war between India and Pakistan; in the middle of the Biafra War; the Vietnam War; and a large number of wars of national liberation in Africa and elsewhere. Third World States felt that this was not being taken into consideration and that the laws of war were outdated. So when I was asked to help I thought it was a very good opportunity to reflect the interests of the Third World in this area, and indeed I accepted and we did the report. Of course the UN formatted it by making it less sharp – that's the UN and you cannot do anything about it. But the General Assembly liked it very much and commended it, asking for a second report concentrating on wars of national liberation – that is on wars resulting from denial of self-determination. So the Human Rights Division asked me again to do the report, which I did, but they didn't like it. They considered it too partisan. It was not that they kept my contribution out, but they referred to it as 'one expert said'. So I was furious and published an article on the subject entitled 'Wars of National Liberation and the Laws of War',[16] which was widely cited and reprinted in several collections later on. In a way, that was a contribution to the awakening of consciousness and raising awareness. It was also an example of the 'legal feasibility studies', showing why and how wars of national liberation can and should be classified as international armed conflicts.

As a result of this article, I got into the Egyptian Delegation to the Diplomatic Conference on the Reaffirmation and Development of International Humanitarian Law (1974–1977). The Egyptian Foreign Ministry doesn't usually call on people from the outside. But the head of the delegation was my former professor, Dr Hamed Sultan, and I told him, 'wars of national liberation is a very important issue, you should concentrate on it, and here is an article with all the arguments'. This was at the preliminary stage, before the Diplomatic Conference itself started, at a conference of government experts as they called it. When he came back to Cairo, he went to see the Minister, Dr Mourad Ghaleb, and said 'I have a former student teaching in Geneva who knows all about the subject, and he will not cost you anything because there is no air ticket and per diem as he lives in Geneva. Could you put him on the delegation?' So, I was on the delegation, and when the Diplomatic Conference started in 1974 we had the first group meetings.

Members of the Group of 77 were worked up about wars of national liberation and Tanzania had prepared a draft amendment concerning the subject. The ICRC, which is very diffident, did not touch the subject in the Draft Protocols it prepared as bases of discussions for the Conference, but we wanted to introduce it. I was asked to speak in the name of the Group of 77. It took the whole first session, three months of discussions – a war on wars of national liberation. At the beginning the West did, as they do with many Third World issues, try to shrug it off, saying this is political and it should be treated in the General Assembly rather than at a legal conference where we should discuss exclusively legal matters. A first lesson to be learnt here is that you have to be rigorous in your legal expertise. When I formulated the case for wars of national liberation as international armed conflicts from a legal perspective, they understood they had to answer; they could not simply push it aside. And we ended up winning this battle and having recognition in the First Protocol of wars of national liberation as a species of international wars. So this case ended with a victory. How it was applied in practice is a different matter, but we have no time for that here.

The other example of speaking through the oracle of the UN Secretary-General goes back to the 1980s, just at the beginning of what I called the Second Act, the counteroffensive (or the Empire strikes back) after the elections of Thatcher followed by Reagan, who tried to push aside 'all this Third World nonsense'. And here the Philippines put on the agenda of the Sixth Committee of the UN General Assembly the subject of 'progressive development of principles and norms of international law relating to the New International Economic Order', which was rather unwelcome in the new prevailing ambiance. The General Assembly asked the Secretariat to do a report. The legal advisor at the time was averse to dealing with this very hot potato. He said 'we have nobody to do that, so outsource it'. It ended up somehow, via the UNITAR, with me. So I did the report and I think the report is a very good legal blueprint of the NIEO. The Resolution had enumerated seven principles, starting with permanent sovereignty over natural resources. What I tried to do was first to identify clearly the components of each normative principle; then try to evaluate the degree of maturation of these components into positive law. This leads to the question: what are the processes by which this maturation or transformation takes place? And what are the means by which we can act upon them to accelerate the transformation when it has not been completed? This is an example of the larger problématique of the passage of perceived social values and interests into law, and whether we can somehow gauge the degree or stage of this passage from one state into the other. A principle like permanent sovereignty over natural resources is sufficiently crystallised, so it could be treated as a legal principle; but others were much less so. The Assembly took note and commended the report. But nothing further was done about it, given the then prevailing mood. However, the report is still there as a feasible blueprint of the NIEO, if and when there is sufficient will to transform it into living law.

I am not going to speak of the two Secretary-Generals who are my close friends, Boutros Boutros-Ghali and Kofi Annan. That I leave, like Chateaubriand, to *Mémoires d'outre-tombe*.

That much for my first example of an activist role, as ghost writer of the UN Secretary-General, if one has the occasion to deliver his message through the oracle of a personality that can direct or influence practice. The second example of an activist role is by direct participation in the decision-making process through one's membership in a country's negotiating team. I told you about my participation in the humanitarian law conference. The role I played in that conference led to my election in 1993 by the General Assembly as one of the founding judges of the ICTY, which brings me to the third model of activist role, through direct participation in decision-making as judge or arbitrator.

However, before turning to that, I would like to refer to another role at one remove from the decision-maker, that of counsel and advocate in international litigations. This is the popular image of the lawyer stricto sensu. But I have to admit this not my cup of tea. I came to study law as a kind of public philosophy, the most rational and equitable way of ordering society, and not as a prelude to a career as a practicing lawyer.

However, at some stage of one's career as a professor, one cannot avoid solicitations to act as advocate and, according to the circumstances of the case, the invitation can be tempting. Moreover, it is always enriching to see how the concepts one articulates and teaches fare in practice. So, I accepted to appear in a few cases, but I kept it consciously a minor activity. My mental reservation basically was that normally, as an advocate, one has to defend the private interests of one party against those of the other, rather than speak for the public interest as she or he sees it. Thus I accepted cases where I saw that the interests of the party that I represented coincided with my view of the public interest, particularly if that party was a Third World country, though in some instances both parties were Third World countries.

In any case, I try to be consistent with my general attitude and interpretations of the law, never attempting to ply the law to serve the case at hand. Moreover, a good part of the cases I dealt with were delimitation cases where the public interest was to make legality prevail over effectivity, which in general serves the stronger party who usually imposes a status quo of her or his own doing, or rather often her or his misdoings.

Appearing in two types of cases gave me particular satisfaction: cases where I felt I was exercising self-defence, as an Egyptian and Arab, using law as a weapon to repel aggression and its after effects, as in the *Taba* arbitration between Egypt and Israel (1988),[17] and the advisory proceedings on the *Legal Consequences of the Construction of a Wall in the Occupied Palestinian Territory*[18] where I served as lead counsel of the Palestinian Authority; or cases which gave me the opportunity to speak to general issues I felt strongly about, particularly in advisory proceedings, such as the one on the *Wall* just mentioned (about the law of occupation), and the advisory proceedings on the *Legality of the Threat or Use by a State of Nuclear Weapons in Armed Conflict*[19] in which I presented the observations of Egypt, an oral pleading that I consider my finest hour in court, notwithstanding the legal and logical aberration of the Advisory Opinion that followed.[20] What I said as advocate in both those advisory proceedings was a continuation of the work I did in the diplomatic conference on humanitarian law; the same as my work as a judge on the Appeals Chamber of the International Criminal Tribunal for the Former Yugoslavia (ICTY).

This brings me to the last activist role in decision-making as judge or arbitrator, a role that raises most acutely the question: where to situate oneself alongside the spectrum of the subtitle of this speech, 'confrontation, participation, or operation behind enemy lines'? Indeed, it could be at any one or a combination of them. However, when it comes to my role on the ICTY bench, it does not fall into any of them. It was not only participation, but I admit unashamedly to collaboration, not only with my close friend Professor Antonio Cassese, whom we elected as President, but also with most of the judges who were inhabited by the same pioneering spirit. For here was a unique opportunity for institution building and rapid law development; an opportunity for 'teething' the revamped international humanitarian law (in the Geneva Conference) by providing an effective means of sanctioning its egregious violations in the form of criminal individual prosecution.

In spite of my short period on the bench, I managed to play an active role, as rapporteur of the Rules Committee, in drafting the first comprehensive code of international criminal procedures; and more particularly in drafting the first and most illustrious pronouncement of the Appeals Chamber, its *Decision on the Defence Motion of Interlocutory Appeal on Jurisdiction* in the *Tadic* Case.[21]

My other short experience on the bench, twice as judge ad hoc in the ICJ, is easier to situate on the spectrum. I would describe it as relaxed 'participation', without (at least overt) confrontation, and a fortiori far from operating behind enemy lines. There are of course deliberations, which start usually after the oral pleadings, where every judge has the latitude of saying what she or he wants. There is no pressure or anything of that sort. But of course, the decision is collective, and what one has to say is either reflected in the decision itself, if one is in the majority, or one can always express it in a separate or dissenting opinion.

The two cases on which I sat were both boundary disputes between two African newly-independent states. The first of which, *Frontier Dispute (Burkina Faso v Rėpublic of Mali)*,[22] was also the first African land boundary case to come before the ICJ where problems ensuing from colonial arbitrary divisions were compounded with great difficulties of establishing facts, geographic, historical, or otherwise. Law and facts, as well as evidence, were messy.

As a neophyte, apprehensive of the solemnity of the setting, I tried to clear up matters for myself by drawing up in my Note (which every judge has to write addressing the different issues raised in the case as a prelude to substantive deliberations) a template of delimitation of land boundaries under such conditions: the relative weights of different legal titles and types of evidence; the limited role of colonial law; and particularly the interaction between legal title and effectivities, which is, as mentioned earlier, the most sensitive issue. To my delight, this was largely reflected in the judgment, which has been considered thence as locus classicus on land delimitations.

This case was decided by a chamber of five judges. The other case I sat on, the *Territorial Dispute (Libya v Chad)*,[23] was decided by the full court and did not raise particularly complex problems. Thus, as mentioned before, my experience as judge ad hoc of the ICJ can be classified on the spectrum of the subtitle as relaxed participation.

The third alternative or position on the spectrum, to which I will dedicate the remaining time, is operating behind the enemy lines. And that is what I felt when I was asked whether I would like to sit on the Appellate Body of the WTO.

I started teaching in 1963. In 1964 there was the United Nations Conference on Trade and Development (UNCTAD), which carried with it a lot of the hopes of the Third World. It was at that time the largest conference in the UN, before the marathons which succeeded it, because it lasted for three months, had more than 1000 delegates, including several important personalities. The most impressive one was Che Guevara, who was there as Minister of Industry of Cuba. At night, he would meet with us, the young people from the Third World, to discuss, and it was a very inspiring experience. I went every day to the Conference, except for my lecture hours, as I intended to write a book about it. But I ended up writing a long article. All of my professional life I thought of myself as an 'UNCTADian' and was feeling very sorry for the decline of UNCTAD particularly since the creation of its opposite number, opposite in the real sense, the WTO. And they asked me to sit on the Appellate Body of the WTO. I hesitated. It was one of my old teachers and a very respectable person, Professor Said el Naggar, then outgoing member of the Appellate Body, who suggested insistently that I succeed him. Then Faiza Abul Naja, who was the Egyptian ambassador in Geneva and a former student of mine, also spoke to me. And the then Foreign Minister Amr Moussa, an old friend from Cairo Law School, prodded me to accept. So I did, saying to myself that I'll consider myself a guerrilla parachuted behind enemy lines.

When I started the worst thing was the hermetic character of the products. If any one takes the trouble of reading a report of the Appellate Body, particularly an older one, it's really like reading Chinese for a non-Chinese speaker. Everything is almost in cipher. One of the great lessons I learned is that if you have a standing body then you can influence it much better than an ad hoc body. Because a standing body has to develop its own judicial policy, and if you have strong arguments, even in a body which decides by consensus as is the case of the WTO, you can make a dent, though progress is very incremental. And indeed there proved to be a narrow opening for progress, in making reports a little more transparent and writing them in a way that is more understandable, because, after all, judicial decisions are not only for the cognoscenti but for those who will suffer or benefit from them.

Secondly, and more importantly, the trade lawyers knew very little about international law. When they had to apply Article 31 of the Vienna Convention on the Law of Treaties on interpretation, they understood it as three completely water tight compartments: you look first at the text; and only if the text is not clear you go into the context; and only if the context is not clear, you go beyond that. I kept arguing that interpretation is a holistic operation, you have to look at the whole thing at the same time; and I'm very gratified that, even after I left, they are still saying that interpretation is a holistic operation. Moreover, there was an opening up to general international law and a realisation that the WTO law is a part of it.

Thirdly, there was a modest opening up to non-trade concerns. There is greater awareness of human rights, development, and environmental imperatives. I am particularly proud of two decisions: *Brazil – Retreaded Tyres* and *European Community – Tariff Preferences* about GSP.[24] By the way, Judge Abdulqawi Yusuf had written his thesis with me some 30 years ago about GSP, the general preference scheme.[25]

Thus, while the agreements are rather tilted against the Third World, the Appellate Body, as a standing organ, could develop a judicial policy of interpreting them in a more balanced way. And here I have a comment about reformism. If you accept to sit on a bench, you have to accept its terms of reference. And if you want to improve things, it has to be done within these terms of reference. I proceed on the basis of a famous dictum of a great Marxist legal thinker, Pashukanis, who once wrote that the rules of law are armistice agreements. I think, as long as they stand, let us get the best out of them within the amenable margin of interpretation. If we can change them, that is all the better. But this is not within the judge's purview.

My very last point is that, in contrast to the WTO – where I came out with being less of a saboteur behind enemy lines than I had expected – when it comes to ICSID arbitrations, the enemy is clearly there. Not only is the procedure tilted in favour of foreign investors (for example, they can initiate arbitration against the host State, but the reverse is not possible), but so are also a good majority of the players in the system, who do not hesitate grossly to misinterpret the rules of international law to suit their private purposes. This is because of *inter alia* the 'moral hazard' in ad hoc arbitration, arbitration by a panel which is formed to deal only with one case; of arbitrators deciding the case while thinking 'what I'm going to say now will affect the possibility of my being appointed in the next case'. This applies unfortunately even to great names. My experience in ICSID made me lose respect for several persons I previously held in high esteem.

In many cases there is nothing that can be done except to follow what a famous leftist French lawyer, Jacques Vergès – who defended the Algerians during the Algerian war of liberation – called *la stratégie de rupture*. Vergès used it to delegitimise the whole process, that is to say, the prosecution of Algerian guerrilla by French courts. But it could also be used to delegitimise the output of the process, that is to say the judicial decision or award. And sometimes this is the only alternative left in ICSID arbitrations, in the face an implacable majority of two, heedless of legal and logical imperatives. The strategy thus joins the third alternative of the title 'operating behind the enemy lines', or rather within these lines, in enemy territory, by targeting the output or the award. But to do that, one has to be there, to stand his ground in spite of the unpleasantness of the situation and, as I said before, to expose high and loud what went wrong and the legal failings and defects of the award, to undermine its credibility and legitimacy.

These are some examples, from my personal experience, of the diverse roles that can be played by Third World intellectuals in trying to transform their theories into social practice. Of course whatever one does is no more than a drop in the ocean. But if every one of us does what she or he can, the drops may converge to set off a forceful current.

Disclosure statement

No potential conflict of interest was reported by the author.

Notes

1. Abi-Saab, 'Newly Independent States and the Scope of Domestic Jurisdiction.'
2. Ibid; Abi-Saab, 'Newly Independent States and the Rules of International Law'; Abi-Saab, 'Peaceful Change and Integration'; Abi-Saab, 'Inner Wandel Internationale Rechtsordnung'; Abi-Saab, 'Third World and the Future.'
3. Abi-Saab, 'Newly Independent States and the Rules of International Law.'
4. Anand, "The Role of the 'New.'"
5. Syatauw, *Newly Established Asian States.*
6. *Basic Law of the Federal Republic of Germany*, Article 67(1).
7. Gramsci, *Prison Notebooks*, 9.
8. Ibid., 4.
9. *Shorter Oxford English Dictionary.*
10. See Note 2 as well as subsequent footnotes addressing specific topics.
11. Abi-Saab, 'War of National Liberation.'
12. Abi-Saab, 'Legal Formulation of Right to Development.'
13. United Nations General Assembly, 'New International Economic Order.'
14. Yusuf, *Pan Africanism and International Law.*
15. See Kohen's locus classicus, *Possession contestée et souveraineté territoriale.*
16. See Note 11.
17. Taba Arbitration, 20 *UN Report of International Arbitral Awards* 1–118.
18. *Legal Consequences*, ICJ Report 3.
19. *Legality of the Threat*, ICJ Report 46.
20. I later published this pleading, with a commentary on the Advisory Opinion, in Abi-Saab, 'Court and the Bomb.'
21. *Tadic Case*, ICTY, Case No IT-94–1-AR72, Decision of 2 October 1995. For an evaluation of the contribution of the Tribunal to the development of international humanitarian law, see my *Separate Opinion* attached to the above decision. See also Abi-Saab, 'International Criminal Tribunals.'
22. *Frontier Dispute*, ICJ Report 554.
23. *Territorial Dispute*, ICJ Report 6.
24. Appellate Body Report, *Brazil – Measures Affecting Imports of Retreaded Tyres*, WT/DS332/AB/R, adopted 17 December 2007, DSR 2007:IV, 1527; Appellate Body Report, *European Communities – Conditions for the Granting of Tariff Preferences to Developing Countries*, WT/DS246/AB/R, adopted 20 April 2004, DSR 2004:III, 925.
25. Yusuf, *Legal Aspects Trade Preferences.*

Bibliography

Abi-Saab, G. "The Newly Independent States and the Scope of Domestic Jurisdiction." *Proceedings of the American Society of International Law* 54 (1960): 84–90.

Abi-Saab, G. "The Newly Independent States and the Rules of International Law: An Outline." *Howard Law Journal* 8 (1962): 95–121.

Abi-Saab, G. "Peaceful Change and the Integration of the Newly Independent States in the International Community." *Yearbook of the AAA* 32/33 (1962–63): 172–178.

Abi-Saab, G. "Inner Wandel und Internationale Rechtsordnung: Eine Perspektive der Dritten Welt." [Inner Change and International Law: A Third World Perspective]. In *Recht und Sozialer Umbruch* [Legal and Social Upheavals], edited by C. Walther, 21–36. Frankfurt: Lembeck, 1971.

Abi-Saab, G. "War of National Liberation and the Laws of War." *Annals of International Studies* 3 (1972): 93–117.

Abi-Saab, G. "The Third World and the Future of the International Legal Order." *Revue Egyptienne De Droit International* 29 (1973): 27–66.

Abi-Saab, G. "The Legal Formulation of a Right to Development." In *The Right to Development on the International Level*, edited by R. J. Dupuy, 159–175. The Hague: Martinus Nijthoff, 1979.

Abi-Saab, G. "The Court and the Bomb: A Case of Mutual Deterrence?" *Transnational Law and Contemporary Problems* 7 (1997): 429–457.

Abi-Saab, G. "International Criminal Tribunals and the Development of International Humanitarian and Human Rights Law." In *Liber Amicorum Judge Mohammed Bedjaoui*, edited by Emile Yakpo, and Tahar Boumedra, 649–658. The Hague: Kluwer, 1999.

Anand, R. P. "The Role of the 'New' Asian-African Countries in the Present International Legal Order." *American Journal of International Law* 56 (1962): 382–406.

Basic Law of the Federal Republic of Germany. Brazil – Measures Affecting Imports of Retreaded Tyres. Appellate Body Report. WT/DS332/AB/R, adopted 17 December 2007, DSR 2007:IV, 1527.

European Communities – Conditions for the Granting of Tariff Preferences to Developing Countries. Appellate Body Report. WT/DS246/AB/R, adopted 20 April 2004, DSR 2004:III, 925.

Frontier Dispute (Burkina Faso V Republic of Mali) 1986. ICJ Report 554.

Gramsci, A. *The Prison Notebooks: Selections*. New York: International Publishers, 1971.

Kohen, M. *Possession contestée et souveraineté territoriale* [Contested Possession and Territorial Sovereignty]. Paris: Presses Universitaires de France, 1997.

Legal Consequences of the Construction of a Wall in the Occupied Palestinian Territory 2004. ICJ Report 3.

Legality of the Threat or Use by a State of Nuclear Weapons in Armed Conflict. 1996 ICJ Report 46.

Shorter Oxford English Dictionary. 6th ed. Oxford: Oxford University Press, 2007.

Syatauw, J. G. G. *Some Newly Established Asian States and the Development of International Law*. The Hague: Nijthoff, 1961.

Taba Arbitration. *20 UN Report of International Arbitral Awards* 1–118, 1988.

Tadic Case (Decision on the Defence Motion of Interlocutory Appeal on Jurisdiction). ICTY, Case No IT-94-1-AR72, Decision of 2 October 1995.

Territorial Dispute (Libya V Chad) 1994 ICJ Report 6.

United Nations General Assembly, "Progressive Development of the Principles and Norms of International Law Relating to the New International Economic Order." Report of the Secretary-General, Annex III Analytical Study (prepared by G. Abi-Saab). UN Doc A/39/504/Add1 (1984).

Yusuf, A. *Legal Aspects of Trade Preferences for Developing Countries: A Study in the Influence of Development Needs on the Evolution of International Law*. The Hague: Nijhoff, 1982.

Yusuf, A. *Pan Africanism and International Law*. The Hague: Hague Academy of International Law, 2014.

On fighting for global justice: the role of a Third World international lawyer

M. Sornarajah

ABSTRACT
The life of a Third World international lawyer is devoted to resistance to the norms of international law designed by agents with power to promote the interests of the powerful sections of the international community. Increasingly the instrumental norms of international law are fashioned through the use of private power, making the positivist claim that public international law is a law between states illusory. The task of this paper is to identify a framework of common concerns so that a collectivity of Third World lawyers can work together, examine how mechanisms of power can be countered, and devise a confrontational strategy.

In this contribution I build on the themes I raised during my keynote remarks to the Cairo Conference on Third World Approaches to International Law (TWAIL): 'On Praxis and the Intellectual'. I was asked to reflect on the issue of praxis in light of my own experience as a teacher of international law, an academic researcher in the subject, and as a practitioner of international law. This experience indicates that the life of a Third World international lawyer should be devoted to resistance to the norms of international law designed by agents with power to promote the interests of the powerful sections of the international community.[1] In advocating resistance to norms of power, it is inevitable that a call be made to reject such norms and to give reasons for their rejection. In this sense this contribution becomes a manifesto, containing prescriptions as to what an aspiring Third World international lawyer should do in order to resist the instrumental use of international law by countering norms of power with norms of justice.

Norms of power undermine the interests of people in poverty. Such norms are intent on continuing a hierarchical structure of states and peoples that were created during the era of European colonialism through the instrumentality of international law. Although colonialism has been dismantled, the legal structures associated with it remain. These structures are restated and enforced in insidious ways so as to give them the appearance of legality in a modern and ostensibly postcolonial world. In this structure poorer states are condemned to remain at the bottom. As a consequence, international law becomes a purveyor of poverty. It is necessary to resist the formation of these norms. If they are already formed, it is necessary to fight for change. The notion of justice here is not complicated. It is universally accepted that a dominance of one people by another, or one group by another, must be ended so that equality is restored. It is unnecessary to enter into debates about the different theories of global justice that exist, for international law has overtly recognised imperialism as a wrong and inequality as a situation that must be ended. If the proposition that international law is a purveyor of poverty is shown, its violation of standards of global justice has to be conceded.[2] The Third World international lawyer should find means of redressing this injustice.

It is necessary to understand the agenda or the strategy that a Third World international lawyer should work through. It is not suggested that the agenda should be the same for everyone. Every single Third World international lawyer should work this out in accordance with her own preferences, expertise and inclinations. But a framework of common concerns must exist so that a collectivity of such lawyers may work together. The objectives of a movement like TWAIL should be to act as the focus of such a group of international lawyers who work for humanity, not as the narrow sectional interests of groups in power. The task of this paper is to identify this framework.

The first part of the paper looks at the liberation of the colonial people through their freedom struggles. The triumphalism generated by this historical change often dims the fact that the struggle between power and justice is a continuous one that requires vigilance in order to resist the machinations of power, which takes multifarious forms because of its mutability to suit circumstances and its agility in shaping the course of events as yet unforeseen by the rest. Extensive historicisation defeats the larger aim of ensuring that the legal cloak that enables the pushing of people into poverty that occurs in the present is not addressed.[3] The past must only be a guide to the present. In the second part the ideological guises in which power has sought to shape international law in the present are indicated. It is necessary to know this ideological basis thoroughly, so that justice based responses can be made. This part identifies the strategies adopted by hegemonic power in shaping the law. Its use of theoretical devices in order to support the system it creates is analysed and the manner of the refutation of these methods is looked at. The third part looks at how such mechanisms of power can be countered. The enemy will seek to scuttle the well-laid plans of Third World warriors of international law. Past efforts are surveyed and possibilities are indicated. The need not only to be defensive but to be confrontational of adverse norms and creative of new, favourable norms is asserted.

Origin of the Third World through resistance

The origin of the Third World lies in the resistance of its people to the norms of international order that justified their subjugation. From initial European contacts first with Latin America and then with Asia and Africa, the norm that supported the subjugation of the cultures of these people has been driven by the superiority of Europe and its self-assumed civilisational responsibility to lift the peoples of these regions to Europe's level. The assumption of this civilisational responsibility was an altruistic cloak to plunder the wealth of the people of Africa and Asia, for there is nothing to show that the organisational levels of the peoples of the subjugated regions were inferior or that their practices were lacking in civilisational standards when compared to the genocidal plunder that the Europeans embarked on. The early theorists of Europe condoned the activities of successive colonial powers through the formulation of doctrines relating to differences in standards of civilisation. They justified intrusions into the lives of the larger sections of humanity living in Latin America, Africa and

Asia on the basis that they were acting for the good of these people and elevating them into a higher sphere of living. The reason was the same, whether given by Vitoria to justify the brutal massacres of the Incas and Aztecs,[4] or by Grotius to justify Dutch penetration of Southeast Asia, or by the English international lawyers to justify the Opium Wars, the genocide of the Tasmanian aboriginals, the subjugation of India, or the plunder of the natural resources of Africa.

The early justifications were based on natural law ideas that there was a common right to use the resources of the world, that the denial of trade was illegitimate, so force could be used to open entry to trade and, above all, that enlightenment in the form of Christianity and governance standards similar to those of European states should be brought to all non-European peoples. In the context of this evolution of international law and its continuation in similar vein through the colonial period there was no hope for the people of the colonies except through resisting these laws. Resistance was what took place and it is through that resistance that the people of the Third World wrested their freedom from the domination of the European powers. Military power had conquered them. The power of the law had kept them in bondage by providing justifications for colonialism. However, despite decolonisation, the West continues to impose standards on others, although standards of civilisation have been replaced with standards of governance.

The resistance that led to decolonisation involved an assertion of the norm of self-determination. In its earlier incarnation the principle was intended to apply only to Europe. Its wide espousal by the Afro-Asian states, the resistance to colonialism that resulted in non-violent Gandhian protests, as well as bloody wars as in Indonesia, and the weakened condition of European states to fight any longer after the exhaustions of the Second World War, resulted in the freedom of the colonies. The ending of imperial control over Asia and Africa, the consequent creation of new states, the coming together in conferences like the Bandung Conference, and their formation of the Non-Aligned Movement resulted in the possibility of the use of collective power to change the existing order.

The first generation of Third World international lawyers was active in bringing about change. They believed that international law could be changed so that it benefited the whole of humanity, not just the people of the former colonial states. This may be because they believed in universality and the possibility of a plurality of laws for the whole of mankind based on justice and equality. They believed that the emerging Third World would be an agent of change that would benefit the whole of mankind, not just a section of the rich world and the elite of that world. Therein also lay a socialist agenda, for these leaders were imbued with a socialist bent and their movements were supported by socialist sections of the Western world.[5] But universality also meant permitting the powerful the means of ensuring that they became the leaders of the world once any countervailing power was removed. This unfortunately did happen when Third World cohesion and Soviet communism collapsed around the same time, ensuring the predominance of the USA as the sole hegemonic power.

But that came after. Third World leaders chose to remain within the system and to make changes to the existing system without seeking to replace it. This is a paradox, for it was the very system that had been used to exploit them in the past that they sought to continue.[6] The founding of the United Nations and the rise of Third World power within the General Assembly were factors that contributed to this strategy, one that may have worked to their detriment later. Third World leaders accepted the borders of the states the Europeans had drawn for them, without any regard to the ethnic or religious composition of these states.

They all subscribed to the *uti possidetis* principle, which required that existing borders be regarded as sacrosanct. Third World leaders did little to ensure that internal issues relating to the political balances between ethnic and other groups were addressed at the outset. The issue festered through history and affected the progress of newly independent states. A mechanism to resolve these issues still remains to be worked out.

As much as there was a deficiency in addressing internal issues, there was alacrity in the preservation of the newly acquired political independence, and the assertion of the need to ensure economic independence from companies of the metropolitan states. Self-sufficient agricultural economies were replaced during imperial times with new forms of economic activity, either through the planting of new crops such as tea or rubber, or the mining of natural resources. The social and economic changes effected by colonialism still continue as these sectors remain the backbone of the economies of most developing states. Economic dependence was created as both the new plantation sector and the natural resources sector were dependent on exports to developed states. The marketing of these resources, despite decolonisation, was still controlled by multinational corporations of the erstwhile colonial powers. It was necessary to break this control.

The recovery of economic control, without which political independence would be meaningless, required changing existing international law that favoured the maintenance of economic control of the resource and agricultural sectors of newly independent countries. It was at this stage that there was a decision to confront the norms of the existing structure by putting up a system of counter-norms. The incipient resistance on the basis of a new parallel package of norms, articulated on the basis of justice, began with the New International Economic Order (NIEO) resolutions. These caused consternation among the developed states. The vigour of their reaction attests to the force with which the claims to the NIEO were made. The NIEO is an important turning point in Third World resistance. It marked the end of seeking reforms within the existing system of international law. It began the idea of structuring oppositional norms to those based on power in the belief that the justice considerations inherent in these oppositional norms would ensure their triumph. As it turned out, justice considerations without sufficient authority to back them up do not prove too successful in the face of intransigence.

The NIEO was an accumulation of existing notions, many of which were contained in already existing General Assembly resolutions. A resolution on economic self-determination in the form of a right of a state to exploit its natural resources without hindrance had been passed regularly in the General Assembly from 1952.[7] Such resolutions culminated in the Resolution on the Permanent Sovereignty over Natural Resources. Thereafter came the Resolutions on the New International Economic Order (NIEO) and the Charter of Economic Rights and Duties of States (CERDS). But the manner of the statement of these existing norms in a package that was supported by the rhetoric of justice was what made the NIEO different. The leading developing country international lawyers of this generation concentrated their efforts on ensuring the success of this project to change the structure of the international economic system.[8] They realised that they should have the right to control their own economies, which were befuddled by alliances with foreign multinational corporations. For their economies to prosper there should be fairness in international trade. The concentration was therefore justified that effort should be made to ensure that the rules of the international economic order should be changed. This effort of the first generation of international lawyers of the independent Third World must be studied with care. They addressed norms of change on the basis of justice. The appeal to justice is the only way to counter the norms of power. Appeals to justice themselves generate power by marshalling empathy in the majority of mankind. The NIEO was able to have an impact as a result. The lesson to be learnt from this experience is to press strongly for a desired norm on the basis of justice, to marshal support for it from the academic community and, more importantly, tro ensure that there is sufficient state support and subsequent state practice that follows the norm. This will ensure that the norm matures into a rule and will withstand any oppositional rules that the power-based system has put up.

The NIEO cannot be erased as it forms a part of the constitutions of many Third World states. These states recognise the principle of sovereignty over natural resources and the primacy of domestic courts in dealing with disputes arising from their exploitation. Also, contract practices were changed on the basis of the norms of the NIEO, with states ensuring greater control over resources through new contractual techniques. Thus the production-sharing agreement in the oil sector is clearly based on the ownership of oil vesting in the state oil corporation until it is put on board a tanker at port. Despite the gleeful reports of the demise of the NIEO, its principles lived on through important changes effected in the practice of states. They were eclipsed as a result of events that took place in the 1990s. In the 1990s the espousal of neoliberal philosophies by many states of the Third World put the NIEO into abeyance. The principles of the NIEO have remained dormant. They could yet be woken up when shifts occur in power equations and justice-based norms become ascendant once more.

It is also necessary to understand the reasons why the NIEO went into eclipse in the last decade of the 20th century. There was a coincidence of events that presaged a change. Change occurs when such a confluence takes place. The fall of the USSR ended the need for a non-aligned group. The Cold War ceased to be. It left the USA as the sole hegemonic power. This signalled 'the end of history', leaving the capitalist system triumphant.[9] Petrodollar loans to the developing countries could not be serviced by the developing states. This created a sovereign lending crisis. With the passing of the first-generation leaders of Africa and Asia, the fervour for Third World solidarity ended. With the rise of strong leaders in the West committed to neoliberalism – Reagan in the USA, Thatcher in the UK, Kohl in Germany – aid to developing countries dried up. The Kuwait war in 1990 demonstrated the absolute military might of the USA. East European states, newly created through the dissolution of the USSR, competed with developing states for aid and foreign investment.

With these events taking place almost together, their momentum led to the collapse of Third World solidarity. The purposeful move of Western states to destroy the NIEO and Third World solidarity seemed to have succeeded.[10] Developing countries adopted the twin principles – democracy and market capitalism – without protest. What we have in that period from 1990 until about 2008, the year of the global economic crisis, is the making of an international law with the USA in the driver's seat. The guiding principles were provided by neo-conservatism, with democracy as its main thrust, and by neoliberalism, with market fundamentalism as its main philosophy. The instrumental use of international law ensured that rules are created in order to advance an order that was in conformity with the interests of the USA. The outlines of this new order, created to displace the vision contained in the NIEO, may be briefly traced.

The ascendance of the USA, as indicated, coincided with a confluence of circumstances. It enervated the enthusiasm of the Third World for collective action. With the sudden formation of new states following the dissolution of the USSR, they had to compete in the international economy with these new states for the only form of capital that was available – the assets by way of investment and trade that multinational corporations of the West possessed. The two financial institutions, the World Bank and the IMF, were egging them onto accept the neoliberal tenets that had made the USA and its European allies seemingly successful. Neoliberalism was touted as possessing the formulae for success.

The developing countries accepted neoliberalism and the international law principles devised on its basis without protest. Thus, the World Trade Organization (WTO)and its principles on intellectual property and services were accepted, although, as events were to show, they were harmful to the development of the poorer countries. They protected genetically modified seeds, which affected agriculture and ruined the livelihood of farmers. They made medicines essential to the cure of epidemics unavailable to the poor because of high costs. They created artificial markets in luxury goods available to the conspicuously consuming rich in the developing countries.[11] The developing states began signing bilateral investment treaties rapidly. The number of treaties, around 400 in 1990, had shot up to 3000 by the end of that decade. These included treaties signed by Latin American states, previously adherents of the Calvo Doctrine. That doctrine had required investment disputes to be settled by domestic courts. The investment treaties required submission of such disputes to foreign arbitration at the instance of the foreign investor. In the course of the interpretation of these treaties a handful of arbitrators had created rules through interpretation entirely favourable to multinational investors.[12] The awards involved huge sums as damages. As to the use of force, the doctrine of humanitarian intervention and the Bush doctrine of pre-emptive force enabled the use of the awesome military might of the USA without restraint. The use of force in the Middle East was intended to enable Western control of the resources of the region. It has badly misfired but doctrine had been created to justify the use of force to control the region. As in the days of imperialism trade and investment rules favoured the developed states. If there was a need, the rules on the use of force were kept sufficiently malleable so that force could be used to back the national interests of the rich states. Force always followed trade and investment in the past; it does so in the present and will do so in the future unless clear doctrines prohibiting its use can be advanced. The picture that emerged involved the reversal of any progress made under the NIEO principles.

In 2008 the neoliberal agenda, progressively weakening thanks to a succession of economic crises in Asia, Russia and Argentina, came to be challenged in the developed world as well, via what is referred to as the 'global economic crisis'. There was nothing global about the crisis. Asia and many other countries weathered it well. They had instituted financial and other safeguards following their earlier crises at the end of the 1990s so that they were saved from the effects of the 2008 crisis. The USA and Europe, which had kept away from regulating markets in accordance with neoliberalism, suffered most. It was a European–American crisis rather than a global crisis. They quickly went back to regulating the markets, nationalising affected banks and reordering their economies. But the effects of neoliberalism lingered on, particularly in international law. Its rationale in international law was to ensure that the developing countries and their economies remained under the control and tied to the markets of developed states. It was necessary to keep the system going.

It is interesting to look at the industry that the developed country international lawyers invested in making arguments that would ensure the continued existence of the system of control that had been created through international law. It shows the manner of operation of developed country international lawyers. The notion of a college of international lawyers that stands as a bulwark against injustice is an ideal. It has never happened that way. Periodically, no doubt, as at the conclusion of the two world wars, there has been an emotive sense of recovering the ethical roots of humanity in order to bring about a system that benefits mankind. But this is a rarity. Most of the time, from Vitoria to Grotius to modern day international lawyers, the majority has invested effort in keeping up a law that ensures the privileges of the rich in their countries. The exercise can be seen in a frenetic way in the formulation of theory supporting the retention of the neoliberal norms created in the period between 1990 and 2008. It is best to itemise the techniques that were used to conserve the rules created on the basis of the neoliberal thrust.

Resurrecting the neoliberal order

Despite the fact that the neoliberal order that was created during the era of the sole hegemonic power of the USA was shown to be a failure, the rules it had generated proved too tenacious to dismantle, both on the domestic and the international scene. On the domestic scene it is back to business as usual, with banks passing off the debts they had incurred to the public. Governments of developed states, always closely linked to business, complacently watched the restoration of the system that had brought about economic chaos, transferring the burden of recovery to the public through austerity measures.

It was so also on the international scene. International law based on neoliberalism continues with vigour. It has been bolstered through the floating of ideas now familiar as variations on the same theme of altruism and the bringing about of a standard of civilisation that is beneficial to all. The same music is played with different harps. It takes the different forms that are described below.

There are global governance rules

The suggestion is that activity inspired by neoliberalism brought about global governance principles such as the respect for property and contracts of foreign investment and international business, protection of intellectual property, and the liberalisation of the movement of capital and assets. Global progress, it is claimed, cannot be achieved without the recognition of a common core of rules on these important concepts. Since these uniform rules are ostensibly for the betterment of the world, they should be regarded as global governance principles.

There is a *déjà vu* feeling about this argument, as it reiterates the standard of civilisation that provided a justification for the maintenance the imperial system of international law. The construction of these standards of governance has not been accomplished through the standard norms of public international law. Rather, the most that could be said is that they were accomplished through the exploitation of the low-order sources of public international law – judicial decisions and the writings of highly qualified publicists, which look primarily only to Western international lawyers and decisions of tribunals. Both can be manipulated by private power. Multinational corporations and large law firms can create law through these means by hiring 'highly qualified publicists' to write briefs and then convert them into academic articles, indicating what the rules of global governance are. Or arbitration tribunals, manipulated through capricious appointments by institutions of neoliberalism and multinational corporations, make awards containing law that is foisted on the international community as beneficial rules contributing to standards of governance.

The proliferation of international tribunals has led to making new international law rapidly. Theory is made in order to ensure that the decisions these tribunals make in accordance with favoured principles of hegemonic powers are given legitimacy by investing them with a power to act as if they had a law-making role. Academic lawyers of this ilk would refuse such power to bodies of states, like the UN General Assembly. The decisions of these new tribunals are passed off as precedents. The classic example occurs in the field of investment arbitration, which comes about as a result of bilateral investment treaties. The intellectual abilities of the people sitting on these tribunals are seldom scrutinised. The heavy writings of the so called 'highly qualified publicists' often, hired hands, who have appeared as counsel in cases on behalf of private power, are used in support of these precedents. Often the same person writes the book, argues cases and sits on the tribunals.[13] It would appear that international law is made by a collectivity of like-minded individuals who promote each other's capacity to be the arbiters of what the law should be for the world. It is an interesting way of making international law. The rest of the world must seemingly accept this charade.

Standards created through the manipulation of low-order sources of law are suspect when it comes to democratic legitimacy, as the law is made for the world by a handful of persons to promote the interests of the rich of the world, at a time when the claim is made that increasingly the top 1% of the world's wealthy control more wealth than the rest.[14] International law, then, is made to suit the top 1% of the people. It is then argued that the rest of the world should accept it on the grounds that it is to their benefit, as wealth created always trickles down. Galbraith defined the theory in terms of the horse and the sparrow: 'If you feed the horse enough oats, some will pass through to the road for the sparrows'.[15] Rules of governance ensure that the poor of the world remain sparrows feeding on the remnants of what is given to them by the rich. Clearly, the situation is unpalatable to the vast majority of the people of the world. Global justice requires the dismantling of these rules of governance. Resistance to such rules maintained as rules of governance is justifiable on the grounds that it promotes the achievement of global justice.

The rules are made by tribunals with constitutional authority within regimes

The fragmentation of international law into specialist areas, each with its own rules and tribunals, disadvantages poor states that lack the capacity to master each of these fragmented sectors. The making of laws in these sectors, which are converted into separate regimes, becomes easier for powerful states both with their army of experts in the sector and the law relating to the sector. Indeed, some writers see the proliferation of arbitration tribunals and dispute-settlement mechanisms by treaties as creating constitutional regimes, within which law is constructed by these judicial mechanisms.

Regimes are developed when national interests coincide to such an extent that treaties create an institution that makes further rules as to how activity should take place in a particular area. For example, with regard to international civil aviation, the Chicago Convention on International Civil Aviation, the International Civil Aviation Organisation (ICAO), further conventions sponsored by the ICAO and the rules made by it, together constitute a regime that has been accepted by states and other relevant actors as governing international activity in this field. This phenomenon of regime making has taken place successfully in areas where there is conformity in national interests to ensure common rules. The Universal Postal Union and International Maritime Organization are also examples.

The making of such regimes in other areas, where there is an absence of such coincidence of national interests would be problematic. Investment and trade are such areas. Yet some scholars argue that the fact that there is machinery devised through tribunals created by treaties to enforce laws indicates consent that such tribunals should also have a free rein in creating rules. The tribunals are thus understood as having a constitutional function to play. According to this thesis, an investment tribunal would have the authority to extend the scope of international investment law through the interpretation of treaties. A trade tribunal, likewise, would have constitutional authority to extend the law on the basis of its understanding of the objectives of the regime within which it functions.

Neoliberalism in domestic spheres was able to thrive through the idea of legal extensions made through judges. In this context judges took upon themselves the role of extending rules on the ground that were desirable to further the policy of the law. The assumption is that there would be greater acceptance of the law because of the respect community shows towards courts. The safer course for the fashioning of neoliberal norms is to have judges, who have a class bias towards such norms, to achieve the function of extension of the neoliberal system, than for the executive or the legislature to attempt to do this. This may be permissible in the domestic sphere because, if the extension is not acceptable, it could be corrected by the legislature. This assumption does not stand in cases where an international tribunal extends the law, as where an investment treaty tribunal extends the law through interpretation. There is no mechanism for correction of law, so extended and democratic legitimacy is lacking. Yet the neoliberal vision is to ensure that the law is so made and that a network of such law is created for the world through awards passing into precedents that are followed by later tribunals.

The rule of law argument

The rule of law, redefined to suit neoliberalism, takes the form of ensuring the protection of property and contract, on the grounds that these are sacrosanct concepts without which international business cannot function. Devices such as global administrative law, and international constitutional principles extracted from systems of Europe, are brought in to construct this understanding of the rule of law. When it comes to comparative public law, there does not seem to be agreement, even among Europe's legal systems, about the extent to which protection should be given to property and contract. But that has proven to be no deterrent to the making of the argument that there are now global public law principles that support them.

The global administrative law argument

The proliferation of international tribunals within regimes created by treaties is seen as a sign of inevitable progress within the international community. The growth of administrative law within the domestic sphere occurred when the state assumed welfare functions. The role of administrative discretion in disbursing welfare needed to be exercised with fairness. Consequently a system of administrative law developed to enable courts to oversee the exercise of administrative discretion in the employment of welfare resources. It would be possible for a person excluded from welfare facilities to question the exercise of the administrative discretion against him. Relatively uniform rules may have developed in this area in some states. The similarity between domestic systems of administrative law is that they seek to guard the small fry against the might of the state.

It is argued by some that, in the international context, the various tribunals that have mushroomed within the international community perform precisely similar functions. The analogy is inexact. The private power that comes to be protected by a trade or investment tribunal is by no means unequal to the state against which it claims protection. Tribunals in the international sphere do not deal with entitlements that are being disbursed to the least able members of society. Rather, they often deal with the protection of interests of the powerful to access markets or the protection of the foreign investment of multinational corporations. Yet these tribunals are seen as performing benign and protective functions in the same way that the domestic courts apply administrative law against the state. Through the global administrative law argument, concern with the decisions of international tribunals in highly fragmented sectors of international law is diverted.

Increasingly, as a result of globalisation, the instrumental norms of international law are fashioned through the use of private power. This makes the positivist claim that public international law is a law between states made through custom and treaties of states illusory. In international law relating to the protection of foreign investment, techniques have been devised for the direct protection of such investment by multinational corporations. The law now grants such corporations unilateral recourse to tribunals to apply pre-determined standards of protection. These corporations have been vested with sufficient personality to be invested with such rights. There is no similar recourse given to states to sue the corporations when they cause massive damage to the people of the host states.[16] In the area of international trade the lobbying power of these multinational corporations has resulted in the formulation of rules of protection such as those on patents for drugs that affect the ordinary person. The rules are enforced through access to tribunals with effective enforcement mechanisms. The origins of imperialism lay in the roles that the Dutch and British East India Companies and other multinational corporations played in the conquest of the peoples of Africa and Asia. We now live in an age in which the role of the multinational corporations in fashioning the rules of the international order is no less effective. Either directly or through the extensive power they possess in dictating political outcomes in the Western states, multinational corporations exert power in shaping the rules of international law.

Habituating the middle ground

When all else fails, the strategy is to drive the argument to the middle ground so as to escape controversy. Such a move may ensure consensus, as there will be reluctance to continue the enervating effects of conflict. This was the domestic strategy to escape socialism. When the right wing felt political pressure from the populace, favouring a socialist solution, it moved towards the middle ground, adopting some socialist measures. The pressure was eased and a solution with which the right wing could live was achieved. The same technique is adopted in international law. When arguments are made that are unanswerable, there is a shift to a middle position so as to counter any pressure that may have been created.

One example will suffice. The rule that nationalisation of foreign property should be subject to compensation became unstuck through the assertion of the exception that a regulatory expropriation, made in the public interest, is not a compensable expropriation. Since most expropriations in modern times are made in the public interest, they would be non-compensable, a rule that would have disastrous consequences for investment arbitration and for investment protection. The reaction was to create the rule of proportionality from some European legal systems and argue that the rule would apply only in situations where the regulatory taking was proportionate to the public interest objective sought. The proportionality assessment indicates a middle ground which enables some compensation to the foreign investor.

Another example in the area would be the so-called balanced treaties on investments. While some states withdraw from making treaties or withdraw consent to arbitration when faced with the fact that arbitrators are overstepping their mark by making favourable and expansionist interpretations of investment treaties, states which want to persevere with the system of investment treaties seek to bring about a balance between the need for conserving the regulatory power of the state and the need for investment protection. They make treaties which state the standards of investment protection but at the same time also make state-wide defences to liability that justify the use of the regulatory power of the state. Again, the technique seeks a middle ground. The difficulty with such solutions is that the accommodation usually serves neither side's interest but the appearance of some movement is given. Chances are that the old law is conserved as such compromises enable decision makers to continue as if nothing has happened.

This section has outlined some of the techniques that adherents of neoliberal, or perhaps neo-imperial, international law have used in order to conserve legal principles promoting neoliberalism when they are subjected to attack. They often succeed in protecting them or, at the least, ensure their vitality in hopes that they may be revived at a later stage when the cycle turns favourable. As in the case of the NIEO, the cycle will change. It is good strategy on the part of the international law of the rich world to keep the norms viable until such a change occurs. It is necessary to examine what the response of Third World international lawyers should be to the use of such techniques. Ideally they should seek to administer a *coup de grace* to neoliberal principles but this may prove difficult to accomplish for, in some corner, neoliberal principles will continue to smoulder until aroused again, as long as laws based on neoliberal principles continue to exist.

Countering dominant international law

In the first section the article argued that the battle lines between developed states and developing states had been drawn in the period after decolonisation. It was shown that there were cyclical movements towards and away from stances based on justice advanced by developing states. The NIEO declined when a confluence of circumstances led to the rise of neoliberalism. With the succession of economic crises, neoliberalism was dented. But neoliberal norms have proved to be tenacious and have been kept alive through various means. In the second section the ways in which the norms of neoliberalism continue to be maintained were detailed. The task of the Third World international lawyer is to be aware of the techniques that have come to be used to maintain the norms favourable to private power and to the states which support such private power. Essentially the role of such norms has been to continue the imperial structure of Eurocentric international law in heavily disguised forms, ensuring that structural inequalities remain within international law. Third World international lawyers must devise strategies to counter neoliberal international legal principles.

Countering the techniques of sustaining neoliberal principles

As indicated above, there is a concerted effort to sustain the neoliberal principles through the devising of theoretical notions such as standards of governance, rule of law and the emergence of a global public law. These are false constructs. Standards of governance are no different from the standard of civilisation that was used to impose and maintain imperialism. They are constructed on the basis of the existence of a single standard that must apply to the whole world, regardless of disparate cultures, different political systems and stages of development. Each people must be able to develop in the manner it chooses. That is the essence of the principle of self-determination. There is a significant body of literature in economics that indicates that there is no uniform panacea for development. Neither is there a single political system that needs to be considered superior to another. All peoples must have the right to choose the system that they prefer to live under and not have it prescribed from above. This, it must be remembered, was a central tenet of the NIEO. The present hegemonic order will be replaced as a result of decline in the power of the USA with a multipolar world. This is an opportune time to revive the basic tenets of the NIEO, namely that there could be diverse methods for the solution of the different problems of states.

The standard of governance in the guise of the rule of law states as an inflexible proposition that the world must aspire to the preferences of the neoliberal system for liberalisation of capital assets: the protection of property and the sanctity of contracts. It is difficult to find uniform principles in all legal systems on concepts such as property or contract. It would be difficult, in the context of the success of legal and political systems such as that of China, to say that there must be a uniform, global system for states to succeed. There is no accepted core of principles with universal validity, apart from the principles that are accepted as *ius cogens* principles. There is no process by which the preferred principles of neoliberalism can be converted into universally applicable rules.

Neoliberal principles do not become international law even if the exercise of showing that they are part of European legal systems can be convincingly demonstrated. Often it cannot be demonstrated that there are uniform principles in the European systems supporting a particular principle or rule. There are, for example, no uniform principles that support the sanctity of contract, which neoliberals tout as a general principle of law. Progress in modern systems of contract law has been achieved through the erosion of the notion of the sanctity of contracts. Likewise constitutional systems do not recognise an inviolable right to property. They subject it to a variety of exceptions based on public interests. Even if there are principles common to regional systems like European law, it is difficult to demonstrate that they have global application. Gone are the days when it was possible to say that European principles constitute general principles of law and are therefore part of international law. It must be shown that the rules are applicable in and acceptable to other legal systems of the world.

Countering the techniques supporting neoliberal principles is not difficult. They are weak ideas dressed up in jargon. Removed of jargon, the content in the ideas such as global governance principles or the rule of law are slim. Ruthless challenging of the jargon and the demonstration of the paucity of substance in the principles must follow such exposure.

Given the extent of the competing literature in politics and economics, as well as in law, generated by liberal academics and others in both the First and the Third World, this task will become increasingly easier.

Demonstration of new justice-based principles countering neoliberalism

The rules of European international law, from their origin, were based on power, with a fictitious moral basis that imperial extension was to bring civilisation to the peoples of Asia and Africa. The new manifestation of this earlier justification is that there are uniform rules, tested and proven in the developed states, which will spread prosperity and development to all people. Proving these justifications to be false and replacing them with justice-based principles is a task that Third World international lawyers must perform with vigour. There are examples of this having been done in the past. The successful use of the principle of self-determination and the principles associated with the NIEO are instances. But one has to view these attempts in the context of the future. A criticism that can be made of TWAIL is that it is backward looking, continuously harping on the harm that colonialism has done to the Third World. This can become a long and futile wail if new prescriptions are not advanced to counter the instrumental use of international law by hegemonic powers. Obviously the theme of imperialism is an important one, as it is the continuation of laws developed during the imperial times that the hegemonic powers continue to use. Despite new guises and rationalisations, there is nothing innovative in these legal devices. While in the past, gunboat diplomacy was used to protect European investments, in modern times, instead of soldiers in fatigues, arbitrators in well-tailored suits protect foreign investments with conveniently crafted rules.

Thus, the oft-used rhetoric that the rules of power have been replaced by the rule of law is a hollow justification for the use of hegemonic power to make new laws in the field of investment and trade. The mere fact that arbitrators in pin-striped suits have replace soldiers in fatigues does not hide the fact that the objectives of the two groups are the same – to ensure that trade and investment are opened to multinational corporations of the First World and that they are conducted under rules entirely favourable to the interests of these corporations. Very often the UN itself is unable to act to bring about a just system that ensures that private power is not abused. Whereas international law now has an effective system of protecting foreign investment from measures taken by the host state through a system of arbitration based on treaties, the UN is only able to bring about a non-binding code of conduct for multinational corporations.

Much international law making in the modern world has been transferred to international institutions and international tribunals. Both are non-representative and are capable of being manipulated to serve the interests of the alliance between the hegemonic public power of First World states and the private power of multinational corporations. This is evident in fields such as investment and trade. In investment the leading institutions are the World Bank and the IMF, both non-democratic institutions having weighted voting on the basis of contributions made by member states. The USA has dominant power within these institutions so that these institutions carry out the objectives set by the USA. The World Bank's tribunal settling investment disputes, the International Centre for the Settlement of Investment Disputes (ICSID), virtually creates principles that favour the protection of foreign investment, creating an impediment to the exercise of the regulatory power of host states against foreign investors. The role of the WTO in international trade is similar. Its instruments are invasive of sovereignty. Some of the disputes taken to its dispute settlement board reflect the interests of large multinational corporations, ensuring that the most effective dispute settlement mechanism so far devised in international law is ultimately a servant of private power.

The work of these institutions is often justified on the basis of global governance standards and the rule of law. The undemocratic law made through processes controlled by these institutions, and the techniques of justifying them, lack legitimacy. Governance standards need to have the acceptance of the governed. They cannot be imposed from above, as these global institutions do. Merely invoking the mantra of the rule of law cannot convert an illegitimate process into a legitimate one. The process is fundamentally inconsistent with the rule of law.

In addition to TWAIL and other critical approaches to international law, objections to these developments have also been articulated by a liberal group of mainstream Western international lawyers.[17] They are stated in a manner that is not too destructive of the existing system as these well-intentioned lawyers cannot feel the pain of developing states at what is happening. Third World international lawyers must be in the forefront articulating objections to the techniques of law making that favour hegemonic power. They must point out the lack of legitimacy of the processes that are used. These processes themselves involve power. International law is fragmented so that expertise can be built up in every nook of the fragmented law through the abundant resources in expertise that the First World possesses. The Third World cannot muster similar resources. What is more, the best lawyers of the Third World thirst to join the institutions set up by the First World, and become betrayers of their own people. There must be early training in the universities of the Third World to prevent such tendencies. The instilling of a sense of global justice is central to the project. Courses in international law must emphasise the nature of the continuing domination through international law of the interests of the people of the Third World.

The history of international law shows that Third World resistance can lead to a change of international law based on power. The employment of justice as an argument against the rule of power lends great force to such resistance. It will also draw liberal international lawyers to support such moves. The increasing number of non-governmental organisations that operate to further just ends in human rights, the environment and poverty alleviation will also provide support. Enough countervailing power could be built up to support change. A field in which this is happening is the international law on foreign investment, where the laws built up on neoliberal principles by agencies of power like ICSID are coming to be dismantled through resistance.[18] The resistance comes from states, no doubt, but, also at the lower levels, protests by tribal people affected by mining, protests against land grabs to erect new manufacturing plants for multinational corporations, prevention of sweated labour at multinational factories, and farmers' protests at lowering tariff barriers that affect prices of their produce, have had effects for change. Third World international lawyers must articulate in legal terms the changes that are needed to reflect these protests.

Healing oneself

Arjuna, a central figure in the Indian epic, the *Mahabharata*, which has wide influence in Asia, is the epitome of an Indian warrior. He does penance before he gets his powers as a warrior so that he may be deserving of those powers. It was to him that the text of the *Baghavad Gita* was preached on the battlefield by Krishna because Arjuna questioned the righteousness of the killings he was to embark upon. In the course of providing justifications to him, Krishna preaches the path of righteousness.

The penance for the Third World lawyer is to ensure that her own country and her region live according to the just norms of international law. One must heal oneself and one's country before one can venture to heal others. We must know our own weaknesses, an idea that is common to all philosophies. These weaknesses often stem from the fact that postcolonial states inherited problems from colonial times. But that was long ago. One has to stop blaming colonialism for defects that should have been remedied by now. Third World states have created for themselves weaknesses such as excessive corruption, an intolerance of minorities arising from chauvinistic politics, and elite rule that drives divisions on the basis of wealth. Domestic elites form associations with foreign elites to ensure that their collective wealth remains intact. Other internal injustices persist, such as discrimination on the basis of gender, ethnicity, religion and caste, as well as the disempowering of tribal peoples. These internal defects within the constitutional structures must be removed so that the people of the Third World can express themselves freely with a concerted voice.

A primary duty of the Third World international lawyer is to ensure that her own country and region live in accordance with the normative principles of justice which she advocates for the world. She must grasp the progressive and people-oriented principles of modern international law by whomsoever made. Its core principles are in international human rights law and the emerging international criminal law. Eschewing their political elements, the core values of these areas of international law should be received into domestic legal systems so as to promote constitutional principles which will enable corruption to be defeated, elite abuse to be punished, multinational corporations held accountable for their misconduct, and a network of international principles developed to safeguard the people against governmental abuse. The protection of human dignity must underlie this project. Ensuring that natural resources are used to the betterment of the whole people and not only the elite of states, that tribal rights are adhered to and that minorities are treated equally are some of the functions that the Third World international lawyer has to perform. It is only when her own country has stature in the world that she can speak with a voice that attracts attention. Leaving aside debates as to the formation of human rights law and the imbalances it contains, there is an essential core in them that must be observed by developing states if they are to avoid cruelty to their own people. It is necessary to accept such law as applicable to the Third World so that its states can be rid of tyrants, ethnic chauvinists and the corrupt.

Supporting liberal stances of First World international lawyers

It must not be forgotten that First World international lawyers are increasingly speaking out for an inclusive approach towards international law. Where such an approach is taken and it is favourable to the interests of the Third World, it must receive the support of Third World international lawyers. But there must be a careful examination of whether these approaches tie in with the interests of the Third World. Often they move international law to the middle ground without necessarily indicating an active effort to promote Third World interests. The middle ground is static. There must be movement away from the static position to an active position that promotes the interests of the Third World. Movement must be towards the establishment of substantive principles that would actively aid in the creation of definite obligations, such as poverty reduction, transfer of technology, active control over natural resources and access to markets, the prohibition of the use of force, and the promotion of development. In this sense the articulation of the NIEO principles constitutes an example of the assertion of normative principles that requires affirmative action towards a goal of economic development. Such norms must be identified and promoted. A start could be made with the revival of the principles of the NIEO.

Conclusion

The battle lines in modern international law remain hidden. Positivism has presented international law as a neutral discipline which enhances human welfare without favouring any state. This cloak has hidden the inequities that have existed in international law. From its inception international law has ensured that imperial interests are furthered through legal rules. Empire was ended. But the rules that were fashioned during imperial times either remain or have morphed into principles that conserve hegemonic power. As in imperial times, private power has been able to exert itself through international law by ensuring that rules favourable to its dominance continue. The task of the Third World international lawyer is to resist them through appeals to justice. Change can be effected when justice-based norms counter those based on power, particularly if there is unity in the making of the claims that such norms should replace the norms based on power.

Anti-colonial struggles provide examples of change of the dominant rules of international law, which justified imperialism. The people of these regions had to fight against the collective might of European states arraigned against them. For the period thereafter they had to fight against the power of the USA, the new hegemonic leader of the Western world, and its allies in order to resist the use of international law as an instrument to replicate rules similar to those that existed under colonialism. Whereas under colonialism there was a more direct control of the people of the colonial world, the instrumentalism of international law cloaks iniquitous systems in legitimacy and seeks to habituate people of the Third World into a belief that the system must be just because it is maintained through international law. International law becomes a washing machine through which unjust laws are laundered to give them an appearance of being clean and legitimate. Armies of academic and practising international lawyers employ themselves in the perpetuation of this system with many iniquitous rules. The struggle of the Third World international lawyer must be to prevent the laundering of the law through instruments of legitimacy to give it an appearance of justice when, in fact, the law that is foisted on the peoples ensures that they continue to be in bondage, without access to their rights and without development that uplifts them from poverty.

TWAIL must set itself the agenda of resisting international law norms based on power by setting up a system of norms based upon justice. Justice has countervailing power, particularly when people support the changes that are sought. History has demonstrated the power of justice-based norms to effect change. As the conservation of power-based norms through the articulation of new doctrines takes place, it is imperative that TWAIL set itself the task of countering these new doctrines and putting up alternatives that enhance the interests of the majority of the people of the world, so that the protection of private power ceases to be the objective of international law.

Disclosure statement

No potential conflict of interest was reported by the author.

Notes

1. The Third World is no longer confined to geographical areas that were considered poor in the past. These were the former colonies in Asia, Latin America and Africa. The Third World now also includes the poor in the developed regions such as Europe and North America. As such, the Third World international lawyer is one who seeks to resist instrumental international laws that serve the rich, and to replace them with norms that ensure global justice through eliminating poverty and promoting the protection of the environment and human rights. She is not identified in terms of geography.
2. Pogge, *World Poverty and Human Rights Reform*. The dispute between political philosophers as to global justice uniformly recognised that poverty involves global injustice. Any norm or regime that creates poverty must be regarded as being in violation of global justice.
3. This is a mild criticism of the TWAIL movement, which is strong on addressing past inequities. TWAIL's leading texts are intent on addressing such inequities. This phase must be ended as there is sufficient literature on that aspect. It is more important to address the inequities that are extended into or created in modern international law through the instrumental use of power.
4. Anghie, *Imperialism, Sovereignty*.
5. The two leaders of the Third World were India and China, both adherents of socialism. The founding philosophy of *pancha sila*, which forms the basis of the Bandung Declaration, was earlier stated in a 1952 treaty between China and India. The two states played leading roles in the Non-Aligned Movement. China continues to state *pancha sila* as the cornerstone of its policy.
6. The Declaration of the Bandung Conference is instructive. It articulated 10 principles but they are largely assertions of the Westphalian model of state sovereignty and the principle of non-interference. The assertion of equality is to flow from the newly acquired sovereignty of the Third World states.
7. "Right to Exploit Freely Natural Wealth and Resources." General Assembly Resolution 626, UN GAOR, 7th Sess., Supp. No. 20, UN Doc. A/2361 (December 21, 1952).
8. We now have literature on the works of the leading Third World lawyers of this generation. For Mohammed Bedjaoui, see Bedjaoui et al., *Liber Amicorum Judge Mohammed Bedjaoui*. For Kamal Hossein, see Sornarajah, "The Return of the NIEO."

9. Fukuyuma, *The End of History*.
10. There is evidence of this purposeful move. Arguments were made that the UN General Assembly could not make binding rules but only recommendations. In *Aminoil v. Libya* these arguments were given legal form, with the NIEO being considered a set of aspirational norms, not having legal status.
11. Sun et al., *The Luxury Economy and Intellectual Property*.
12. The course of this expansionary law is described in Sornarajah, *Resistance and Change*.
13. Puig, "Social Capital in the Arbitration Market."
14. Stiglitz, *The Great Divide*.
15. Galbraith, "Recession Economics."
16. Ecuador was able to establish massive environmental pollution and destruction of the homelands of its aboriginal people by petroleum companies before its domestic courts. But, it did not have standing to establish these facts before arbitral tribunals before which the petroleum companies sued.
17. For example, Stewart, "Remedying Disregard in Global Regulatory Governance"; Benvenisti, "The Law of Global Governance"; and Benvenisti and Downs, "The Empire's New Clothes."
18. The process is traced in Sornarajah, *Resistance and Change*.

Bibliography

Anghie, Antony. *Imperialism, Sovereignty and the Making of International Law*. Cambridge: Cambridge University Press, 2005.

Bedjaoui, Mohammed, Emile Yakpo, and Tahar Boumedra. *Liber Amicorum Judge Mohammed Bedjaoui*. The Hague: Kluwer Law International, 1999.

Benvenisti, Eyal. "The Law of Global Governance." *Hague Academy Recueil des Cours* (2014): 59.

Benvenisti, Eyal, and George Downs. "The Empire's New Clothes: Political Economy and the Fragmentation of International Law." *Stanford Law Review* 60 (2007): 595–631.

Fukuyuma, Francis. *The End of History and the Last Man*. New York: Penguin Books, 1992.

Galbraith, John. "Recession Economics." *New York Review of Books*, February 4, 1982.

Pogge, Thomas. *World Poverty and Human Rights: Cosmopolitan Responsibilities and Reform*. Cambridge: Polity, 2008.

Puig, Sergio. "Social Capital in the Arbitration Market." *European Journal of International Law* 26 (2015): 387–424.

Sornarajah, Muthucumaraswamy. *Resistance and Change in the International Law on Foreign Investment*. Cambridge: Cambridge University Press, 2015.

Sornarajah, Muthucumaraswamy. "The Return of the NIEO and the Retreat of Neo- liberal International Law." In *International Law and Developing Countries: Essays in Honour of Kamal*, edited by Sharif Buiyan, Philippe Sands and Nico Schrijver, 32–59. Berlin: Brill, 2014.

Stewart, Richard. "Remedying Disregard in Global Regulatory Governance: Accountability, Participation and Responsiveness." *American Journal of International Law* 108 (2014): 211–145.

Stiglitz, Joseph. *The Great Divide*. London: Allen Lane, 2015.

Sun, Haochen, Barton Beebe, and Madhavi Sunder. *The Luxury Economy and Intellectual Property: Critical Reflections*. New York: Oxford University Press, 2015.

Regulation of armed conflict: critical comparativism

Nesrine Badawi

ABSTRACT

This paper calls for comparative analysis of international humanitarian law and Islamic laws regulating armed conflict by focusing on the underlying assumptions and interests informing both systems (rather than on rule-based comparison). It argues that examination of the biases inherent to each legal system can potentially inform scholars to understand better the paradigms shaping each of them. In doing so, the paper builds on contextual and critical interpretations of both fields of law to assert the need for 'critical comparativism' rather than functionalist comparativism. Unlike functionalist comparativism, which treats international law as the 'objective' benchmark against which other legal traditions are measured, 'critical comparativism' treats the two legal systems examined as alternative manifestations of power structures which, when contrasted against each other, help shed more light on the inherent bias in each legal system.

Introduction

Jihād has often received prominent attention throughout the history of Islamic jurisprudence. As many have noted, the term 'jihād' applies to all aspects of Muslim conduct, by demanding that Muslims exert their best effort to satisfy the divine will.[1] However, most legal works have tended to focus on jihād as armed conflict conducted in accordance with God's ordinances. While classical Muslim jurists focused primarily on the rules and regulations governing the conduct of armed conflict,[2] modern writings have concentrated rather on when it is justifiable for Muslims to engage in armed conflict and have neglected the significant body of work undertaken by former classical jurists. As argued by Hashmi, this shift in focus has probably been triggered by modern Muslim writers being 'fixated upon reinterpreting the grounds for *jihād* in light of modern sensibilities on wars of religion'.[3] This paper argues, as others have done, that Islamic jurisprudence was heavily responsive to its socio-political context; thus the paper examines the notion of jihād as approached in early jurisprudential works as a legal system devised primarily to regulate the conduct of Muslims in their armed conflicts with others. Because of the undeniable continued authority of formative and classical jurisprudence as the primary authorities of legal interpretation, and of the rising interest in understanding legal regulations governing Muslim conduct in war, the paper focuses on jihād (also often referred to as *siyar* or *qitāl*) as the branch of Islamic law dealing with the conduct of Muslims in armed conflict. In this paper I argue that much of the literature examining Islamic jurisprudence on armed conflict falls short of comprehending the nature of the Islamic legal system and, in the attempts to relate it to modern international humanitarian law (IHL),[4] is unable to explore the dynamics of development of Islamic jurisprudence on conflict. Because of this, modern understandings of jihād 'conflate the social, economic, political and legal realities of the second/eighth century with those of our own time, thereby producing a "historical Islam" that is reducible to one abstracted essence'.[5]

To some extent the limited literature providing a context-sensitive analysis of the dynamics of Islamic regulation of warfare is attributable to the challenge posed by the task of reading a body of law formulated in a 'pre-modern' context and detaching ourselves from the framework of IHL and its alleged distinction between combatants and non-combatants. More importantly, it is even more difficult for us to be able to imagine the conduct of war without the existence of states as we know them in the modern world, with their modern military apparatus.

In an attempt to squeeze Islamic jurisprudence into an IHL-focused paradigm, insufficient attention has been given to the diversity of juristic works on the matter. This has paved the way for a functionalist approach to examining the Islamic legal system's regulation of warfare. Functionalism in comparative legal analysis is defined as lawyers focusing on legal problems and assessing how different legal regimes solve the problem in question.[6] While not all functionalist literature addressing conduct of war in Islam has adopted a comparativist approach, the influence of what writers perceive as IHL norms and principles can be often discerned. As many scholars have noted, the designation 'functionalism' is perhaps reductionist in its own sense. Here, I use the term to refer to the tendency to assume particular objectives for the legal regime that regulates war, and measuring Islamic law against those objectives. This approach is characterised by arbitrary selectivity of Islamic sources and juridical opinions, in order to fit Islamic regulation of armed conflict into the IHL framework, as well as by an attempt to offer an over-decisive image of the Islamic regime by portraying a source or a ruling on a specific matter as the ultimate Islamic law position. Such approaches do not give the reader an understanding of the extensive disagreements over rules of armed conflict in juristic literature, and disregard the fact that this diversity and disagreement is a fundamental feature of a legal regime that is articulated by independent jurists rather than political authority.

The paper starts with a brief introduction to the rather complex term 'Islamic law'. After this the paper is divided into two main sections. The first offers an overview of the two primary modern approaches to the study of Islamic regulation of armed conflict: the functionalist approach and the contextual approach. I conclude this section by building on numerous works examining the role of context in shaping Islamic jurisprudence with a call for a historicisation of the different Muslim juristic works on war. The second section argues that this alternative approach could aid us in adopting a more critical comparativist approach and in understanding the biases guiding both international law and Islamic jurisprudence on matters relating to armed conflict.

What is Islamic law?

It is almost impossible to offer a unanimously agreed upon definition of Islamic law.[7] Prominent scholars in the field have dedicated significant effort to this issue and it would be impossible to do this incredibly rich intellectual debate justice for the purposes of this paper. Suffice to say, there is no Islamic code and there is no agreed upon manner by which one can claim to understand what the Islamic legal ruling on a particular matter is. Hence, the paper restricts itself to one particular means of understanding Islamic law, which is Islamic jurisprudence, *fiqh*. The term '*fiqh*' literally means 'understanding' or 'comprehension' and it is used to refer to scholarly attempts to develop legal rulings out of the sources of Islamic law. Because of the absence of an agreed upon legal hierarchy for rule articulation and of the development of the Islamic legal system in a manner that was, to a great extent, distant from the Caliph (the ruler), Islamic law was primarily articulated by jurists in the formative period. Most of those jurists were independent from the state and, as a matter of fact, many early prominent jurists are reported to have been in conflict with the state at different stages of their intellectual careers. Thanks to the absence of a state-sponsored legal authority capable of monopolising legal reality, many jurists offered varying understandings of Islamic law. After some time and after going through different stages of development, these varying understandings developed into personal schools of law, ie schools that attribute their authority to a master of jurisprudence. However, in many instances opinions on legal matters often varied within the school itself. The most established schools of Islamic jurisprudence are the Maliki school (in reference to Mālik ibn Anas, died 795AD), the ḥanafī school (in reference to Abu ḥanīfa, died 767AD), the Shāfi'ī school (in reference to al-Shāfi'ī, died 820AD) and the ḥanbalī school (in reference to Ibn ḥanbal, died 855AD).

As a result of varying interpretive techniques and approaches, even the sources of Islamic law were not unanimously agreed upon but gradually the primary sources among the most salient schools were the Qur'an (the Muslim holy book), Sunna (acts and sayings of prophet Muhammad), juristic consensus and different forms of inferential reasoning.

International law as a yardstick

Most modern literature attempts to squeeze the Islamic legal system into the international legal paradigm and draws parallels between the two. Whereas some scholars consciously treat Islamic laws of war as a possible legitimating tool for IHL, and in some extreme cases as a possible aid to the development of a singular legal code premised on the principles of humanity articulated in IHL,[8] most scholarship is framed either as a comparative analysis or as an interpretive reading of Islamic law. But, even in these readings, legitimation of Islamic law from an IHL lens is evident. For example, al-Zuḥaylī, a prominent Syrian scholar, makes these objectives clear in a paper written for the *International Review of the Red Cross*:

> While the voices of 'the clash of civilizations' are echoing loud, and the so called 'war on terror' is influencing the fate of some communities and many groups of individuals in various countries of the world, it is appropriate to recall the humanitarian values that rally nations and peoples around them.[9]

In order to achieve this reconciliatory objective, some scholars adopt a selective functionalist approach in their review of Islamic regulation of armed conflict. The term 'functionalism' here refers to assumed similarities in legal problems, and accordingly to assessment of how different legal systems address similar problems.[10] This approach assumes the existence of agreed upon 'social needs', 'an objective, determined, progressive, social evolutionary path' and that 'legal systems should be described and explained in terms of functional responsiveness to social needs'.[11] In order to establish a basis for comparison, the comparativist functionalist approach generally tends to focus on similarity and to ignore differences.[12]

Thus, instead of attempting to understand the difference in objectives and paradigms of the Islamic legal system, scholars accept the modern paradigm and principles of IHL as a statement of the 'legitimate' approach to 'agreed upon' societal needs in the regulation of conflict, and attempt to either prove or disprove Islamic law's conformity. As mentioned by Legrand, this functionalist approach prevents the reader from understanding the legal system under study, because it is 'inevitably socially, historically, culturally and epistemologically situated'.[13]

For example, in order for al-Zuḥaylī to establish equality between Muslims and non-Muslims, he addresses Islamic practice with 'others' and relies on respect for a pact or *'ahd* in Islamic law to conclude that Islamic law upheld equality between the 'Islamic state' and other 'states'.[14] This approach not only assumes the existence of states and the materialisation of the notion of equal sovereignty; more importantly, it falls short of recognising the different principles governing the conclusion of treaties as developed by Muslim jurists. For example, al-Shāfi'ī, the figurehead of the Shāfi'ī school, argues that an imām may only enter into a truce with another nation for a limited period of time to regroup his forces, and that the imām is obliged to refrain from renewal of the agreement once he believes it is feasible to resume fighting.[15]

With regard to defining combatants, Abū Zahra, a prominent Egyptian scholar in the 1960s, argues that Islam allows fighting to prevent aggression and threats to Muslim individuals' faith, and concludes that 'this objective limits war through prohibition of killing those who do not fight or participate in the war in any manner, and restriction of its domain to the battlefield'.[16] However, Abū Zahra's definition contradicts definitions provided by other scholars such as Hamidullah, arguing that a combatant is the individual capable of fighting and not necessarily participating in conflict.[17] More importantly Abu Zahra's definition shows a lack of sensibility to pre-modern warfare techniques by assuming the existence of a distinguishable battlefield and organised troops engaged in conflict, which conflicts with historical studies of Arabian practice in war.[18]

Other scholars tend to reduce the two legal regimes, IHL and Islamic law, to 'static monolithic systems' in order to achieve a functionalist comparison.[19] Hamidullah argues that the Islamic legal system was the first to acknowledge the rights of other nations and that it granted other nations equal rights, because 'Islam has rather been fortunate in discarding, from the very first day, difference of race and colour, country and language, in favour of the universal brotherhood of the faithful'.[20] In order to achieve a parallel between Islamic law and international law, Hamidullah focuses his comparative analysis on a specific principle – equality – disregarding any other competing principles in both legal systems that might limit the application of this particular principle. For example, he does not address how the notion of sovereignty in international law limited equality between different types of political communities, and how that same notion legitimised asymmetrical rights and privileges during internal armed conflicts.[21] At the same time he does not show how these asymmetrical privileges are almost reversed in Islamic law, where internal Muslim conflicts offer both parties more privileges and protections than conflicts engaging non-Muslim adversaries. The same approach is largely employed by Niaz Shah in his comparative analysis of IHL and Islamic law, where he largely reduces international law to *jus cogens* norms and Islamic law to the primary definitive Islamic texts, in order to 'find out which rules of Islamic law are compatible with international law and how international law can be applied in Muslim states in a compatible fashion'.[22]

Even when there is an attempt to highlight differences, examination of the Islamic legal regime is still conducted through a functionalist lens, where scholars seem reluctant to detach themselves from the paradigm of modern international law. For example, the simple fact that Islamic law is not reliant on state practice, in contrast with customary international law, leads Mayer to argue that 'instead of examining the actual conduct of governments, succeeding generations of Islamic jurists tended to perpetuate the ideas that had been set forth by their predecessors in the first centuries of Islam without bothering to take into account altered political circumstances'.[23] Mayer's claim is contentious because, until now, whereas there are numerous studies that assert the political responsiveness of Muslim jurists to the socio-political context, there has been no study detailing the different factors influencing early juridical works on matters relating to armed conflict, with the exception of Abou El Fadl's elaborate study of rebellion in Islamic law. Additionally, there is evidence of Sunni juristic reliance on the actions of al-Khulafā' al-Rāshidūn, the Rightly Guided Caliphs, as authoritative sources. Finally, the statement suggests bias towards international law and its development process, as shown by a lack of interest in the dynamics through which the Islamic legal system developed and in the evolving role of political authority in a divine system. Moreover, even if Meyer's claim holds, this specific detachment from state practice was, according to Hallaq, one of the main factors allowing for Muslim juristic creativity and the establishment of an early system of rule of law.[24]

Limited static views of IHL are also applied by scholars aiming to establish the difference between the Islamic legal regime and international humanitarian law. Attempting to prove limited protection for 'non-combatants' under Islamic law, Landau-Tasseron argues that, in the case of international law, 'non-combatants may not be harmed intentionally. By virtue of not being involved in warfare, they are considered to have immunity'.[25] Alternatively, she argues that in the case of Islamic law, 'prohibition against killing has the validity of law in regard to Muslims and their allies, but it is merely a general and non-binding directive in regard to others'.[26] In order to prove this argument, Landau-Tasseron partially relies on the lack of legal punishment for violating the rules of warfare in Islamic law. However, she disregards the fact that there are also no directives for violations of the rules of *baghy* (conflicts with Muslim rebels)'. Landau-Tasseron's approach also ignores the limitations in IHL to her statement that non-combatants may not be harmed intentionally. While in principle non-combatants may not be targeted, the principle is severely limited by the notion of proportionality of the attack to the attacker's military objectives. Perhaps the best illustration of these limitations is the *ICJ Advisory Opinion on the Legality of the Threat or Use of Nuclear Weapons*, which refused to 'reach a definitive conclusion as to the legality or illegality of the use of nuclear weapons by a State in an extreme circumstance of self-defence, in which its very survival would be at stake',[27] despite the indiscriminate nature of these weapons. Additionally, she makes a positivist claim that Islamic rules regulating warfare are mere directives lacking a legal nature because of the lack of punishment. Yet international law had no established collective system for punishment of violations of IHL until the recent introduction of the International Criminal Court, which still only punishes violations with regard to a limited set of circumstances and actors. In brief, Landau-Tasseron disregards the intricate relationship between *jus ad bellum*[28] and its ability to limit *jus in bello* regulation and the legacy of state-centric tendencies in international law governing punishment of war crimes. This disregard helps her assume a simple function for IHL – in this case protecting non-combatants – and to measure Islamic law against this function, without any regard for the fact that the objective of protection of non-combatants is not the primary or sole objective of IHL.

Selective comparison

Functionalist approaches to the conduct in war in Islamic law adopt a highly selective approach in their analysis of the rules of Islamic laws of war. For example, al-Zuḥaylī is highly selective in his reliance on particular Islamic sources and classical jurisprudence. In his treatment of Sunna, he relies on the prophet's famous speech to military leaders urging them not to mutilate and not to kill women and children.[29] However, he avoids any reference to the Hadīth indicating that the prophet allowed the death of women and children in the process of raiding villages at night, despite wide juristic reliance on this Hadīth.[30]

Moreover, he argues that property may not be destroyed,[31] but he avoids reference to an incident where the prophet reportedly burnt the Banū Naḍīr's palm trees in his battle with them,[32] an incident again widely relied on by many jurists to legitimate destruction of property. The same approach to destruction of property is adopted by Munir, who argues that the destruction of property is prohibited because it 'amounts to *fasad fi al ard*' (destruction on earth),[33] but fails to make any reference to textual sources contradicting his hypothesis.

Al-Zuḥaylī's selective approach is not only limited to sources, but includes his choice of the issues to ensure functional parallels. Rather than attempting to provide the reader with an overview of all the issues relating to the conduct of hostilities in Islam, al-Zuḥaylī chooses to highlight segmented aspects supporting his thesis and to ignore contradictory ones. For example, when he argues, as mentioned above, that destruction of property in armed conflict is illegal in Islamic law, a claim contentious in itself, he blurs the juristic position on property by drawing on modern IHL's position on the matter of destruction of property, but fails to recognise classical scholarship's agreement on the acquisition of the enemy's property as booty.[34]

In al-Zuḥaylī's case his selectivity is illustrated by his duality of tone depending on his audience. For example, his English article written for the Red Cross offers a vague position on prisoners of war and argues that 'they are often either released through grace bestowed on them without any return, or are exchanged for money or in return for other captives'.[35] He does not mention that male prisoners of war may be killed. On the other hand, his Arabic book, *Athār al-Ḥarb*, offers a more detailed analysis of the matter, examining positions taken by different jurists on the killing of fighting men, showing that the majority of jurists allow the killing of male captives and acknowledging the reports that the prophet allowed this practice.[36] In this text al-Zuḥaylī's analysis of juristic works argues that the killing of captives was only permitted in instances of necessity. He avoids these contentious points when addressing a 'Western' audience but is more willing to engage with contradictions in his Arabic book. This selectivity recurs in several other works, as noted below.

When scholars purposefully seek to provide a modern reading of Islamic law reconcilable with international law, they are unable to avoid what may appear an arbitrary selection of sources. One of the most evident is scholarly reliance on the acts of 'Umar ibn al-Khaṭṭāb. For example, Bennoune argues that Muslims rejected treachery and refused to use deceit in the treatment of the enemy, using a reliance on 'Umar's instructions to one of his military commanders.[37] At the same time Bennoune argues that 'women, children, and other non-combatants were recognized as a separate category of persons entitled to various degrees of immunity from attack',[38] but he disregards a precedent attributed to 'Umar instructing the killing of all adult men and sparing women and children.[39] Equally Abū Zahra relies on 'Umar's removal of Khālid ibn Al-Walīd as the head of the army for his merciless killing to prove that Islam prohibited unnecessary suffering,[40] but disregards 'Umar's instructions to his army to target and kill everyone except for women and children. Bassiouni also claims that respect for prayer houses is established by 'Umar's reluctance to pray in a church in Jerusalem upon acquiring the city,[41] but makes no reference to the controversial pact argued to have been given by 'Umar to Christians, denying them the right to build new churches and to have church bells ring loudly. Unlike Abdulrahman, who has provided interesting arguments to doubt the authenticity of this pact,[42] Bassiouni selectively relies on portions of that precedent.

As in the case of al-Zuḥaylī, classical and medieval scholars are relied on selectively to fit the agenda of the writer. For example, Hamidullah relies on the Mālikī jurist Ibn Rushd's alleged rejection of decapitation of war captives to prove that killing them is prohibited,[43] although elsewhere he seems to refer primarily to the Ḥanafī positions. In many instances early juristic opinions are disregarded completely. Abū Zahra also avoids reference to the juristic tradition dealing with killing captives and simply relies on the Qur'ānic verse dealing with the issue to argue that Islamic laws of war prohibited the killing of prisoners of war,[44] but makes no reference to juristic views challenging the view that the verse prohibited killing.[45] Yet, when it comes to the matter of cutting down trees in war, he provides a survey of scholarly difference and lists the various arguments supporting the conflicting scholarly positions.[46] From his selective survey of the juristic tradition it would seem that Abū Zahra allows his own personal views of an acceptable image for Islamic jurisprudence to interfere with the consistency of his methods. In other words, it may seem more acceptable for a modern writer to acknowledge the readiness of Muslim jurists to allow the cutting of trees, but portraying their willingness to kill war captives conflicts with modern perceptions of the 'ethical' conduct of warfare.

Reasons for selectivity

From these examples it is evident that this trend of scholarship in the analysis of Islamic law is committed to reconciliation between Islamic law and international law. In the case of Muslim scholars such as Abū Zahra and Al-Zuḥaylī, one can see that they are likely to have been influenced by their motivation to promote an understanding of Islamic law that fits 'modern' regulations of warfare and to defend Islam against non-Muslim claims of disregard for 'humanitarian principles'. This objective is traceable in the tone used by some of these scholars. For example, al-Zuḥaylī argues that Islamic law

> has a universal tendency, for it aspires to see welfare prevail and Muslim principles spread throughout the entire world. It does so not for economic, material, racial, imperialist or nationalistic interests, but in order to achieve salvation, happiness, welfare, justice and prosperity for humanity as a whole.[47]

This language reveals the treatment of the system as a divine law and a view that this divine law must at the least match man-made law in its respect for agreed upon social objectives. It also reveals an interest in defending this religion against 'defamation' by non-Muslims. In fact, al-Zuḥaylī makes this objective very clear when he sets out his purpose for writing the book, *Athār al-Ḥarb*:

> A lot of them [orientalists] wrote on some areas of it [Islamic law] in accordance with what their fanaticism, personal prejudice and hatred dictated, as they wish to fight Islam on the basis of its intellectual scientific origin.[48]

On the other hand, non-Muslim institutions seem to have been guided by different objectives. The Red Cross, for example, in choosing to publish al-Zuḥaylī and Munir's articles cannot be expected to be aiming at proving the correctness of Islamic law. Rather, the 'guardian of IHL' is presumably interested in legitimating it in the Muslim world through support of the congruency thesis between the two systems and to undercut the rising wave of violence committed under the banner of Islam. The US military, on the other hand, is more likely to have been influenced by a different yet not conflicting agenda. Facing the challenge of militant Muslim groups relying on an alternative legal regime, the US military may validly be expected to highlight every possible tool of limitation on the conduct of these groups. This objective is stated by Aboul-Enein and Zuhur, who argue that 'understanding the importance of the classic Islamic texts and the ultimate goals of Islam itself – peace and social equity – will enable us to fight terrorism through information operations combined with other means'.[49]

Suppression of diversity

Scholars' unwillingness to confront the different interpretations also offers a reading of Islamic law that strips it of its plurality. Islamic law is a legal system that was shaped by influential Muslim jurists, who have at many times provided different opinions on matters relating to the conduct of hostilities. Proposing a question regarding Islamic law's position on any matter would not only need to be qualified by asking about the position of a certain school of Islamic law, but even by asking about the position of a certain jurist. At many times jurists from within the same school disagreed with each other over particular issues.[50] The selectivity of the modern scholar can lead to confusion about conflicting opinions.

Perhaps the issue of the definition of a combatant best illustrates this confusion. Some scholars, like al-Zuḥaylī, argue that a 'non-combatant who is not taking part in warfare, either by action, opinion, planning or supplies, must not be attacked'.[51] Hamidullah, on the other hand, argues that 'combatants are only those who are physically capable of fighting'.[52] The distinction between defining a combatant as one participating in fighting, and alternatively as one capable of fighting, leads to dramatically different outcomes on the battlefield. While both arguments show reliance on sources and earlier juridical works, both views are presented as the definitive position in the jurisprudence of war rather than possible readings thereof. The decisiveness of the tone in these works puts the reader in the difficult position of being unable to understand how combatants are expected to be treated. Can any able bodied man be killed, or are Muslims only allowed to kill those who participate in fighting?

The confusion caused is an outcome of modern authors' failure to acknowledge and address the diversity of juristic positions in the field. Islamic law is an extremely plural field, full of different and distinct views regarding every aspect of legal regulation, including the conduct of warfare. Unless a modern scholar is willing to engage in a close reading of the extensive list of sources relating to the matter, it is almost impossible to determine the position of Islamic laws of war towards a matter such as the definition of a combatant. While the existence of a unified position is highly contentious, authors' pretence that their interpretation is the 'true' one causes confusion among readers when they witness contradictory readings that equally claim authenticity and legitimacy. Aside from the awkwardness of applying a modern definition of who a combatant is to the Islamic legal system articulated centuries before war as we know it, one can hardly provide an answer to who may be targeted during war according to Islamic law. While al-Shāfiʿī argued that older men may be killed,[53] al-Sarakhsī, the Ḥanafī scholar, argued that they shouldn't be targeted,[54] while Ibn Ḥazm argued that all men, including priests and monks, could be killed.[55] In brief, diversity and conflicting positions have always existed in juristic interpretations of the sources of the law.[56] However, current scholarship suppresses this diversity in order to promote specific readings congruent with their perceptions of societal needs for the regulation of warfare.

Context and details matter

The social context of jurisprudence

While functionalist literature seems to have been assessing the conduct of hostilities in Islam against assumed social objectives of warfare limitation derived from the IHL tradition, other scholars have attempted to locate Muslim jurisprudence within its historical context. In addition to numerous valuable works attempting to examine the relationship between Islamic law and its context,[57] several works have instead looked at the context of law in terms of the relationship between Western law and Islamic law,[58] as well as the relationship between Islamic law and international law.[59] More specifically there have also been several examinations of the role of the socio-political context in the development and the articulation of Islamic laws on armed conflict, as noted below. It has been mentioned by more than one scholar that Islamic law was responsive to societal norms and standards,[60] and that the jurisprudence reflected interaction between the Arab Islamic culture and the culture of new converts.[61] Khadduri suggests that 'there is ample evidence to show, however, that Islamic law evolved from Arab customary law and that, after the expansion of the Islamic state, Islam absorbed the local custom and practices of the conquered territories no less than other religious systems had done'.[62]

Abou El Fadl's discussion of juristic discourse on issues relating to armed conflict is indeed nuanced and detailed in its examination of the dynamics of the development of the juridical tradition. He argues that jurists were interested in balancing what they perceived as inalienable moral principles with utilitarian functional needs and that their reasoning was focused on resolving the tension between the two.[63] How those interests played out with each jurist is still unclear, since Abou El Fadl's article posits a hypothesis based on a general survey of the literature and calls for a detailed linguistic study of juristic works in order to understand the dynamics of his proposed mechanism.[64]

It should be noted, however, that the contextual analysis of jurisprudence in no way promotes a limited understanding, with Islamic law as synonymous with Islamic jurisprudence. I agree with newer trends in Islamic legal historiography that the actual practice of Muslim societies, whether in conflicts, or in court proceedings relating possibly to the division of the booty (if it exists), as well as correspondences with non-Muslim empires and the caliphs' treatment of rebellion, are equally indicative of Islamic law,[65] and that a focus on the jurisprudence does not comprehend the full complexity of this legal system. But awareness of this structure does not, at the same time, undermine the jurisprudence as an essential component of this legal structure that deserves analysis and deconstruction, especially in light of the prevalent modern assertion of its prominence.

Relationship with international law: from inferiority to critical engagement

While critical of existing comparative works, this paper doesn't deny the potential for comparative analysis here. To the contrary, I believe that, once an extensive study of Islamic jurisprudence is conducted and once we are able to understand the different factors shaping juristic views, we can attempt to use Islamic jurisprudence and IHL as alternative frameworks that address the use of force and that can potentially legitimate particular approaches to conflict. The alternative frameworks adopted by each of these two regimes can aid us in understanding the biases of each of them or, as Karen Engle defines it, to engage in mutual self-reflection.[66] In other words, both legal regimes can lead us to understand that the adopted approach to violence in one of them is neither inevitable nor the most protective and can thus be built on to help us see the tendency of each regime to recognise and tolerate particular patterns of violence.

Commentators often assume that the two primary principles of IHL are its universal application and its humanitarian objective. The assumption is that international law is the legal system devised by states to govern relationships between equal states,[67] and to minimise the casualties of war to the most feasible extent possible. Contrasted with this legal system, Islamic law is positioned as either an archaic legal system that fails to set the same constraints on armed conflict or as an equal to international law in its assertion of humanitarianism.

This section offers an alternative comparative approach premised on the perception of a legal system as responsive to and constructive of social 'reality'. To do so, it pays attention to how law plays a major role in engineering society and legitimising social arrangements by persuading people that the existing structure is inevitable.[68] I argue that contrasting power arrangements in both systems can help challenge this perceived inevitability. I also argue that comparative work examining the relationship between those two legal systems should move beyond measuring Islamic law against international law's yardstick, not just because it clouds our analysis of Islamic law, but also because it contributes to a fanciful understanding of international law, an understanding that fails to acknowledge the implications of this legal regime in modern conflict. As Kennedy notes, 'Law is perhaps the most visible part of military life when it privileges the killing and destruction of battle. If you kill this way, and not that, here and not there, these people and not those – what you do is privileged. If not, it is criminal.'[69] Thus this section calls for critical engagement between the two legal systems, whereby such engagement exposes the biases of each and reveals to each the potential for alternatives.

Nothing is better suited to this alternative comparative analysis than the contrast between the regulation of international and non-international armed conflicts in international law, on the one hand, and the regulation of wars with non-Muslims and of *baghy* (wars between Muslims) in classical Islamic jurisprudence, on the other hand. As Berman, and others,[70] argue, the view of international law as an outsider to war, attempting to regulate and humanise it, fails to account for the project's implication in the construction of war as a separate legal sphere where certain acts and actors of violence are condoned and others overridden. 'Rather than *opposing violence*, the legal construction of war serves to *channel violence* into certain forms of activity engaged in by certain kinds of people, while excluding other forms engaged in by other people.'[71] According to Berman, the regime of war reflects clear statist bias, a bias that ends up delegitimising forms of violence that do not conform to the established legal construct through denial of applicability of the law. For example, before the 1948 Geneva Conventions, war only existed, legally, between recognised states, hence denying the applicability of the rules of war to colonial conflicts.[72] Anghie and Chimni show how this bias is an example of international law's colonial civilising mission, where it is 'the "other", the non-European tribes, infidels, barbarians, who are identified as the source of all violence, and who must therefore be suppressed by an even more intense violence.'[73] According to Berman, even later attempts in the 1948 Geneva Conventions and its additional protocol to regulate, albeit in a more limited fashion, intra-state conflicts were still 'based on the state-like quality of the participating entities…In other words, the statist bias would be mitigated only by the governmental bias.'[74] For example, Common Article 3 of the Geneva Conventions and the Second Additional Protocol may still allow the state to prosecute rebels for the mere act of rebellion.[75]

On the other hand, classical Islamic jurists do not uphold state-centric biases of IHL in their approach to conflicts between parties within the Islamic Umma (nation). Unlike international law, a system devised by and for states, Islamic jurisprudence on rebellion was developed by jurists, who were relatively autonomous from the ruling authority.[76] These jurists developed a system that denies the ruler the power to prosecute rebels once they put down their arms.[77] Unlike non-Muslims, their property may not be confiscated and their women and children may not be taken as captives.[78] Arguably the regime developed by many of the jurists examined was interested in establishing outside control of the authority of the ruler,[79] as well as an emphasis on the relative sanctity of Muslim life and property.

More important than the inclination towards immunity for rebels from criminal liability for the act of rebellion, many Muslim jurists allow for more significant protection frameworks for rebelling parties and those who fall under their control, in comparison with conflicts with communities outside the Muslim nation. For example, whereas most jurists are reluctant to accept enslavement of captives taken by rebels because of their adherence to the Islamic faith,[80] the same jurists grant the imām wide discretion in the enslavement of captives taken after a conflict with a non-Muslim entity.[81] Additionally, some scholars show a relative reluctance to the employment of tactics that are likely to incur some damage to those in proximity to rebels, but show less reluctance towards resorting to such weapons with non-Muslims. For example, al-Shāfiʿī argues that, in *baghy* wars, indiscriminate weapons such as mangonels (rock hurling machines) may only be resorted to in reciprocity or to avert serious damage to the imām's people.[82] In wars with non-Muslims al-Shāfiʿī argues that the prophet only prohibited the deliberate singling out of women and children as targets.[83] To prove this assertion, he relies on several prophetic traditions that include the use of hurling machines against the people of Ṭā'if and Banū al-Naḍīr,[84] and on a Ḥadīth attributed to the prophet, in which the prophet is reported to have been asked regarding the death of women and children during night raids, and responded by stating that 'they [women and children] are from them.'[85] This Hadīth is understood by al-Shāfiʿī and others to indicate that non-Muslim women and children may be killed during relatively indiscriminate use of weapons during conflict.

> And if the enemy shields itself...there is nothing wrong with attacking them with mangonels, catapults, fire, scorpions, snakes or anything they hate, or open up water on them so that they

drown or get buried in mud, regardless of whether they have children, women or monks with them.[86]

Similarly Ibn Qudāma, despite being one of the more restrictive interpreters of the use of indiscriminate weapons during conflict with non-Muslims, still accepts the use of mangonels against non-Muslims, regardless of whether or not it is necessary.[87] However, he argues that the use of such weapons against Muslim rebels should be refrained from unless necessary.[88] Ibn Ḥazm argues that flooding and burning may not be resorted to if the rebels are not solely confined to the targeted area, in order to prevent the infliction of damage on those in the area. He even argues that, if a fire is lit around the targeted area, an exit point must be created, in order to guarantee the opportunity for Muslim rebels to repent and refrain from their rebellion.[89] At the same time, Ibn Ḥazm, who is relatively brief on the issue of damage inflicted upon un-targetable categories in non-Muslim land, argues that non-Muslim women and children may be unintentionally killed during night raids.[90]

On the other hand, al-Shaybānī, a Ḥanafī jurist closely affiliated with the Abbasid Caliph, al-Rashīd, shows a relative inclination to accept the infliction of damage on rebels and their surroundings. Whereas the regime provided for by al-Shaybānī still offers a degree of protection and legitimacy to rebels, it also seems clearly in its interest to give a certain level of freedom, though limited, to the political authority. His work refers extensively to the conduct of 'Alī (the fourth caliph) with rebels and his unilateral promise to rebels that 'whoever flees [from us] shall not be chased, no [Muslim] prisoner of war shall be killed, and no wounded in the battle shall be despatched'.[91] Nevertheless, an innovative approach is adopted to limit the power of the rebels and set a condition for the non-existence of a group of rebels 'with whom refuge might be taken, but if a group of them has survived with whom refuge might be taken, then their prisoners could be killed, their fugitives pursued and their wounded dispatched'.[92] This approach not only deprives the rebels of the alternative to cease fighting but also allows the death of Muslim bystanders who might happen to be in the rebel camp, including Muslim women and children. However, this different approach employed by al-Shaybānī arguably proves the claim that there is a direct correlation between the relative independence of jurists from the political authority and inclinations to devise a system that limits the discretion of the caliph in his conduct of armed conflict with rebelling parties since, from the examples mentioned above, al-Shaybānī was the closest to the political authority of his time.

This quick survey of the different jurisprudence works on *baghy* (rebellion) and wars with non-Muslims indicates, as earlier stated, a diverse and plural legal tradition. Detailed examination of such juristic works is beyond the scope of this paper. However, even a brief survey indicates that none of the conclusions of the abovementioned jurists was inevitable or directly extrapolated from their theoretical positions on Islamic jurisprudence methodology.[93] Rather they indicate varying degrees of inconsistency and the influence of several factors outside the domain of formalist legal interpretation. For the purposes of this paper two important conclusions may be drawn: that international humanitarian law is more state-centric than Islamic jurisprudence on armed conflict; and that both legal regimes reflect varying manifestations of power structures in the societies concerned and that such manifestations were meant to protect particular interests.

State centrism of international humanitarian law

One of the potential conclusions that can be drawn from the study of the Islamic jurisprudence on armed conflict is that regulation of armed conflict does not have to stem from the political authority. There is evidence of deviations by political authority from juristic views on rebellion as well as on armed conflict with non-Muslims. Nevertheless, the legal system articulated by jurists of classical Islamic jurisprudence defies the logic that, since states enjoy monopoly over the legitimate use of force, the best way of minimising war casualties is to rely on state consent to the regulation of violence. In fact, Islamic jurisprudence indicates that the political authority may be a subject of the legal regime rather than an articulator of it.

Different protective interests

The examples above show the inevitability of legal systems channelling and legitimising particular types of violence in conflict situations at the expense of others. In contrasting the biases of the two regimes of IHL and Islamic jurisprudence, we are confronted by the fact that both systems are influenced by factors other than humanitarianism and the value of human life. Both systems are interested in advancing particular political objectives and the legal regime is designed to ensure that the paths to those political objectives are clear.

For example, the protection afforded to rebellion in Islamic jurisprudence indicates that IHL's inclination to curtail combatant immunity in rebellion, and its reluctance to articulate a system of equal protection in situations of internal armed conflict, deliberately tolerates the state's discretion to inflict damage on those who rebel against it. It also indicates that combatant immunity in international conflicts is designed to expand the legitimate resort to violence by the warring parties in such situations. Conversely, the IHL framework helps us see the bias evident in Islamic jurisprudence, which inclines towards more protection for Muslim lives, and asserts, as Abou El Fadl argues, that the caliph should be scrutinised in his resort to violence against his opponents. Ultimately the regulations of IHL and Islamic jurisprudence are equal and alternative expressions of underlying power structures and ideological constructions of war.

The analyses of Berman, Anghie and Chimniare are insightful in their exploration of how IHL advances states' interests and of how this bias can be traced back to the colonial project and the use of IHL to justify the violence of empire and delegitimise the violence of colonial subjects. Berman also shows how this colonial project translated into modern day biases against unlawful combatants in the 'war on terror'.[94] But these analyses are challenged by traditionalist views of international law that argue that the current system is the only feasible and working system, in which states are and will continue to be the sole shapers of international law.[95] This is where reliance on Islamic jurisprudence as an example of an alternative system of governance of war can be useful.

This paper also rejects the calls for interaction between the two legal regimes and the assumption that the two systems should cooperate to achieve a more humane world.[96] The two legal regimes are about the promotion of different power structures that might at times have coinciding interests. Our understanding of what constitutes humane is shaped in part by these existing structures. Thus, rather than cooperating to cover up the biases of each, I propose academic exposure of tension between the two, that is to say, a critical engagement. This critical engagement must assert the lack of moral superiority of either over the other to ensure that Islamic law, pushed to the background for decades because of the assumed supremacy and universality of international law, is not relegated to the position of an inferior legal system attempting to prove its congruency with the other.

Comparative critical engagement can also empower Muslim jurists to challenge what some of them regard as a cultural assault on their legal traditions. From a state-centric and colonial perspective international law has been most successful at eroding the legitimacy of alternative legal regimes through its claim to positivist objectivity and equality between states.[97] Juxtaposing those two legal regimes against each other and exposing their biases could help erode the legitimacy of international law as an alternative civilising legal regime.[98] But, much like international lawyers, in order for Muslim scholars to succeed in challenging the international legal framework, they must engage in self-criticism and acknowledge the susceptibility of any legal project, including Islamic law, to political influences that shape legal reasoning and outcomes. It is this critical engagement between the two regimes that is necessary to help international and Islamic lawyers see their blind spots.

Legal structures serve particular power interests and are disguised as apolitical and objective legal projects. The revelation or exposition of these biases helps challenge prevailing powers and deny them the claim of objectivity. Rather than debating whether Islamist militants have the right to inflict damage on particular groups under Islamic law or IHL, the debate instead shifts towards the different interests involved in the infliction of such damage. Rather than debating whether IHL allows states to restrict unlawful combatants to a grey area between international and domestic law, the debate instead focuses on what is achieved and for whom by withholding legal protection from certain groups.

Such comparative work could alert the advocates of harmony between the two legal systems to the dangers of those projects. By exposing the biases of both systems, comparative critical work will help alert humanists asserting international law's 'universalist' values to the underlying ideological foundations of the international legal doctrine. The debate on the 'war on terror' is best suited to illustrating the shortcomings of universalist claims. For example, Bennoune, who published an article in the early 1990s on Islamic law's congruency with international humanitarian law, later published another calling upon international lawyers to assert the relevance of international law to Muslim fundamentalism. Bennoune is critical of international lawyers' condemnation of the 'war on terror' and its violations of international law while they remain silent on violations committed by Muslim fundamentalists. She goes on to argue that such silence risks the assertion of the existence of 'an undifferentiated Muslim population'.[99]

Bennoune is correct in asserting the need for empowerment of Muslim voices fighting al-Qaeda. Nevertheless, her endorsement of international law's universal spirit, and her attribution of international lawyers' silence about al-Qaeda to a self-conscious ambivalence about international law's imperial heritage,[100] fails to account for the role of contemporary international law in creating such silences. First, given that most international lawyers reject the critical and Third World approaches denounced by Bennoune, it is unlikely that such approaches silenced them on al-Qaeda's actions. Rather, it is the doctrine of international law itself that allows for such silence through, among other thing, the distinction made between international and internal conflicts. As Berman and Megret point out, modern day terrorists are simply extensions of the unprivileged colonised 'Others' of international law – Others who are left hanging in the cracks of the system in a manner convenient for states in their conduct of armed conflict with non-state actors.[101] This silence is, as elaborated earlier, best demonstrated through contrast with the Islamic jurisprudential approach to rebellion and its relative protection of life and property during rebellions.

Muslim fundamentalists undeniably 'pose particular threats to the human rights of free thinkers, women, religious minorities, [and] LGBT persons',[102] but the solution is not to wholeheartedly endorse a legal system that often poses threats to those same groups. For example, one potentially interesting project is to examine how both legal systems contribute to discrimination against women. Much can be said about Islamic jurisprudence's exception of women from targetable groups, in contrast with IHL's relative silence on the disproportionately gendered outcome of violence during wartime. Such an approach would contribute to the debate on the role of protectionist, gendered stereotypes on one hand, and the role of liberalism and blind equality in reproducing gender hierarchies on the other hand.[103]

Finally, this critical assessment could help Islamic legal scholars employ *ijtihād*[104] and articulate modern jurisprudence that is freed from the pretence of adherence to classical scholarship. In fact, comparative critical examination of the two legal regimes could help Islamic legal scholarship articulate a new regime that does not claim objectivity, but one that is willing to embrace and acknowledge its subjectivity, while benefiting from a primary advantage denied to international lawyers: playing the role of the modern jurist, the jurist who enjoys enough distance from power to promote the interests of those disadvantaged by it, and to do so by drawing on the diverse nature of Islamic jurisprudence that helps defuse authority. Of course, there are several obstacles to such a romantic view of modern Muslim scholarship, including the privileged positions enjoyed by many scholars, the ongoing encroachment by many Muslim states on intellectual freedom and, last but not least, the reluctance of most traditional scholars to such a radical reorientation of the field. But if Islamic law is to become relevant in modern times without falling prey to the ongoing legitimacy battle between the mainstream and the militant approaches, then 'debunking' the tradition is necessary.

Disclosure statement

No potential conflict of interest was reported by the author.

Acknowledgements

I would like to thank Lynn Welchman, Vanja Hamzic, Ali Hammoudi, Sujith Xavier, Amar Bhatia, Adil Khan, Adrian Smith, Mazen Masri, Robert Knox, Usha Natarajan, Nahed Samour, John Reynolds and the attendees of the Second Cambridge Journal of International Law Conference and the 2015 Third World Approaches to International Law conference for their valuable and insightful feedback on this paper. It goes without saying, however, that all shortcomings in the paper are, in spite of their excellent feedback, the responsibility of the author.

Notes

1. For an examination of the history of jihād, see, for example, Bassiouni, "Evolving Approaches to Jihad"; Reiter, *War, Peace & International Relations*, 16–18; and Johnson and Kelsay, *Cross, Crescent and Sword*.
2. Abou El Fadl, "Between Functionalism and Morality," 113. For the purposes of this paper, 'classical' refers to jurisprudence from the formative and medieval eras.
3. Hashmi, "Saving and Taking Lives," 129.
4. Whereas the paper predominantly uses the term 'international humanitarian law' to refer to the international legal framework governing the regulation of armed conflict, it also uses the terms 'laws of war', 'law of armed conflict' and the Latin term '*jus in bello*' (laws in war).
5. Hallaq, *Sharī'a*, 340–341.
6. Frankenberg, "Critical Comparisons," 436.
7. See, for example, Hallaq, "*Shar ī'a*"; and Shalakany, "Islamic Legal Histories."
8. See Evans, "The Double Edged Sword'; and Shah, *Islamic Law*, 30–91.
9. Al-Zuḥaylī, "Islam and International Law," 269. For consistency with other works by the author, I am using the proper transliteration. It should be noted, however, that the article was published by the Red Cross under the name of al-Zuhili.
10. Frankenberg, "Critical Comparisons," 436.
11. Gordon, "Critical Legal Histories," 61–62.
12. Frankenberg, "Critical Comparisons," 436.
13. Legrand, "How to compare Now," 238.
14. Al-Zuḥaylī, "Islam and International Law," 269.
15. Al-Shāfi'ī, *Al-Umm*, 4: 270.
16. Abū Zahra, *Al-'Ilaqāt Al-Dawliyya fī Al-Islam*, 97.
17. Hamidullah, *Muslim Conduct of State*, 195.
18. Firestone, *Jihād*, 34.
19. Cockayne, "Islam and International Humanitarian Law," 597.
20. Hamidullah, *Muslim Conduct of State*, 46.
21. Anghie and Chimni, "Third World Approaches."
22. Shah, *Islamic Law*, 4.
23. Mayer, "War and Peace," 196.
24. Hallaq, *The Origin and Evolution of Islamic Law*, 193.
25. Landau-Tasseron, "Non-combatants," 1.
26. Landau-Tasseron, "Non-combatants," 2.
27. ICJ, *Nuclear Weapons*, para 97.
28. Latin term referring to the legal regulation of the use of force.
29. Al-Zuḥaylī, "Islam and International Law," 282.
30. Al-Shāfi'ī, *Al-Umm*, 4: 337.
31. Al-Zuḥaylī, "Islam and International Law," 282.
32. Al-Shāfi'ī, *Al-Umm*, 4: 390.
33. Munir, "Suicide Attacks," 88.
34. See, for example, Ibn Ḥazm, *al-Muḥalla*, 7: 335; Ibn Qudāma, *Al-Mughnī*, 13: 107; Al-Shāfi'ī, *Al-Umm*, 4: 257; Al-Shaybānī, *The Islamic Law of Nations*, 77; and Mālik, *Al-Mudawwana*, 1: 503.
35. Al-Zuḥaylī, "Islam and International Law," 283.
36. Al-Zuḥaylī, *Athār Al-Ḥarb*, 432.
37. Bennoune, "As-Salāmu 'Alaykum?," 625.
38. Bennoune, "As-Salāmu 'Alaykum?," 623.
39. Ibn Ḥazm, *Al- Muḥalla*, 7: 299.
40. Abu Zahra, *Al-'Ilaqāt*, 102.
41. Bassiouni, *The Sharī'a and Islamic Criminal Justice*.
42. Sālim, "Bayn Al-'Uhda Al-'Umarīya."

43. Hamidullah, *Muslim Conduct of State*, 206. Ibn Rushd himself acknowledges that the majority of jurists allowed the killing of captives and that there is a consensus that they could be killed if their threat was established. See Ibn Rushd II, *Bidayāt al-Mujtahid*, 2: 145.
44. Abu Zahra, *Al-'Ilaqāt*, 115.
45. Ibn Rushd II, *Bidāyat*, 2: 145.
46. Abu Zahra, *Al-'Ilaqāt*, 99–102.
47. Al-Zuḥaylī, "Islam and International Law," 270.
48. Al-Zuḥaylī, *Athār Al-Ḥarb*, 19.
49. Aboul Enein and Zuhur, *Islamic Rulings on Warfare*, 29.
50. Khadduri, "Introduction: Shaybani's Siyar," 58.
51. Al-Zuḥaylī, "Islam and International Law," 282.
52. Hamidullah, *Muslim Conduct of State*, 195.
53. Al-Shāfi'ī, *Al-Umm*, 4: 340.
54. Al-Sarakhsī, *Al-Mabsūṭ*, 10: 34.
55. Ibn Ḥazm, *Al-Muḥalla*, 7: 296.
56. Hallaq, *Sharī'a*, 76.
57. See, for example, Hallaq, "What is Shari'a?"; Zaman, *Religion and Politics*; and Rahman, *Islamic Methodology in History*.
58. See Abou Odeh, "Comparatively Speaking," 287–307.
59. Emon et al., *Islamic Law*.
60. Sachedina, "The Development of Jihad," 36.
61. Donner, "The Sources of Islamic Conceptions," 32; Khadduri, *War and Peace*, 20, 33; and An-Naim, *Towards an Islamic Reformation*, 2.
62. Khadduri, *War and Peace*, 20. For similar contextual readings, see An-Naim, *Towards an Islamic Reformation*, 142; Peters, *Jihad in Classical and Modern Islam*, 2; Al-Dawoody, *The Islamic Laws of War*, 143; and Hallaq, *Sharī'a*, 324.
63. Abou El Fadl, "Between Functionalism and Morality," 105.
64. Abou El Fadl, "Between Functionalism and Morality," 121.
65. Shalakany, "Islamic Legal Histories," 79–80.
66. Engle, "Comparative Law," 366.
67. Sassoli, *Transnational Armed Groups*, 4.
68. Gordon, "Critical Legal Histories," 106, 109.
69. Kennedy, "Modern War," 179.
70. See, for example, Escorihuela, "Humanitarian Law."
71. Berman, "Privileging Combat?," 5, emphasis in original text; See also Kennedy, *Of War and Law*, 36–37; and Anghie and Chimni, "Third World Approaches," 80.
72. Berman, "Privileging Combat?," 15.
73. Anghie and Chimni, "Third World Approaches," 85.
74. Anghie and Chimni, "Third World Approaches," 19.
75. Berman, "Privileging Combat?," 20.
76. Abou El Fadl, *Rebellion*, 327.
77. Despite the potential for the application of other legal regimes in Islamic jurisprudence, such as the harsher regime of *ḥirāba*, normally reserved for highway robbery or apostasy, to incidents of rebellion, this paper is premised on the primary regime addressing rebellion in Islamic jurisprudence, which is *baghy*.
78. Al-Shaybānī, *Siyar*, 231–232; Al-Shāfi'ī, *Al-Umm*, 4: 311–312; Ibn Ḥazm, *Al-Muḥalla*, 11: 102; and Ibn Qudāma, *Al-Mughnī*, 12: 254.
79. Abou El Fadl, *Rebellion*, 326.
80. Al-Shaybānī, *The Islamic Law of Nations*, 231–232; Al-Shāfi'ī, *Al-Umm*; 4: 311–312, Ibn Ḥazm, *Al-Muḥalla*, 11: 102; and Ibn Qudāma, *al-Mughnī*, 12: 254.
81. Al-Shaybānī, *The Islamic Law of Nations*, 97–98; Al-Shāfi'ī, *Al-Umm*, 4: 335; Ibn Qudāma, *Al-Mughnī*, 13: 44–47; and Ibn Ḥazm, *Al-Muḥalla*, 7: 324.
82. Al-Shāfi'ī, *Al-Umm*, 4: 311.
83. Al-Shāfi'ī, *Al-Umm*, 4: 347–348.

84. Al-Shāfi'ī, *Al-Umm*, 4: 347.
85. Al-Shāfi'ī, *Al-Umm*, 4: 337.
86. Al-Shāfi'ī, *Al-Umm*, 4: 347. The Editor of *Al-Umm*, Maḥmud Mutrajī, provides evidence that this prophetic tradition was abrogated by other traditions. See *Al-Umm*, 4: 337–338, footnote 3.
87. Ibn Qudāma, *Al-Mughnī*, 13: 138–140.
88. Ibn Qudāma, *al-Mughnī*, 12: 247
89. Ibn Ḥazm, *Al-Muḥalla*, 11: 116–117
90. Ibn Ḥazm, *Al-Muḥalla*, 7: 296.
91. Al-Shaybānī, *The Islamic Law of Nations*, 231 (clarifications in brackets in original translations).
92. Al-Shaybānī, *The Islamic Law of Nations*, 232.
93. Badawi, "Sunni Islam," 301–370; and Abou El Fadl, *Rebellion*, 62–100.
94. Berman, "Privileging Combat?," 69.
95. Simma and Paulus, "Symposium on Method," 303–304.
96. Baderin, "Religion and International Law," 652.
97. Anghie, "Peripheries."
98. Megret, "Savages," 35.
99. Bennoune, "Remembering the Other's Others," 642.
100. Bennoune, "Remembering the Other's Others," 661.
101. Berman, "Privileging Combat?," 69; and Megret, "From Savages to Unlawful Combatants," 37.
102. Bennoune, "Remembering the Other's Others," 650–651.
103. For feminist readings of the biases of the laws of war, see Charlesworth, "Symposium on Method," 379–394; Gardham, "A Feminist Analysis," 265–278; and Chinkin, "Gender-related Violence," 75–81.
104. Whereas the terms ijtihad and jihad stem from the same arabic source (j.h.d), for effort, ijtihad is a technical term for the process of studying and understanding God's laws.

Bibliography

Abou El Fadl, Khaled. "Between Functionalism and Morality: The Juristic Debates on the Conduct of War." In *Islamic Ethics of Life: Abortion, War and Euthanasia*, edited by Jonathon E. Brockopp, 103–128. Columbia, SC: University of South Carolina Press, 2003.

Abou El Fadl. *Rebellion and Violence in Islamic Law*. Cambridge: Cambridge University Press, 2002.

Abou Odeh, Lama. "Comparatively Speaking: The 'Honor' of the 'East' and the 'Passion' of the 'West'." *Utah Law Review* (1997): 287–307.

Aboul-Enein, H. Yousuf, and Sherifa, Zuhur. *Islamic Rulings on Warfare*. Darby, MT: Strategic Studies Institute, US Army War College/Diane Publishing, 2004. http://www.fas.org/man/eprint/islamic.pdf.

Abū Zahra, Muḥammad. "Al-Ilaqāt Al-Dawliya fī Al-Islām." In *Majma' Al-Buḥuth Al-Islāmīya First Conference*. Cairo: Al-Azhar, 1964.

Al-Dawoody, Ahmed. *The Islamic Law of War: Justifications and Regulations*. Palgrave Macmillan, 2009.

Al-Sarakhsī, Muḥammad Ibn Aḥmad Ibn Abī Sahl. *Al-Mabsūṭ*. Beirut: Dār Al-Kutub Al-'Ilmīya, 2001.

Al-Shāfi'ī, Muḥammad Ibn Idrīs. *Al-Umm*. Edited by Maḥmūd Mutrajī. Beirut: Dār al-Kutub Al-'Ilmiya, 1993.

Al-Shaybānī, Muḥammad Ibn Al-Ḥasan. *The Islamic Law of Nations: Shaybānī's Siyar*. 2nd ed. Translated by Majid Khadduri. Baltimore, MD: Johns Hopkins University Press, 1966.

Al-Zuḥaylī, Wahba. *Athār Al-Ḥarb fī Al-Fiqh Al-Islāmī*. 3rd ed. Damascus: Dār Al-Fikr, 1981.

Al-Zuḥaylī, Wahba. "Islam and International Law." *International Review of the Red Cross* 87, no. 858 (2005): 269–283. https://www.icrc.org/eng/assets/files/other/irrc_858_zuhili.pdf

Anghie, Antony. "Finding the Peripheries: Sovereignty and Colonialism in Nineteenth Century International Law." *Harvard International Law Journal* 40, no. 1 (1999): 1–80.

Anghie, Antony, and B. S. Chimni. "Third World Approaches to International Law and Individual Responsibility in Internal Conflicts." *Chinese Journal of International Law* 2 (2003): 77–103. doi:10.1093/oxfordjournals.cjilaw.a000480.

An-Naim, Abdullahi Ahmed. *Towards an Islamic Reformation: Civil Liberties, Human Rights and International Law*. Cairo: American University in Cairo Press, 1992.

Badawi, Nesrine. "Sunni Islam. Part I: Classical Sources." In *Religion, War and Ethics*, edited by Gregory Reichberg and Henrik Syse, 301–369. Cambridge: Cambridge University Press, 2014.

Baderin, Mashood A. "Religion and International Law: Friends or Foes?" *European Human Rights Law Review*, no. 5 (2009): 637–658. doi: 10.2139/ssrn.1621375

Bassiouni, M. Cherif. "Evolving Approaches to Jihad: From Self-defense to Revolutionary and Regime-change Political Violence." *Chicago Journal of International Law* 8, no. 1 (2007). http://chicagounbound.uchicago.edu/cjil/vol8/iss1/8

Bassiouni, M. Cherif. *The Shari'a and Islamic Criminal Justice in Time of War and Peace*. Cambridge: Cambridge University Press, 2014. Kindle Edition.

Bennoune, Karima. "'As-Salāmu 'Alaykum? Humanitarian Law in Islamic Jurisprudence." *Michigan Journal of International Law* 15 (1993–94): 605–643.

Bennoune, Karima. "Remembering the Other's Others: Theorizing the Approach of International Law to Muslim Fundamentalism." *Columbia Human Rights Law Review* 41 (2009–10): 635–698.

Berman, Nathaniel. "Privileging Combat? Contemporary Conflict and the Legal Construction of War." *Columbia Journal of Transnational Law* 43 (2004–05): 1–71. https://www.law.upenn.edu/live/files/2145-berman-privileging-combatpdf.

Charlesworth, Hilary. "Symposium on Method in International Law: Feminist Methods in International Law." *American Journal of International Law* 93 (1999): 379–394. http://www.jstor.org/stable/2997996.

Chinkin, Christine. "Gender-related Violence and International Criminal Law and Justice." In *The Oxford Companion to International Criminal Justice*, edited by Antonio Cassese, 75–81. New York: Oxford University Press, 2009.

Cockayne, James. "Islam and International Humanitarian Law: From a Clash to a Conversation between Civilizations." *International Review of the Red Cross* 84, no. 847 (2002): 597–626. https://www.icrc.org/eng/resources/documents/misc/5fld2f.htm.

Donner, Fred. "The Sources of Islamic Conceptions of War." In *Just War and Jihad: Historical and Theoretical Perspectives on War and Peace in Western and Islamic Traditions*, edited by John Kelsay and James Turner Johnson, 31–69. New York: Greenwood Press, 1991.

Emon, Anvor, Mark Ellis, and Benjamin Glahn (eds.). *Islamic Law and International Human Rights Law*. Oxford: Oxford University Press, 2012.

Engle, Karen. "Comparative Law as Exposing the Foreign System's Internal Critique: An Introduction." *Utah Law Review* (1997): 359–369.

Escorihuela, Alejandro Lorite. "Humanitarian Law and Human Rights Law: The Politics of Distinction." *Michigan State Journal of International Law* 19, no. 2 (2011): 299–407.

Evans, Carolyn. "The Double Edged Sword: Religious Influences on International Humanitarian Law." *Melbourne Journal of International Law* 6 (2005): 1–32.

Firestone, Reuven. *Jihād: The Origin of Holy War in Islam*. New York: Oxford University Press, 1999.

Frankenberg, Gunter. "Critical Comparisons: Re-thinking Comparative Law." *Harvard International Law Journal* 26 (1985): 411–455.

Gardham, Judith. "A Feminist Analysis of Certain Aspects of International Humanitarian Law" *Australian Yearbook of International Law* 12 (1988–89): 265–278.

Gordon, Robert W. "Critical Legal Histories" *Stanford Law Review* 36 (1984): 57–125.

Hallaq, Wael. *The Origin and Evolution of Islamic Law*. 2nd ed. Cambridge: Cambridge University Press, 2006.

Hallaq, Wael. *Sharī'a: Theory, Practice, Transformations*. Cambridge: Cambridge University Press, 2009.

Hallaq, Wael. "What is Sharia?" *Yearbook of Islamic and Middle Eastern Law* 12 (2005–06): 151–180.

Hamidullah, Muhammad. *Muslim Conduct of State*. Lahore: Kashmiri Bazar, 1945.

Hashmi, Sohail M. "Saving and Taking Lives in War: Three Modern Muslim Views." In *Islamic Ethics of Life: Abortion, War and Euthanasia*, edited by Jonathon E Brockopp, 129–154. South Carolina: University of South Carolina Press, 2003.

Ibn Ḥazm, Alī Aḥmad. *Al- Muḥalla Bī Al-Athār*. Beirut: al-Maktab al-Tijārī lil-Tiba'ah wa Al-Nashr, 1969.

Ibn Qudāma, Mūwaffaq al-Dīn Abī Muḥammad Abd Allāh ibn Aḥmad ibn Muḥammad. *Al-Mughnī* [The Sufficient]. Riyadh: Dār 'Ālam al-Kutub, 1999.

Ibn Rushd II, Abū Al-Walīd Muḥammad Ibn Aḥmad. *Bidāyat Al-Mujtahid wa Nihāyat Al-Muqtaṣid*. Cairo: Dār Al-Ḥadīth, 2004.

ICJ Advisory Opinion on the Legality of the Threat or Use of Nuclear Weapons. Advisory Opinion. ICJ Rep.226 (1996). Accessed July 20, 2011. http://www.icj-cij.org/docket/index.php?p1=3&p2=4&k=09&case=95

Johnson, James Turner, and John Kelsay, eds. *Cross, Crescent and Sword: The Justification and Limitation of War in Western and Islamic Tradition*. New York: Greenwood Press, 1990.

Kennedy, David. "Modern War and Modern Law". Speech given at the University of Baltimore School of Law, October 26, 2006. Published in *University of Baltimore Law Review* 36 (2007): 173–194.

Kennedy, David. *Of War and Law*. Princeton, NJ: Princeton University Press, 2006.

Khadduri, Majid. *War and Peace in the Law of Islam*. Baltimore, MD: Johns Hopkins University Press, 1955.

Landau-Tasseron, Ella. 'Non-Combatants in Muslim Legal Thought.' Center on Islam, Democracy and the Future of the Muslim World Monographs. Series no. 1, Paper 3 (2006). Accessed March 9, 2007. http://www.futureofmuslimworld.com/research/pubID.60/pub_detail.asp

Legrand, Pierre. "How to Compare Now." *Legal Studies* 16 (1996): 232–242.

Mālik ibn Anas, Al-Mudawwana al-Kubra lī al- Imām Mālik ibn Anās al-Aṣbaḥī. *The Grand Document of the Imām Mālik ibn Anās al-Aṣbaḥī*. Beirut: Dār al-Kutub al-'Ilmīya, 1994.

Mayer, Ann Elizabeth. "War and Peace in the Islamic Tradition." In *Just War and Jihad: Historical and Theoretical Perspectives on War and Peace in Western and Islamic Traditions*, edited by John Kelsay and James Turner Johnson, 195–226. New York: Greenwood Press, 1991.

Megret, Frederic. "From Savages to Unlawful Combatants: A Post-colonial Look at International Humanitarian Law's Other." In *International Law and its Others*, edited by Anne Orford, 265–317. Cambridge: Cambridge University Press, 2006.

Munir, Muhammad. "Suicide Attacks and Islamic Law." *International Review of the Red Cross* 90, no. 869 (2008): 71–89.

Peters, Rudolph. *Jihad in Classical and Modern Islam: A Reader*. Princeton, NJ: Marcus Wiener, 1996.

Rahman, Fazlur. *Islamic Methodology in History*. 3rd ed. Islamabad: Islamic Research Institute, 1995.

Reiter, Yitzhak. *War, Peace & International Relations in Islam*. Brighton: Sussex Academic Press, 2011.

Sachedina, Abdul Aziz. "The Development of Jihad in Islamic Revelation and History." In *Cross, Crescent and Sword: The Justification and Limitation of War in Western and Islamic Tradition*, edited by James Turner Johnson and John Kelsay, 35–50. New York: Greenwood Press, 1990.

Sālim, 'Abdul Raḥmān. "Bayn Al-'Uhda Al-'Umarīya wa 'Ahd Muḥammad Al-Fātiḥ lī Ahālī Al-Qusṭanṭīniya." *Al-Majlis Al-A'la lī al-Shū'un Al-Islāmīya*. Sixteenth Conference: 1075. Accessed June 7, 2011. http://www.elazhar.com/conf_au/16/conf_16.pdf.

Sassoli, Marco. *Transnational Armed Groups and International Humanitarian Law*. HPCR Occasional Paper Winter 2006. http://www.hpcrresearch.org/sites/default/files/publications/OccasionalPaper6.pdf.

Shah, Niaz. *Islamic Law and the Law of Armed Conflict: Armed Conflict in Pakistan*. Abingdon: Routledge, 2011.

Shalakany, Amr. "Islamic Legal Histories." *Berkley Journal of Middle Eastern and Islamic Law* 1 (2008): 2–82. doi: 10.15779/Z38CC7W

Simma, Bruno, and Andreas L. Paulus. "Symposium on Method in International Law: The Responsibility of Individuals for Human Rights Abuses in Internal Conflicts – A Positivist View." *American Journal of International Law* 93 (1999): 303–304.

Zaman, Muhammad Qasim. *Religion and Politics under the Early Abbasids: The Emergence of the Proto-Sunni Elite*. Leiden: Brill, 1997.

Decolonisation, dignity and development aid: a judicial education experience in Palestine

Reem Bahdi and Mudar Kassis

ABSTRACT
Taking Palestine as the focus of inquiry, and drawing on our experiences as co-directors of Karamah, a judicial education initiative focused on dignity, we reflect on the attributes of colonisation and the possibilities of decolonisation in Palestine through development aid. We conclude that decolonisation is possible even within development aid frameworks. We envision the current colonial condition in Palestine as a multi-faceted, complex and dynamic mesh that tightens and expands its control over the coveted colonial subject but that also contains holes that offer opportunities for resistance or refusal. We turn to Karamah to illustrate how some judges have insisted on a professional identity that merges the concepts of human dignity and self-determination and ultimately rejects the colonial condition inherent in both occupation and development aid. We conclude that in this process of professional identity (re)formation, members of the Palestinian judiciary have helped reveal the demands of decolonisation by demonstrating their commitment to realising human dignity through institutional power, and bringing occupation back into international development discourse.

> For two-thirds of the people on earth, this positive meaning of the word 'development'...is a reminder of *what they are not*. It is a reminder of an undesirable, undignified condition. To escape from it, they need to be enslaved to others' experiences and dreams (Emphasis is in the original).[1]

Introduction

Is it possible to participate simultaneously in development aid and decolonisation? Several decades of development aid have produced significant disappointments. Indeed, far from liberating and benefiting the Global South, development aid can entrench colonial forms.[2] Aid is ultimately a problematic construct that should be replaced with solidarity. But praxis scholars cannot ignore development aid in anticipation of new South–North engagement frameworks. Rather, emancipatory actors need strategies to harness existing frames against their colonial tendencies, remaining critical but not overly sceptical about the possibilities of decolonisation.

Given that occupation has produced de-development in Palestine, the withdrawal of development aid has significant consequences, including the risk of economic collapse. The possibility of participating in development aid in Palestine thus creates tensions for those committed to praxis and decolonisation. Ignoring or refusing to participate in development aid simply cedes space to those who will take it up without a critical lens or a commitment to decolonisation. But engaging on the terms set by development aid orthodoxies amounts to neo-colonial co-optation.

In this paper we reflect on the attributes of colonisation and decolonisation through development aid in Palestine. Borrowing from studies of indigenous assimilation,[3] we envision the current colonial condition in Palestine as a multi-faceted, complex and dynamic mesh. This mesh tightens and expands its control over the coveted colonised subject, but it also contains holes or spaces that offer up opportunities for resistance and refusal. We examine the requirements of decolonisation in the Palestinian context and draw on some of our experiences with the Karamah initiative to illustrate ways in which members of the judiciary have helped advance decolonisation through a dignity lens. Karamah, which means 'dignity' in Arabic, was a judicial education initiative organised by Birzeit University, Palestine and the University of Windsor, Canada that focused on promoting dignity in the Palestinian justice system through judicial education. We are of course not suggesting that judicial references to dignity have exhausted the decolonisation project in Palestine. Far from it. We argue that members of the Palestinian judiciary, through the various ways and sites in which they invoked dignity, helped make visible the parameters of the decolonisation project in Palestine against the intentions of colonial actors whose assumptions and agendas work towards denying the existing colonial condition in Palestine.

The colonial condition in Palestine

While we cannot completely map the elements and consequences of the colonial condition in Palestine, we highlight the basic features of the colonial terrain in this section. We do so for several reasons. An expansion of the colonial condition over the past several decades has made decolonisation more complicated. Ending the occupation no longer encapsulates this struggle, although, of course, it remains a vital part. By unravelling and naming the elements of the colonial condition in Palestine we identify the nature and scope of required decolonisation responses and emphasise the urgency of taking up opportunities for decolonisation.

The current colonial condition in Palestine includes traditional colonial structures as well as neo- and postcolonial forms perpetuated by a multiplicity of actors. Israeli occupation represents colonialism in its classic form. While its modalities and effects have varied over time and across Palestinian geography, Israel's occupation has consistently aimed at territorial imperialism using military might. As an occupying state, Israel has, for example, annexed Palestinian land and resources; built walls, settlements, roads, checkpoints and other structures that divide Palestine into enclaves resembling 'bantustans'; governed Palestine through a legal system that is largely bereft of justice or due process; used military weaponry against the West Bank and Gaza; and systematically defied Palestinian individual and collective human rights.[4]

Israel also relies on neo-colonial practices to discipline and control Palestine. Neo-colonialism is evident in Israel's relationship with the Palestinian Authority. Israeli leaders imagine the Palestinian Authority as the long arm of Israeli occupation and work to keep the Authority under Israeli control. Critics point to security cooperation between Israel and the Palestinian Authority as the quintessential example of neo-colonialism at work. They describe the ways in which Palestinian security forces have been deployed against Palestinians, ostensibly as part of an effort to support peace negotiations, but ultimately to the benefit of Israel's security at the expense of Palestine and Palestinians.[5]

The Palestinian justice system offers another example of the ways in which Israel assumes neo-colonial control over Palestinian institutions. Like their counterparts in other jurisdictions, Palestinian judges need to travel to attend court, engage in education and other professional development activities, manage justice institutions and promote strategic development at the institutional level. Unlike most judges around the world, however, Palestinian judges must receive permission to travel – whether abroad, to or from Gaza or, given checkpoints and closures, within the West Bank – from the occupying power rather than their own national institutions. The Palestinian justice system, like the larger project of Palestinian public institution building, has thus remained directly dependent upon permission from Israel for its vitality. Similar measures of Israeli control mark the Palestinian forensic system, the police and the Prosecution.

Occupation's classic colonial and neo-colonial forms are bound together through Israel's legal system, particularly its courts, which rationalise the individual and collective violence perpetrated against Palestinians by Israeli policies and practices. For example, Israel's Supreme Court has ruled in favour of the wall.[6] Moreover, Israeli judges, most often military judges sitting in military courts, dispense violence against Palestinians from the bench. For example, military judges sentence Palestinian youth who throw stones at the wall to harsh punishment.[7] Military courts retain broad jurisdiction over Palestinian life, particularly in matters involving Jerusalem, family reunification, taxation, permits, Israeli settlers or security.[8] Notwithstanding the existence of the Palestinian Authority, the Israeli legal system thus ensures that Israel retains control over structures that sustain the occupation and that affect the daily lives of Palestinians, regardless of where they live.

Israeli occupation also assumes the colonial forms identified by Edward Said and others: stereotypes, biases and images of the other as less knowledgeable, less moral and less worthy.[9] The ontology of Israeli occupation posits a hierarchy of being or worth between Israelis and Palestinians and translates this ontology into politics through policies and practices that subjugate Palestinian rights and interests to Israeli rights and interests. Imagination thus proves inextricably linked with the conventional violence of colonialism and its neo-colonial counterparts.

Beyond the occupation development aid provides another vehicle for the neo-colonial project in Palestine. Development aid entrenches colonialism in various ways. Sometimes, development aid buttresses the occupation. For example, development aid has helped Israel cover the financial cost of its occupation. As an occupying state, Israel has obligations under international law to the Palestinian community, including obligations to maintain infrastructure and civilian services. By offering development assistance to the Palestinian Authority the international community has *de facto* relieved Israel of its obligations without simultaneously requiring the end of occupation.

Development aid has also created 'facts on the ground', which have helped cement the occupation. Roads financed by USAID, for example, are built to bypass settlements and make travel between West Bank enclaves more bearable for Palestinians. While they make life easier in the short run, these roads extend the 'facts on the ground' strategy that has been employed by Israel for decades as part of its territorial expansion campaign. The roads entrench settlements, one of the main barriers to the creation of a contiguous and viable Palestinian state.

Significant development aid also goes to Palestinian security apparatuses, which police and control Palestinians, again relieving Israel of the cost of doing so.[10] And development assistance presents an opportunity to expand the security apparatus and bureaucracy beyond formal state agents. Since international donors prohibit aid-implementing agencies from hiring individuals or organisations listed on domestic or UN-designated terrorist lists, aid workers are solicited into the security agenda without additional costs to Israel or to international donors.[11] Overall, to put it colloquially, Israel gets to have its cake and eat it too. It comes as no surprise therefore that Israel welcomes development aid to the Palestinian Authority.[12]

Development aid has also deflected attention away from the occupation *qua* occupation. Aid thus has a direct relationship with classical colonialism, helping further Israeli imperialism and even abetting its military aggressions. This link between development aid and colonialism is nuanced and multifaceted; it exists as a hybrid between classical and neo-colonial practices. Our experience in Palestine indicates that aid-focused engagement between a donor country and Palestine privileges a discourse that furthers Israel's political aims. In Canada, for example, recent discussions about how much aid to offer Palestine have come to prevail in political and public spaces over the past 10 years. This aid-centred discourse has eclipsed discussions of previous years about whether Canada was living up to its foreign policy *vis-à-vis* Israel and Palestine.[13] Discursive reshaping of donor states' political horizons aligns well with Israel's efforts to refocus attention away from the occupation through a 'rebrand Israel' public relations campaign, and helps it 'define a narrative for the occupation on its own terms: one that refers to an illusory "peace process," "capacity-building" and "development projects" that mask a [colonial] reality'.[14]

Moreover, donor states can rationalise inaction, including failure to act against Israeli political and military aggression, through the aid spectrum. Canada and the USA chose to offer development aid to Palestinians while giving unequivocal political support to Israel, even as the latter stepped up its military assault on the Gaza Strip and the West Bank.[15] Between 2003 and 2014 Canada increased its aid to Palestinians, while justifying heightened Israeli military aggression and continued territorial expansion.[16] Aid to Palestine is also conditioned to further support Israeli occupation. Unlike other peoples, Palestinians have been required to prove their readiness for statehood by building public institutions and negotiating their self-determination with the very state that occupies them – two conditions that are at least implicitly attached to the receipt of international development aid envelopes.[17] The moral dimensions, legal requirements and socio-political conditions of occupation are largely side-lined in this framework, which treats the Palestinian Authority and Israel as entities with largely equal bargaining power, partly on the theory that international aid should equalise the playing field.

Development aid entrenches colonial forms in other ways. Development aid works as a postcolonial force that mirrors the ontology of occupation even as it differs from occupation in its objectives, impacts and methods. As we discuss below, one can see this postcolonial condition practised in Palestine by examining the modalities of development aid programming and the assumptions of 'the other' on which they are built. A rich body of literature has critiqued the ways in which development aid deems whole groups more or less knowledgeable, moral and worthy, permitting the possibility of redemption when the recipient of aid has been recast into the image made by the centres of control.[18] Donors define development processes to replicate their interests through neo-colonial conventions that ensure their continued control. Development aid programmes establish the frames through which donors deem decisions by local actors legitimate and validate locally valued results.

The basic impulse of seeking control over subjects deemed to be incomplete until they replicate the values and practices of the metropole represents the *sin qua non* of colonisation.[19] At root this hierarchy dehumanises the other and denies responsibility for suffering,[20] tracing an unsatisfactory socioeconomic or political state of affairs back to local rage, strife, corruption and/or the incompetence of those deemed in need of development. Knowledge transfer, technical training and the external consultant represent the main modalities of this postcolonial form.[21] Palestine is no exception.

Within the knowledge transfer paradigm context must be minimised as a necessary corollary of expert knowledge transfer. The implicit assumption is that context is not relevant or that it is only relevant to the extent that it can be gathered and managed by external experts; knowledge is a commodity that can be produced in one place and consumed in another.[22] International consultants thus move from one location to another, imparting knowledge as though time, place, personalities, histories and politics did not matter to the degree that they do.

Given the prevailing donor premise that the end of occupation is to be negotiated with Israel, it should be clear that development aid is rarely given to those who explicitly and directly work towards ending the occupation. Against this complex, shifting and often overwhelming colonial reality, the dilemma for praxis scholars is whether to engage in development aid projects that share in the colonial condition. Can one take development aid and reframe its terms to further decolonisation in Palestine? In particular, can praxis scholars help reveal and disentangle themselves from the postcolonial structures that underlie both occupation and development aid, both of which posit Palestinians as "less than." Is it possible to maintain a focus on occupation as a mischief to be remedied in Palestine even within a development aid project that is not specifically focused on Israel and the occupation? To what extent can development aid programming be used to keep alive and model a vision of Palestine that understands political power as a public good? Our experience with Karamah and judicial education in Palestine suggests that such possibilities exist and can contribute to the decolonisation project.

The Palestinian judiciary: between occupation and development aid

The rule of law and judicial education

Limited Palestinian self-rule gave the Palestinian judiciary some measure of control over its institutional practices and mandates, even as its jurisdiction over matters pertaining to the occupation remain limited by the Oslo Process and Israeli military jurisdiction. The Palestinian judiciary enhanced efforts in the early 2000s to develop unified judicial institutions, further professionalise its judiciary through continuing education, define the relationship between the judicial and executive authorities, and enhance public trust in the Palestinian legal system.[23] Around the same time foreign and donor interest in building Palestinian state institutions burgeoned.[24]

As in other parts of the world, building the rule of law became the rallying cry for reform and judicial capacity building formed the core of rule of law programming.[25] Donors supported rule of law programming on the assumption that such programming would: *inter alia*, bring stability to the West Bank and Gaza by promoting good governance;[26] stimulate the economy;[27] promote human rights;[28] support peace;[29] and help prepare Palestine for statehood.[30] But a largely unspoken and hence unresolved conceptual schism in the meanings attached to 'the rule of law' existed. Given that Israeli occupation advanced through law, the rule of law in Palestine invoked images of violence and unbridled power.[31] Scepticism extended to human rights norms and systems.[32] From a community-based perspective credible attempts at building the rule of law through development aid had to address the occupation.

International donors, however, tended to understand the rule of law problem largely as an institution-building or capacity-building problem, stripped away from the context of Israeli occupation and the larger colonial condition. The way in which problems are conceptualised defines their purported solutions and structures implementation activities. The development aid solution to the rule of law problem thus emphasised filling capacity gaps with knowledge, or presumed knowledge; since such knowledge did not exist in 'the field', it would have to be imported from abroad. Consistent with historical colonial practices, education became a favoured instrument of development's civilising mission.[33] Development aid programmes in Palestine reached into familiar development aid toolkits and picked up knowledge transfer as the main response to the rule of law problem as they perceived it. The external or foreign consultant thus becomes central to the development aid response. The consultant, who often knew little about the local context but was willing to share the information s/he had picked up in other contexts, usually for significant financial profit, was presented as the solution to the capacity gap. The consultant embodied and signified the continuous flow of information (as opposed to knowledge) to Palestine from abroad. To complete the tautology, Palestinian judges were imagined as largely empty vessels to be filled with external knowledge.[34]

Reliance on knowledge transfer as the main modality of judicial education in Palestine had practical, ethical and political consequences. Judges quietly complained that the education offered to them by external consultants was of limited use or relevance to the issues that confronted the bench. Judicial education offered significant information but not necessarily knowledge, in part because programming too often ignored the fact that, while knowledge can be gained across contexts, information without context is not knowledge. Moreover, given its reliance on knowledge transfer, programming tended to replicate occupation's hierarchical ontological structures: it placed the Palestinian judge in a colonial relationship to the foreign trainer who was positioned as the expert-knower while the judge was to be the passive recipient of whatever information the expert had to dispense. Finally, judicial education programming assumed political significance; the emphasis on capacity building helped mute the occupation as a subject of discussion in favour of emphasising the places and spaces in which Palestinian judges lacked capacity. In short, occupation figured in international development programming primarily as a logistical challenge to activity planning.

Shaped by development aid and knowledge transfer orthodoxy, much of the early judicial education programming in Palestine proved impractical to implement, because those with authority lacked knowledge and those with knowledge had insufficient authority. It was also conceptually incoherent because it purported to curb arbitrary power while side-lining the occupation as a source of the rule of law problem in Palestine and it was ethically suspect because it assumed a colonial stance towards Palestine and Palestinians. Despite the significant funds funnelled to judicial education efforts throughout the late 1990s and early 2000s, Palestinian judges largely resented judicial education programmes and Palestinian human rights organisations continued to complain about the judiciary and the judicial system.

Towards a new judicial education model

Karamah sought to respond to the shortcomings of the knowledge transfer paradigm. In 2010 Karamah and the Palestinian Judiciary launched the Candidate Master Trainers (CMT) model of judicial education as an alternative to the prevailing knowledge transfer paradigm. Karamah rejected knowledge transfer because it implied hierarchical relationships between Canadians and Palestinians.[35] Instead, Palestinian interdisciplinary expertise displaced international expertise as the main project modality. Philosophers, lawyers, pedagogues, political scientists and sociologists, mostly from Birzeit University, all played key roles in supporting the development of a locally designed and implemented judicial education programme. Palestinian judges organised themselves into working groups to develop professional education courses for their peers. Combining leadership and learning, the CMT produced curricula in areas such as employment law, landlord–tenant law, juvenile justice and insurance law. These areas were identified as priority areas by the Palestinian judiciary – all 146 judges in the West Bank were surveyed.

Each working group lasted for roughly a year. CMT judges were provided with the resources they needed to develop and deliver educational sessions. Palestinian pedagogues worked with the judges in developing their own teaching skills and visualising learning as a process of self-empowerment. The judges also had the support of a team of Palestinian legal researchers, all from Birzeit University, who effectively took on the role of clerks. Highly skilled and dedicated judges from Canada volunteered ongoing advice, support and exchange of experience. They treated the Palestinian judges as colleagues and interacted with them as participants in a transnational judicial dialogue.

Karamah adopted dignity as its overriding theme. Who could object? To some commentators relying on dignity as a theme was attractive because it meant nothing more than education around the technicalities of human rights. Canadian officials tended to emphasise that Canadian values would be imported overseas, as the Supreme Court of Canada had proclaimed that dignity defined Canada's legal system. Karamah, however, adopted dignity as its unifying theme for different reasons. Dignity in the Palestinian context proved particularly appealing because 'human rights' had become increasingly bogged down with its own form of scepticism, particularly after the failure of the Oslo Accords and the failure of Western governments to counter Israel's occupation.[36] Dignity, moreover, offered a discourse through which popular priorities and aspirations could be articulated beyond the technicalities of human rights law and dignity stood as antidote to the Palestinian occupation experience, which Palestinians generally experienced as humiliation.

The CMT process allowed the judges the resources and opportunity to examine the status quo from the lens of human dignity. They were given the opportunity to explore various issues of law within their working groups. The approach was not prescriptive. They were not lectured about human rights nor directed towards a particular result. They were simply asked to think about how examining a particular legal problem through the lens of dignity might frame their analysis or decision making. Ultimately the CMT process cemented or, in some cases, introduced an aspect of professional judicial identity that permitted the demand for human dignity to emerge as a personal, professional, communal and national priority rather than a consumable slogan served up by experts from abroad.

Roughly one year after the CMT process ended an independent agency conducted an external evaluation of the CMT programme and confirmed that the CMT judges had adopted human dignity as a lens through which they made their decisions. Though engaged in judicial education in one aspect of the law, CMT judges applied the dignity lens to their analysis across legal subjects and approaches to particular legal problems were documented across several areas of law.[37] As one judge put it, 'my approach to all cases changed'.[38]

Human dignity, professional identity and collective aspirations

As we point out in the first part of this paper, the colonial condition in Palestine represents a multi-faceted web that is bound together by the notion that those over whom power is exercised are less worthy than those who exercise power. We also point out that the Palestinian judiciary, unlike judges in other jurisdictions, have limited jurisdiction over matters that affect the lives of Palestinians, because Israel has retained authority over vital issues that sustain its occupation. In this section we highlight the ways in which members of the Palestinian judiciary harnessed dignity to their limited institutional power to question the colonial condition in Palestine and model the relationship between dignity and power. Dignity appealed to members of the Palestinian judiciary because dignity resonated with their personal and professional desire to reject the occupation experience, fashion a different relationship between Palestinian people, align their institutional power with recognition of the inherent, equal worth the Palestinian people, and allow them to speak truth to power despite the particular confines of the Palestinian judicial office.[39]

As Robert Cover has so eloquently explained, judges are people of violence.[40] Through their decision making they wield 'power-over' (see below) others and inflict state-sanctioned violence. The bench thus offered the most obvious site from which the CMT judges could demonstrate or model the ways in which dignity can mitigate power over others. Inspired by a deepened sense of personal and professional empowerment, and increasingly aware of their responsibility and ability to exercise power to enhance dignity, CMT judges viewed decision making as an obligation to respect dignity.

They developed new ways to bring a measure of dignity to the legal system, given their power through the judicial office. Several judges emphasised rehabilitation over retribution as the underlying principle in juvenile justice cases and considered the conditions of detention in rendering sentencing decisions.[41] Other examples include:

- ordering *in camera* testimony for witnesses in sexual assault and juvenile cases;
- reducing sentences or offering alternative sentencing for young offenders;
- introducing the 'best interests of the child' analysis;
- assessing the power imbalance between litigants;
- ensuring faster decision making and better case management, especially in cases involving sexual assault and sexual harassment;
- avoiding detention in debtor–creditor cases and attempting to resolve disputes through other means;
- improving treatment of litigants and witnesses by explaining their rights and considering their special needs in the court room;
- applying the human rights provisions of the Basic Law;
- moving away from literal or rigid readings of the law and applying the purpose or spirit of the law to the facts of the case.[42]

Beyond the bench the CMT judges declared in interviews and in public statements that they regarded themselves as social leaders who should help define the aspirations of the Palestinian states. Human dignity, to the extent that it represented an antidote and opposition to the dehumanisation known through occupation, invited a conceptual departure from the colonial past and hinted at a nascent future in which the judges could have some influence on shaping people's lives and the lives of those who came before them.

Dignity thus sparked the emancipatory imagination in Palestine, as it had in jurisdictions such as post-apartheid South Africa and post-Nazi Germany, which sought a break from an undesirable past marred by the dehumanisation of perceived others. CMT judges proposed that the Palestinian people, because they had endured the humiliation of occupation, deserved a legal system that valued and delivered human dignity. The judicial leadership suggested that the Palestinian judiciary could make a positive difference in the lives of ordinary people by taking up the professional mantle of human dignity.

CMT judges encouraged a particular professional identity. As one judge put it, 'We need to see judges as providing a service to society, not as an authority with the right to impose his/her will on parties in court'.[43] Another judge stated: 'We serve to protect human dignity; in our analysis of the case and interpretation of law we need to side with human dignity.'[44] Not surprisingly the professional identity of the CMT judges became inextricably linked with national emancipation, as the appeal to dignity could not ignore the indignities of the everyday. A senior judge, for example, emphasised at Karamah's closing conference that the Palestinian judiciary have an 'additional' reason to ensure justice for the Palestinian people to 'compensate' for a history of injustice:

> Building judicial capacity is part of building our state and we are honoured to be chosen for this mission. It is our duty to bring to our society strong and merciful judges, judges who are able to protect the dignity of Palestinian citizens...The Palestinian people have suffered significantly and their dignity has been abused continuously by an occupier that treats the Palestinian people as if they have no dignity and ignores or abuses Palestinian rights without mercy...In this context, we as judges should be the address for human dignity, through our practice at court and through our efforts in building the capacity of new judges...We should remember that we are the servant of the people, not their master. This is how Palestine should be, and this is how the Palestinian judiciary should be.[45]

Dignity was posited as the opposite of occupation. By emphasising that 'we need to see judges as providing a service to society' and insisting that they are 'servants of the people, not their masters', judges committed to using their institutional power to further the interests of individual justice and collective aspirations.

Judges explicitly tied judgement through a human dignity lens to national self-determination and the desire to break from Israeli occupation by behaving differently from the occupier rather than seeking revenge and reproducing the violence of the occupier. Where occupation is premised on the degradation of the other and relies on dehumanisation at all levels – personal, professional, structural, individual and collective – human dignity invited an examination of the circumstances of a person's life, a search for legal principles that would recognise the humanity of the people before the court, and recognition of the responsibility for law's impact on people's lives.

Several judges explained that their decision making benefited not because they had gained knowledge of new legal rules. They noted that they had instead come to see 'the human side of cases' and linked this perspective to the need for national self-determination.

> The CMT programme focused on looking at the human side of cases. This is very important to us as a nation because we went through tough times. It has affected the way I look at all cases and has had a lasting impact on me.[46]

Like other CMT judges, s/he linked a willingness and ability to see the 'human side' to the national struggle for liberation and the move away from structural suffering.

Judges reasoned that treating claimants with dignity not only brought justice to the individual, it would also create positive social bonds. One judge explained this relationship in the context of juvenile justice cases.

> Looking at the human side of a case and looking at rehabilitation rather than punishment when dealing with juveniles helps enhance justice…When the juvenile himself recognises that the aim of the decision is rehabilitation and not punishment for the sake of punishment, he will start to look at things differently himself. He will start to appreciate the value of human dignity and justice in society.[47]

The external evaluation of Karamah cited similar examples of judges behaving in ways towards witnesses that helped model social and political respect.

> A judge explained how he integrated human dignity in procedures by dealing with each witness and suspect or litigant with respect. He also started to recognize power relations in court and started to make sure not to abuse his power as judge when questioning witnesses.[48]

Journalists and civil society organisations noted that judges treated those who came before them in respectful ways that mirrored desired social outcomes.[49]

Decolonisation?

Karamah ended its activities in 2012. Because Karamah was a judicial education initiative, resources could not be directed towards advocating the end of occupation, even though we fully understood that occupation represented a negation of dignity in all its forms and even as we continued to speak against occupation in our capacities as scholars and social commentators. We accepted that the struggle to support decolonisation within development aid initiatives in Palestine required strategic compromises, although we were not advocating 'a least of all possible evils' strategy or suggesting that one give up on aspects of self-determination or decolonisation.[50] Rather, we worked on the theory that one must sometimes accept that successes will be limited, while remaining committed to advancing one's ultimate goals at every opportunity. In this section we examine whether judicial invocations of human dignity as described above furthered decolonisation.

Unlike the capacity-building approach, which would inquire *whether* human dignity had become part of judicial decision making, the decolonisation question focuses on *why* the judges took up human dignity in their professional practice. The decolonisation question focuses on the why in part because judges in jurisdictions around the world have cited dignity without much relevance to decolonisation. Indeed, sometimes dignity is used regressively in that it is attached to a particular group but ignored in relation to the claims of other groups.[51] Alternatively dignity is used narrowly as a substitute for a particular, often narrowly construed human right such as liberty.[52] In both instances the power status quo is preserved. In discussing decolonisation and dignity, therefore, our method is not to simply ask about the instances in which judges used dignity in their decision making. Instead, by focusing on how judges invoked dignity, our methodology requires an examination of the relationship between dignity, colonisation and decolonisation.

In the first part of this paper we demonstrated that occupation and development aid employ their power, to varying degrees, to reinforce a group-based hierarchy of being or existence. Colonial actors, in Kantian terms, perceive the colonised as having price rather than inner worth. The undoing of colonisation thus requires different ways of deconstructing and engaging with power, recognises the interdependence of all actions, and orients actors with relative power towards their responsibility for others. We label the varying relationships between formal power, forms of violence, oppression and dehumanisation as 'power-over' and 'power-for'. Colonisation is inextricably linked with power-over. Those who exercise power as 'power-over' seek to deny the suffering created by their exercise of power, presenting it as either a natural mishap or the fault of the sufferer. By contrast, power-for, because it dissects and rejects the notion that power should be exercised to preserve group-based hierarchies, is an instrument of decolonisation. Power-for recognises that individuals and institutions with power have an ethical and professional responsibility to those over whom they exercise power. Power-for recognises the equal worth of self and other, and challenges the monopoly of institutional power by emphasising that its purpose and legitimacy derives from the populace. Through their invocation of dignity, members of the Palestinian judiciary rejected the exercise of power as power-over and helped make visible the parameters of the decolonisation project in Palestine. Dignity provided the judges with a language that could be spoken to coloniality's power in its various sites.

Members of the judiciary worked away at the knot that binds together occupation and development: the notion that power exercised must be of the power-over variety. Dignity helped unsettle hierarchical notions of being and challenged the power-for relations that define coloniality. Decolonisation re-centres analysis and action on the needs of those over whom power is exercised, regardless of who exercises it. In other words, it involves the whole complex spectrum of life activities, perceptions, values and, of course, relations. The judges who adopted human dignity as an aspect of their professional identity helped build a dignity jurisprudence in Palestine that rejected law and the rule of law as an oppressive, power-over force. They did so in part by self-imposing limits on the way in which they exercised their own power and by seeking to inject dignity analysis into the relationship between the parties in both civil and criminal contexts. They furthered dignity in the lives of Palestinians who found themselves, for various reasons, forced to engage with the legal process in Palestine. But the decolonising move involved more than decision making from the bench. The judges who harnessed the dignity concept to their decision making helped loosen the colonial mesh in other ways.

Palestinian dignity jurisprudence, even in its nascent form, reflected the view that the national Palestinian struggle is not simply aimed at achieving a state or even a sovereign state and that building state institutions is not, as capacity-building programmes would have it, largely a bureaucratic task of adding up knowledge and skills to power. The national struggle requires the achievement of a just and decent state, and the building of national institutions requires a particular relationship between those institutions and the Palestinian people, one rooted in and aiming at popular dignity. The judges who declare that 'they are the servants of the people, not their masters', are modelling this possibility for the larger judiciary and for the Palestinian Authority more generally. They emphasise that breaking with the colonial past begins with recognising and guarding the equal dignity and worth of the other over whom formal power is exercised.

In the Palestinian context breaking with the colonial past requires a rejection of the relationship between hegemonic power and the community that colonialism engenders, and that Israeli occupation presumes and perpetuates. The judges who accepted dignity as the mediating principle between state power and the Palestinian people over whom they held power exhibited a trend towards recognising the need for an epistemological break with colonial discourse, where the question is no longer a question of struggle over who is dominant, but rather about rejecting domination. The judges who adopted human dignity as their professional identity were also thus affirming a founding principle for Palestine.

Moreover, the development of dignity as a professional identity, and not simply as a legal concept or legal right, by at least some judges opened up the possibility of a judiciary that continues to pursue its independence from other state structures and ultimately proves willing to challenge executive decisions in the name of dignity. Of course, a distance remains between affirming dignity as the founding principle for Palestine and fully bringing that philosophy to bear on the judiciary's relationship with other branches of the state. Palestinians have indicated that they trust the judiciary as compared to other parts of the Palestinian justice system,[53] but the judiciary as a branch of the state continues to be implicated in the Palestinian Authority's shortfalls and abuses.[54] To the extent that decolonisation involves exposing and rejecting abuse of power by the Palestinian state, the adoption of dignity as a professional identity by members of the judiciary offers some hope. Experiences with judges in diverse jurisdictions have demonstrated that professional identity plays a profound and lasting role in defining the ethos and shaping practices of judicial institutions.[55] Simply put, judges who develop a professional identity that links judicial legitimacy to the general will rather than to executive dictates are more likely to think and act independently of the executive branch of the state.

The adoption of dignity as a professional identity by members of the judiciary also furthered decolonisation by giving the judges a platform and a conceptual lens through which they could remain respectful of the limits of their judicial office while still reminding the world of the Palestinian narrative. By invoking human dignity as an antidote to occupation, the judges also insisted on 'speaking truth to power', including to development aid practitioners and Israel. Both have worked to redefine the occupation as nothing more than a neutral back-drop for 'state building' or a 'peace-process'. By pitting occupation against dignity, the judges offer a reminder that the occupation remains a race-based construct that denies the equal worth of individuals because of their identity.

Reminding observers that occupation defiles dignity, the judges were committing a 'profanation' in Agambenian terms. Sacred things, Agamben explained, are removed from common use. 'Once profaned, that which is unavailable and separate loses its aura and is returned to use'.[56] Within donor discourse and development aid programming, occupation had assumed an untouchable, almost sacred status. Occupation had been rendered untouchable by classical colonial violence and its less visible neo- and postcolonial forms. Significantly the judges reclaimed discussions of occupation as a legitimate and necessary subject of development aid projects and the subject of legitimate judicial commentary, even in the absence of formal jurisdiction.

Scholars of colonialism in other contexts have demonstrated the efficacy of speaking truth to power and the insistence on telling one's narrative as a form of resistance.[57] In response to the question, 'whose reality counts?' members of the Palestinian judiciary insisted that the national experience of occupation, which they knew well, would not be side-lined by an imagined rule of law problem that could only contemplate pedagogy stripped of politics as development's contribution to dignity in Palestine.

Notwithstanding their socio-political status, Palestinian judges directly experienced the power-over oppression and humiliation of Israeli occupation. As members of the Palestinian community, Palestinian judges and their families were/are imprisoned, subject to closures, checkpoints, military assaults, home demolitions and confiscations, permits, restrictions on travel, interruptions in education and military violence. But the judges did not limit their invocation of human dignity to their own personal or institutional needs, legitimate as those needs might be. Rather, they used the dignity concept to turn the lens, using the platforms provided by development aid, back onto the Palestinian people.

Palestinian judges emphasised that Palestinians deserve well-functioning and just institutions, including legal systems, in particular, *because of* the occupation experience. Judges thus rejected the 'reality' presumed by international donor agencies that defined the rule of law, rule of law programming and judicial education as activities that take place largely outside the colonial framework. The judges also implicitly refused the notion that Palestinian public institutions should be built to secure Israeli confidence. The rights and interests of the Palestinian people also deserved consideration in assessing the efficacy of Palestinian public institutions. Without stepping outside the confines of their judicial offices, members of the judiciary refused to be framed or disciplined by international development's assumptions. They asserted control over the narrative that they wanted to tell the world, their state and their people.

Conclusion

Development aid presents a particular dilemma for praxis scholars. Praxis, by definition, demands engagement with colonial conditions in an effort to introduce transformative change. The very act of engaging with colonial contexts opens up the possibility of perpetuating through practice the colonial structures that one rejects in principle. In every context praxis involves risks and a willingness to work with paradoxes. Praxis scholars have not yet clearly articulated, *ex ante*, the concrete conditions that make praxis possible. Indeed, it may not be possible to do so because every context and every engagement is different.

Praxis demands an understanding of the colonial terrain. In Palestine this terrain has become all the more complex and, arguably, entrenched with the rise of development aid programming. While there are of course differences between occupation, state power and development aid, their hegemonic structures intersect and reinforce each other in multiple ways. But development aid also creates opportunities to undercut the colonial condition even as it partakes in that condition. The Karamah initiative represented an attempt to further decolonisation through praxis by resisting the basic assumptions of development aid and highlighting the depth and the contingency of the dehumanising frames that sustain the colonial condition. By demonstrating how and why power can be exercised through a dignity lens, even in a development aid framework that minimises dignity, members of the Palestinian judiciary helped make visible the parameters of the decolonisation project in Palestine.

Disclosure statement

No potential conflict of interest was reported by the authors.

Notes

1. Sachs, *The Development Dictionary*, 10.
2. Escobar, *Encountering Development*; Cowen and Shenton, *Doctrines of Development*; and Cooke, *From Colonial Administration to Development Management*, 8.
3. Woolford, *This Benevolent Experiment*.
4. "Occupied Palestinian Territories Homepage"; Playfair, *International Law*; Kretzmer, *The Occupation of Justice*; Shehadeh, "The Lucrative Arms Trade," 25; Weizman, *Hollow Land*; and "Occupied Palestinian Territory."
5. Nafi and Purkiss, "Palestinian Security Cooperation."
6. *International Legality of the Security Fence*.
7. Sedley et al., *Children in Military Custody*.
8. Rayyes, "The Rule of Law and Human Rights"; Kelly, *Access to Justice*; Weill, "The Judicial Arm of the Occupation"; Military Court Watch, "Fact Sheet"; Bahdi, "Phosphorus and Stone," 171; and Hajjar, *Courting Justice*.

9. Said, *Orientalism*; Said, *Culture and Imperialism*; and Cohen, *States of Denial*.
10. Zanotti, *US Foreign Aid to the Palestinians*.
11. See ibid., 4 for an uncritical illustration.
12. Ben-Ari, "Israel's Statement."
13. Engler, "Aid to Palestine or Israel?"; and Ziadah, "What Kind of Palestinian State?"
14. Wildeman, "Why Aid Projects in Palestine are doomed to Fail."
15. Al-Haq, "Briefing Note I." See also Shlaim, "How Israel brought Gaza to the Brink."
16. Kennedy, "The Harper Doctrine"; and "PM Stephen Harper urges World Leaders." On increasing aid to Palestine, see Goodman, "Stephen Harper offers $66 million in New Aid."
17. See, for example, Canadian Department of Foreign Affairs, Trade and Development, "West Bank and Gaza."
18. Easterly, *The White Man's Burden*.
19. Kothari and Wilkinson, "Colonial Imaginaries and Postcolonial Transformations."
20. Cohen, *States of Denial*.
21. Easterly, "The Ideology of Development," 32.
22. Kothari, "Authority and Expertise."
23. For a discussion of current activities and priorities generally, see the website of the Palestinian High Judicial Council at http://www.pcpsr.org/.
24. Rocard and Siegman, *Strengthening Palestinian Public Institutions*; Gompert et al., *Building a Successful Palestinian State*; and Bouris, *The European Union and Occupied Palestinian Territories*.
25. Nicholson and Low, "Local Accounts of Rule of Law Aid."
26. See, for example Gompert et al., *Building a Successful Palestinian State*, 23.
27. The World Bank links justice-sector reforms to economic growth. World Bank, *Sustaining Achievements in Palestinian Institution-building*.
28. Samuels, *Rule of Law Reform*; and United Nations, *Rule of Law Development*.
29. Bouris, *The European Union and Occupied Palestinian Territories*, 15, n. 28.
30. Fayyad, *Ending the Occupation*.
31. Institute of Law, *'Al'Kada' Gayrel Nethamee*, 8, 41; and Khalil, "(Rule of) Law and Development in Palestine."
32. Allen, *The Rise and Fall of Human Rights*.
33. Woolford, *This Benevolent Experiment*.
34. For example, see NETHAM, *Rule of Law Program*.
35. Easterly, *The White Man's Burden*, Chap. 1; Sayer and Campbell, *The Science of Sustainable Development*, 77–78; and Cooke and Kothari, *Participation*.
36. Allen, *The Rise and Fall of Human Rights*.
37. Just Governance Group, *Evaluation of the Project on Judicial Independence*.
38. Ibid.
39. Uma Kothari reminds us that the political narrative is often stripped away from development undertakings, thus rendering them colonising rather than liberating. See Kothari, 'Authority and Expertise', describing how participatory approaches to development discipline and co-opt those who believe themselves to be acting outside the mainstream.
40. Cover, "Violence and the Word."
41. Just Governance Group, Evaluation of the Project on Judicial Independence, 55.
42. Ibid.
43. Ibid.
44. Ibid.
45. *Presentation by Judge Mahmoud Jamous, Head of the First Instance Court, Ramallah and Head of the Judges' Panel on Criminal Cases, at Karamah's closing conference. The full text of Justice Jamous' presentation is available on the website of the Palestinian High Judicial Council.*
46. *Judge One, interviewed by Karamah, March 2012.*
47. *Judge Two, interviewed by Karamah, March 2012.*
48. Just Governance Group, *Evaluation of the Project on Judicial Independence*, 54.
49. Ibid.
50. See Weizman, *The Least of All Possible Evils*.

51. See, for example, the remarks of former Chief Justice of Israel, Aaron Barak. Barak, *Human Dignity*.
52. See Jordaan, "Autonomy as an Element of Human Dignity."
53. Arab World Centre for Research and Development, *Perceptions of the Palestinian Authority Judiciary*; and Turner, *Public Perceptions*.
54. 'Findings of the third quarter of 2015 indicate that two thirds of the public demand the resignation of president Abbas and two thirds do not believe his current resignation from the PLO Executive Committee is real.' "Palestinian Public Opinion Poll No. 57, October 6, 2015." Palestinian Centre for Policy and Survey Research, http://www.pcpsr.org/.
55. Vigour, "Professional Identities and Legitimacy Challenged."
56. Agamben, *Profanations*, 77.
57. Cooke and Kothari, *Participation*, 15, n. 47; Sium and Ritskes, "Speaking Truth to Power"; and Kohn and McBride, *Political Theories of Decolonization*.

Bibliography

Agamben, Giorgio. *Profanations. Translated by Jeff Fort*. Cambridge, MA: MIT Press, 2009.

Allen, Lori. *The Rise and Fall of Human Rights: Cynicism and Politics in Occupied Palestine*. Stanford, CA: Stanford University Press, 2013.

Al-Haq. "Briefing Note I: The Destruction of Water and Sewage Infrastructure under International Humanitarian Law." *Al-Haq Briefing Note Special Series: Legal Analysis of Israeli Attacks against the Occupied Gaza Strip*. July 26, 2014. http://www.alhaq.org/advocacy/topics/gaza/833-al-haq-briefing-note-special-series-legal-analysis-of-israels-attacks-against-the-occupied-gaza-strip.

Arab World Centre for Research and Development. *Perceptions of the Palestinian Authority Judiciary: A Survey of Judges, Lawyers, Court Users, Court Staff, and the Public*. Ramallah, April 2009. http://www.lacs.ps/documentsShow.aspx?ATT_ID=1567.

Bahdi, Reem. "Phosphorus and Stone: Operation Cast Lead, Israeli Military Courts and International Law as Denial-maintenance." In *Criminal Justice in International Society*, edited by Willem de Lint, Marinella Marmo and Nerida Chazal, 171–191. New York: Routledge, 2014.

Barak, Aaron. *Human Dignity: Constitutional Value and Constitutional Right*. Cambridge: Cambridge University Press, 2015.

Ben-Ari, Yaffa. "Israel's Statement to AHLC: Ministerial Meeting." Remarks at the Ministerial Meeting of the Ad Hoc Liaison Committee, New York, September 30, 2015. http://mfa.gov.il/MFA/ForeignPolicy/Peace/Humanitarian/Pages/Israel-statement-to-AHLC-ministerial-meeting-30-Sep-2015.aspx.

Bouris, Dimitris. *The European Union and Occupied Palestinian Territories: State-building without a State*. New York: Routledge, 2014.

Canadian Department of Foreign Affairs, Trade and Development. "West Bank and Gaza." Accessed October 6, 2015. http://www.international.gc.ca/development-developpement/countries-pays/westbankgaza-cisjordanie.aspx?lang=eng.

Cohen, Stanley. *States of Denial: Knowing about Atrocities and Suffering*. Cambridge: Polity Press, 2001.

Cooke, B. *From Colonial Administration to Development Management*. IDPM Discussion Paper Series, Working Paper 63. Manchester, NH: Institute for Development and Policy Management, University of Manchester, 2001.

Cooke, Bill, and Uma Kothari (eds.). *Participation: The New Tyranny?*. London: Zed Books, 2001.

Cover, Robert M. "Violence and the Word." *Yale Law Journal* 95 (1986): 1601–1629.

Cowen, M. P., and R. W. Shenton. *Doctrines of Development*. London: Routledge, 1996.

Easterly, William. "The Ideology of Development." *Foreign Policy* 161 (July/August 2007).

Easterly, William. *The White Man's Burden: Why the West's Efforts to Aid the Rest have done so much Ill and so little Good*. New York: Penguin Press, 2006.

Engler, Yves. "Aid to Palestine or Israel? Ottawa delivered Millions in Aid to Palestinian Authority to advance Israeli Interests." *Global Research*. July 22, 2013. http://www.globalresearch.ca/aid-to-palestine-or-israel-ottawa-delivered-millions-in-aid-to-palestinian-authority-to-advance-israeli-interests/5343529.

Escobar, Arturo. *Encountering Development: The Making and Unmaking of the Third World*. Princeton, NJ: Princeton University Press, 1995.

Fayyad, Salam. *Ending the Occupation, Establishing the State: Program of the 13th Palestinian Government.* Palestinian National Authority Two-Year Plan, August 2009. http://www.jmcc.org/documents/Fayyadplan.pdf.

Gompert, David, Kenneth Shine, Glenn Robinson, C. Richard Neu, and Jerrold Green. *Building a Successful Palestinian State.* Santa Monica, CA: Rand Corporation, 2005.

Goodman, Lee-Anne. 2014. "Stephen Harper offers $66 in New Aid to Palestinians but refuses to criticize Israel during West Bank Visit." *National Post*, January 20. http://news.nationalpost.com/news/canada/canadian-politics/stephen-harper-visits-west-bank-city-offers-66-million-in-new-aid-to-palestinians.

Hajjar, Lisa. *Courting Justice: The Israeli Military Court System in the West Bank and Gaza.* London: University of California Press, 2005.

Institute of Law. *'Al'Kada' Gayrel Nethamee: Seyadat al-Kanun wa-Hal al Niza'at Fee Falasteen'* [Informal Justice: Rule of Law and Dispute Resolution in Palestine]. National Report on Field Research Results. Birzeit: Institute of Law, Birzeit University, 2006.

International Legality of the Security Fence and Sections near Alfei Menashe. Israel High Court Ruling Docket H.C.J. 7957/04, September 15, 2005. http://www.zionism-israel.com/hdoc/High_Court_Fence.htm.

Jordaan, Donirch W. "Autonomy as an Element of Human Dignity in South African Case Law." *Journal of Philosophy, Science & Law* 9 (2009): 1–15.

Just Governance Group. *Evaluation of the Project on Judicial Independence and Human Dignity (KARAMAH).* April 2012.

Kelly, Tobias. *Access to Justice: The Palestinian Legal System and the Fragmentation of Coercive Power.* Crisis States Research Centre Working Papers Series 1, 41. London: Crisis States Research Centre, LSE, 2004.

Kennedy, Mark. 2014. "The Harper Doctrine: Why Canada's Prime Minister supports Israel." *Ottawa Citizen*, April 3. http://ottawacitizen.com/news/national/the-harper-doctrine-why-canadas-prime-minister-supports-israel.

Khalil, Asem. "(Rule of) Law and Development in Palestine". Paper presented at the Colloquium on Law and Development in the Middle East and North Africa, Cornell University Law School, April 20, 2010. http://www.researchgate.net/publication/228275625_%28Rule_of%29_Law_and_Development_in_Palestine.

Kohn, Margaret, and Keally McBride. *Political Theories of Decolonization: Postcolonialism and the Problem of Narrative.* New York: Oxford University Press, 2011.

Kothari, Uma. "Authority and Expertise: The Professionalisation of International Development and the Ordering of Dissent." *Antipode* 37, no. 3 (2005): 425–446.

Kothari, Uma, and Rorden Wilkinson. "Colonial Imaginaries and Postcolonial Transformations: Exiles, Bases, Beaches." *Third World Quarterly* 31, no. 8 (2010): 1395–1412.

Kretzmer, David. *The Occupation of Justice: The Supreme Court of Israel and the Occupied Territories.* Albany: State University of New York Press, 2002.

Military Court Watch. "Fact Sheet." 2015. http://www.militarycourtwatch.org/page.php?id=a6r85VcpyUa4755A52Y2mp3c4v.

Nafi, Ahmad, and Jessica Purkiss. 2015. "Palestinian Security Cooperation with Israel." *Middle East Monitor*, October 28.

NETHAM. *Rule of Law Program: Justice and Enforcement.* West Bank and Gaza, USAID, Twentieth Quarterly Report, July 1–September 30, 2010. http://pdf.usaid.gov/pdf_docs/Pdacs623.pdf.

Nicholson, Pip, and Sally Low. "Local Accounts of Rule of Law Aid: Implications for Donors." *Hague Journal on the Rule of Law* 5, no. 1 (2013): 1–43.

"Occupied Palestinian Territories Homepage." United Nations, Office of the High Commissioner for Human Rights. http://www.ohchr.org/EN/Countires/MENARegion/Pages/PSIndex.aspx.

"Occupied Palestinian Territory." United Nations Office for the Coordination of Humanitarian Affairs. http://www.ochaopt.org/index.aspx.

Playfair, Emma, ed. *International Law and the Administration of Occupied Territories: Two Decades of Israeli Occupation of the West Bank and Gaza Strip.* Oxford: Oxford University Press, 1992.

"PM Stephen Harper urges World Leaders to side with Israel." *Toronto Star*, July 13, 2014. http://www.thestar.com/news/canada/2014/07/13/pm_stephen_harper_urges_world_leaders_to_side_with_israel.html.

Rayyes, Naser. "The Rule of Law and Human Rights within Palestinian National Authority Territories: The Palestinian Judiciary is fighting an Uphill Struggle to keep Control over the Increasingly Fragmented Territories." *Palestine–Israel Journal of Politics, Economics, and Culture* 10, no. 3 (2003). http://www.pij.org/details.php?id=27.

Rocard, Michel, and Henry Siegman. *Strengthening Palestinian Public Institutions: Report of an Independent Task Force Sponsored by the Council on Foreign Relations*. Washington, DC: Council on Foreign Relations, 1999.

Sachs, Wolfgang. *The Development Dictionary: A Guide to Knowledge as Power*. 2nd ed. London: Zed Books, 2009.

Said, Edward W. *Culture and Imperialism*. New York: Random House, 1994.

Said, Edward W. *Orientalism*. New York: Random House, 1979.

Samuels, Kirsti. *Rule of Law Reform in Post-conflict Countries: Operational Initiatives and Lessons Learnt*. Social Development Papers: Conflict, Prevention & Reconstruction 37. Washington, DC: October 2006. http://siteresources.worldbank.org/INTCPR/Resources/WP37_web.pdf.

Sayer, Jeffrey, and Bruce Campbell. *The Science of Sustainable Development: Local Livelihoods and Global Environments*. Cambridge: Cambridge University Press, 2004.

Sedley, Stephen, Patricia Scotland, Frances Oldham, Marianna Hildyard, Judy Khan, Jayne Harrill, Jude Lanchin, Greg Davies, and Marc Mason. *Children in Military Custody*. Delegation of British Lawyers on the Treatment of Palestinian Children under Israeli Military Law, June 2012. http://www.childreninmilitarycustody.org.uk/wp-content/uploads/2012/03/Children_in_Military_Custody_Full_Report.pdf.

Shehadeh, Raja. "The Lucrative Arms Trade behind the Occupation must End." *Tikkum* 30, no. 4 (2014): 25.

Shlaim, Avi. 2009. "How Israel brought Gaza to the Brink of Humanitarian Catastrophe." *Guardian*, January 7. http://www.theguardian.com/world/2009/jan/07/gaza-israel-palestine.

Sium, Aman, and Eric Ritskes. "Speaking Truth to Power: Indigenous Storytelling as an Act of Living Resistance." *Decolonization: Indigeneity, Education & Society* 2, no. 1 (2013): 1–10.

Turner, Lucy, ed. *Public Perceptions of Palestinian Justice and Security Institutions*. United Nations Development Program, March 2012. http://www.ps.undp.org/content/dam/papp/docs/Publications/UNDP-papp-research-Survey.pdf.

United Nations, Office of the Special Coordinator in the Occupied Territories. *Rule of Law Development in the West Bank and Gaza Strip: Survey and State of the Development*. May 1999. https://unispal.un.org/DPA/DPR/unispal.nsf/2ee9468747556b2d85256cf60060d2a6/7968e954038f503785256b1f0058556f?OpenDocument.

Vigour, Cécile. "Professional Identities and Legitimacy challenged by a Managerial Approach: The Belgian Judicial System." *Sociologie du travail* 51, supplement 2 (2009): 136–154.

Weill, Sharon. "The Judicial Arm of the Occupation: The Israeli Military Courts in the Occupied Territories." *International Review of the Red Cross* 89, no. 866 (2007): 395–419.

Weizman, Eyal. *Hollow Land: Israel's Architecture of Occupation*. London: Verso, 2007.

Weizman, Eyal. *The Least of All Possible Evils: Humanitarian Violence from Arendt to Gaza*. London: Verso, 2012.

Wildeman, Jeremy. 2012. "Why Aid Projects in Palestine are doomed to Fail." *The Electronic Intifada*, September 6, 2012. https://electronicintifada.net/content/why-aid-projects-palestine-are-doomed-fail/11642.

Woolford, Andrew. *This Benevolent Experiment: Indigenous Boarding Schools, Genocide and Redress in Canada and the United States*. Winnipeg: University of Manitoba Press, 2015.

World Bank. *Sustaining Achievements in Palestinian Institution-building and Economic Growth: Economic Monitoring Report to the Ad Hoc Liaison Committee*. September 18, 2011. http://siteresources.worldbank.org/INTWESTBANKGAZA/Resources/WorldBankAHLCReportSep2011.pdf.

Zanotti, Jim. *US Foreign Aid to the Palestinians*. Congressional Research Report. Washington, DC: CRS, July 3, 2014.

Ziadah, Rafeef. "What Kind of Palestinian State in 2011? Neoliberalism and World Bank Diktats." *Global Research*, April 13, 2010. http://www.globalresearch.ca/what-kind-of-palestinian-state-in-2011-neoliberalism-and-world-bank-diktats/18638.

The conjunctural in international law: the revolutionary struggle against semi-peripheral sovereignty in Iraq

Ali Hammoudi

ABSTRACT
This article will detail an event of revolutionary action in the historiography of anti-colonial and anti-imperial struggle in Iraq, namely *al-Wathba* ('the leap') of 1948, utilising it as an example to address the limitations of the methodology and analysis of Third World Approaches to International Law (TWAIL) scholarship. I will argue that there is a disconnect between notions of agency and structure in TWAIL analyses and that therefore TWAIL scholars should consider studying the conjunctures that allowed certain movements ample room to struggle against the imperialism of international law in the first place. I will use the example of the *Wathba* to illustrate how a conjunctural analysis may be undertaken, analysing its implications for the international legal order. I will then move to highlight the significance of labour to the conjuncture in question. Finally, I will demonstrate how events like the *Wathba* illuminate the transient and provisional nature of the foundations of international law, while emphasising its structural constraints.

Introduction

> We do not know – are we independent or colonized? ('Saniyya' in the novel *The Hand, the Land and the Water* by Dhu Nun Ayyub)[1]
>
> Men make their own history, but…they do not make it under circumstances chosen by themselves, but under circumstances directly encountered, given and transmitted from the past. (Karl Marx)[2]
>
> No longer may…international law be… understood merely as the history of the law of nations to the entire exclusion of the law of peoples. (Upendra Baxi)[3]

During the third session of the United Nations General Assembly held in Paris in 1948, the delegate for the Philippines, Carlos Romulo, insisted on a broad interpretation of the ambiguous Chapter XI of the UN Charter, emphasising that 'the force of history which had brought about many changes in the British Empire was far stronger than legal or constitutional barriers'.[4] Romulo was directly referring to what he called the 'impetus of revolutionary forces', which was bringing about transformations on the ground in the Third World, to make a legal argument.[5] This 'non-juridical' approach, which was used extensively by the 'Afro-Asian bloc' in the UN, demonstrates that the anti-colonial and anti-imperial struggles unleashed by Third World peoples at the time could not be ignored and had direct implications for international law and its interpretation.

This paper is concerned with the question of revolutionary agency within international legal scholarship relating to the Third World. I will address certain limitations in the methodology and analysis of Third World Approaches to International Law (TWAIL) scholarship by detailing an event of mass working-class agency in the historiography of anti-colonial and anti-imperial struggle in Iraq, namely the *Wathba* of 1948, situating it broadly within the international conjuncture of decolonisation. The *Wathba* of 1948 was a great popular uprising of the Iraqi underclasses that successfully prevented the imposition of a revised, unequal treaty between Iraq and Britain (the Anglo-Iraq Treaty), sparking the revolutionary process that would eventually overthrow the British-sponsored monarchy a decade later. The *Wathba* will be shown to be one historical manifestation of a wider conjuncture against international law in the Third World. I will argue that TWAIL must begin undertaking the study of the conjunctures that allowed certain movements ample room to act and manoeuvre against the structures of imperialism of international law. It is only through an examination of these past conjunctures that the present conjuncture can be understood and the future transformed.

The limitations of the study of revolutionary agency in TWAIL analysis

TWAIL scholars have been at the forefront of exposing how colonialism and imperialism are constitutive of the history and discipline of international law.[6] They have done so by reverting to an examination of history to expose the legacy of imperialism in international law. In fact, it is this particular method of historical analysis that has been said to be 'the feature most fundamental' to TWAIL scholarship,[7] one which regards 'historical perspective' as the 'key technique' in understanding the current features of international law.[8] TWAIL encompasses a political commitment to counter traditional approaches that have disregarded the colonial past and considered it of trivial concern to international law. Moreover, international law as a discipline tends, through its positivist predisposition, to repress this colonial past, constructing and reproducing the version of the past that is better suited to its hegemonic discourse.[9] TWAIL analysis resists this process and aims to expose the hidden colonial origins of international law. Most importantly it emphasises the *continuity* of 'colonial relations' in the contemporary structures of international law.[10]

Despite this radical commitment of the TWAIL analysis, there still appear to be considerable limitations to it. This is primarily a result of the manner in which TWAIL scholars often approach the question of agency in their analysis. As Owen Taylor has argued, TWAIL scholars tend to invoke notions of 'resistance' (the word most often used to evoke agency) that are highly selective of the conceptual history of revolution.[11] In other words, when TWAIL scholarship turns from an analysis of the structures of imperialism within international law to address the issue of agency, it does so in a highly idealised manner that locates the agency of social movements within a narrative of 'resistance' as a 're-conceptualization [of law] as an act of will', while emphasising the necessity of 'radical legal pluralism' as fundamental to emancipation.[12] Balakrishnan Rajagopal, for example, takes such a position in situating the revolutionary potential of social movements in 'non-institutional, non-party, and cultural terms'.[13] This narrow conception suggests that, as long as revolutionary agency or resistance is 'sanitised' (ie spontaneous, without central or party organisation, and non-violent), then it will bring about true political and democratic change *within* the liberal promise of international law, whatever the state of the structures in question.[14]

The problem with this approach is that it assumes that law is abstract and can be re-conceptualised into an emancipatory plural form, rather than *already* entrenched (and so constrained) within certain material social conditions and forms. What this also does is ignore the connection between agency and structure – ie the conjuncture – leading to a fanciful situation whereby 'any kind of agency' becomes possible and 'the structure becomes entirely contingent'.[15] The reality is that different forms of action may be effective depending on the particular structural conditions pertaining at any given time.[16] This article is concerned with this latter disconnect between the notions of structure and agency that is prevalent in TWAIL scholarship. My argument is that TWAIL scholars should shift their focus to a study of what I refer to as 'conjunctural resistance' or 'conjunctural agency' rather than focusing on 'plural resistance' (or agency) that is waged against international law at any given time. To do this is to realise that it is the conjuncture that should be studied to understand agency.

The concept of the conjuncture is derived here from Marxist theory and analysis, in particular from the formulations of VI Lenin and, later, Antonio Gramsci. Louis Althusser defines the conjuncture as denoting, 'the exact balance of forces, state of overdetermination of the contradictions at any given moment to which political tactics must be applied'.[17] Referring to Lenin's approach in the 1917 Russian Revolution, Althusser demonstrates how 'the history of imperialism' was analysed by Lenin in its current conjuncture, as opposed to the way it was theorised by the typical Marxist theoretician and historian, who was merely concerned with historical knowledge: 'Lenin meets Imperialism in the modality of a *current* existence: in a concrete present. The theoretician of history or the historian meet it in another modality, the modality of non-currency and abstraction.'[18] He goes on to argue that Lenin's (conjunctural) approach to the 'current situation' at that time was unique, as he was concerned with the 'typicality of the contradictions, with their displacements, their condensations and the "fusion" in revolutionary rupture that they produced…[in other words] what makes it possible to act on History from within the sole history present…not [merely] to demonstrate or explain the "inevitable" revolutions *post festum*, but to make them in our unique present.'[19] As Stuart Hall makes clear, the conjuncture is the product of 'many determinations', not of one.[20] Conjunctural thinking therefore involves 'clustering' or assembling elements into a particular formation.[21] In this way the concept of the conjuncture can be used as an analytical tool for identifying strategic sites of political action that have emerged and, when used properly, can open up possibilities for transformation.

TWAIL analysis has, for the most part, disregarded the significance of the conjunctures that allowed for the possibilities of 'resistance', and their implications within the context of international law. By shifting the focus on to the conjuncture, TWAIL scholars would become more attentive to the pressing question of political action. Of course, TWAIL scholarship has often concerned itself with the question of the agency of Third World peoples, and there have been a significant number of works that have examined the role of *social* movements in the development of international law.[22] What I am concerned with here, however, is the necessity of locating agency conjuncturally within the wider narrative of the imperialism of international law put forward by TWAIL. My intention in this article, therefore, is to extend certain aspects of the conjunctural analysis to TWAIL approaches, so that one may more effectively grasp (and more importantly apply the lessons of) the history of revolutionary action and 'resistance' to international law's imperialism in the present conjuncture.

What follows is a detailed account of the *Wathba*, a revolutionary event of 'conjunctural resistance' in Iraq, which started out against the extension of an (unequal) treaty between Iraq and Britain 'under the guise' of its revision.[23] The *Wathba* eventually turned into the rejection of the 'semi-peripheral sovereignty' that was granted to Iraq through the Mandate system in 1932. I refer to 'conjunctural resistance' as a kind of counterweight to TWAILian 'plural resistance' to illuminate the fact that it is the conjuncture that should inform one's understanding of agency rather than its plural character. It will be clear from my analysis that resistance can only be said to be constitutive of international law (if at all) *at certain conjunctures* and not *tout court* (as TWAIL scholarship suggests). I will use the *Wathba* to illustrate an example of how a conjunctural analysis could be undertaken in relation to the history of Iraqi resistance to imperialism and international law. After detailing this story, I will return to the present analysis to tease out the unique conjunctural characteristics of this event by assessing how working-class agency (through the labour movement) attempted to subvert the imperialism of international law, eventually situating it more broadly within the conjuncture of decolonisation in the shifting international legal order.

The making of semi-peripheral sovereignty in international law

Al-Wathba (literally, 'the leap') was a social uprising initially sparked by news of negotiations and then the signing of a revised unequal treaty between Iraq and Britain in 1948. To understand the significance of this treaty and its centrality to the colonial and imperial domination of Iraq, I will briefly examine the history of treaty making and its consequences in the context of the formation of the Iraqi state and the Mandate system. The purpose of this section is to trace the evolution of the unequal treaty and its role in the manufacturing of what I call Iraqi 'semi-peripheral sovereignty', a form of sovereignty that was unique to the geopolitical specificities of the semi-peripheral Middle East. This is vital in order to situate the *Wathba* in its proper context. It is also needed to understand how the imperialism of international law functioned in Iraq at the time, so as to appreciate why the Iraqi masses decided to wage a struggle against it.

Once the Hejazi Emir Feisal was handpicked at the 1920 Cairo Conference as the new King of the Iraqi state, the British decided to use the instrument of the treaty to express their Mandatory relationship. The British brought past colonial practices from their long experiences in colonial administration, in particular in India and Egypt, to the Iraqi situation. The instrument of the treaty and its legal structures was used in the 19th century to create 'native states' in India that were, as Lauren Benton has shown, distinguished from the purview of international law.[24] This generally led to the construction of the notion of 'divisible sovereignty', which asserted that sovereignty could be held in degrees, with full sovereignty reserved for the imperial power.[25] While the instrument of the treaty was used to exclude the non-European from international law and its order in the 19th century, in the case of Iraq the treaty was brought in to do the opposite: to express the Mandatory relationship that would eventually create Iraq as a 'sovereign state' and lead to its incorporation into international society.

Iraqi nationalists were vehemently opposed to any form of mandatory relationship, demanding nothing less than complete independence. The first Anglo-Iraqi Treaty was eventually signed in 1922.[26] The treaty created an ambiguous situation whereby the British had 'a mandate for Iraq vis-à-vis the League, and not one vis-à-vis Iraq'.[27] The cornerstone of indirect control in the treaty was the requirement that the Iraqi government appoint British advisors to every governmental post. This parallel British advisory system became the backbone of the Iraqi state. The mandate remained the operative document, defining the obligations of the British government towards the League and its Covenant.[28] The treaty provided that Iraq was to maintain its *indivisible* sovereignty as a constitutional monarchy with a representative government.[29] The instrument of the treaty was therefore used to distance Iraq from the Mandate, while at the same time constructing a limited sovereignty in form, which would give the British some control. The difference here was that the sovereignty given was not divisible, but rather indivisible, with constraints imposed by the treaty.

The contents of the treaty maintained British dominance of the new Iraqi state and its institutions, limiting the state's constitutional structures. It was consequently intertwined with the 1925 Iraqi Constitution or Organic Law, enshrining wide executive powers and constricting parliamentary sovereignty, so as to allow the King and Cabinet to uphold the provisions of the treaty. The Constitution ensured that the entire relationship between the Iraqi state and Britain remained outside the constitutional order, wholly governed by the treaty, which was a product of international law.[30] In September 1929 Britain agreed to support Iraq's entry to the League of Nations and in turn its formal independence by 1932.[31] There was hence the need for a new treaty detailing the arrangements of the relations between the two states after formal independence. The Anglo-Iraqi Treaty of Alliance was ratified in 1930 only after the most trusted of the King's court, Nuri al-Said, headed the cabinet and used his infamous firm tactics to stifle any parliamentary opposition. The treaty's contents maintained a 'close' alliance between the two states.[32] Iraqi sovereignty was therefore conditional and riddled with contradictory constraints – particularly the British right to move troops over Iraqi soil and the continued employment of some British judges and advisors.[33]

After several years of a seemingly permanent impasse, the British government finally decided that it was committed to the opinion that Iraq was ready to be admitted to the League. It consequently deployed its entire diplomatic arsenal to lobby the Permanent Mandate Commission (PMC) (the main body tasked by the League to make recommendations as to Iraq's independence under international law) to this conclusion. *The Special Report...on the Progress of Iraq, 1920–1931* submitted to the PMC painted an auspicious picture of the progress of the Iraqi state and its institutions as having 'all the working machinery of a civilized government'.[34] The British government asserted that it had appropriately fulfilled its Mandatory obligations. By June 1931 the PMC, which had been sceptical throughout its deliberations, paradoxically only agreed to admit Iraq after a declaration confirming Britain's continuing 'moral responsibility' to the implications of Iraq's independence.[35] In October 1932 Iraq became the first Mandate state to gain formal independence through the processes of the Mandatory system. In this manner Iraqi semi-peripheral sovereignty was manufactured, turning into the model for the region.

The members of the PMC in Geneva developed within international law a unique form of sovereignty that would generally ensure economic dominance over the semi-peripheral Middle East. If one closely examines the PMC reports and the sophisticated legal reasoning therein, it is evident that most economic considerations of the emerging 'independent' state, particularly in relation to oil, were reconciled with this form of semi-peripheral sovereignty.[36] The 1925 Iraqi Petroleum Company (IPC) oil concession, and later the 1931 pipeline agreement were (legally) distinguished from the principle of the open door – the main economic principle of the Mandate system, which was meant (at least in theory) to protect mandatory territories from economic exploitation by a Mandatory power.[37] The PMC eventually established that there was no violation of the open door with regard to the 1925 oil concession.[38] By 1931 the Iraqi government, crippled by a high deficit, had no choice but to agree to sign a revised concession with the IPC in exchange for a modest cash advance. The revised concession was heavily biased in favour of the company as it eliminated all taxation of the company's profits, removed the minimum production obligation and allowed the company to maintain control over undeveloped plots.[39]

The subjugating structures embedded within this concession would extend to the entire region through auxiliary pipeline conventions, signed by the other 'A' Mandate states in the region. The 'A' Mandate system linked the three Mandate areas economically by an oil pipeline from the Mosul oilfields in Iraq to the ports of Haifa in Palestine and Tripoli in Syria to the Mediterranean Sea.[40] In that way the semi-peripheral sovereignty that was juridically constructed to ensure Iraq's 'independence' was in reality made *to legitimise and legalise* the extraction, production and transportation of Iraq's most valuable natural resource (oil) across the region to the world – to the benefit of the world economy. Hence, international law through the Mandate system produced a unique form of semi-peripheral sovereignty out of the Iraqi experience. However, this was not possible without the use of the old colonial instrument of the treaty, which ultimately ensured that the Iraqi state not only appeared independent but also was 'independent' under international law, although in reality it remained subservient to imperialism.

The British Empire's 'new clothes of treaties and pacts' and the leap of the Iraqi masses

Although throughout the period described above Iraqis were continuously resisting the 1930 Treaty and its wide reach into every aspect of their lives, it was the event of the massive *Wathba* uprising that was the defining moment of revolutionary struggle against imperialism. Despite its heterogeneous character, the working-class was the *Wathba*'s quintessence. It was a robust alliance between workers and students, which led the massive demonstrations on the streets of Baghdad. In the gripping words of Hanna Batatu, 'an atmosphere redolent of social revolution enveloped Baghdad' during the *Wathba*, as it was

> the most formidable mass insurrection in the history of the monarchy…It was the social subsoil of Baghdad in revolt against hunger and unequal burdens. It was the students and the Schalchiyyah workers braving machine guns…and dying for their ideas…[I]t was the political representatives of the various layers of the middle class…resentful of constraints or plotting for political gains. It was the privileged stratum [of the ruling and landowning classes]…menaced in their political power and social interests. It was British overlordship shaken, the Anglo-Iraq Treaty of 1930 sapped, and the Portsmouth Agreement of 1948 abolished.[41]

Once the British and their Iraqi counterparts had agreed that they needed to revise the now visibly outdated and much hated 1930 Anglo-Iraq Treaty, secret negotiations commenced. Although the new treaty promised the eventual withdrawal of British troops and the surrendering of military bases to Iraq, it gave the British a say in Iraq's military planning through the establishment of a Joint Defence Board and the continued employment of British 'experts'. The treaty made it clear that Iraqis must surrender their bases to Britain in wartime, making it impossible for a stance of neutrality.[42] It also safeguarded British influence 15 years beyond the time limit of the old treaty.[43] The Portsmouth Treaty as it came to be known turned out to be no more than an extension of the 1930 treaty couched in 'new-fashioned terminology' that did not alter much of the old relationship.[44] The revision of the treaty was clearly meant to ensure the continuation of British intervention in Iraqi affairs.

The struggle of common Iraqis against the treaty started the day after the official announcement of negotiations on 5 January 1948. Mass demonstrations originated at the Law College of Baghdad. Law students left their classes to demonstrate against both the treaty and the partition of Palestine. [45] In no more than 10 days these seemingly circumscribed student demonstrations would erupt into an unprecedented fervour of discontent, composed of the majority of the underclasses of Iraq. Following a government clamp-down at the law school, the opposition – in particular the outlawed but popular Iraqi Communist Party (ICP) – began organising all workers on the ground. The 'Cooperation Committee', which united most leftist and nationalist parties under its leadership, had been formed a few months earlier; now an adjunct 'Student Cooperation Committee' was created and joined with it.[46] These two committees would lead the movement's demonstrations and strikes throughout the *Wathba*. The illusive stillness of the following week was broken when the official announcement was made on 16 January that the Portsmouth Treaty had been signed in London the previous day. Strikes and demonstrations exploded instantaneously. The protestors called for the resignation of the cabinet and the cancellation of the Portsmouth Treaty. On 20 January the *Schalchiyyah* workers[47] and the famished *sarifa-dwellers* (squatters) joined the protests for the first time, broadening the event beyond the narrow confines of parliamentary politics. It was also the day that police shot into the crowd. The masses became bitter but remained defiant. Eventually more Baghdadis from other walks of life joined the protests. The *Wathba* spread to other parts of the country.[48]

Overwhelmed, and against the advice of the British, the Regent capitulated, renouncing the treaty in a public statement, and guaranteed that it would not be ratified against the will of the people.[49] This led to a splintering of the opposition, as some of the right-wing nationalist parties recoiled. The left, led by the communists, refused to retreat, considering the Regent's statement a mere tactic. Furthermore, the protests were now calling for more than the cancellation of the new treaty, but for the end of British imperialism and the formation of a truly national democratic government. Their calls were not merely concerned with 'political freedoms'; at their core were issues relating to economic injustice. This could be ascertained especially by their calls for 'bread'. The *Wathba* quickly turned from a demand to replace the cabinet to a call for a profound transformation of the social and political order.[50]

The respected social democrat and lawyer, Kamil Qazanchi, who was the head of the movement's Coordination Committee, addressed the cheering crowd, asserting: 'You must declare a great people's revolution, and struggle to establish a people's government that represents these [labouring] classes'.[51] Qazanchi emphasised that the cancellation of the Portsmouth Treaty was in fact more about the liberation of the country from imperial and semi-colonial rule than the negotiation of the contents of the treaty. The statement released by the social democratic National Democratic Party explains this well, plainly stating that 'the truth of the matter is that the British , since its occupation of Iraq, intended to make this country a strategic site in the Middle East, for its own interests…to exploit their resources, and control their markets'. It goes on to argue that the British were in fact merely 'dressing up colonial [imperial] control with the new clothes of treaties and pacts'. The Portsmouth Treaty was therefore merely 'a new colonial [and imperial] project…a blatant attack on Iraq's very being, its sovereignty and political future'. For this reason it should be resisted by Iraqis with all their might.[52]

The *Wathba* came to a bloody culmination on 27 January 1948 when police, some stationed on roofs and minarets, had express orders to break up demonstrations and shoot to kill if necessary. Huge crowds gathered on both sides of the entrance of the Ma'mun Bridge. As the crowds courageously moved towards the centre of the bridge to join their comrades, the police sprayed bullets in their direction. An estimated 300 to 400 died on the bridge that day.[53] The 'Day of the Bridge', as it came later to be known, endures in the annals of Iraqi history and folklore as the moment when ordinary unarmed Iraqis gave their lives to rid themselves of the chains of imperial and semi-colonial rule. Although the cancellation of the Portsmouth Treaty was achieved, the new 'caretaker' government ultimately clamped down on all forms of dissent, declaring martial law, and shutting down newspapers and trade unions on the basis of national security. Despite the slow strangulation of the movement, it was the *Wathba* that was the spark that ignited the revolutionary process that would materialise in the July Revolution a decade later during the turbulent year of 1958.

The *Wathba* has been largely interpreted as a nationalist anti-colonial struggle for the assertion of the constitutional rights of the Iraqi people, which were infringed and weakened by the 1930 Treaty.[54] However, it also contains a unique labour narrative underlying its history, which had a particular significance for the conjuncture in question. In other words, one way to understand the *Wathba* is through the lens of the labour struggle against semi-peripheral sovereignty and its social and economic implications for the lives of the ordinary Iraqi working classes. As Eric Davis has emphasised, workers provided 'the backbone' of the *Wathba*.[55] The Iraqi labour movement was making strides in its continuous struggle against the British employers of the colossal industrial enterprises (namely the port, railways and oil refineries). Even before the *Wathba*, continuous labour strikes in these enterprises were rapidly becoming a concern for the British authorities.[56] The workers were not merely angered by their wretched conditions, but were also able, because of their unique position within the semi-colonial system of capitalist exploitation, to make a direct correlation between their immediate material conditions and the far-reaching issue of imperialism.

To understand the role of the labour movement in the *Wathba*, one must begin with its organising efforts several years earlier. The years leading up to the *Wathba* found the workers developing certain organisational tactics and strategies that demonstrated that they were becoming more cognisant of the direct relationship between British imperialism and the Iraqi state. One could begin with the 1945 railway strike, which was eventually suppressed, and led to the intensification of 'hatred towards British colonialism and imperialism' within the Iraqi working-class.[57] The Railway Directorate was deemed a 'colonial entity' and the 1930 treaty that maintained it under British control was considered a direct cause of their dire conditions.[58] The Port Workers' Union, which organised a strike the same year and was similarly suppressed, released a petition that described the conditions of workers in the following manner: 'Our workers have lived under the shadow of the British directorate that controls the Port, a life of misery and despair and slavery…representing the cruellest form of colonial exploitation…a life that…does not fit with [the principles of international law and] human rights of our age today'.[59] The radicalisation of the Iraqi working class was deepened even further after the violent Gawurbaghi Strike at the Kirkuk oilfields in 1946, which ended in a bloodbath as police violently shot into a peaceful gathering of striking workers, killing 10 and injuring dozens. Although this massacre forced the IPC temporarily to give in to some of the workers' demands, the union was eventually suppressed. Despite the government inquest, and the workers placing responsibility on a 'high-up combination of government and company,' no company or British official was ever held accountable under Iraqi law, thanks to the rigid protections provided by the provisions of the treaty.[60]

It is in this manner that Iraqi workers were slowly becoming aware that the withdrawal of their labour would strike a powerful blow to imperialism in the region as a whole. Timothy Mitchell illustrates this perspective well when he writes:

> in building the infrastructure of oil, the petroleum companies were also laying the infrastructure of political unrest. The points of vulnerability, where movements could organize and apply pressure, now included a series of oil wells, pipelines, refineries, railways, docks and shipping lanes across the Middle East. These were the interconnected sites at which a series of claims for political freedoms and more egalitarian forms of life would be fought.[61]

During the *Wathba* workers' strikes continued throughout the country in the months after the 'Day of the Bridge', reaching 'unheard-of proportions' despite the martial law in place, leading to the famous oil strike at the K3 pumping-station, a vital oil pipeline near Haditha (as it was 'the point of bifurcation of the Kirkuk–Haifa and Kirkuk–Tripoli pipelines').[62] The strike, demanding the rights to a union, sickness and disability insurance, and a pension, involved 3000 workers and lasted over a month. The workers were successful in their goal of completely shutting down the station, picketing all exits to ensure that not 'even a pint of gasoline' got out.[63] After the authorities cut water and food to their camps, the workers were forced to march to Baghdad, about 250 km away. The police eventually caught up with them and arrested them 70 km from their destination in Fallujah. This celebrated labour episode of the enduring *Wathba* narrative has been considered 'an Iraqi variant on a diminutive scale of the Chinese epic of the Long March'.[64] It is therefore not an overstatement to consider the *Wathba* as the wider reflection of a labour struggle against the semi-peripheral sovereignty that gave the juridical and ideological cover needed for the imposition of the capitalist economic structures on Iraq.

The wider implications of the Wathba and its contribution to the conjuncture of decolonisation in international law

I will now return to my earlier analysis of TWAIL and its methodology by inserting the social and juridical implications of the *Wathba* into my theoretical argument. My contention was that TWAIL scholars should begin the study of the conjuncture in the history of international law – connecting their concern for the 'micro-histories of resistance' to a much broader understanding of the conjuncture in question. This would allow for the bridging of all these micro-histories into an overarching understanding of agency. Consequently, the conjunctural moment, which allowed anti-colonial and anti-imperial resistance to materialise in Iraq cannot be explained without an attempt to understand the *wider* conjuncture of decolonisation in the region and the Third World. Decolonisation, as Mohammed Bedjaoui reminds us, is by its very definition a 'structural revolution *on a world scale*'.[65] For this reason a conjunctural analysis must begin 'at the level of the international itself', ascertaining 'a dominant combination of causes', while evaluating 'the period characterized by the working out of that combination'.[66] It entails the necessity of simultaneously 'looking inwards to examine the detailed movement of a given period and outwards to locate that period in the longer historical process of which it forms a part'.[67]

A conjunctural analysis in international law, therefore, would have to be attentive to the organic movement within this wide scale, while analysing agency, focusing, in the words of Negri and Hardt, on the 'intersections' and the 'accumulation of struggles' against international law.[68] Although TWAIL scholars are generally familiar with such an analysis – one which Gramsci would refer to as the study of the 'long waves' of history[69] – (for instance Anghie's return to the thought of Francisco de Vitoria in the 16th century), what tends to be missing in general is how this connects to agency (or, using TWAIL vocabulary, to resistance). The conjuncture therefore acts as a bridging device for one's analytic lens in relation to the notion of agency that can be used in tandem with the study of the imperial structures of international law. It is nevertheless not merely a matter of contextualisation, but rather about continuously being attentive to the question of agency and action in one's wider analysis. Before moving to assess Iraqi working-class agency, I will first address the structural implications of the *Wathba* on a variety of different interconnecting and intersecting levels – the Iraqi, regional and international.

On the Iraqi level the *Wathba* contained the origins of the revolutionary process that culminated in the overthrow of the British-sponsored Monarchy by the 1958 July revolution. It certainly inspired and stimulated the Free Officers to take matters into their own hands to defend the people from 'the incubus of injustice that weighed upon them'.[70] I would go as far as to argue that the *Wathba* could be considered the 'dress rehearsal' for the 1958 revolution, especially if one was to consider that the revolutionary process of struggle was sustained throughout the decade, resurfacing as mini-*Wathba*s – namely, the Intifada of 1952 and the Uprising of 1956. In many ways it was the spark that started the process of the brewing and making of the revolution. It is in this sense that the *Wathba* and the revolution are part of the same Iraqi conjuncture. The July revolution was a genuine revolution that broke with the *ancien régime*. The Proclamation No 1 read out on Baghdad Radio announced the establishment of a republic, promised that the Iraqi people would participate in shaping their own future, and established a neutralist foreign policy ending its close alliance with the West.[71] The revolutionary processes began with the drafting of a Provisional Constitution barely two weeks after the revolution, frustrating the subjugating structures of the old constitution or Organic Law, which limited popular sovereignty, as shown above. Furthermore, the new Agrarian Reform law ended the 'semi-feudal' system that was the foundation of British policy and control, destroying the social power of the landed sheikhs by finally bringing the countryside under the purview of state law.[72] Finally, the position of urban workers and the working-class was significantly enhanced by the revision and enactment of an updated progressive labour law for the protection of workers' rights and their trade unions. As for the anti-hegemonic impact of the *Wathba* on the region, this was apparent in the way it inspired countless sympathy strikes and demonstrations in Beirut, Damascus and Cairo. A revealing clipping from a Cairo newspaper read, 'the Iraqi people did not only save itself, but saved the entire Arab world from remaining under Western colonial subjugation'.[73]

To situate the *Wathba* internationally, one would need to analyse how its revolutionary impetus was partially successful in striking at imperialism by preventing the imposition of a revised treaty. To do that it would be necessary to understand other regional and international events that rendered it the appropriate moment to attack (British) imperialism. Here, the weaving of other events of conjunctural resistance against imperialism and the international legal order that occurred in the Third World that year is necessary, in order to grasp the vulnerability of British imperialism at that particular moment. Frank Furedi has detailed the conjuncture that emerged during that unique year of 1948 for anti-colonial and nationalist liberation struggles in the Third World.[74] He demonstrates how 1948 was a year of widespread panic in Whitehall as a crisis of imperial rule emerged unexpectedly, where anti-colonial and anti-imperial resistance reached its utmost intensity: 'No part of the empire seemed immune from what appeared to be an epidemic of unrest'.[75] Twelve days before the *Wathba*, Burma rejected Commonwealth membership, while February saw riots in Accra and in June emergency rule was established in Malaya.[76] Of course, regionally 1948 was the year that the tragic Palestinian *Nakba* (catastrophe) was unfolding. More than anything else this event represented the injustices of colonialism and imperialism for the Arab peoples. A focus on the manifestation of the conjuncture on the international scale would take all these events into account in the analysis of this particular moment of Iraqi agency against the imperialism of international law.

The *Wathba* could be situated in the conjuncture that was emerging within the international legal order and which was manifested in the signing of the 1960 Declaration on the Granting of Independence to Colonial Countries and Peoples (General Assembly Resolution 1514).[77] The significance of this document – sometimes referred to as the 'Magna Carta' of decolonisation – should not be understated.[78] The UN Charter of 1945 failed to clearly condemn colonialism, and its imposition of a duty of administration of specific colonies could arguably be construed as recognising the legality of colonialism.[79] The 1960 Declaration was therefore the first instrument in the history of international law in which colonialism and imperialism were deemed unlawful. As Christopher Quaye has observed, the preamble of the Declaration, 'decried colonialism…by observing the universal position against perpetuation of colonialism and expressing belief in liberation from anything that is colonial'.[80] In its words, the declaration: '*Solemnly proclaims* the necessity of bringing a speedy and unconditional end to colonialism *in all its forms and manifestations*' .[81] Despite its significance in international legal history, the Declaration did not fully accelerate the process of decolonisation at a pace corresponding to the hopes of the peoples under colonial rule, as its implementation had to be continuously fought for by the bloc over the next few years.[82] Nevertheless, the contribution of the Iraqi anti-colonial and anti-imperial struggle to this Declaration, as will be shown below, was clear.

The *Wathba* and its revolutionary consequences on the Iraqi plane was only one event among a series of similar revolutionary events in other parts of the Third World that had a direct influence on the way the representatives of the Afro-Asian bloc in the UN, adhering to the Bandung Spirit, was aggressively arguing for the drafting and liberal interpretation of this Declaration, while maintaining a firm anti-colonial stance.[83] It was clear that legal arguments were specifically made on the basis of 'the political weather outside the [UN] Headquarters'.[84] In other words, not only was the law rejected as a mechanism for dealing with the question of colonialism and imperialism, but the myriad events of decolonisation on the ground were considered necessary sources for the drafting and moulding of international law and its instruments. The bloc continuously insisted that these anti-colonial struggles must be unconditionally recognised as legitimate – international 'law should be modified according to changed circumstances'.[85]

The permanent representative of the revolutionary government of Iraq in the UN, Adnan Pachachi, took part in the drafting of the 1960 Declaration.[86] The Iraqi delegation, together with a number of Asian and African states, ended up co-sponsoring the Declaration when it was presented to the General Assembly. In an impassionate and eloquent speech to the

Assembly, the new Iraqi Foreign Minister, Hashim Jawad, began by recounting the long history of colonialism in the Arab world, beginning with the first experience of European imperialism with the French conquest of Algeria in 1830, eventually referring to the Mandate system as 'a new form of colonialism' that was imposed on the peoples of the Middle East.[87] Jawad accordingly directly rejected the semi-peripheral sovereignty that the Iraqi masses had attempted to abolish with their blood, sweat and tears during the *Wathba* and thereafter. He went on to state that, although the Mandate in Iraq was terminated in 1932, it was replaced by a new relationship that retained for the former Mandatory Power great influence in the internal affairs of the country, emphasising that 'it took another twenty-six years and our great July Revolution of 1958 for the people of Iraq to rid the country finally of the last vestiges of foreign domination and influence'.[88] Jawad then emphasised how he regarded all struggles for decolonisation as interconnected by specifically referring to the Arab and Iraqi experience:

> I do not think I exaggerate when I say that few nations in the world have suffered as much as the Arab nation under colonial rule…the Arab people have known colonialism in its worst forms and manifestations. They have experienced at first hand its oppression and treachery and have suffered from it physically, materially and spiritually as few others have. This is one of the reasons why we have such a deep sympathy and understanding for the struggle of the other nations for freedom and independence.[89]

He went on to make clear that it was this unique 'extensive' and 'tragic' experience of (semi) colonialism in the Arab world in general and in Iraq in particular which solidified his delegation's belief in the importance of an unequivocal anti-colonial wording in the Declaration.[90]

The Iraqi contribution to the drafting of this document was hence in ensuring that the semi-peripheral sovereignty that was skilfully woven into international law in Geneva and granted to Iraq in 1932, as a recognised form of 'independence', would be unequivocally rejected in the Declaration. International law should instead postulate concrete sovereignty and full independence. NM Perrera, the representative for Ceylon (present-day Sri Lanka) plainly explained the meaning of this part of the Declaration when he emphasised that reference to the 'manifestations of colonialism' specifically refers to 'the various methods, procedures and legal figments which are used by colonial powers to cover the nakedness of rank colonialism'.[91] The semi-peripheral sovereignty described earlier and which was a significant part of the Iraqi experience was one of these more sophisticated legal figments that were recognised under international law. It is in this way that the Iraqi experience of the *Wathba* and its revolutionary consequences, in rejecting semi-peripheral sovereignty on the ground, may be linked through a conjunctural analysis to the wider changes within the international legal order.

The significance of labour and working-class agency to the conjuncture of decolonisation

The conjunctural analysis above has clearly shown how 'resistance' or, more broadly, revolutionary agency is only conducive within a particular conjuncture that emerges from the structures in question. TWAIL scholars would traditionally have analysed the *Wathba* in isolation of these structures, concentrating on certain characteristics of agency as being external and not contingent to these structures (in particular its spontaneity, non-violence and heterogeneity). However, this narrow approach differs from the conjunctural analysis that brings agency and structure into *one* fold, while it romanticises agency, approaching it as a form of resistance that is devoid of any revolutionary content. Many TWAIL scholars cannot conceive of emancipation without or beyond the law or the international legal order, despite it being the very target of their critique.[92] The *Wathba*, however, emerged for the very reason that the legal mechanisms of the state that were being manipulated by imperial instruments of international law were inept and completely dysfunctional. The *Wathba* eventually became about the subversion of the law rather than its mere reform. Furthermore, it demonstrated that the effectiveness of what I refer to as 'conjunctural resistance' in the context of revolutionary action depends on its organisational capacity. It is not enough to put one's hopes in the spontaneity of action, as TWAIL scholars tend to do, for, despite the unforeseen nature of the *Wathba*, the movement took off at that particular moment because it was able to readily organise into effective steering committees. This was certainly possible because of some of its participants' past experiences, especially those of the workers. In this manner, therefore, romanticising the spontaneity of agency ignores the fact that spontaneity and organisation must come together within a particular conjuncture to be effective.

I want to end by briefly returning to the significance of labour to the specific conjuncture in question. A focus on labour and working-class agency in this analysis demonstrates the strong affinity between capitalism, imperialism and international law, especially in the semi-periphery. This is what explains the significant role of labour in countering the manifestations of the international legal order within the conjuncture in question. I have already shown how semi-peripheral sovereignty in the Iraqi context was manufactured as a mechanism to control the semi-colonial Middle East. The 'independence' of Iraq was more a mechanism to legalise the control of Iraqi oil and to regulate its transportation across the region. While the Anglo-Iraq treaty maintained this control juridically, Iraqi labour was exploited to superintend the everyday functioning of this infrastructure of economic dominance. In this way colonial and racial relations remained intact after Iraqi 'independence', especially in the colossal private enterprises and factories. The Anglo-Iraq treaty ensured British control of the most important economic sites of production and trade in the country. Even within a semi-colonial context of 'independent Iraq' this created an atmosphere of racism that was common elsewhere in the Empire. A British official visiting the oil company sites appallingly observed that, 'the relation between management and labour is outwardly that of "sahibs" and "niggers", and this aspect is accentuated by the luxury in which management and British staff live, and their remoteness: In brief, my impression was of what our Russian friends would call capitalism at its worst, and foreign capitalism at that'.[93] These workers, like their counterparts elsewhere in the Third World, embodied the contradictions of the capitalist system within the (semi) colony, experiencing at first hand the effects of imperialism and racism in their everyday lives. Thus it should not be surprising that they would lead a significant role within the nationalist liberation movement.

Iraqi workers reconstituted the question of labour as an anti-colonial and anti-imperial one. This is why their rejection of the Anglo-Iraq treaty was a rejection of the entire international legal and economic order imposed on the region. Yusuf Salman Yusuf (aka Fahad), the secretary-general of the Iraqi Communist Party, reveals the way the workers were thinking when he wrote: 'the working class did not separate the national [political] from the social [economic] content of liberation…[For them] national liberation is but a starting point of a fundamental change in the life of the people'.[94] The Iraqi labour movement combined claims of higher wages and better living conditions with anti-colonial demands for national liberation, ensuring its 'full integration into the national movement'.[95] This wide analytic lens was unique to the international conjuncture in question. It was prevalent at the time in other parts of the Third World.[96] Furedi has characterised this conjuncture as a 'radical moment in anti-colonial politics', where there was a 'tendency of protests to acquire a more fundamental anti-systemic and anti-imperialist orientation, accompanied by increasing erosion of the boundaries between economic and political demands.'[97] This explains how 'relatively ordinary demands could mushroom into a major challenge to imperial authority'.[98] Iraqi workers, therefore, were unable to articulate their rejection of their social, living and working conditions without at the same time rejecting the entire international legal and economic order that was imposed upon them.

The British came to the conclusion that there needed to be an extensive development policy towards labour that would 'ameliorate the dire labour conditions' and 'fend off Communism'.[99] It is revealing that, before the eruption of the *Wathba*, the British were in the process of advising the Iraqi government on drawing up 'regulations for the whole field of labour in Iraq' and for the establishment of an arbitration procedure that would address workers' grievances.[100] It is this ultimately unsuccessful policy of development and conciliation that dominated British policy towards the region in the next decade. In a similar vein a development framework was manifest within international law and its institutions. The International Labour Organization, for example, sent technical assistance missions to advise on labour and social issues in the Middle East. The ILO's technical assistance programmes were conceived in the context of constricted notions of social and economic development, with the aim of fighting the growing influence of communism.[101] Moreover, the 1961 Declaration of the United Nations Development Decade (General Assembly Resolution 1710) ensured that the effects of the 1960 Declaration would be limited in that it 'bound together decolonization and development with a firm yoke'.[102] This maintained the subordination of society to the discipline of economics, and led to the continuation of the development of underdevelopment.[103] Most importantly, this was what prevented the materialisation of an alternative international economic order from the 'salt-water' decolonisation that was won. In this way the conjunctural shift did not ultimately produce the revolutionary changes sought, whether within the international legal order or in the Iraqi experience, where revolutionary processes were interrupted by a CIA-sponsored military coup in 1963.

Conclusion

The history of the *Wathba* recounted above is an illustration of how revolutionary action may be undertaken within a specific conjuncture to subvert the effects of the imperialism of international law. Although this affirms the transient and provisional nature of the foundations of international law, it is only in relation to the structures in question that agency may be evaluated.[104] It is nevertheless important to recall Gramsci's warning that 'a common error...consists in an inability to find the correct relation between what is organic and what is conjunctural. This leads to...[either]...an excess of "economism"...[or]...an excess of "ideologism". In the first case there is an overestimation of mechanical causes, in the second an exaggeration of the voluntarist and individual element.'[105] It is necessary in the end to find an accurate correlation between the (organic) structure and (conjunctural) agency in one's analysis if one is to correctly evaluate how agency was (or is to be) deployed *within* the structural constraints of the international legal, political and economic order.

The prominent Iraqi poet Mohammed Mahdi al-Jawahiri recited a celebrated poem eulogising those who died on the bridge during the *Wathba*, his brother among them. He begins with the following line: 'Are you aware or not, that the wounds of martyrs are a mouth?'[106] It is not only a matter of allowing this 'mouth' to speak in one's scholarship, but rather to focus on the very conjunctures that allow those who take action to liberate themselves (becoming 'wounded martyrs'). It is, in other words, the opening (or 'mouth') of the conjunctures that should be one's point of departure.

Disclosure statement

No potential conflict of interest was reported by the author.

Acknowledgements

An earlier draft of this paper was presented at the 'Third World Approaches to International Law Conference' at the American University of Cairo, February 2015. The author would like to thank participants at the writing workshop of the Transnational Law Summer Institute at King's College, London, in June 2015, as well as the TWAIL Conference workshop at the University of Maynooth, Ireland, in September 2015 for all their comments on earlier drafts. Special thanks to Nesrine Badawi, Susan Drummond, Adil Hasan Khan, Robert Knox, John Reynolds, Alice Riccardi, Adrian Smith and Sujith Xavier for their useful feedback and/or suggestions.

Notes

1. Ayyub, *al-Yad, al-Ard wa'l Ma'*, 286.
2. Marx, *The Eighteenth Brumaire of Louis Bonaparte*, 15.
3. Baxi, "What may the 'Third World' Expect?," 720.
4. Romulo, quoted in El-Ayouty, *The United Nations and Decolonization*, 35.
5. Romulo, quoted in El-Ayouty, *The United Nations and Decolonization*, 34.
6. For a good overview of the literature, see Gathii, "TWAIL."
7. Mickelson, "Rhetoric and Rage," 406.
8. Okafor, "Newness, Imperialism and International Legal Reform," 178.
9. Anghie, "The Evolution of International Law."
10. Ibid.
11. Taylor, "Reclaiming Revolution."
12. Ibid., 273.
13. Rajagopal, *International Law from Below*, 293.
14. Taylor, "Reclaiming Revolution," 263.
15. Taylor, "Reclaiming Revolution," 274.
16. Taylor, "Reclaiming Revolution," 271.
17. Althusser, *For Marx*, 250.
18. Althusser, *For Marx*, 178.
19. Althusser, *For Marx*, 180 (emphasis in the original).

20. Koivisto and Lahtinen, "Historical–Critical Dictionary of Marxism," 274.
21. Ibid.
22. See Parmar, *Indigeneity and Legal Pluralism in India*.
23. Batatu, *The Old Social Classes*, 546. It should be noted that I am not referring to the 'event' here in the same manner as Alain Badiou does.
24. Benton, "From International Law to Imperial Constitutions," 599.
25. Ibid.
26. Anglo-Iraq Treaty of Alliance [1922] Cmd. 2370.
27. Wright, *Mandates under the League*, 60.
28. *League of Nations Official Journal*, Vol. V, at 1217.
29. Treaty with H. M. King Faisal [10 October 1922] Cmd. 1757.
30. Brown, "Constitutionalism, Authoritarianism, and Imperialism," 936.
31. See Pederson, "Getting out of Iraq."
32. Treaty of Alliance between United Kingdom and Iraq [1929–1930] Cmd. 3627.
33. Ibid.
34. Colonial Office, *Special Report*, 11.
35. Permanent Mandates Commission (PMC), "Minutes," XX, 134.
36. See PMC, "Minutes," Sess. 18, 19, 20.
37. See PMC, "Minutes," Sess. 20, 168–176.
38. Ibid.
39. Mitchell, *Carbon Democracy*, 47, 102.
40. Bentwich, "The Termination of the A Mandates," 191.
41. Batatu, *The Old Social Classes*, 544, 551.
42. Marr, *The Modern History of Iraq*, 103.
43. Ibid.
44. Batatu, *The Old Social Classes*, 550.
45. Humaidi, *Al-Tatwurat*, 519–525.
46. Ibid.
47. Schalchiyyah is a working-class neighborhood in Baghdad.
48. Batatu, *The Old Social Classes*, 551.
49. Ibid.
50. Batatu, *The Old Social Classes*, 553.
51. Humaidi, *Al-Tatwurat*, 533.
52. For the full text, see al-Hasani, *Tarikh al-Wizarat*, 249.
53. Batatu, *The Old Social Classes*, 557.
54. Al-Chadirji, *Mudhakkirat*.
55. Davis, "History for the Many?," 293.
56. British Embassy, Baghdad to Foreign Office, 21 May 1948, enclosing minute on strikes at IPC [FO 371/68479].
57. Al-Nou'aman, *al-Hizb al-Shyou'i al-Iraqi*, 126.
58. Ibid.
59. Quoted in al-Nou'aman, *al-Hizb al-Shyou'i al-Iraqi*, 123.
60. Batatu, *The Old Social Classes*, 622, 624.
61. Mitchell, *Carbon Democracy*, 103.
62. Batatu, *The Old Social Classes*, 622.
63. Batatu, *The Old Social Classes*, 625.
64. Batatu, *The Old Social Classes*, 563.
65. Bedjaoui, *Towards a New International Economic Order*, 88 (emphasis in the original).
66. Justin Rosenberg, quoted in Koivisto and Lahtinen, 'Historical–Critical Dictionary of Marxism,' 273.
67. Ibid.
68. Hardt and Negri, *Empire*, 263.
69. See Finocchiaro, *Gramsci and the History of Dialectical Thought*, 164.
70. Col. Abdul Karim Qassim's words, quoted in Batatu, *The Old Social Classes*, 806.

71. See Romero, *The Iraqi Revolution of 1958.*
72. Marr, *The Modern History of Iraq*, 105.
73. *al-Nida'* newspaper (Cairo, February 5, 1948), quoted in Humaidi, *Al-Tatwurat*, 546.
74. Furedi, *Colonial Wars*, 4, 88–108.
75. Furedi, *Colonial Wars*, 89.
76. Ibid.
77. Declaration on the Granting of Independence to Colonial Countries and Peoples, GA Res. 1514 (XV), UN GAOR, 15th sess., 947th plenary meeting, UN Doc. A/RES/1514 (XV) (14 December 1960).
78. Quayson-Sackey, cited in Quaye, *Liberation Struggles in International Law*, 111.
79. Quaye, *Liberation Struggles in International Law*, 108–109.
80. Quaye, *Liberation Struggles in International Law*, 112.
81. Declaration on the Granting of Independence.
82. Sharma, *Afro-Asian Group in the UN*, 205.
83. Ibid.
84. El-Ayouty, *The United Nations and Decolonization*, 60.
85. Anand, "Attitude of the Asian-African States," 14.
86. Pachachi, *Iraq's Voice at the United Nations*, 9.
87. UN GAOR, 15th Sess., 937th plenary meeting, UN Doc. A/PV 937 (6 December 1960), 120–138.
88. Ibid.
89. Ibid.
90. Ibid.
91. UN GAOR, 15th Sess., 926th plenary meeting, UN Doc. A/PV 926 (28 November 1960), 1002.
92. See, for example, Eslava and Pahuja, "Between Resistance and Reform"; Chimni, "Third World Approaches"; and Anghie, *Imperialism*.
93. Minute by Wells (Embassy, Baghdad), 7 April 1948, F0 624/130, quoted in Fuccaro, "Reading Oil as Urban Violence," 228.
94. Batatu, *The Old Social Classes*, 589.
95. Farouk-Sluglett and Sluglett, "The Social Classes," 127–128.
96. Rodney, *How Europe underdeveloped Africa*, 276.
97. Furedi, *Colonial Wars*, 38.
98. Ibid.
99. British Embassy to Baghdad to Rt. Hon. E. Bevin, Foreign Secretary, "Street Demonstrations in Baghdad," London, 2 July 1946, [FO 371/52406].
100. D. L. Busk, Baghdad to Rt. Hon. E. Bevin, Foreign Secretary, London, 21 August 1946 [FO371/52456].
101. Maul, "The Morse Years," 54.
102. Pahuja, "Decolonization and the Eventness of International Law," 99.
103. Ibid.
104. Marks, "False Contingency," 10.
105. Gramsci, *Selections from the Prison Notebooks*, 178.
106. See Jayussi, *Trends and Movements*, 199.

Bibliography

al-Chadirji, Kamil. *Mudhakkirat Kamil al-Chadirji wa Tarikh al-Hizb al-Watani al-Dimuqrati [The Memoirs of Kamil al-Chadirji and the History of the National Democratic Party]*. Beirut: Dar al-Tal'ia, 1970.

al-Hasani, Abdul Razzaq. *Tarikh al-Wizarat al-Iraqiya [The History of the Iraqi Cabinets]*. Vol. 3. Baghdad: Dar al-Su'oun al-Thaqafiya al-'Ama, 1974.

al-Nou'man, Salim. *al-Hizb al-Shyou'i al-Iraqi bqayadat Fahad [The Iraqi Communist Party under the leadership of Fahad]*. Damascus: al-Mada, 2007.

Althusser, Louis. *For Marx*. London: Verso, 2005.

Anand, R. P. "Attitude of the Asian–African States towards Certain Problems of International Law." In *Third World Attitudes toward International Law: An Introduction*, edited by Frederick E. Snyder and Sathirathai Surakiart, 5–22. Dordrecht: Martinus Nijhoff, 1987.

Anghie, Anthony. *Imperialism, Sovereignty and the Making of International Law*. Cambridge, MA: Cambridge University Press, 2005.

Anghie, Anthony. "The Evolution of International Law: Colonial and Postcolonial Realities." *Third World Quarterly* 27, no. 5 (2006): 739–753.

Ayyub, D. N. *al-Yad, al-Ard wa'l Ma' [The Hand, the Land and the Water]. In al-Athar al-kamila li-adab Dhi al-Nun Ayyub [The Collected Heritage of D. N. Ayyub]*, 1978. Reprint, Baghdad: Wizarat al-I'lam, 1948.

Batatu, Hanna. *The Old Social Classes and the Revolutionary Movements of Iraq: A Study of Iraq's Old Landed and Commercial Classes and of its Communists, Ba'thists and Free Officers*. Princeton, NJ: Princeton University Press, 1978.

Baxi, Upendra. "What may the 'Third World' expect from International Law?" *Third World Quarterly* 27, no. 5 (2006): 713–725.

Bedjaoui, Mohammed. *Towards a New International Economic Order: New Challenges to International Law*. New York: Holmes & Meier, 1979.

Benton, Lauren. "From International Law to Imperial Constitutions: The Problem of Quasi-sovereignty, 1870–1900." *Law and History Review* 26, no. 3 (2008): 595–619.

Bentwich, Norman. "The Termination of the A Mandates." *Zeitschrift für Ausländisches Recht und Völkerrecht* 3, no. 2 (1932): 176–191.

Brown, Nathan. "Constitutionalism, Authoritarianism, and Imperialism in Iraq." *Drake Law Review* 53 (2005): 923–941.

Colonial Office. *Special Report by His Majesty's Government in the United Kingdom of Great Britain and Northern Ireland to the Council of the League of Nations on the Progress of Iraq During the Period 1920–1931*. London: H.M. Stationery office, 1931.

Chimni, B. S. "Third World Approaches to International Law: A Manifesto." *International Community Law Review* 8 (2006): 3–27.

Davis, Eric. "History for the Many or History for the Few? The Historiography of the Iraqi Working Class." In *Workers and Working Classes in the Middle East*, edited by Z. Lockman, 271–301. New York: State University of New York Press, 1994.

1960 Declaration on the Granting of Independence to Colonial Countries and Peoples. GA Res. 1514/UN GAOR, 15th Sess., Supp. No. 16/UN Doc. A/4684 (1960) 66.

El-Ayouty, Yasin. *The United Nations and Decolonization: The Role of Afro-Asia*. The Hague: Martinus Nijhoff, 1971.

Eslava Luis, and Sundhya Pahuja. "Between Resistance and Reform: TWAIL and the Universality of International Law." *Trade, Law and Development 3*, no. 1 (2011): 103–130.

Farouk-Sluglett, Marion, and Peter Sluglett. "The Social Classes and the Origins of the Revolution." In *The Iraqi Revolution of 1958: The Old Social Classes Revisited*, edited by Robert Fernea and Roger Louis, 118–142. London: I. B. Tauris, 1991.

Finocchiaro, Maurice. *Gramsci and the History of Dialectical Thought*. Cambridge: Cambridge University Press, 2002

Fuccaro, Nelida. "Reading Oil as Urban Violence: Kirkuk and its Oil Conurbation, 1927–1958." In *Urban Violence in the Middle East: Changing Cityscapes in Transition from Empire to nation State*, edited by Ulrike Freitag, Nelida Fuccaro, Claudia Ghrawi, and Nora Lafi, 222–242. New York: Berghahn Books, 2015.

Furedi, Frank. *Colonial Wars and the Politics of Third World Nationalism*. London: I. B. Tauris, 1994.

Gramsci, Antonio. *Selections from the Prison Notebooks*. London: International Publishers, 1971.

Gathii, James. "TWAIL: A Brief History of its Origins, its Decentralized Network, and a Tentative Bibliography." *Trade Law and Development* 3, no. 1 (2011): 26–64.

Hardt Michael, and Antonio Negri. *Empire*. Cambridge, MA: Harvard University Press, 2000.

Humaidi, Ja'afar Abbas. *Al-Tatwurat al-Syasisya fi al-Iraq, 1941–1953 [The Political Developments in Iraq, 1941–1953]*. al-Najaf: Matb'at al-Ni'aman, 1976.

Jayyusi, Salma Khadra. *Trends and Movements in Modern Arabic Poetry*. Leiden: Brill, 1997.

Koivisto, J., and M. Lahtinen. "Historical-Critical Dictionary of Marxism." *Historical Materialism* 20, no. 1 (2012): 267–277.

Marks, Susan. "False Contingency." *Current Legal Problems* 62 (2010): 1–22.

Marr, Phebe. *The Modern History of Iraq*. Oxford: Westview Press, 1985.

Marx, Karl. *The Eighteenth Brumaire of Louis Bonaparte*. New York: International Publishers, 1963.

Maul, D. "The Morse Years: The ILO 1948–1970." In *ILO Histories: Essays on the International Labour Organization and its Impact on the World during the Twentieth Century*. Bern: Peter Lang, 2010, 365–400.

Mickelson, Karin. "Rhetoric and Rage: Third World Voices in International Legal Discourse." *Wisconsin International Law Journal* 16, no. 2 (1998): 353–419.

Mitchell, Timothy. *Carbon Democracy: Political Power in the Age of Power*. London: Verso, 2011.

Okafor, Obiora. "Newness, Imperialism and International Legal Reform in our Time: A TWAIL Perspective." *Osgoode Hall Law Journal* 43, nos. 1–2 (2005): 171–191.

Pachachi, Adnan. *Iraq's Voice at the United Nations 1959–69: A Personal Record*. London: Quartet Books, 1991.

Pahuja, Sundhya. "Decolonization and the Eventness of International Law." In *Events: The Force of International Law*, edited by John Fleur, Richard Joyce and Sundhya Pahuja, 91–105. Abingdon: Routledge, 2011.

Parmar, Pooja. *Indigeneity and Legal Pluralism in India: Claims, Histories, Meanings*. Cambridge: Cambridge University Press, 2015.

Pederson, Susan. "Getting out of Iraq – in 1932: "The League of Nations and the Road to Normative Statehood." *American Historical Review* 115, no. 4 2010: 975–1000.

Quaye, Christopher. *Liberation Struggles in International Law*. Philadelphia, PA: Temple University Press, 1991.

Rajagopal, Balakrishnan. *International Law from Below: Development, Social Movements and Third World Resistance*. Cambridge, MA: Cambridge University Press, 2005.

Rodney, Walter. *How Europe underdeveloped Africa*. Washington, DC: Howard University Press, 1981.

Romero, Juan. *The Iraqi Revolution of 1958: A Revolutionary Quest for Unity and Security*. Lanham, MD: University Press of America, 2011.

Sassoon, Joseph. *Economic Policy in Iraq, 1932–1950*. London: Frank Cass, 1987.

Sharma, D. N. *Afro-Asian Group in the UN*. Allahabad: Chaitanya Publishing, 1969.

Taylor, Owen. "Reclaiming Revolution." *Finnish Yearbook of International Law*. Vol. 22, 259–292. Oxford: Hart Publishing, 2011.

Wright, Quincy. *Mandates under the League of Nations*. New York: Greenwood Press, 1930.

Mir-Said Sultan-Galiev and the idea of Muslim Marxism: empire, Third World(s) and praxis

Vanja Hamzić

ABSTRACT
This paper revisits the idea of Muslim Marxism, as espoused through the life and work of the Tatar Muslim and Bolshevik intellectual and revolutionary Mir-Said Sultan-Galiev (1892–1940). I argue that Sultan-Galiev's oeuvre – a unique synthesis of Marxist, Muslim modernist, anti-colonial and Third World praxis – represents a path-breaking take on Muslim selfhood and practices of belonging.

Marxist and Muslim lifeworlds do not converge a lot nowadays. They are generally thought so much apart, both in theory and practice, that any mention of 'Muslim Marxism' appears hopelessly oxymoronic. Marx's denunciation of religion as 'the opium of the people',[1] and countless accounts of religious persecution under communist rule are often invoked as a grim reminder of the supposed incompatibility of Marxist and Muslim ideas. Yet, historically, such incompatibility is tenuous. Not only did many Muslim thinkers *tend* towards Marxism (a tendency so neatly captured by the French adjective *marxisant*[2]) and vice versa, in more ways than one;[3] there also emerged, especially in the Worlds designated as Third,[4] idiosyncratic forms of individual and collective praxis whose transformative potential resulted precisely from the idea that rudimentary Marxist views on social and economic justice can and must be reconciled with those of Muslim political and social consciousness.

Nowhere can this bold idea – the idea of Muslim Marxism – be better traced than to the eventful life and legacy of the controversial Tatar Muslim and Bolshevik political and social reformer, Mir-Said Sultan-Galiev (in Tatar: Mirsäyet Soltanğäliev; 1892–1940). Caught between the demise of one long-standing empire and the rapid rise of another, that is, between the unmaking of czarist Russia and the making of the USSR, Sultan-Galiev's story is that of a personal and ideological struggle in an inauspicious time, a story of an avant-garde take on Muslim subjectivity, tradition and revolutionary potential, albeit with a tragic ending.

Sultan-Galiev's good repute among the Muslims and communists alike of the revolutionary and post-revolutionary Russia of the early 20th century, earned in an unusually rapid fashion, made him a chief authority on the so-called 'Eastern Question', which in the Soviet context mainly related to the USSR's vast eastern territories, populated, among others, by millions of Muslims, largely of Turkic origins. It was this anxiety of the emerging Soviet state about its Eurasian Muslim populace – famously exemplified in Lenin's observation that one has to be a thousand times more careful and accommodating than usual when dealing with these 'national minorities'[5] – that provided Sultan-Galiev and other like-minded Muslim activists with an opportunity to negotiate a unique, even if short-lived, position for Soviet Muslims, one not only of relative freedom of worship and association in an age of militant atheism but also one of increasing participation in the state's political and military affairs. Sultan-Galiev's ambitions were, however, much greater and, had he managed to retain the trust of Stalin and his inner circle towards the close of the interbellum period, he might have wrestled an even greater autonomy for Soviet Muslims. Indeed, he might even (as he would later be accused of planning) have spearheaded a revolutionary insurgency of his own, which, in all likelihood, would have been Muslim and Third World socialist in nature.

The intent of this article is to provide a preliminary critical reassessment of the rise and fall of Muslim Marxism of Sultan-Galiev's type. Sultan-Galiev's own works, spanning a variety of genres from poetry and prose in Muslim social and educational magazines to relentlessly Bolshevik political writing in state-sanctioned journals such as *Zhizn' natsional'nostei* (*The Life of Nationalities*), offer a rich source of analysis in their own right, and are particularly useful when compared with archival data on his party work, trials and prison notes, including an autobiographical letter.[6] Most of these sources are still available in Russian and Tatar only. However, this is not to say that some of Sultan-Galiev's works have not been of interest to a much wider scholarly and activist community;[7] my argument is, rather, that specifically Muslim dimensions of his social and political mission were more often than not sidelined in contemporary accounts of his life and work, or were given unduly literalist explanations.[8]

I would like to propose that such readings of Sultan-Galiev's thought and actions fail to take into account his extraordinarily difficult political position, as a chief mediator between, on the one hand, an increasingly autocratic Soviet socialist elite, bearing all the hallmarks of Said's *Orientalism* and Great-Russian chauvinism, and the reform-minded Muslim Eurasians, on the other. This is particularly true with regard to his interpretation of Muslim subjectivity, which uses but ultimately transgresses the early 20th-century concepts of ethnic, national and religious belonging in order to reimagine and give primacy to Muslim political – and, indeed, revolutionary – *umma* (community). It is equally evident in his formative years, which involved Muslim religious schooling of the so-called *jadīd*ist type, thus inextricably linking his educational experience with the work of an earlier Muslim reformer, Ismail Gasprinskiĭ (in Turkish: İsmail Gaspıralı, 1851–1914), a Crimean Tatar deeply invested in a Muslim modernist educational, linguistic and cultural project that had transformed beyond recognition the educational landscape of late tsarist Russia.[9]

I argue that the *uṣūl al-jadīd*, or 'new method', that Gasprinskiĭ had introduced to Muslim schools and popularised, as a form of critical thinking, among the Muslim intelligentsia in the turbulent *fin-de-siècle* period immediately preceding the fall of the Russian Empire, had given Mir-Said Sultan-Galiev an invaluable model for his future work. A key element of this model, befitting the trying times and circumstances of both Gasprinskiĭ's and Sultan-Galiev's lifeworlds, is that of *satr*, or 'concealment' for the greater good, which the two reformers exercised and perfected in their own idiosyncratic ways, thus escaping censorship and other, ostensibly more serious, forms of repression. In Gasprinskiĭ's case, it enabled the gradual introduction of over 5000 *uṣūl al-jadīd* schools in Russia by 1916 and the creation of an important intellectual movement that in many ways assisted the survival of Muslim social and political life in the times to come. In Sultan-Galiev's case, it evolved into a full-fledged revolutionary methodology of rare sophistication; so rare, in fact, that it continues to befuddle the connoisseurs of his work until this very day. I will propose here, albeit with some caution, that the strategic deployment of *satr* by Gasprinskiĭ and Sultan-Galiev, which only a careful deduction can reveal, as it is never explicitly stated, is reminiscent of the *satr* that used to be a staple of Ottoman social relations, as stated, for example, around the year 1601, by the Ottoman jurist 'Ālī al-Qārī' al-Harawī.[10] In a sense, then, Gasprinskiĭ's and Sultan-Galiev's uses of concealment for the 'greater good' represent a revival of an important principle from a milieu not entirely strange to either of the two reformers.

What follows, then, is an attempt to re-contextualise Sultan-Galiev's oeuvre with a particular focus on its Muslim-specific elements. I will first introduce his take on Muslim subjectivity and praxis, which I understand to be an amalgamation of his personal experience of class-based injustice, his *jadīd*ist views and his deeply felt revolutionary cause directed at liberating Muslims from colonial oppression, first in respect to his own (Tatar and Bashkir) populace struggling under Russian imperialism, and then in respect of Muslims in the Third World(s) writ large, with Euro-American capitalist imperialism and the native metropolitan bourgeoisie identified as their arch-enemies. I will then address Sultan-Galiev's political interventions, aimed specifically at building a Muslim socialist movement. After initial success, this would become a vexed matter, involving, shortly before its downfall in the hands of the Stalinist state, a series of clandestine interactions that ultimately cost Sultan-Galiev his life, as well as the lives of much of his family and his real or imagined political inner circle. Finally, I will briefly reflect on some of the afterlives of Muslim Marxism in places geographically far away but close in terms of religious and political belonging to Sultan-Galiev's homeland, and on their enduring, if uncanny, relevance for the contemporary reformulations of Muslim religious, political and social selfhood.

Sultan-Galiev's early life and directions

Mir-Said Sultan-Galiev was born in 1892 in the Bashkir village of Elembet'evo in the Ufa governorate, which was then part of the Russian Empire. His father, a respected schoolteacher, followed Gasprinskiĭ's 'new method' in teaching his Muslim pupils, including the young Mir-Said.[11] Apart from what was called 'Islamic history and methods of thought', the curriculum included a variety of social and natural sciences as well as languages other than Russian, such as Tatar and Arabic.[12] Mir-Said's particular passion was Russian literature, which he was able to read in its original language from an early age, as well as Muslim folk stories and customs. The *jadīd*ist schooling taught him critical thinking, however, and some of his earliest contributions to the Muslim press were directed against customary practices that he thought repugnant to modern Muslim culture, such as the *ḥudūd* punishments for the offence of *zina*.[13] His further education, directed towards his becoming a teacher himself, as well as his literary and journalist work, quickly gained support from the Tatar *jadīd*ist intelligentsia. Yet his own class experience gave him an opportunity to reflect upon an element that was still clearly missing from Muslim Tatar life – that of social equality and economic justice.

Sultan-Galiev was born into a 'mixed' family of a father who proudly called himself a Mishar (Mişär), a member of a Tatar peasant community,[14] and a mother who came from a Tatar noble family. In an autobiographical letter Sultan-Galiev reflected upon the continuous bullying he was subjected to by his mother's cousins at her father's estate as formative of his early class-consciousness. 'Thus', he wrote in 1923, 'the farmstead of my grandfather was for me the first and most realistic revolutionary school, cultivating in me a feeling of class hatred'.[15] It is, one can assume, this feeling of his – and the lack thereof in his Tatar intellectual circles – that pushed Sultan-Galiev towards Marxist literature, which he read very sparsely. Surprisingly, perhaps, this literature did not impress him very much. What he was after was a social and political movement able to tackle class difference in everyday life and, in his *jadīd*ist mind, one that could simultaneously respond to colonial injustices felt by Muslims everywhere. In his own words, written in 1917, Sultan-Galiev attested that he had discovered such a movement in the form of the Bolsheviks, because 'they had done more for the Muslims than anyone else':

> Only they are striving to transfer the nationalities' fates into their own hands. Only they revealed who started the world war. What doesn't lead me to them? They also declared war on English imperialism, which oppresses India, Egypt, Afghanistan, Persia and Arabia. They are also the ones who raised arms against French imperialism, which enslaves Morocco, Algeria and other Arab states of Africa. How could I not go to them? You see, they uttered the words that have never been uttered before in the history of the Russian state. Appealing to all Muslims of Russia and the East, they announced that Istanbul must be in Muslims' hands.[16]

This confession reveals some of the elementary tenets of Sultan-Galiev's revolutionary project. His first concern, even when it was not explicitly stated, seemed always to be for Muslims, whose subjectivity he loosely construed as one marked by continuous class and colonial oppression. They were, for him, the most perfect example of Third World proletariat, whose history and social cohesion had made them uniquely placed to ignite and lead world revolution. Although he frequently used concepts such as 'nationality' and showed special interest in the liberation of Turkic nations from tsarist colonialism and then from post-revolutionary Russian hegemony, in all likelihood he saw pan-Turkism, of which he was often accused, as but one of the potential avenues towards global Muslim socialist uprising.

Race, class and the Colonial International

Another struggle, directly associated with Sultan-Galiev's project of world revolution, which was often hinted at but, yet again, somewhat obliquely formulated in his writing, was the struggle for racial equality. He wrote of colonialists 'domestic' and 'foreign', as it were, as white racists, who exploited non-white populations of the East, in which he occasionally included the native populations of the Americas, simply on the basis of perceived racial difference.[17] It is plain that he had excluded Turkic and Caucasian Muslims from his definition of 'colonial whiteness'. In his vision of the Colonial International, which was to cooperate with or even replace the Third International (1919–43),[18] racial and class difference were to be concomitantly tackled. In an almost prophetic gesture,[19] Sultan-Galiev denounced Eurocentric models of class struggle as a *contradictio in terminis* when applied in the East:

> We think that the plan to replace one class of European society by the world dictatorship of its adversary – that is, by another class from this same society – will bring no significant change in the situation of the oppressed part of humanity. Even if there would be a change, it would be for the worse, not for the better.[20]

Class differences in the East were, for Sultan-Galiev, inextricably linked to European colonialism and the urban–rural divide this had exacerbated, 'the parasitism and reactionary foundations of the material culture of the metropolis [being] a chief factor of today's global [capitalist] development'.[21] In this context, anti-colonial, racial and class struggle could not be artificially separated from one another.

It is interesting that further social revolution, which for the majority of his Bolshevik comrades undoubtedly meant the demise of all religions, including Islam, was not for Sultan-Galiev something worth pursuing before world revolution.[22] On closer inspection one realises that for him this may not have been something worth pursuing at all.[23] Yet, as the highest-ranking Muslim of the Soviet communist state,[24] which advocated fervent 'atheisation' of its citizens, Sultan-Galiev could not but accept, if only in principle, this tenet of Bolshevik modernity.

But to understand the very possibility of merging Bolshevik and Muslim modernities in a single revolutionary praxis, one needs to take a step back and consider the larger context in which such interventions were taking place.

On *jadīds* 'on the left' and Bolsheviks turning 'eastwards'

The strand of *jadīd*ism into which Mir-Said Sultan-Galiev was (quite literally) born was distinct from that of Gasprinskiĭ's in the Crimea and still different from the *jadīd* thought in Central Asia. As one of the foremost scholars of this intellectual tradition has noted, *jadīd*ism 'was a coherent movement to the extent that it was (or came to be) embedded in a set of self-reproducing institutions (eg new-method schools that recruited their own graduates to teach in them). Beyond that, it is difficult to impute any unity to the "movement"'.[25] Even the names the *jadīds* commonly called themselves – *ziyālilar* (intellectuals) and *taraqqiparwarlar* (progressives)[26] – attest to a pluralist community of reformers loosely united (but) by a set of common principles. These included their dedication to new methods of production and transmission of knowledge, especially by means of print, translation and pedagogy. Gasprinskiĭ's attempts to achieve greater unity among the *jadīds* through a common literary language did not go down well (especially among the Volga Tatars), neither did the later efforts at creating a number of distinct 'nationalities' out of an irreverently fluid sense of self that seems to have prevailed among the late tsarist and early Soviet Muslims. In fact, in many *jadīd* writings in a variety of Turkic and other languages and dialects, 'the distinction between Islam as a faith and Muslims as a community disappears completely'.[27] Moreover, such Muslim pluralist 'communalism' was not uncommon in many other Third World contexts and was often considered a hallmark of Muslim modernity.[28]

While *jadīd*ism was coterminous with the rising awareness among Muslims of the increasing political and social importance of concepts such as 'nation' (*millat*, *millet*) or 'homeland' (*watan*, *vatan*),[29] many *jadīds*, along with some other Muslim intellectuals, refused to take such concepts for granted. Instead, they sought to measure them against the perceived borderlines of their imagined *community* (religious, 'ethnic', linguistic or otherwise) and to point to such concepts' numerous shortcomings. Conflating the old Ottoman concept of *millet* with the term 'nation' was seen as particularly dangerous,[30] since it could have undermined the greater unity (in diversity) and communality of Muslims.[31]

Besides, *jadīd*ism rose and was in many ways a response to the late 19th and early 20th century disintegration of Muslim imperial subjecthood in both Russian and Ottoman empires. The new nation-based concepts of empire explored both in the early Soviet and Turkish states met with a mixed response, with some Muslim intelligentsia lamenting the loss of the caliphate,[32] while others saw an opportunity for a reformulation of Muslim identity *tout court*. The precursors of such debates, including Ismail Gasprinskiĭ, while toying with ideas such as pan-Turkism, always kept in mind the 'big picture', ie the Muslim *umma* as a whole, which needed to be revived from its perceived *rigor mortis*.[33] Many members of the later generations of *jadīds*, especially some notable contemporaries of Sultan-Galiev, saw the Russian Revolution of 1917 as an opportunity to do just that,[34] and 'joined it as soon as it was possible'.[35] No doubt the idea of a Muslim socialist revolution, which the *jadīds* sought to ignite, differed from that of the Bolsheviks. But, importantly, the two factions shared a vested interest in 'revolutionising the East'. For the Bolsheviks the Third World was increasingly becoming a substitute for their (failed) efforts to revolutionise Europe, while the *jadids* increasingly saw the Russian Revolution as an opportunity to 'help liberate Muslims of India and the Middle East from the tyranny of the British' and the French.[36] It is in this context that ideas about anti-colonialism and communism, which the *jadids* sought to link with their Muslim and Turkic 'communalism', began to converge, thus preparing the ground for further cross-fertilisation.

At first, the *jadids* and other Muslim intellectuals 'on the left' sought to preserve the plurality of their approaches to socialism. Thus, for example, a Muslim Socialist Committee (*Müsülman Sosialist Komitesi*), which formed in 1917 in Kazan and which Sultan-Galiev soon joined, espoused a great internal diversity of views.[37] What brought them together was the idea of a common revolutionary agency that was Muslim, Third World and socialist/communist in nature. 'In order to prevent the oppression of the toiler of the East', averred Sultan-Galiev in 1918, 'we must unite the Muslim masses in a communist movement that will be our own and autonomous'.[38] A few years later, however, even he began to understand that such a project would require a great deal of manoeuvring within an increasingly hostile Soviet state.

While the Bolsheviks continued to provide concessions for Muslims, including a short-lived return of *sharī'a* courts and administrative councils,[39] and made every effort to forge lasting ties with 'the peoples of the East',[40] the 1920s brought a sway of state policies aimed at an ever-increasing central control that saw Muslim intellectuals, including Sultan-Galiev, wary as to the future of their revolutionary project.[41] With such concerns in mind, Sultan-Galiev and some other Tatar functionaries proposed, in October 1922, that the unfair division of Soviet peoples into 'step-sons and true sons' be corrected,[42] by allowing the existing autonomous republics and oblasts 'to enter the Soviet Union directly, that is, to be removed from the RSFSR [Russian Soviet Federative Socialist Republic]' – a proposal Stalin angrily rejected.[43] By then, however, Sultan-Galiev's activism had moved mostly underground, as if in anticipation of his imminent fall from grace with the Soviet state.[44]

Sultan-Galiev and other Muslim intellectuals 'on the left' become aware of the imperial nature of the rising Stalinist regime very early on:

> The theories of the Muslim…communists in the 1920s were always tempered by hard realism… Above all, they understood that the Great-Russian imperial tradition was ongoing: that once a territory fell under Russian control it remained for all times a part of the imperium…Theory and practice served the same purpose – to neutralize Great-Russian imperialism at its source, or, if that failed, to defeat it by forming new alliances and new coalitions.[45]

Sultan-Galiev's work in these troubled times followed two major directions: a turn inwards, towards rethinking Muslim subjectivity and praxis, and a dedication to the sophisticated, if dangerous, *jadīd*ist art of concealment (*satr*).

***Double entendre* with a tragic ending**

Indicative of his intricate role in mediating between the Soviet and Muslim spaces in his immediate political milieu are Sultan-Galiev's 1921 articles in *Zhizn' natsional'nostei* on the supposed 'Methods of Antireligious Propaganda among the Muslims'.[46] Although he is quick to concede some utility of such propaganda and, indeed, to declare himself atheist, Sultan-Galiev goes to great pains in these articles to explain to his Bolshevik readership that Islam is the youngest and by far the most vigorous of all the great world religions, and one harbouring distinct socialist values at that. '*Sharī'a*, or Islamic law', he informs the reader,

> governs all aspects of Muslim life on earth…And, of course, among these laws, there are many that are, in essence, positive. Suffice it here to list: compulsory education…compulsory industriousness and work…the parental duty to educate their children until they have reached adulthood; acceptability of civil marriage; denial of private ownership of land, water and forests; repudiation of superstition; prohibition of witchcraft, gambling, luxury, extravagance, gold- and silver-wearing, drinking, bribery and cannibalism…[and] the establishment of an elaborate progressive tax system …Even family and inheritance laws of Islam [were progressive for their time]. For example, the researchers interpreted Muḥammad's *ḥadīth* on polygamy as effectively delimiting the then widespread polygamous practice.[47]

Sultan-Galiev goes on to praise the Muslim 'clergy', exemplified in the positionalities of the Tatar *mullā* and the Uzbek *'ālim*, who, unlike the Russian Orthodox clergy, generously perform numerous useful positions in the Muslim society, including that of 'priest', teacher, administrator, judge and even doctor, if need be.[48] The Muslim 'clergy', concludes Sultan-Galiev, consider themselves 'servants' of the people and listen to their constituents' voice, and are, therefore, far more democratic and enjoy much greater respect and influence than their Russian Orthodox counterparts.[49]

The researchers who denounce Sultan-Galiev on the basis of these articles as a militant atheist and therefore firmly on the outside of the Muslim tradition fail, in my view, to understand the true nature of such an intervention in times of most ardent anti-religious sentiments actively encouraged by the Soviet state. Far from being yet another piece of anti-religious propaganda, the primary concern of Sultan-Galiev's articles was with painting an overwhelmingly positive picture of Islam and Muslim communities that could, and indeed did, justify their still relatively protected position in an increasingly violent anti-religious state. Declarative atheism with which the author assures his readers of his Bolshevik credentials was doubtless just that – a faithless expression of faithlessness to secure the necessary, even life-saving, authority of his account.[50]

To understand this peculiar *double entendre* one needs to comprehend the value of *satr* (concealment) in the *jadīd*ist tradition.[51] The famous Bashkir historian, Turkologist and, at a later stage, leader of the anti-Bolshevik and anti-Soviet revolutionary Basmachi Movement (1916–34), Ahmet-Zeki Validov (in Bashkir: Äxmätzäki Wälidov; in Turkish: Zeki Velidi Togan; 1890–1970), with whom Sultan-Galiev confessed to have maintained 'a complicated relationship',[52] once intimated to one Ebubekir the following opinion of Ismail Gasprinskiĭ:

> İsmail *Bey* Gaspıralı had been too servile!…It was dangerous for us to encourage the Russians to approach us in the guise of a 'big brother'…[and] make love to us in order to betray us. It was better for the future of the colonial peoples to refrain from close mingling, as the English did.[53]

Ebubekir replied: 'The ideas of those times were different; moreover, had İsmail *Bey* said that, his [publications] would never have passed the censorship. In bad times he brought us at least some comfort!'[54] Gasprinskiĭ's talent for evading censors even at the cost of some unseemly alliances has been described by one commentator as 'political quietism'.[55] That could, indeed, be another name for political *satr*, which the *jadīds* employed with great skill and success,[56] although at times to the dismay of their more openly confrontational comrades.

Mir-Said Sultan-Galiev's *satr* was of an even more sophisticated type. There could be no doubt that he was aware at all times how dangerous a game this was, especially since 1923, the year in which he was arrested for the first time for – allegedly – conspiring to create 'an [anti-Soviet] organisation of the Validov type' and subsequently expelled from the party.[57] Sultan-Galiev's arrest was ordered after the infamous Soviet secret service, GPU (Gosudarstvennoe politicheskoe upravlenie; State Political Administration), had intercepted his coded letter enjoining an Iranian communist, Tajī Bakhshī, 'to get in touch with Afghani, Indian, Arab and Turkish revolutionaries', supposedly for the purposes of creating the Colonial International.[58] The letter warned its reader: 'Only in the unity of revolutionary Eastern countries lies the guarantee of success in the struggle for liberation. And only in that. Never forget this.'[59]

It is nothing short of a miracle that Sultan-Galiev survived this episode and even managed to secure his release and regain, at least partly, Stalin's trust. Yet it is precisely his extraordinary talent in keeping up certain outward appearances while concealing from the Soviet regime his less palatable plans and activities that put the final phase of his gradual departure from the Bolshevik ideology *almost* within reach. If it were not for an additional set of letters intercepted by the ever-watchful GPU, some of which were making clear requests to 'make a connection with Zeki Validov', leader of the Basmachi Revolt,[60] Sultan-Galiev might even have succeeded in creating a Muslim Third World insurrectionary socialist movement within and beyond the Soviet state. Instead, following a series of further arrests, his death by firing squad was finally authorised by the Stalinist regime and carried out in January 1940. His elimination was accompanied by what was by then the typical Stalinist *chistka* (purge), in which numerous members of the Sultan-Galiev family, as well as the Tatar Muslim intelligentsia found guilty of *sultangalievshchina* (Sultan-Galievism), were sent to their deaths.

Epilogue

Thus ended Sultan-Galiev's experiment with Muslim Marxism, or at least this is how its interbellum phase was finished off. Its legacies, however, have extended far and wide, especially during the era of decolonisation in the 1960s and, even before that, through the revolutionary work of many a non-Soviet student at the Communist University of the Toilers of the East (or KUTV, Kommunisticheskiĭ universitet trudyashchikhsya Vostoka), at which the likes of Tan Malaka, Hồ Chí Minh, Liu Shaoqi, Magomet Mamakaev, Khalid Bakdash, Manabendra Nath Roy and Nazım Hikmet attended Sultan-Galiev's lectures on the 'Colonial East and World Revolution' course.[61] His work was also reclaimed by Gamal Abdel Nasser, Ahmed Ben Bella and other political leaders experimenting with various forms of Arab socialism. Both Nasser and Ben Bella are said to have kept Sultan-Galiev's portraits in their offices,[62] but the influence of his ideas may not have extended much beyond this symbolic gesture, nowadays easily comparable with the penchant for Che Guevara's portraits, to whom, incidentally, Sultan-Galiev bore a striking physical resemblance.

The peculiarity of Muslim Marxism as espoused by Sultan-Galiev lay not only in its methodological idiosyncrasy, which saw principles such as that of *satr* skilfully employed, in times of trouble, to assist the revolutionary cause. It also lay in its early and in many ways avant-garde awareness of the religious, cultural and racial connotations of class struggle in colonial and postcolonial contexts. In his unfinished 1924 work entitled 'Theses on the Basis of Socio-Political, Economic and Cultural Development of the Turkic Peoples of Asia and Europe',[63] Sultan-Galiev wrote of the need to reclaim historical materialism as an Eastern intellectual tradition, in a move resembling contemporary calls to end the hegemony of global Northern epistemologies in academia and beyond.[64] Muslim insurrectionary subjectivity, upon which Sultan-Galiev had placed all his hopes and dreams of global socialist freedom, had always been for him an intrinsically complex and multifaceted phenomenon, embodying at once a wide range of ethnic, national and religious practices of belonging, which in turn were conducive to a specifically socialist, and indeed revolutionary, Muslim praxis.

Yet, if one is to recast the Muslim Marxism of Sultan-Galiev's strand as an expression of radical reform *within* the Muslim tradition, one ultimately needs to resolve the question of declarative atheism that some have understood as constituting a rapid and irreversible exit from Muslim hieropraxis, *tout court*. Given the specific context in which it was made, I am reluctant to ascribe to Sultan-Galiev's one-time declaration any significance other than that of a strategic move, taking the practice of *satr* to an extreme level. That all of Marxism does not have to be atheist or agnostic has since been proven, particularly in the various Muslim contexts, just as it is, indeed, obvious that being Muslim entails an infinitely complex web of practices of belonging. For all these reasons Mir-Said Sultan-Galiev's idea of Muslim Marxism has much to offer to contemporary attempts at reformulation and reimagination of Muslim post-imperial, religious, political and social selfhood.

Disclosure statement

No potential conflict of interest was reported by the author.

Acknowledgements

Earlier versions of this paper were presented at 'Reformers and Intellectual Reformulation in Contemporary Islam', SOAS and Queen Mary, University of London, 29–30 January 2015; the TWAIL conference 'On Praxis and the Intellectual', American University in Cairo, 21–24 February 2015; and 'Islamic Law and Empire', 1–2 June 2015, held as a part of IGLP: The Conference at Harvard Law School. My thanks are due to the organisers and participants of the exhilarating TWAIL Writing Workshop for this special issue of *Third World Quarterly* for their very helpful comments and suggestions. Of course, all errors are mine and mine alone.

Notes

1. Marx, "Zur Kritik der Hegel'schen Rechts-Philosophie," 72.
2. Cf. Bennigsen and Lemercier-Quelquejay, *Sultan Galiev*, 278.
3. See generally Rodinson, *Marxism and the Muslim World*.
4. As is undoubtedly known to the readership of this journal, the geopolitical designation 'Third World' is as problematic as it is helpful to describe global power relations. There were many Worlds in the Cold War context that were Third in their relation to the First World powers, some even located *within* the First and Second Worlds. I use the singular and the plural versions of this designation concomitantly, to underline this plurality. Sultan-Galiev did not use the designation in question, instead opting for 'the East', which, as we shall see, meant for him something rather similar to the later concept of Third World, including with regard to its inherent geopolitical plurality. Today's overall preference for the concept of 'Global South' is fraught, and perhaps blessed, with similar ambiguities.
5. See generally Sagadeev, "Mirsait Sultan-Galiev."
6. The most comprehensive collection of Sultan-Galiev's oeuvre is available in Sultan-Galiev, *Izbrannye trudy*. This publication also contains a comprehensive bibliography of academic works on Sultan-Galiev at pp 703–710. A still relevant critical analysis of sources on Sultan-Galiev (despite being published in 1986) can be found in Bennigsen and Lemercier-Quelquejay, *Sultan Galiev*, 289–300.
7. See especially Bennigsen and Lemercier-Quelquejay, *Les mouvements nationaux*; Bennigsen and Lemercier-Quelquejay, *La presse et le mouvement national*; Bennigsen and Lemercier-Quelquejay, *Le soufi et le commissaire*; Bennigsen and Lemercier-Quelquejay, *Sultan Galiev*; Bennings and Wimbush, *Muslims of the Soviet Empire*; Benningsen and Wimbush, *Muslim National Communism*; Benningsen et al., *Soviet Strategy and Islam*; Carrère d'Encausse, *Islam and the Russian Empire*; and Carrère d'Encausse, *The Great Challenge*. For an interesting work of fiction, see Tengour, *Sultan Galièv ou la rupture de stocks*.
8. See, for example, Froese, "'I am an Atheist and a Muslim'."
9. For two seminal studies on Ismail Gasprinskiĭ in English, see Lazzerini, "Ismail Bey Gasprinskii"; and Lazzerini, "Ismail Bey Gasprinskii's *Perevodchik/Tercüman*."
10. al-Harawī, *Fatḥ bāb al-'ināyah bi-sharḥ al-Niqāyah*, 195.
11. In the Crimea in the 1880s Gasprinskiĭ championed a new (phonetic) method (*uṣūl al-jadīd*) of teaching the Arabic alphabet, from which the name of the larger Muslim reformist movement (*jadīd*ism) was derived. *Jadīd* activities primarily concerned Muslim communities in the late Russian Empire and the early Soviet state, but were also present in some other centres of Islamic learning, such as Istanbul and Cairo.
12. See generally Keller, *To Moscow, Not Mecca*, 20–25. For a detailed analysis of the *jadīd* educational reforms, albeit with a focus on Central Asia, see Khalid, *The Politics of Muslim Cultural Reform*, 155–183.
13. Sultan-Galiev, *Izbrannye trudy*, 27. In Islamic law, the *ḥudūd* (lit. 'limits') offences are considered to be the most serious transgressions, for which the penalties are interpreted as prescribed in the Qur'ān itself. *Zina* is one such offence, relating to adultery or fornication.
14. A community distinct from the (other) Volga Tatars who have seemingly (better) preserved 'their Finnic ethnic type and speak a special (western) dialect of the Kazan Tatar' language. Bennigsen and Wimbush, *Muslims of the Soviet Empire*, 233.
15. Sultan-Galiev, *Izbrannye trudy*, 476.
16. Sultan-Galiev, *Izbrannye trudy*, 108.

17. Sultan-Galiev, *Izbrannye trudy*, 217–218. See also note 4.
18. Bennigsen and Wimbush, *Muslim National Communism*, 58.
19. That is, long before the Non-Aligned Movement of the 1960s would tackle the very same problematic. It is for this reason that Maxime Rodinson famously branded Sultan-Galiev 'a forgotten precursor', while Bennigsen and Lemercier-Quelquejay published a book entitled *Sultan Galiev, le père de la révolution tiers-mondiste*. See Rodinson, *Marxism and the Muslim World*, 133–141; and Bennigsen and Lemercier-Quelquejay, *Sultan Galiev*.
20. Attributed to Sultan-Galiev by his adversary Tobolev in a propaganda publication called *Kontrrivolutsiyon Soltangäliefcheleke karshy* [Against the Counterrevolutionary Sultan-Galievism], published in Kazan in 1930 and cited in Bennigsen and Wimbush, *Muslim National Communism*, 58. Despite the nature of this publication, there is little doubt that this was, indeed, Sultan-Galiev's view on Eurocentrism. See, for example, Sultan-Galiev, *Izbrannye trudy*, 215–222.
21. Sultan-Galiev, *Izbrannye trudy*, 529.
22. See generally Sultan-Galiev, *Izbrannye trudy*, 525–538.
23. Ibid.
24. Mir-Said Sultan-Galiev 'took part in the First All-Russian Muslim Congress of May 1917 in Kazan and in July 1917 became one of the leading members of the Muslim Socialist Committee of Kazan. In November 1917 he entered the [Russian Communist Party (Bolshevik)] and, because of his exceptional gifts for organization, rapidly became the highest-ranking Muslim in the CP hierarchy – member of the Central Muslim Commissariat, chairman of the Muslim Military Collegium, member of the Little Collegium of the Narkomnats [People's Commissariat of Nationalities], editor of *Zhizn' natsional'nostei*, the official organ of the Narkomnats, and member of the Central Executive Committee of the Tatar Republic'. Bennigsen and Wimbush, *Muslim National Communism*, 207–208. For an alternative short account of Sultan-Galiev's many functions within the Soviet state, see Davletshin, *Sovetskiĭ Tatarstan*, n. 19, 133–134.
25. Khalid, *The Politics of Muslim Cultural Reform*, 8–9; See also Akademiiu nauk Tatarstana, *Islam v istorii i kul'ture tatarskogo naroda*; Mukhametshin, *Islam v tatarskoĭ obshchestvennoĭ mysli nachala XX veka*; Vahidov, *Prosvetitel'skaia ideologiia v Turkestane*.
26. Khalid, *The Politics of Muslim Cultural Reform*, 93.
27. Khalid, *The Politics of Muslim Cultural Reform*, 193. Even the language in which such writings appeared was often called 'Muslim language' (*musulmān tili, müsülman tili, musul'manskiĭ iazyk*).
28. Muslim modernity (or Islamic modernism) is often described as an *idée reçue*, based on both traumatic and 'productive' Muslim experiences with European Enlightenment, modernity and colonialism. The phenomenon is, however, much larger in scope, and can arguably be traced back to various historical Muslim polities long before the late 19th century, ie before the time of the well-established Muslim modernist reformers, such as Muḥammad 'Abduh (1849–1905) and Jamāl al-Dīn al-Afghānī (1838–1897). As such, Muslim modernity can be compared to other historical examples of 'early modern' phenomena around the world. See, for example, Goldstone, "The Problem of the 'Early Modern' World," 249–284. With his ideas about progress and reform, Ismail Gasprinskiĭ can certainly be counted among the Muslim modernists of his time.
29. See especially Khalid, *The Politics of Muslim Cultural Reform*, 184–187; and Critchlow, "*Vatan* and the Concept of 'Homeland' in the Muslim Soviet Republics," 481–488.
30. The Ottoman usage of the word *millet* before the Tanzimât (1839–76) primarily related to the (legal) concept of a separate confessional community, self-governed via its own system of personal laws. The Tanzimât brought a new usage of the term, more akin to the concept of 'nation', although a number of communities it pertained to were still primarily confessional. In modern Turkish, *millet* translates as 'nation'.
31. Thus, for example, in Ottoman Turkish a separate word for 'nation' – *milliyet* – was used to distinguish it from the more open-ended concept of *millet*. See Meyer, *Turks across Empires*, 120–121.
32. Centuries-long Ottoman sultans' claim to caliphal authority ended in 1924, when Mustafa Kemal Atatürk abolished the office of the caliph, to great dismay across the Sunnī Muslim world. The

caliph (in Arabic: *khalīfa*) is traditionally considered to be the Prophet Muḥammad's deputy, or successor, on Earth, and thereby a rightful ruler over the Muslim *umma*.

33. Gasprinskiĭ claimed that, after the third century AH, 'the Muslim world was reduced to (a condition of) *rigor mortis*', a condition he thought he could change with his 'reason-centred' educational and social policies. Lazzerini, "Ismail Bey Gasprinskii," 157. However, Gasprinskiĭ did not think that such change could be brought about by means of socialism, which he rejected as an illusion. Ibid., 163.
34. That is, both the February Revolution in March 1917 and the October Revolution in November the same year.
35. Khalid, *The Politics of Muslim Cultural Reform*, 288.
36. Khalid, *Islam after Communism*, 56.
37. Bennigsen and Quelquejay, *Les mouvements nationaux*, 70–71.
38. Sultan-Galiev, cited in Bennigsen and Wimbush, *Muslim National Communism*, 46. In March 1918 Sultan-Galiev founded the Muslim Communist–Socialist Party, which maintained its independence from the Russian Communist Party for some time. See Carrère d'Encausse, *The Great Challenge*, 141.
39. For an example from Turkestan, see Khalid, *Islam after Communism*, 61.
40. Of which the Congress of the Peoples of the East in Baku in September 1920, organised by the Communist International, was perhaps the most symbolic, if eventually unsuccessful, project. The capital of Azerbaijan was, in that period, hailed as a 'Mecca of the anti-imperial struggle' for the sheer number of Muslim revolutionaries present there. See Dumont, "Bakou, carrefour révolutionnaire, 1919–1920," 414.
41. One such policy was *razmezhevanie* (delimitation), which led, *inter alia*, to the dissolution, in 1924, of the Turkestan Soviet Socialist Republic into several smaller Soviet republics and oblasts. The dissolution of Turkestan was seen by many Soviet Muslims as an attempt by the early Stalinist state to exert greater control over their affairs.
42. Sultan-Galiev, *Izbrannye trudy*, 409.
43. Martin, *The Affirmative Action Empire*, 397.
44. Unfortunately for Sultan-Galiev, his 'going underground' did not go unnoticed. Several months before denouncing Sultan-Galiev in a speech to the delegates of the Fourth Conference of the Central Committee of the Communist Party of the USSR, on 10 June 1923, Stalin himself apparently warned Sultan-Galiev that he was 'playing a dangerous game'. See Baker, "Did he really do It?," 599. For the full transcript of Stalin's speech, in which he accused Sultan-Galiev of both pan-Turkism and pan-Islamism, see Stalin, "Rights and 'Lefts'," 308–319.
45. Bennigsen and Wimbush, *Muslim National Communism*, 51.
46. Sultan-Galiev, *Izbrannye trudy*, 363–374.
47. Ibid.
48. Sultan-Galiev, *Izbrannye trudy*, 364.
49. Ibid.
50. Alternatively the possibility of a faithless Muslim may have signalled the forging of a radical take on Muslim subjectivity, which, while persistently denounced in the mainstream Muslim traditions, would not be dissimilar to explorations of agnosticism and atheism in other Abrahamic traditions, most notably in liberal Jewish theology. See, for example, Kaplan, *The Meaning of God*.
51. In the larger Islamic tradition the *jadīds*' and Ottoman art of *satr* (concealment) could be compared to the Sunnī legal and philosophical device of *iḍṭirār* (compulsion) and the Shīʿī concept of *taqīyya* (dissimulation) – both of which render concealment of one's true religious beliefs and hieropraxis permissible in times of extreme danger and duress.
52. Sultan-Galiev, *Izbrannye trudy*, 511–512.
53. Velidi Togan, *Bugünkü Türkili (Türkistan) ve Yakın Tarihi*, 556.
54. Ibid.
55. Kuttner, "Russian *Jadīdism* and the Islamic World," 384.
56. The employment of *satr* is certainly not the only example of the *jadīds*' giving an old (in this case Ottoman) social tool a new use. Writing about the early 20th-century Central Asian *jadīd*

discourse, Adeeb Khalid describes how the *jadīds* 'had appropriated the literary device of *ibrat* – taking admonition from noteworthy example – which had deep roots in Islamic tradition but was now given a new form'. Khalid, "Representations of Russia," 197.

57. Rossiiskaya kommunisticheskaya partiya (bol'shevik), cited in Baker, "Did he really do It?," 599.
58. Sultanbekov and Sharafutdinov, cited in Baker, "Did he really do It?," 601.
59. Ibid.
60. Sultan-Galiev, *Izbrannye trudy*, 471.
61. Tagirov and Sultanbekov, "Velikiĭ providets," 7.
62. Ibid. For an overview of Arab communist ideas and movements in the 20th century and their relations with Sultan-Galiev's oeuvre, see Ismael, *The Communist Movement in the Arab World*.
63. Sultan-Galiev, *Izbrannye trudy*, 525–538.
64. See, for example, de Sousa Santos, *Another Production is Possible*; Comaroff and Comaroff, *Theory from the South*; and Chakrabarty, *Provincializing Europe*.

Bibliography

Akademiiu nauk Tatarstana. *Islam v istorii i kul'ture tatarskogo naroda*. Kazan: Shkola, 2000.

al-Harawī, 'Ālī ibn Sulṭān al-Qārī'. *Fatḥ bāb al-'ināyah bi-sharḥ al-Niqāyah*. Vol. 3, c. 1601. Reprint, edited by M. N. Tamīm and H. N. Tamīm. Beirut: Dār al-Mu'arrikh al-'Arabī, 1997.

Baker, Mark R. "Did he really do It? Mirsaid Sultan-Galiev, Party Disloyalty, and the 1923 Affair." *Europe-Asia Studies* 66, no. 4 (2014): 590–612.

Bennigsen, Alexandre, and S. Enders Wimbush. *Muslim National Communism in the Soviet Union: A Revolutionary Strategy for the Colonial World*. Chicago, IL: University of Chicago Press, 1979.

Bennigsen, Alexandre, and S. Enders Wimbush. *Muslims of the Soviet Empire: A Guide*. Bloomington: Indiana University Press, 1986.

Bennigsen, Alexandre, and Chantal Lemercier-Quelquejay. *La presse et le mouvement national chez les musulmans de Russie avant 1920*. Paris: Mouton, 1964.

Bennigsen, Alexandre, and Chantal Lemercier-Quelquejay. *Le soufi et le commissaire: les confréries musulmanes en URSS*. Paris: Éditions du Seuil, 1986.

Bennigsen, Alexandre, and Chantal Lemercier-Quelquejay. *Sultan Galiev, le père de la révolution tiers-mondiste*. Paris: Fayard, 1986.

Bennigsen, Alexandre, and Chantal Quelquejay. *Les mouvements nationaux chez les musulmans de Russie: Le 'sultangalievisme' au Tatarstan*. Paris: Mouton, 1960.

Bennigsen, Alexandre, Paul B. Henze, George K. Tanham, and S. Enders Wimbush. *Soviet Strategy and Islam*. London: Macmillan, 1989.

Carrère d'Encausse, Hélène. *Islam and the Russian Empire: Reform and Revolution in Central Asia*. Translated by Quintin Hoare. Berkeley: University of California Press, 1988.

Carrère d'Encausse, Hélène. *The Great Challenge: Nationalities and the Bolshevik State, 1917–1930*. Translated by Nancy Festinger. New York: Holmes & Meier, 1992.

Chakrabarty, Dipesh. *Provincializing Europe: Postcolonial Thought and Historical Difference*. Princeton, NJ: Princeton University Press, 2000.

Comaroff, Jean, and John Comaroff. *Theory from the South: Or, how Euro-America is evolving toward Africa*. Boulder, CO: Paradigm, 2012.

Critchlow, James. "*Vatan* and the Concept of 'Homeland' in the Muslim Soviet Republics." In *Passé turco-tatar, présent soviétique: Études offertes à Alexandre Bennigsen*, edited by Ch. Lemercier-Quelquejay, G. Veinsten and S. E. Wimbush, 481–488. Leuven: Éditions Peeters, 1986.

Davletshin, Tamurbek. *Sovetskiĭ Tatarstan: Teoriia i praktika Leninskoĭ politiki*. London: Our World, 1974.

de Sousa Santos, Boaventura. *Another Production is Possible: Beyond Northern Epistemologies*. Vol. 3. London: Verso, 2006.

Dumont, Paul. "Bakou, carrefour révolutionnaire, 1919–1920." In *Passé turco-tatar, présent soviétique: Études offertes à Alexandre Bennigsen*, edited by Ch. Lemercier-Quelquejay, G. Veinsten and S. E. Wimbush, 413–433. Leuven: Éditions Peeters, 1986.

Froese, Paul. "'I am an Atheist and a Muslim': Islam, Communism, and Ideological Competition." *Journal of Church and State* 47, no. 3 (2005): 473–501.

Goldstone, Jack A. "The Problem of the 'Early Modern' World." *Journal of the Economic and Social History of the Orient* 41, no. 3 (1998): 249–284.

Ismael, Tareq Y. *The Communist Movement in the Arab World*. London: Routledge, 2005.

Kaplan, Mordecai M. *The Meaning of God in Modern Jewish Religion*. 1947. Reprint, Detroit, MI: Wayne State University Press, 1995.

Keller, Shoshana. *To Moscow, Not Mecca: The Soviet Campaign against Islam in Central Asia, 1917–1941*. Westport, CT: Praeger, 2001.

Khalid, Adeeb. "Representations of Russia in Central Asian Jadid Discourse." In *Russia's Orient: Imperial Borderlines and Peoples, 1700–1917*, edited by Daniel R. Brower and Edward J. Lazzerini, 188–202. Bloomington: Indiana University Press, 1997.

Khalid, Adeeb. *The Politics of Muslim Cultural Reform: Jadidism in Central Asia*. Berkeley: University of California Press, 1998.

Khalid, Adeeb. *Islam after Communism: Religion and Politics in Central Asia*. Berkeley: University of California Press, 2007.

Kuttner, Thomas. "Russian *Jadīdism* and the Islamic World: Ismail Gasprinskii in Cairo, 1908." *Cahiers du Monde russe et soviétique* 16, nos. 3–4 (1975): 383–424.

Lazzerini, Edward James. "Ismail Bey Gasprinskii and Muslim Modernism in Russia, 1878–1914." PhD diss., University of Washington, 1973.

Lazzerini, Edward J. "Ismail Bey Gasprinskii's *Perevodchik/Tercüman*: A Clarion of Modernism." In *Central Asian Monuments*, edited by Hasan B. Paksoy, 143–156. Istanbul: Isis Press, 1992.

Martin, Terry. *The Affirmative Action Empire: Nations and Nationalism in the Soviet Union, 1923–1939*. Ithaca, NY: Cornell University Press, 2001.

Marx, Karl. "Zur Kritik der Hegel'schen Rechts-Philosophie." *Deutsch-Französischen Jahrbücher* 1, no. 1 (1844): 71–85.

Meyer, James H. *Turks across Empires: Marketing Muslim Identity in the Russian-Ottoman Borderlands, 1856–1914*. Oxford: Oxford University Press, 2014.

Mukhametshin, Rafik. *Islam v tatarskoĭ obshchestvennoĭ mysli nachala XX veka*. Kazan: Iman, 2000.

Rodinson, Maxime. *Marxism and the Muslim World*. Reprint, 2015. London: Zed Books, 1972.

Sagadeev, Artur Vladimirovich. "Mirsait Sultan-Galiev: Revoliutsioner i myslitel'." *Nasha rodina i sovremennyĭ mir* 20, no. 3 (1998): 38–52.

Stalin, J. V. "Rights and 'Lefts' in the National Republics and Regions: Speech on the First Item of the Conference Agenda: 'The Sultan-Galiyev Case', June 10." In *Works*. Vol. 5, 308–319. Moscow: Foreign Languages Publishing House, 1953.

Sultan-Galiev, Mir-Said K. *Izbrannye trudy*. Edited by I. G. Gizzatullin and D. R. Sharafutdinov. Kazan: Izdatel'stvo Gasyr, 1998.

Tagirov, Indus, and Bulat Sultanbekov. "Velikiĭ providets." In *Izabrannye trudy*, by Mir-Said Sultan-Galiev, edited by I. G. Gizzatullin and D. R. Sharafutdinov, 5–8. Kazan: Izdatel'stvo Gasyr, 1998.

Tengour, Habib. *Sultan Galièv ou la rupture de stocks: Cahiers, 1972/1977*. Paris: Sindbad, 1985.

Vahidov, H. *Prosvetitel'skaia ideologiia v Turkestane*. Tashkent: Uzbekistan, 1979.

Velidi Togan, Zeki. *Bugünkü Türkili (Türkistan) ve Yakın Tarihi*. Istanbul: Arkadaş/İbrahim Horoz ve Güven Basımevleri, 1942.

International lawyers in the aftermath of disasters: inheriting from Radhabinod Pal and Upendra Baxi

Adil Hasan Khan

ABSTRACT
In the present lives in the postcolony are beset by relentless disasters, generating great suffering and loss. How should an international lawyer conduct herself in response? Resisting the urge to construct these times as entirely unprecedented, this article attempts a response by drawing out the conduct of two ancestral Third World international lawyers responding to disasters in their own time. It reveals how disasters never simply occur but are actively produced by particular modes of conduct deployed by international lawyers. From their conduct we learn how to attend to the tasks of justice and responsibility in the aftermath of disaster by being responsive to the suffering and by recognising the disastrous effects of our action. We also learn how attending to the tasks of inheritance is vital for this.

Introduction

We are said to inhabit 'disastrous times'.[1] Taking disasters to be 'the widespread disruption of the conditions that render life to be livable', we find that, from unending global wars to ever more frequent climate change-related catastrophes, 'industrial accidents' and disastrous austerity regimes being unrolled in the wake of the (re)current financial crisis, we are confronted by an ever accumulating series of disasters.[2] The injury and loss, or the suffering, produced by these disasters in the Global South has been particularly egregious.

Given this dizzying accumulation of catastrophes, the basic question of how to conduct oneself in the wake of disasters assumes great significance. In particular, asking the conduct question become pressing because of a sense of disorientation and flux in the wake of disasters – times when praxis itself emerges as a problem.[3] It is this problem that this article attempts to confront, with a specific focus on the conduct of those occupying the office of international lawyers.[4] The overarching question it asks is: how does one conduct oneself as an international lawyer in the aftermath of disasters?

However, this immediately raises several other prior questions. Where does one turn to for guidance on how to conduct oneself? Can some inherited past, namely in the form of the exemplary conduct of ancestral international lawyers, possibly serve as a source of guidance? A brief perusal of the existing literature in the field of international law around this question of conduct reveals two distinct lines of response.

One model, which constitutes the dominant orientation in the field of international law, by way of fixating on the experience of temporal flux and disorientation experienced in the wake of disasters, constructs each disaster as an unprecedented event that creates entirely new configurations and problems, and asks entirely different questions from earlier disasters. In specifically temporal terms each disaster thus gets constructed as a rupture in time, which creates entirely novel grounds for action.[5] Determining how to act in the present, in response to 'our' disasters, by drawing out the conduct of international lawyers past in response to 'their' disasters would be entirely redundant to this mode of responding to disasters. In other words, for this model, engagement with inheritance offers no vital training for conduct in the present.[6]

However, in the scholarship of international lawyers belonging to the Third World Approaches to International Law (TWAIL) network and tradition, we are presented with an alternative model, in which we not only find a powerful critique of the ideology of 'newness' underlying the previous model,[7] but also a significant engagement with how ancestral figures past conducted themselves in order to fashion one's own conduct in the present.[8] It is this tradition that this article chooses to take up and inherit in order to respond to the problem of conduct.

Once we adopt this alternative approach, the question that then arises is whether there exists such a model for conduct or ethos in our inheritance as TWAILers? It is my contention that in the ancestral figures of Radhabinod Pal and Upendra Baxi and the mode of conduct that they displayed in their own 'disastrous times' we encounter exactly such a vital inheritance that can guide and train our own conduct for our present. In what follows I will attempt to narrate their conduct and to draw out two significant facets of the training that they bequeath to us.

Judge Radhabinod Pal presided over the International Military Tribunal for the Far East (Tokyo Tribunal), which was established in April 1946 to respond with criminal justice to the catastrophic violence that occurred in the Pacific theatre of the Second World War. He delivered the sole dissenting judgment, acquitting all of the Japanese accused, in November of 1948, as a representative of independent India. The writing of his judgement took shape amid the aftermath of the nuclear holocaust in the Japanese cities of Hiroshima and Nagasaki and the extensive firebombing by the allies of Tokyo itself in 1945.[9] In 1955 he went onto publish *Crimes in International Relations*, his only book-length engagement with international law, in which he further ruminated upon the issues and question raised in his dissenting judgment.[10]

Similarly, in 1984, Professor Upendra Baxi was one of the leading jurists in India, a country that had recently become the recipient of several IMF loans which, among other things, required it to dilute its regulatory regimes for the multinational corporations (MNCs) it hosted on its territory.[11] In December of that year occurred one of the most horrific mass industrial disasters in history, which became (in)famous as the 'Bhopal Catastrophe'.[12] The immediate cause of the spectacular disaster was the leakage of a deadly gas from a chemical plant being operated by the subsidiary, Union Carbide India Limited (UCIL), of a controlling MNC, Union Carbide Corporation (UCC), in Bhopal.[13] In its tortuous aftermath survivor groups other activists, public intellectuals and lawyers, prominently including Baxi himself, brought to the public's attention how, in the lead-up to the catastrophe UCC had been engaged in actively diluting various safety measures at the plant and reducing supervisory staff in an effort to shore up profits from the plant.[14] In addition to producing a voluminous body of ground-breaking scholarship critically engaging with the key problematics relating to this catastrophe, especially around the liability of MNCs, Baxi has also been a committed participant in the social movement that has emerged to demand justice for the survivors.[15]

Attentiveness to the legacies of the past in the aftermath of disaster

The past is never dead. It's not even past. (William Faulkner, *Requiem for a Nun*, 1951)

The aftermaths of disasters are times palpably haunted by the past,[16] hauntings that intimate the great suffering, loss and trauma produced by disasters. For an international lawyer this raises the problem of how she must conduct herself in response to this 'disastrous suffering'. At a fundamental level this is the problem of justice. In this section it is my argument that both Pal and Baxi provide us with training in conduct as international lawyers that responds to the suffering in the aftermath of disasters, and attends to the task of justice.

Apprehension of life and suffering

Before proceeding any further, we need to ask a prior question relating to the very apprehension of this lingering suffering. This prior step concerns the dominant structures of framing the apprehension of certain lives as lives in the first place, ie a framing 'according to which certain "lives" are perceived as living while others, though apparently living, fail to assume perceptual form as such'.[17] It is this prior framing which powerfully structures any response to 'disastrous suffering', since, by denying certain lives the status of being lives, the suffering generated by their loss or injury in disasters also simply gets ignored and those disasters that affect such 'disposable' populations are also not apprehended as being disasters to begin with.[18] I would argue that the operation of such powerful exclusionary frames in the international legal field does indeed structure the dominant response among international lawyer to 'disastrous suffering' – a response which is non-responsive to the suffering engendered by certain disasters as it simply fails to apprehend it as actual human suffering.[19]

A containment of disasters

Another way in which this dominant framing structure structures the response to 'disastrous suffering' is that it produces a truncated and episodic construction of disasters. Disasters in this dominant framing are spectacular events causing overt loss of life and suffering (a loss that is itself selectively recognised), disassociated from longer histories of everyday or structural violence and the lingering aftermaths of past disasters, and considered amenable to having their aftermath sutured through the heroic actions of international lawyers and the 'international community' – a romantic myth of overcoming aided in no small measure by the non-recognition of any lingering and less visible suffering.[20] As Hillary Charlesworth noted in her classic critique of this mode of framing disasters:

> It leads us to concentrate on a single event or series of events and often miss the larger picture. We have a penchant for cutting crises down to bite-size pieces...We stay glued to specific, climactic events and fail to see the larger picture.[21]

However, as suggested by the previous point, even when it comes to these 'spectacular disasters', we find that even their recognition is selective. While certain disasters and their effects find a temporal longevity in the official memories of international lawyers, others, those construed as 'ordinary disasters' on account of the identity of those affected by them,[22] elicit a fleeting memory. In Bhopal this was in evidence in the assertions that the gas disaster no longer had any claims upon the present only a few years after the immediate catastrophe, with UCC officials simply claiming that 'Bhopal is history now'.[23]

Enframing suffering

It is not my contention here that these powerful frames entirely exclude and elide suffering. Rather, it is that particular suffering becomes enframed by them – an active process that suggests a particular shaping of suffering in order for it to get into the frame and be recognised.[24] The suffering that does get recognised by the disaster frames operating in the international legal field is characterised by a loss or lack of autonomy and sovereignty. Constitutively attached to this frame is the aspirational vision of 'liveable life', beyond or before disaster, that is entirely non-relational and autonomous, and bereft of any vulnerability and dependence on the world outside of it, ie a world housed by disembodied sovereign subjects whose self-mastery is what marks their character as subjects of law.[25] The suffering recognised by this frame thus assumes the form of what is the 'other' of masterful autonomy – namely passivity – being entirely deprived of agency, complete dependence on the outside world for mere survival and abject victimhood.[26]

Dominant mode of justice: as progressive overcoming of vulnerability

Following from this, the dominant response of international lawyers to 'disastrous suffering' takes the form of a mode of justice that attempts to restore, or achieve in a redemptive flourish, sovereign autonomy for the suffering 'victim subjects' and, in doing so, entirely overcomes suffering as vulnerable relationality and dependence.[27] It is a temporally progressive response to suffering that attempts to rupture the present from the disastrous past by way of the instrumentality of law, including forgetting past violations and violence in order to bring about a truly self-determining subject who is not bound by other ties of sociality that undermine her autonomy (eg kinship or blood relations that speak of the 'archaic logic' of vengeance) and who does not continue to be a backward looking prisoner of the past.[28] In order to achieve this eternal *telos* of invulnerability and sovereign mastery, one which goes by various names – including being developed, being modern, being civilised and achieving universal peace and security – this response invariably justifies the (temporary) sacrifice of those whose lives are deemed to be 'disposable'.[29]

We thus have cases of the firebombing and nuclear bombing of entire cities, sought to be justified on the grounds of achieving world peace and security, and the exposure of sections of the urban population to the risk of poisoning justified on grounds that the increased production of pesticides will ultimately defeat famines 'caused' by 'food shortages' and help overcome 'abject poverty'.[30]

In certain cases it also includes a retributive mode of justice that seeks to punish those 'criminal' individuals who aggressively violate the security of other sovereign subjects and cause injury through such 'external' interventions.[31] In effect it is a mode of responding to suffering in the aftermath of disasters that authorizes dismantling the relationality and social conditions of the liveability of life and generating suffering on the grounds of entirely overcoming suffering.[32]

Aftermaths and fractured frames

However, if we delve further into this dominant mode of (non)responsiveness to suffering in the aftermath of disasters, we find that more active work of repression takes place exactly at those times when these exclusionary frames must be produced anew and are particularly susceptible to disruption and breakage. After all, the intense haunting experienced in any aftermath takes the form of a 'leakage or contamination',[33] whereby spectral figures constantly trouble, transgress and exceed the borders between the living and not living that these frames otherwise try to hold in place. In the aftermath of disasters these frames are never quite securely in place and in such times their borders actually structure the response of international lawyers by operating as the fault-line for struggles among different groups of lawyers – struggles to either further disrupt these frames and actually be more open and responsive to the suffering, or those to reproduce these frames and repress and actively contain the suffering and its apprehension.[34] It is my argument in this section that from the conduct of both Pal and Baxi in the aftermaths of disasters we receive training in the former.

Past reckoning mode of justice

It is exactly this conduct that was displayed by Pal in his Tokyo Tribunal dissent. His dissent was dissonant in that it sought to interrupt the triumphant temporality that operated in the majority judgmentm which narrated progress from the fallen past of a disastrous war and its spectacular suffering towards the victorious achievement of a just and peaceful 'international community' in the present, a state exemplified in the majority's view by the very fact that such a 'dispassionate' third party Tribunal had actually been set up to mete out justice and overcome suffering.[35] Pal's judgement does not evade the question of justice; but for him the very possibility of achieving such justice is connected to the need to first attend to the longer history of imperial violence and dispossession and not to erase other related disasters that continued to produce suffering for the communities in the Pacific theatre of the Second World War, including that of using nuclear weapons.[36] For Pal this past of imperialist aggression and its disasters continues to haunt, and in many ways structure, the present 'international society'.[37] From his dissent we can discern a disruptive challenge to the truncated construction of the disaster of the war itself.

The same attentiveness to continuing legacies of suffering from past catastrophes is displayed by Baxi in his insistence on the continuing obligations incumbent upon the MNC concerned, their Indian subsidiary, the Indian state and the judicial system to ensure full reparations are made to the survivors of the 'Bhopal catastrophe', that lawful criminal retribution occurs and that efforts are made towards restoring the health of the people still suffering and that of their surrounding environment.[38] In the absence of such efforts he has suggested that the very possibility of begetting new just futures is aborted by the continued leakage of poisons from the past into the present.[39] Furthermore, in a more recent paper, written on the 30th anniversary of Bhopal, Baxi draws attention to how the 'Bhopal catastrophe' cannot be conceived as a single event but should be seen as one which has been repeated several times over on account of the failure to recognise the loss and suffering it has generated and to reckon with the 'slow violence' of its lingering aftermath.[40]

In doing so, he disrupts the attempts to temporally truncate and contain the disaster by way of repressing how it continues to effect suffering into the present. Connecting this to the very possibility of justice, he writes:

> Without memory of violation and victimage...justice is neither possible nor thinkable. Their spectral presence is a necessary condition for thinking and doing justice in society.[41]

Work of mourning

Furthermore, in this conduct that displays an attentiveness to the long temporal expanse of disasters I see both Pal and Baxi as also challenging the non-apprehension of certain lives as not being lives and thus their loss and injury as not being recognised as suffering. They do so by performing the 'work of mourning',[42] which apprehends these lives exposed to suffering in disasters as *valuable* lives and their loss and injury as generating suffering and demanding grieving.[43] For as Baxi observes:

> The work of mourning, this power of creating memory, speaks to grief and bereavement of the past and of their infinite future recurrence. The tasks of justice then are inconceivable outside the frame and the power of civic lamentation.... But how do we mourn for the living dead, those who are *not there*?...These are the truly rightless peoples, peoples who exist only by virtue of their being expendable and disposable, and whose being is indeed a case of not being there... The question is how activist memory workers may affirm the existence of such peoples and persons *who were already there without being there*.[44]

Struggles over temporal transmissions

The attentiveness on Pal's part to the claims of past disastrous suffering in the present provoked several critical reactions from contemporary 'Western' international lawyers. An especially revealing case was provided by Julius Stone, a world-renowned jurist of the time, in his anxious response to Pal's temporal indictment of a justice that is premised upon a refusal to consider and attend to the continuing effects of past disasters associated with imperial violence.[45] Stone observed:

> it is pushing matters *à outrance* to say with Judge Pal...that no present war can be 'unjust' or 'criminal' merely because the present interests of Western Powers in the Eastern hemisphere may have been formerly acquired 'mostly through armed violence' and not 'just' war. Few roots of title of men would sustain an indefinite tracing back in ultimate time; and the general application of the Judge's view would therefore frustrate at the outset all aspirations to either justice or legal order...How far back is any particular man's moral duty to be identified with that of his ancestors, or for that matter the moral right of *the victim* with *his* ancestors.[46]

I would argue that here, in this contestation between Pal and Stone, we witness one of the key sites for both the reproduction and the disruptions of disaster frames. I see this anxiety, an anxiety to measure and draw a line in the temporal sand, beyond which certain claims and normative expectations on account of suffering produced by disasters would be transmitted and as inherited by certain successors (eg alien property rights, investment treaties in the wake of the 'disaster' of decolonisation – inheritances which not incidentally secure sovereign subjecthood) and certain others sought to be contained and deemed to be lost without a trace (eg reparations for the violent disasters of colonialism or compensation for inter-generational poisoning caused by industrial disasters), directing us towards a battle-line in the international legal field marking Third World insurgency and imperial counter-insurgency across different generations.[47]

With this (colonial) structuring of temporal transmissions and their (Third World) disruptions we witness the actual operations of disaster frames in the international legal field, as these struggles over drawing the line in the temporal sand, over where it gets drawn and for what, are basically struggles over what constitutes the boundaries of these frames.

Responsiveness to the suffering

A vital distinction between the mode of conduct displayed by Pal and Baxi and the dominant one concerns how they construe the sufferers. With our ancestral figures the responsive conduct, drawing upon an attentiveness to loss and injury that constitutes the state of suffering, is ultimately towards the sufferers, who are conceived as being acting and struggling agentic communities. Against this, the dominant mode of conduct invokes 'abject victim subjects' who are entirely negatively identified by their states of injury and loss.[48]

Baxi, for instance, counters the dominant frames' construal of those suffering in merely negative and passive terms – ephemeral and incapable of transmitting legacies of liveable life through time. Rather, for him responsiveness to the suffering reveals a certain enduring vitality among the communities of sufferers:

> Even when vanquished, the impoverished are capable of, and daily perform, acts of resistance as myriad ways of protest against their condition. And quite often *they display collective, associational strength so much unexpected of them* as to confuse the dominant interests…The culture of poverty approach altogether obscures from the view *the historic vitality and resilience of the impoverished and the oppressed*.[49]

From this we begin to notice how this responsiveness to the suffering, as active struggling agents who are themselves contesting their own violations and thus responding to the suffering effected by disasters, leads to the approach displayed by these ancestral figures of being guided in their own conduct by these contesting and enduring actions of the sufferers.[50] The response to how to conduct oneself as an international lawyer in the aftermath of disaster is to be open to and let one's conduct be shaped and guided by the conduct of its 'valiant survivors'. This is the training in conduct Pal and Baxi transmit to us.

Following from this the question naturally arises: so how *do* the sufferers survive, endure and resist in the wake of disasters, when the very conditions of livability are disrupted and their lives stand exposed? The response to this query into the endurance of exposed life reveals that the suffers live on by drawing upon the enabling conditions of life being offered by relatedness to others, including collective (as against autonomous) struggle by communities of struggle, by way of transmitted legacies from one generation of the suffering to the next – embodiments that enable living on or 'memory as a resource for doing activism'[51] – that enable the persistent enacting of struggle against injury and violation.[52]

Crucially, in direct contrast to the dominant model for recovery from disasters premised upon creating more autonomous sovereign agents and dismantling relationality, the model of survival and recovery that the suffers themselves display is one based upon the basic vulnerability, relationality and dependency of embodied subjects who always require vital relations with other , relations that constitute the very conditions for survival of life, to recover from disaster.[53]

Taking up responsibility

A hand in things to come. (UCC advertisement slogan)[54]

In the wake of disasters and the suffering they produce the problem pertaining to their causation, namely identifying causal factors and determining any possible responsible conduct and the persons associated with it looms large as a task. This is especially true for those occupying the office of international lawyers and demands responsive conduct on their part. In this section I argue that from both Pal and Baxi we inherit a training in conduct as international lawyers in response to this task, which centres the acknowledgment that particular modes of conduct performed by those occupying the office of international lawyer *produce* disasters and, following on from this, the need for international lawyers to take up responsibility for this causation.[55] This training in conduct posits that our conduct as persons occupying the office of international lawyer is both transformable, ie it entails the making of particular choices and constrained decisions and not the performance of some ineluctable duty, and that this conduct *must* be transformed to prevent the occurrence of future disasters and to heal and halt the ongoing aftermath effects of disasters past.

I contrast this training with the dominant mode of conduct displayed by international lawyers which, even in instances that purportedly centre the self of the international lawyer as an acting, 'public figure', disavow any responsibility of these selves for actions that produce and affect the world, especially when it comes to the more disastrous effects.[56] When it comes to this dominant mode of conduct I would argue that it is determined and enabled by two powerful models for construing the problem of causation of disasters – models for whose operations in the field of international law we find exemplary and inaugural cases in Pal's Tokyo and Baxi's Bhopal.

Criminal model

First, there is the criminal model, exemplified and (partly) inaugurated by the criminal tribunal set-up in Tokyo in the wake of the Second World War, as per which the causation of the disaster in question becomes identified with particular (criminal) individual agents. Herein the disaster is entirely man-made and the 'monstrous' actors in question completely master the action that brings about the disaster. Criminal culpability, it seems, requires largely autonomous action that remains unaffected and undetermined by larger structural processes. Causation thus invariably becomes fixated upon the more immediate factors and more local actors, leaving out longer histories of decisions and actions that find no immediate connection with the spectacular disaster in question.[57] In terms of the 'cutting up' crisis, in this model we find a truncating of the causal factors of the disaster both temporally (only the immediate and instantaneous) and spatially (only the local).[58]

Humanitarian model

Second, there is what I will call the humanitarian model, as per which the causation of the disaster in question cannot be made to lie with any identifiable human agency. In this model disasters are 'tragedies [sic]' which somehow ineluctably befall us on account of some as yet uncontrolled forces of nature, bereft of any space for, and entirely determining decisions and choices associated with, human agency.[59]

This model shifts the response away from determining culpability and accountability to that of rescuing victims, ie away from questions of causation towards urgently responding to the effects of disasters. Articulating this humanitarian model the former CEO of Union Carbide, Warren Anderson, (who, not incidentally, happened to be the prime accused in the criminal cases filed in India) 'magnanimously' preached:

> When you have a disaster in which your company is involved, make everyone understand that the *needs of the victims come first*. Don't get lost in the morass of lawyers, politicians and public relations managers.[60]

In fact, as Kim Fortun has noted, in the wake of the disaster UCC constantly attempted to avoid taking up legal liability for causation by assuming what they termed 'moral responsibility' for rescuing the victims of the disaster – a humanitarian responsibility which, while denying that the actions of the self had produced the disaster, simultaneously sought to authorise action in response to (non-relational and naturalised) 'suffering'.[61]

Shared assumptions

Ultimately both models generate a framework in which there is an elision of the causation of disasters as a consequence of actions undertaken by international lawyers and thus an avoidance of the need for them to take up responsibility. Furthermore, both models generate authorisation for the actions of international lawyers in response to disasters – the action of judging and determining the culpability of (local) 'criminal actors' in international criminal trials and the action of rescuing and protecting the 'victims' of disasters in the wake of humanitarian catastrophes. The combination of the two aspects produces a framework wherein the question of the responsibility for actions is transformed into the responsibility *for* or *over* others: in other words, the authority of international lawyers to protect the 'bare life' of 'victims' of wars and chemical 'accidents'.[62]

Baxi response

In his struggles around the 'Bhopal catastrophe' Baxi has sought to challenge this disavowal of responsibility. Specifically, he has continually struggled against the construction of disasters as being merely accidental and unfortunate 'tragedies' that demand rescue by the legal fraternity.[63] Directly taking on the humanitarian model's obfuscation of the causation of disasters, he has observed of them that they are:

> tendencies towards mass disaster/mass torts *nihilism* that accomplish the production of a belief that most situations entail 'inevitable accidents', signifying 'just an infelicitous combination of natural conditions and innocent human activity', a combination that then leads to the inevitable conclusion that 'responsibility in modern mass torts may be so widespread and diffuse as to be attributable to *no one in particular*'.[64]

In response to the problem of determining causation in the wake of the Bhopal disaster Baxi displays an approach that establishes the connection between the prior exposure of lives to the risk of disastrous injury and the causation of disasters.[65] Following on from this and related to it, by showing how this exposure of lives to the risk of disastrous injury is not something that is inevitable or necessitated by some natural order of things but rather involves a (political) calculus of differentially distributing the risks and rewards/profits of particular activities among different groups and communities of people, Baxi goes on to establish the responsibility for the causation of the disaster with those making these decisions to expose certain lives to risk.[66] Baxi thus disrupts the 'inevitability' or 'ineluctability' thesis of the humanitarian model – one that posits these decisions that produce disasters as entirely determined or non-decisions and thus the disasters as ineluctable though unfortunate events.[67]

So, for Baxi, in the case of Bhopal, when the UCC officials took the decision to dilute safety measures in the chemical plant, they thus (further) exposed the people living around it to a greater risk than there would have otherwise been of an injurious chemical leakage. They acted and their action was neither ineluctable nor 'naturally ordained', as it entailed a distributional decision to shore up the interests of some (by protecting their profits) while exposing others to the risk of injury. Baxi argued therefore that they must bear the liability for the disaster this exposure produced.[68] Furthermore, Baxi's broader scholarship establishes an intimate connection between the state of being impoverished and the exposure to the risk of injury from disasters.[69] In fact, it is the extent and number of those impoverished or exposed to the risk of disastrous injury that determines the spatial and temporal impact or contours of any disaster.[70] From his ground-breaking interventions in the field of 'Law and Poverty' we see how the state of being impoverished or being exposed to the risk of disastrous injury is no natural state but rather one brought about by an active or even planned series of decisions and long-term processes of impoverishment, or an active dismantling of the conditions of liveability, in which lawyers play a key role.[71]

Developing upon this, in his Hague Lectures Baxi specifically focuses on the question of responsibility for the production of 'mass disasters' on the part of the fraternity/field of private international lawyers, including that of so designing the legal framework as to make it possible for global corporations to escape liability and avoid having to pay restorative compensation to those injured.[72]

Pertinently, in the aftermath of the Bhopal disaster, in his careful engagement and fine-grained critique of the legal response to it, he noted how this very response, or 'the catastrophic Bhopal jurisprudence',[73] had impoverished those who had already been violated by the initial Bhopal catastrophe, thus producing *several* Bhopal catastrophes.[74]

Baxi suggests that is only by practising 'institutionalized ethical irresponsibility' that the legal fraternity occludes and disavows its own responsibility for producing disasters.[75] But how exactly does this come to pass? Namely, how do these decisions by international lawyers to expose certain lives to the risk of disastrous injury become elided or naturalised as non-decisions? I would suggest that Baxi's response, one foreshadowed in the previous paragraph, disrupts the other main feature of the humanitarian model, namely its authorisation of the actions of international lawyers to rescue the 'victims' of disasters. It does so by revealing the vicious cycle of how such redemptive actions by purported 'saviours' in the wake of disasters themselves produce future disasters. The key insight is that the distributional decisions taken by international lawyers that impoverish and produce disasters always present themselves as an enactment of an ineluctable duty of 'rescue, protect and prevent' in the wake of disaster. In other words, distributional decisions which selectively impoverish and privilege become ultimately authorised on the grounds of them being the enactment of inexorable tasks for securing the security, growth and protection of all (nation/humanity) by overcoming the possibility of disasters by mastering nature.[76]

Once we take this on board, we begin to perceive how some of the major responses to overcoming suffering in the Third World, namely modernisation and development, entail the exposure of their purported beneficiaries to risks of injury and that they themselves reproduce suffering while claiming to overcome it and to being an unequivocal good that achieves benefits for all, and not a distributional decision that benefits some and exposes others.[77] The decision to expose to injury is grounded and elided by all the sacrificial notions underlying these dominant responses – ie of this suffering being transient, unfortunate but necessary to achieve the ultimate overcoming of 'suffering', or of it being non-suffering as its 'expendable subjects' are less than human, or even as having being produced by acts of the sufferers themselves on account of their natural failings, etc.[78] It is a mode of responding to disasters in which rescue and sacrifice blur into one another, as does the victim and the monster, and the saviour assumes the authority to mete them out *sans* any accountability.[79] If we ourselves apply this training in order to respond to the Bhopal disaster(s), one begins to perceive how the exposure of the impoverished people of Bhopal to the risk of chemical poisoning was itself grounded upon and made to appear ineluctable by presenting it as part of a series of responsive actions in the wake of disasters past – powerfully including the largest agricultural disaster in recorded human history, the Bengal famine of the 1940s, in which over four million impoverished colonised Indians died of starvation.[80]

From Baxi's conduct we learn how all these mystical elisions are just that – mystifications that obfuscate how these not wholly determined actions of international lawyers and others in response to disasters actually produce disasters.

Pal's response

Relatedly, as against an approach that disavows responsibility in the very gesture of claiming responsible authority, Pal articulates a conception of responsibility which is much more capacious and centres the responsibility of the 'self' as the prior condition for authorising the possibility of judging an alleged 'criminal other' for causing disasters. This approach emphasises relatedness, and disrupts the clean dichotomy between the self and the other that the criminal responsibility model is premised upon.[81] In Pal's approach the quest to determine the causation of the disaster of war is expanded both temporally and spatially in a manner that makes several other actors uncomfortable about their own complicity in its creation.[82] Thus, by bringing up how the more immediate and localised actions by the Japanese accused of war crimes could not be addressed without first also taking into account how these actions formed a part of, and were thus determined and enabled by, spatially more expansive and temporally more elongated structures of imperialism, Pal brings into the focus of an enquiry into causation and culpability exactly those more institutionalised webs of decisions and actions at a more global and temporally distanced level that the dominant criminal responsibility model simply 'cuts out'. Such an approach makes it possible to perceive the complicities of actions enacted by a broader and seemingly more distant set of actors, including international lawyers themselves, as well as global imperial powers, in producing disasters.[83]

Disrupting the smooth authorisation of international lawyers' actions in the wake of disaster, such conduct makes it difficult to separate the judging (international lawyer) self from the criminally culpable other and elides the webs of relatedness and chains of culpability. As Nandy observes:

> Pal points out the larger political and economic forces released by the nation-state system, by modern warfare, by the dominant philosophy of international diplomacy, and by the West's

> racial attitude to Japan, all of which helped produce the political response of the accused. The West had to acknowledge that wartime Japan wanted to beat the West at its own game, that a significant part of Japanese imperialism was only a reflection of the West's disowned self... When Pal granted himself the right to judge he was being both an Indian and a Victorian trying to transcend the moral dichotomy of the age. Culpability, Pal sought to argue...could never be divisible, and responsibility, even when individual, could be, paradoxically, fully individual only when seen as collective and, in fact, global.[84]

Conclusion

In concluding this article I would like to briefly dwell upon how this training in conduct pertaining to justice and responsibility come together within the framework of inheritance and with the work of its transmission and reception through time. As has no doubt become clear from the previous sections, we, as inheritors in the wake of disasters, inherit both vital and sordid inheritances, losses and privileges, poisons and nutrients. These transmissions that shape and form us are never entirely within our control. We as inheritors never entirely control what gets transmitted from the past. Yet at the same time we have a measure of choice over which transmitted inheritances we enliven and which we attempt to undo in our conduct of reception as heirs. The problem that confronts all heirs is how to exercise this choice.

More specifically, by combining out previous engagements with the problems of justice and responsibility in the wake of disasters, we arrive at an as yet unarticulated yet pressing problem of conduct for international lawyers. Namely, how does one go about undoing the legacies of those past actions enacted by ancestral figures occupying the office of international lawyers that produced disasters? As we have seen, these were primarily distributional decisions that garnered profit and privilege for certain groups and distributed risks onto others. Those distributed risks brought about disastrous suffering for these unprivileged and impoverished groups and thus they (and their inheritor generations) have inherited suffering in the wake of disaster as a consequence. However, others, invariably including those making these decisions and the heirs to their office, inherit privileges, privileges that include the authority to make these distributional decisions and to determine the response to disasters. The privilege to be audible as the work of picking up the pieces commences. To formulate it in terms of responsibility and justice: how does one take up a responsibility for the effects of ancestral actions that actually does the work of *undoing* the inheritance of these privilege and thus reckons with the legacies of the past in a manner that opens up the present to the possibility of future justice?

Do Pal and Baxi offer us any guidance with regard to this problem? I would suggest that, if we combine their conduct of a responsive justice and that of the taking up of responsibility, we are guided to a mode of conduct in which responsiveness and the taking up of responsibility meet.[85]

To formulate this conduct, I would like briefly to go back to the critique of Pal's judgment put forward by Stone and to draw out what I see as its underlying challenge to such a privilege-undoing exercise: how does one measure how far back in the past we will go in this endeavour? The response offered by Pal and Baxi suggests that such measuring requires a practice of responsiveness towards those who inherit suffering, or what Baxi would call '"infinite responsibility" towards the suffering other'.[86]. Specifically responsiveness in this case to what Baxi has referred to as the 'normative expectations' that these others have of us and our measuring actions, which of course intimately affect their lives.[87] From Pal and Baxi we learn that it is to these expectations that we are accountable and it is they that guide us in the task of measuring and undoing these sordid legacies produced by ancestral action.

That this training itself comes by way of what is itself a transmitted inheritance shows how closely enmeshed the task of undoing and doing of inheritance is.

Disclosure statement

No potential conflict of interest was reported by the author.

Acknowledgments

The writing and fashioning of this piece has naturally not been an isolated exercise and I would like to acknowledge the guidance, conversations and discerning and supporting relations with a community of others who have made it possible. In particular, I would like to acknowledge Prof Upendra Baxi, Prof Sundhya Pahuja, Prof Shaun McVeigh, Julia Dehm, Usha Natarajan, Sujith Xavier, John Reynolds, Sara Dehm, Diego Silva and David Jenkins.

Notes

1. Marks, "International Law in Disastrous Times," 325.
2. My usage of the concept of 'liveable life' throughout this article draws upon the recent work of the philosopher Judith Butler. Butler, "Rethinking Vulnerability and Resistance."
3. Klein, *The Shock Doctrine*.
4. On my use of the terminology of 'office' and 'conduct', see Genovese, "On Australian Feminist Tradition."
5. For a more general account of this model, see Klein, *The Shock Doctrine*, 3–23.
6. For an excellent account of this model, see Charlesworth, "International Law."
7. Okafor, "Newness, Imperialism and International Legal Reform."
8. Mickelson, "Rhetoric and Rage"; Anghie, "C. G. Weeramantry"; Chimni, "The Self, Modern Civilization, and International Law", 1160; and Chimni, "Retrieving 'Other' Visions."
9. Hill, "Reason and Lovelessness," 357–407.
10. Pal, *Crimes in International Relations*.
11. See Baxi, "The Bhopal Victims," iv–v.
12. Fortun, *Advocacy after Bhopal*, xiii–xxi.
13. The chemical plant in which gas leakage occurred during the early hours of 3 December 1984, resulting in the deaths of roughly 20,000 people, mostly inhabitants of densely populated and marginalised neighbourhoods in the heart of the city where it had been set-up, had been engaged in the manufacture of a chemical pesticide that was being promoted as an essential

input to improve the productivity of an industrialising agricultural sector. Rajagopal, "And the Poor get Gassed"; and Fortun, *Advocacy after Bhopal*.

14. Baxi, "The Bhopal Victims." See also Nixon, *Slow Violence*, 45–67.
15. In 1999 he delivered the Hague Lectures in Private International Law on the topic of the liability of MNCs for mass disasters. Baxi, *Mass Torts*, 316.
16. Nixon, *Slow Violence*; and Scott, *Omens of Adversity*.
17. Butler, *Frames of War*, 24.
18. Nixon, *Slow Violence*.
19. Baxi, "Book Review," 125.
20. For the distinction between 'spectacular and instantaneous violence' and 'slow violence', see Nixon, *Slow Violence*, 200.
21. Charlesworth, "International Law," 384, 386. In another section of her article, which deploys the terminology of 'crises' much in the same way as I seek to deploy 'disaster', Charlesworth observes of international lawyers: 'we are preoccupied with great crises, rather than the politics of everyday life. In this way international law steers clear of analysis of longer-term trends and structural problems.' Ibid., 389.
22. . Davis, "Los Angeles after the Storm."
23. This assertion was made by the then UCC CEO, Robert Kennedy, in an interview conducted in 1990. Reisch, "Carbide's Kennedy," 9.
24. Butler, *Frames of War*.
25. Grear, "Vulnerability."
26. Butler, "Rethinking Vulnerability and Resistance."
27. Grear, "Vulnerability."
28. This staging of temporal progress by the majority thus re-enacted the ur-myth of Euro-American modernity, ie the overcoming of endless cycles of violence premised upon the logic of vengeance and revenge, and its triumphant banishing to the past by way of the constitution of a new political order premised upon 'impartial' third-party adjudication of conflicts under an objective, written and general law, thereby achieving justice and freedom. Pertinently this maturation process necessarily demands a certain degree of forgetting or letting go of the past on the part of subjects, especially in terms of injuries and wrongs suffered, from which the subject gains distance, as the right to punish is surrendered to the newly emergent 'sovereign' political order. The subject learns to 'let go' in a process whereby reactive passions give way to greater degrees of self-control and self-limitation. For a useful recent restatement, see Ricoeur, "Justice and Vengeance," 223–231.
29. Baxi, 'Voices of Suffering."
30. Fanning, "The Firebombing of Tokyo"; and Fortun, *Advocacy after Bhopal*. I return to and further develop this mode of authorisation of action in the next section.
31. This model of justice could be said to work on what Butler has identified as the logic of security. Butler, *Precarious Life*.
32. In the next section I will attempt to show how Baxi's conduct with regard to the problem of causation also orientates itself to perceive the operations of this powerful dynamic.
33. Butler, *Frames of War*.
34. To further draw upon Butler's work, these struggles are over the globally 'differential distribution of precarity' and the liveability of certain lives. Butler, *Frames of War*, 25.
35. Varadarajan, "The Trials of Imperialism," 794–795.
36. In doing so, Pal powerfully establishes a connection between the practice of 'colonial domination' and international criminality. See Simpson, *Law, War & Crime*, 96.
37. Pal, *Crimes in International Relations*. See also Varadarajan, "The Trials of Imperialism," 804–807.
38. Baxi, "TLSI Distinguished Lecture."
39. Baxi, "The Bhopal Victims."
40. Baxi, "TLSI Distinguished Lecture." See also Baxi, "Writing about Impunity."
41. Baxi, *Memory and Rightlessnes*, 12.
42. See Derrida, *The Work of Mourning*; and Butler, *Precarious Life*.

43. Here we can adduce several examples of Baxi's 'work of mourning'. Baxi, "Globalization"; Baxi, "The (Im)possibility of Constitutional Justice"; Baxi, *Memory and Rightlessness*; and Baxi, "Constitutional Utopias." In Pal's case, apart from his Tokyo dissent, I find his invocation of the Sanskrit term '*ciradukhini*' (ongoing mourner or griever) to describe the colonised nation as also being suggestive of this openness to lamentation on his part. Nandy, "The Other Within," 55.
44. Baxi, *Memory and Rightlessness*, 12–13 (emphasis in the original).
45. At the time this leading figure associated with the Anglo-American sociological school of law had recently, to great acclaim, delivered The Hague Lecture in Public International Law. Stone, "Problems Confronting Sociological Enquiries."
46. Stone, *Aggression and World*, 143 (emphasis in the original).
47. In terms of temporal transmissions one could note with Baxi that DOW Chemicals, which in 2001 acquired control over the interests of UCC, while assuming the assets and some of its liabilities as 'successor-in-interest', has consistently sought to evade and disavow its inherited responsibilities for the 'Bhopal catastrophe'. Baxi, "Writing about Impunity," 35. This can be connected and compared with the catastrophic aftermaths of Bhopal, both in terms of the health and well-being of subsequent 'wounded generations' born in the vicinity and also in terms of the termination of generational succession as a result of serious birth complications and disorders emerging among survivors. Mukherjee, *Surviving Bhopal*, 7.
48. An illuminating exposition of the consequences of this distinction has been developed by Veena Das, "Suffering, Legitimacy and Healing," 137–175.
49. Baxi, "Introduction," viii (emphasis added).
50. Baxi, *The Future of Human Rights*.
51. Baxi, *Memory and Rightlessness*, 9.
52. Baxi, "TLSI Distinguished Lecture."
53. Hanna, "Bhopal." It is in such a light that I would suggest we can make sense of Pal's statement in his judgment, which perceived in the aftermath of the dropping of the nuclear bombs the arising of a feeling in 'humanity': 'we are a unity of humanity, linked by our fellow human beings, irrespective of race, creed, or colour, by bonds which have been fused unbreakably in the diabolical heat of the explosion'. Hill, "Reason and Lovelessness," 368.
54. Reproduced in Fortun, *Advocacy after Bhopal*, 93.
55. Inheriting this training has in many ways been a central preoccupation for the contemporary generation of TWAILers. See Chimni, "Third World Approaches to International Law"; and Pahuja, "Laws of Encounter."
56. Cassese, *Five Masters of International Law*.
57. The question of responsibility and reckoning in this register of what has been recently described as the 'ethical turn' is projected upon, and confined to, rogue individuals or regimes. See Simpson, *Law, War & Crime*, 54–78. See also Nesiah, "The Trials of History," 127–163.
58. Simpson, *Law, War and Crime*.
59. Marks, "International Law in Disastrous Times," 325.
60. Anderson, cited in Fortun, *Advocacy after Bhopal* (emphasis added).
61. Fortun, *Advocacy after Bhopal*, 98.
62. Orford, *International Authority*; and Pahuja, "Global Poverty."
63. On the pertinent distinction between 'misfortune' and 'injustice', drawing upon the distinction between the merely episodic and the systemic, see Baxi, *Memory and Rightlessness*, 19–23.
64. Baxi, *Mass Torts*, 421 (emphasis in the original).
65. Baxi, *Mass Torts*, 403–423. See also Beck, *Risk Society*.
66. As Fortun observes, the legal response to Bhopal itself was: 'an important precedent for determining how the risks and rewards of globalization would be distributed'. Fortun, *Advocacy after Bhopal*, 54.
67. This orientation on his part has not been limited to the 'Bhopal catastrophe' but has extended to other so-called 'misfortunes' or 'disasters' generating suffering. See Baxi, "Introduction," vi.
68. Baxi, *Mass Torts*.

69. This insight stands reconfirmed in the more recent scholarship of Neil Smith on global disasters, in which he shows with numerous examples how it is the impoverished who bear the inordinate brunt of the injuries generated by disasters. Smith, "Disastrous Accumulation," 782–784.
70. Smith, "Disastrous Accumulation"; and Klein, *The Shock Doctrine*.
71. As he puts it, '*impoverishment is a dynamic process of public decision-making in which it is considered just, right and fair that some people become or stay impoverished*...In other words, impoverishment is a matter of *conscious* planning by those who are not impoverished. Both the state policies and our innumerable daily actions decide *who*, how *many*, to what *extent*, for how *long*, and with what *cost* shall become or remain impoverished' (emphasis added). Baxi, "Introduction", vi–vii. See also Baxi, "Book Review," 118–121.
72. Baxi, *Mass Torts*.
73. Baxi, "Violence, Constitututionalism and Struggle," 18.
74. Baxi, "Justice Deferred," 2.
75. Baxi, "Book Review," 117. See also Baxi, "Liberty, Equality and Justice," 18–21; Baxi, *Mass Torts*; and Baxi, "Writing about Immunity," 40–41.
76. Baxi, *The Future of Human Rights*.
77. See Baxi, "The Uncanny Idea of Development", 76–123.
78. For instance, in a particularly odious editorial published in the *Wall Street Journal* less than a week after the Bhopal catastrophe, it was opined that: 'economic progress is not without its risks. The saving grace is that the benefits outweigh the costs. As a Georgia Tech doctor told the New York Times, "Of those people killed, half would not have been alive today if it weren't for that plant and the modern health standards made possible by the wide use of pesticides"... Simple observation shows that life is better for today's middle class Indian than it was for 19th century rajahs.' Reproduced in Ranjan, 'Disaster, Development and Governance,' 375. See also Baxi, "International Development, Global Impoverishment," 609–610.
79. For a powerful exposition (and critique) of this mode of authorisation, which assumes responsibility for rescue but not for causation, see Baxi, "The 'War on Terror'," 15–16.
80. Thus the UCC plant itself formed part of a series of techno-scientific measures taken in postcolonial India, the so-called 'Green Revolution', that were all in a significant way authorised by invoking particular constructions of the Bengal famine, as well as a purported famine in Bihar in 1966–67. See Cullather, "The Meaning of Famine", 205–231; Gupta, *Postcolonial Developments*, 58. That the 'Bengal famine' itself was very much socially produced and not a result of some 'natural' shortage was of course famously shown by Sen, *Poverty and Famines*, in his now classic book. For a recent work which explores how the war efforts of the British colonial regime played a major role in producing this disaster, one which occurred amid years of over-production, see Mukherjee, *Hungry Bengal*. For the argument that the 'Green Revolution' displaced a more progressive politics of distribution with one that furthered distribution upwards, from small landowning peasants and the rural landless to the large landowners, and that this was elided by way of an ideology of growth or production, see Patel, "The Long Green Revolution." For an early prescient account of this "immiseration of the impoverished" see Baxi, "Introduction", xx-xxii.
81. Nandy, "The Other Within," 49.
82. Hill, "Reason and Lovelessness," 369–376.
83. Nandy, "The Other Within," 49.
84. Nandy, "The Other Within," 65–66.
85. Baxi, "Constitutional Utopias," 22; Baxi, "What May the Third World Expect?", 722; and Nandy, "The Other Within," 57.
86. Baxi, "Book Review," 117, . See also Baxi, *Mass Torts*, 423; Baxi, "Voices of Suffering"; Baxi, "Taking Suffering Seriously"; Pal, "Presidential Address"; and Nandy, "The Other Within," 49.
87. It is exactly this receptiveness that I see Baxi calling forth (and practising) in his exhortation to us to 'listen to the power of lamentation of the millennial losers'. Baxi, "The Colonialist Heritage," 75.

Bibliography

Anghie, Antony. "C. G. Weeramantry at the International Court of Justice." *Leiden Journal of International Law* 14 (2001): 829–850.

Baxi, Upendra. "Taking Suffering Seriously: Social Action Litigation before the Supreme Court of India." *Third World Legal Studies* 4 (1985): 107–132.

Baxi, Upendra. *"Introduction." In Law and Poverty: Critical Essays*, edited by Upendra Baxi, v–xxx. Bombay: N. M. Tripathi, 1988.

Baxi, Upendra. "The Bhopal Victims in the Labyrinth of the Law: An Introduction." In *Valiant Victims and Lethal Litigation: The Bhopal Case*, edited by Upendra Baxi and Amita Dhanda, i–ixix. New Delhi: Indian Law Institute, 1991.

Baxi, Upendra. *Globalization: A World without Alternatives?*. International Centre for Ethnic Studies, Colombo: ICES Annual Lecture, 1992.

Baxi, Upendra. "Voices of Suffering and the Future of Human Rights." *Transnational Law and Contemporary Problems* 8, no. 2 (1998): 125–169.

Baxi, Upendra. *Mass Torts, Multinational Enterprise Liability and Private International Law*. The Hague: Martinus Nijhoff, 2000.

Baxi, Upendra. "The (Im)possibility of Constitutional Justice: Seismographic Notes on Indian Constitutionalism." In *India's Living Constitution: Ideas, Practices, Controversies*, edited by Zoha Hasan, E. Sridharan, and R. Sudarshan, 31–63. London: Anthem Press, 2000.

Baxi, Upendra. *The Future of Human Rights*. New Delhi: Oxford University Press, 2002.

Baxi, Upendra. "The Colonialist Heritage." In *Comparative Legal Studies: Traditions and Transitions*, edited by Pierre Legrand and Roderick Munday, 46–75. Cambridge: Cambridge University Press, 2003.

Baxi, Upendra. "Violence, Constitutionalism and Struggle: Or How to Avoid Being a Mahamoorkha!" In *Liberty, Equality and Justice: Struggles for a New Social Order*, edited by S. P. Sathe and Sathya Narayan, 9–24. Lucknow: EBC Publishing Ltd., 2003.

Baxi, Upendra. *Memory and Rightlessness*. New Delhi: Centre For Women's Development Studies, 2003.

Baxi, Upendra. "The 'War on Terror' and the 'War of Terror' – Nomadic Multitudes, Aggressive Incumbents, and the 'New' International Law: Prefatory Remarks on Two 'Wars'." *Osgoode Hall Law Journal* 43, nos. 1–2 (2005): 7–43.

Baxi, Upendra. "What May the 'Third World' expect from International Law?" *Third World Quarterly* 27, no. 5 (2006): 713–725.

Baxi, Upendra. "The Uncanny Idea of Development." Chapter 3 in Human Rights in a Posthuman World, New Delhi: Oxford University Press, 2007.

Baxi, Upendra. "Book Review: Judging Emmanuel Levinas? Some Reflections on Reading Levinas, Law, Politics." *Modern Law Review* 72, no. 1 (2009): 116–129.

Baxi, Upendra. "Constitutional Utopias: A Conversation with Neelan Tiruchelvam." Tenth Neelan Tiruchelvam Memorial Lecture, January 26, 2009.http://transcurrents.com/tc/NeelanT_Memorial_Lecture.pdf

Baxi, Upendra. "Writing about Impunity and Environment: The 'Silver Jubilee' of the Bhopal Catastrophe." *Journal of Human Rights and the Environment* 1, no. 1 (2010): 23–44.

Baxi, Upendra. "International Development, Global Impoverishment, and Human Rights." In *Routledge Handbook of International Human Rights Law*, edited by Scott Sheeran and Nigel Rodley, 519–613. New York: Routledge, 2013.

Baxi, Upendra. "Justice Deferred – Transnational Lawyering and the Bhopal Gas Tragedy, 30 Years On." TLSI Distinguished Lecture delivered at the Dickson Poon School of Law Transnational Law Summer School, London, July 6, 2015.

Beck, Ulrich. *Risk Society: Towards a New Modernity*. Translated by Mark Ritter. London: Sage Publications, 1992.

Butler, Judith. *Frames of War: When is Life Grievable?*. London: Verso, 2009.

Butler, Judith. *Precarious Life: The Powers of Mourning and Violence*. London: Verso, 2004.

Butler, Judith. "Rethinking Vulnerability and Resistance." Madrid, June 2014. http://www.institutofranklin.net/sites/default/files/files/Rethinking%20Vulnerability%20and%20Resistance%20Judith%20Butler.pdf.

Cassese, Antonio. *Five Masters of International Law: Conversations with R.-J. Dupuy, E. Jiménez de Aréchaga, R. Jennings, L. Henkin and O. Schacter*. Oxford: Hart Publishing, 2011.

Charlesworth, Hillary. "International Law: A Discipline of Crises." *Modern Law Review* 65, no. 3 (2002): 377–392.

Chimni, B. S. "Retrieving 'Other' Visions of the Future: Sri Aurobindo and the Ideal of Human Unity." In *Decolonizing International Relations*, edited by Branwen Gruffydd Jones, 197–218. Lanham: Rowman & Littlefield, 2006.

Chimni, B. S. "The Self, Modern Civilization, and International Law: Learning from Mohandas Karamchand Gandhi's Hind Swaraj or Indian Home Rule." *European Journal of International Law* 23, no. 4 (2012): 1159–1173.

Cullather, Nick. "The Meaning of Famine," Chap. 8 in *The Hungry World: America's Cold War Battle Against Poverty in Asia*, 205–231. Cambridge, MA: Harvard University Press, 2010.

Das, Veena. "Suffering, Legitimacy and Healing: The Bhopal Case." Chap. 6 in *Critical Events: An Anthropological Perspective on Contemporary India*. New Delhi: Oxford University Press, 1997.

Davis, Mike. "Los Angeles after the Storm: The Dialectic of Ordinary Disaster." *Antipode* 27 (1995): 221–241.

Derrida, Jacques. *The Work of Mourning*. Translated by Pascale-Anne Brault and Michael Naas. Chicago, IL: University of Chicago Press, 2001.

Fanning, Rory. "The Firebombing of Tokyo." *Jacobin*, September 3, 2015. https://www.jacobinmag.com/2015/03/tokyo-firebombing-world-war-ii/.

Fortun, Kim. *Advocacy after Bhopal: Environmentalism, Disaster and New Global Orders*. London: University of Chicago Press, 2001.

Genovese, Ann. "On Australian Feminist Tradition: Three Notes on Conduct, Inheritance and the Relations of Historiography and Jurisprudence." *Journal of Australian Studies* 38, no. 4 (2014): 430–444.

Grear, Anna. "Vulnerability, Advanced Global Capitalism and Co-symptomatic Injustice: Locating the Vulnerable Subject." In *Vulnerability: Reflections on a New Ethical Foundation for Law and Politics*, edited by Anna Grear and Martha Fineman, 41–60. Farnham: Ashgate, 2013.

Gupta, Akhil. *Postcolonial Developments: Agriculture in the Making of Modern India*. London: Duke University Press, 2000.

Hanna, Bridget. "Bhopal: Unending Disaster, Enduring Resistance." In *Nongovernmental Politics*, edited by Michel Feher, Yates McKee, and Gaëlle Krikorian, 488–524. Cambridge, MA: MIT Press, 2007.

Hill, Barry. "Reason and Lovelessness: Tagore, the Tokyo Trial and Justice Pal." Chap. 6 in *Peacemongers*. Brisbane: University of Queensland Press, 2014.

Klein, Naomi. *The Shock Doctrine*. London: Penguin Books, 2007.

Marks, Susan. "International Law in Disastrous Times." In *The Cambridge Companion to International Law*, edited by Martii Koskenniemi and James Crawford, 309–326. Cambridge: Cambridge University Press, 2012.

Mickelson, Karin. "Rhetoric and Rage: Third World Voices in International Legal Discourse." *Wisconsin International Law Journal* 16 (1997–98): 353–419.

Mukherjee, Janam. *Hungry Bengal: War, Famine and the End of Empire*. Oxford: Oxford University Press, 2015.

Mukherjee, Suroopa. *Surviving Bhopal: Dancing Bodies, Written Texts, and Oral Testimonials of Women in the Wake of an Industrial Disaster*. New York: Palgrave Macmillan, 2010.

Nandy, Asish. "The Other Within: The Strange Case of Radhabinod Pal's Judgment on Culpability." *New Literary History* 231, no. 1 (1992): 45–67.

Nesiah, Vasuki. "The Trials of History: Losing Justice in the Monstrous and the Banal." In *Law in Transition: Human Rights, Development and Transitional Justice*, edited by Ruth Buchanan and Peer Zumbansen, 289–310. Oxford: Hart Publishing, 2014.

Nixon, Rob. *Slow Violence and the Environmentalism of the Poor*. Cambridge, MA: Harvard University Press, 2011.

Okafor, Obiora Chinedu. "Newness, Imperialism and International Legal Reform in our Time: A Twail Perspective." *Osgood Law Journal* 43, nos. 1–2 (2005): 171–191.

Orford, Anne. *International Authority and the Responsibility to Protect*. Cambridge: Cambridge University Press, 2011.

Pahuja, Sundhya. "Global Poverty and the Politics of Good Intentions." In *Law in Transition: Human Rights, Development and Transitional Justice*, edited by Ruth Buchanan and Peer Zumbansen, 31–48. Oxford: Hart Publishing, 2014.

Pahuja, Sundhya. "Laws of Encounter: A Jurisdictional Account of International Law." *London Review of International Law* 1, no. 1 (2013): 63–98.

Pal, Radhabinod. *Crimes in International Relations*. Calcutta: University of Calcutta, 1955.

Pal, Radhbinod. "Presidential Address: Universal Declaration of Human Rights." In *Lectures on Universal Declaration of Human Rights*, edited by Radhabinod Pal, N. C. Bhattacharya, P. C. Chakravarty, 17–21. Calcutta: Federation Hall Society, 1965.

Patel, Raj. "The Long Green Revolution." *Journal of Peasant Studies* 40, no. 1 (2013): 1–63.

Rajagopal, Arvind. "And the Poor get Gassed: Multi-national Aided Development and the State – The Case of Bhopal." *Berkeley Journal of Sociology* 32 (1987): 129–152.

Ranjan, S. Ravi. "Disaster, Development and Governance: Reflections on the 'Lessons' of Bhopal." *Environmental Values* 11, no. 3 (2002): 369–394.

Reisch, Marc S. "Carbide's Kennedy sees many Challenges for Company, Industry." *Chemical and Engineering News* 68, no. 35 (1990): 9.

Ricoeur, Paul. "Justice and Vengeance." In *Reflections on the Just*, edited by Paul Ricoeur and translated by David Pellauer, 223–231. Chicago, IL: University of Chicago Press, 2007.

Scott, David. *Omens of Adversity*. Durham, NC: Duke University Press, 2014.

Sen, Amartya. *Poverty and Famines: An Essay on Entitlement and Deprivations*. Oxford: Oxford University Press, 1981.

Simpson, Gerry. *Law, War and Crime: War Crimes, Trials and the Reinvention of International Law*. Cambridge: Polity, 2007.

Smith, Neil. "Disastrous Accumulation." *South Atlantic Quarterly* 106, no. 4 (2007): 699–787.

Stone, Julius. *Problems confronting Sociological Enquiries about International Law*. Leiden: A.W. Sijthoff, 1956.

Stone, Julius. *Aggression and World Order: A Critique of United Nations Theories of Aggression*. Berkley, CA: University of California Press, 1958.

Varadarajan, Latha. "The Trials of Imperialism: Radhabinod Pal's Dissent at the Tokyo Tribunal." *European Journal of International Relations* 21, no. 4 (2015): 793–815.

The South of Western constitutionalism: a map ahead of a journey

Zoran Oklopcic

ABSTRACT
In starting from the simple question, 'Why didn't the field of constitutional studies ever generate a school of thought akin to TWAIL?', this article seeks to sketch the contours, obstacles and promises of Southern constitutionalism. In confronting the intra-, meta-, and extra-disciplinary challenges to such a project, the article defines the 'South' of Southern constitutionalism, not the 'South' of the developed 'North', but rather the 'South' of the modernist hopes in – and the post-modernist disappointments with – the templates of Western constitutional imagination.

Introduction: where is the 'TWAIL' of contemporary constitutionalism?

Conceived at the dawn of 'the end of history', Third World Approaches to International Law (TWAIL) quickly established itself as a vibrant 'school of thought' that successfully interrogates the implications of international law in the enduring patterns of Western imperialism, neo-liberal globalisation, and the ideology of human rights.[1] Irrespective of its internal tensions and incongruities, TWAIL endures as an engine of counter-hegemonic intellectual production in the field of international law. While recent attempts have sought to dignify a 'constitutionalism of the global south'[2], nothing of the scale, impact, ambition and dynamism resembling TWAIL has occurred over the last two decades in the field of constitutional law.

For those interested in the possibilities generated by a constitutionalism more attuned to non-Western or anti-capitalist sensibilities, this raises an interesting question: What is the reason behind the conspicuous absence of a TWAIL-like gesture in the constitutional field? Is the habitus of constitutional lawyers simply more conservative than that of their colleagues in international law? Have constitutional lawyers been more receptive to Fukuyama's 'end of history' thesis, unreflectively accepting his verdict about the ultimate victory of liberal democracy as the historically superior form of government? Or, were TWAIL-ers simply more fortunate in being able to draw on the logistical and intellectual support from high-profile academics and Western centres of academic production? Irrespective of the answer, the absence of TWAIL's constitutional cognate is a puzzle worth pondering. Although TWAIL has been subject to a series of important critiques, it has provided an intellectual home for critically-minded scholars, a forum for methodological self-reflection, an antidote to the hegemony of liberalism in international law, and a contribution to intellectual diversity in the field of international law.

In taking this puzzle as a starting point, this article seeks to sketch the contours, obstacles and promises of infusing debates in constitutional law with the spirit of TWAIL. Inspired by the work of Jean and John Comaroff on the 'theory from the South', I call this project *Southern constitutionalism*. Rather than offering a straightforward normative, ontological, prudential or political argument in its favour, I will begin by surveying the disciplinary terrain from which Southern constitutionalism has been absent for more than 20 years. In doing that, the gaze of my exploration will be panoramic, but in a way different from bird's eye surveys of existing disciplinary developments. While 'panoramic' scholarly assessments usually appear as the gesture of 'taking stock' of already well-developed disciplinary debates, the mapping exercise in this article occurs even before we have properly identified the 'South' in the map of contemporary constitutionalism. Instead of asking 'where do we go from here?', this article will ask what is at stake in imagining *the South of Western constitutionalism*. With these questions in mind, this article should be understood both as a work of constitutional imagination, and a reconnaissance report.

The conceptual and political morphology of that 'South' – together with its (inter-)disciplinary location and its anticipated weaknesses and strengths – will emerge in the sections that follow. Tracing this imaginative morphology begins in section I by mapping the developments in comparative constitutional law and theory that have, over the last two decades, taken up the disciplinary space within which a Southern constitutionalism might have otherwise grown. In section II, I will develop this picture further, detecting implicit and explicit intra-, meta-, and extra- disciplinary objections to the project of *Southern constitutionalism*. In sections III, IV, V and VI, I delve into these objections in greater detail. In section VII, I take a step back and reflect on the wider cultural frame that would be hospitable to the project of Southern constitutionalism. In sum, what justifies Southern constitutionalism's space under the disciplinary sun is not its physical but its imaginative referent. The 'South' of Southern constitutionalism – capable of coexisting with its intra- and extra-disciplinary peers – is not the 'South' of the developed 'North', but rather the 'South' of the modernist hopes in – and the post-modernist disappointments with – the templates of Western constitutional imagination.

At the moment, such constitutionalism exists only on Mars, whose constitutional system, unshackled from Western constitutional imagination exhibits a 'whole polyarchic array' of institutions:

> the neighborhood boards, the ag board, the water board, the architectural review board, the project review council, the economic coordination group, the crater council to coordinate all these smaller bodies, the global delegates' advisory board – all that network of small management bodies that progressive political theorists had been suggesting in one variation or another for centuries, incorporating aspects of the almost-forgotten guild socialism of Great Britain, Yugoslavian worker management, Mondragon ownership, Kerala land tenure, and so on.[3]

To imagine it in this world will require reaching out towards other sub-disciplines, such as constitutional ethnography and anthropology of sovereignty which, as I will argue later in the text, can offer a healthy dose of critical distance from the organising concepts and binaries that have marked Western constitutional modernity. While such project does not have to abandon the promise of comparative law, in order escape its 'trap of Western positivism' it should also challenge the organising power of the images of sovereignty, popular self-government and foundational constitutionalism.[4] As 'an experiment in synthesis',[5] it would always be 'catachrestic': 'wrested from its proper meaning' as the product of a sovereign people, and always reliant for its legitimacy on '*other* places'.[6]

I. No space for the South in contemporary constitutionalism?

Asking why a TWAIL-like gesture did not emerge in contemporary constitutionalism might appear strange at first. Constitutional, unlike international law, is almost by definition a parochial discipline, preoccupied with institutional and jurisprudential developments within a domestic political environment. Nonetheless, since the early 1990s, developments in the constitutional field have not only disproved this initial intuition, but have provided us with a first possible reason for the conspicuous absence of a TWAIL-like gesture. The same liberal optimism in international law that has given temporary prominence to the so-called 'right to democratic governance'[7] was equally on display in the constitutional field, increasingly preoccupied with the project of constitutional comparison. Catalysed by the fall of communism, the project of *comparative constitutional law* predominantly focused on the doctrinal, functionalist and normative comparison of the jurisprudence, predominantly coming from a select number of well-developed liberal democracies in the Northern hemisphere. While predominantly focused on the courts of the United States, Canada, Germany, Israel and United Kingdom, the field of comparative constitutional law nonetheless co-opted a small number of peripheral perspectives, as constructive, 'friendly' challenges to the template of liberal democratic constitutionalism. For example, while largely ignoring non liberal-democratic constitutional orders, comparative constitutionalists continued to celebrate the jurisprudence of the South African constitutional court as an exemplar of welcome creativity in the arena of socioeconomic rights, otherwise neglected in Western constitutional discourse. Preoccupied with judicial review and, with time, methodological questions about the migration of constitutional ideas comparative constitutionalism has systematically neglected issues such as poverty, imperialism, or socioeconomic emancipation which have otherwise been high on TWAIL's agenda. Though a number of scholars associated with the comparative constitutionalist movement contributed systematic and innovative theoretical reflections on the nature and functions of constitutional government, none of them challenged the liberal-democratic 'software' of Western constitutionalism.

That blind-spot was gradually challenged in two ways. The first was unintentional, indirect, and unsystematic. Since the early 1990s, a number of constitutional scholars unassociated with the comparative constitutionalism movement have used the phenomenon of European integration as an opportunity to rethink the central building blocks of Western constitutional imagination. Though liberal in their political outlook (and unconcerned with the hegemony of Western constitutionalism as such), their narratives of European constitutionalism have nonetheless chipped away at Western ideas of sovereignty[8], or undivided constitutional authority.[9] Over time, the construction of *geographically* adjectival constitutionalisms proliferated. In addition to European, geographical descriptors have over time included, 'African', 'Andean', 'Caribbean', 'Chinese', 'East Asian' and 'South Asian' variants.[10] Though notionally delimiting the scope of Western (or Northern) constitutionalism, only a smaller number of them were implicated in challenging the hegemony of Western constitutional reason. Only recently has the adjectival gesture become fully self-aware of its own counter-hegemonic potential. In providing an account of 'authoritarian' constitutionalism in the context of Singapore, for example, Mark Tushnet explicitly called for the 'pluralizing' of our understanding of constitutionalism. Beyond the simple contribution to 'analytic clarity', the study of non-liberal constitutionalisms might have 'normative attractions' as well.[11]

The second challenge to the liberal-democratic hegemony of comparative constitutional law has been explicit, methodologically radical, and intellectually and organisationally systematic. As Ran Hirschl argued, the project of comparative constitutional law is methodologically problematic as it draws comparisons among a small number of, often arbitrarily selected, case studies.[12] Politically, in focusing on comparison among the constitutional experiences of leading (mostly Western) countries, it suffers from a 'World series syndrome', where its practitioners, like the aficionados of American baseball, treat the object of their fascination – the courts of leading liberal-democracies – as the representation of the relevant constitutional experiences of the entire world.[13] Its methodological and geographical biases expose comparative constitutional law as 'a political act as much as … a legal or jurisprudential one'. [14]As a result, comparative constitutional law should abandon its parochialism, and establish 'a close dialogue with the social sciences', and become reliant on the 'problem-driven, inference-oriented controlled comparisons'.[15]

Nonetheless, the constructive implication of the critique advanced by the proponents of *comparative constitutional studies* did not culminate in a TWAIL-like *politico*-intellectual gesture. Rather, its political contribution alluded to in the language of its ironic superiority of their project against the emergent 'global south' critique of constitutionalism. As Hirschl argued, 'a large-N research design that is often indifferent to the context and particularities of concrete cases rests on a fundamentally "egalitarian" vision that treats the constitutions of the Gambia and of the United States as two data observations of equal weight'.[16]

Though constitutionalism of the global south, advanced in the eponymous edited volume, may be seen as one of the first collaborative echoes of a TWAIL-like gesture in the constitutional field, I hasten to add that the hegemony of Western, liberal-democratic constitutionalism and comparative constitutional law over the last two decades has been challenged by *individual* contributions, whose sensibilities, in varying degrees overlapped with that of TWAIL.[17] Early on, some scholars, such as Graham Walker, proposed a 'non-liberal', or 'mixed' constitutionalism as an antidote to liberal constitutionalism.[18] Starting from a more open-ended understanding of constitutionalism as a system of government where the exercise of power remains structurally and aspirationally limited, Walker's account critiqued the hegemonic pretentions of the ideas of the separation of power and judicial review, offering a principled accommodation of 'illiberal impulses' and political projects. In the years that followed, such principled revisions of constitutionalist vocabulary have been advanced under the rubric of 'new',[19] 'societal'[20] or 'transformative' constitutionalism.[21] Others, such as Upendra Baxi, articulated constitutionalism as a 'site of state developing practices', charging modern constitutionalism with the suppression of 'lived and generationally embodied histories of collective hurt' of those in the periphery.[22] For Baxi, the 'full potential' of comparative constitutional law can only be accomplished by transcending the 'prescriptive, admonitory knowledges' on which it otherwise relies.[23] Instead of 'Habermasian/Rawlsian essentials', comparative constitutional law should embrace 'imaginary conversations that accord equal discursive dignity to all constitutional discourses'.[24] Baxi's forceful challenge to Western ideological biases, implicit in the project of comparative constitutional law, has only very recently materialised in the collaborative project of 'constitutionalism of the global south'. Even in that case, however, the scope of 'global south' critique was fairly limited. Though nominally far-reaching, 'constitutionalism of the global south' neither offered a different account of constitutionalism, nor did it challenge 'constitutional knowledges' of Western modernity.[25]

Rather than using 'global south' as a privileged point of entry for corroding the hegemony of the constitutional imagination of *Western* constitutionalism – as the ideological frame that *spans* both global south and global North – the main purpose of constitutionalism of the global south has been to raise sensibility to hegemonic patterns of production and dissemination of legal knowledge, between the developed intellectual cores and their peripheries.[26]

II. Southern constitutionalism: intra-, extra- and meta- disciplinary challenges

As in the lives of individuals, timing is equally important in the fortunes of intellectual movements. In the mid-1990s, the identity and the prestige of the field of international law was stable enough to provide an identifiable disciplinary rallying point for a concerted and durable counter-hegemonic intervention by successive waves of TWAIL-ers and their fellow travellers. In contrast, one might argue that a TWAIL-like collective gesture in the constitutional field would arrive at the ((cross-)disciplinary) party at 4am: it would enter the room not only at the moment when the liberal-democratic bias of comparative constitutional law had already been demasked by the empirically-oriented comparative constitutional studies, but also at the moment when the enthusiasm for constitutionalism as the organising frame of government had already diminished among constitutional theorists themselves. Finally, it would attempt to join the party at the moment when the projects from the external fields questioned the sensibility of taking the transformative capacity of constitutionalism seriously. In other words, a 'constitutional' TWAIL would have to confront intra-, meta- and extra-disciplinary challenges. Let me address them in turn.

While recognising the contribution of the 'global south critique' in demasking the 'deep liberal bent' of comparative constitutional law, Hirschl questioned the appropriateness of the geographical referent of 'global south'. Depending on the criterion used – the experience of colonialism, the comparative influence in existing constitutionalist debates, the level of economic development – different polities, irrespective of their geographical location can be subsumed either under the rubric of global north or global south.[27] As a result, the problematic analytical binary between the north and the south must inadvertently result in a theoretically impoverished project, incapable of offering a 'coherent alternative to the liberal-democratic model of constitutionalism'. 'More than anything else', Hirschl concludes, 'the global constitutional south is essentially the global constitutional "non-north"'.[28] Later in the text I will return to the question of whether or how a constitutionalism *from* the South, should aspire to offer a 'coherent alternative to liberal-democratic constitutionalism'. At this point, however, it is worth noting that such a project is made more difficult by the intra-disciplinary mutations in the constitutional field that are occurring at the *meta* level. The prognostications of the 'twilight of constitutionalism'[29] and calls to move 'beyond constitutionalism'[30] have been accompanied by self-doubt among constitutional theorists about the identity and the object of their reflection.[31] Even those who have detected a 'remarkable revival' of constitutional theory,[32] have themselves lost faith in the emancipatory potential of constitutional imagination.[33]

Intra-disciplinary critiques and meta-disciplinary self-doubt complicate the pursuit of the 'South' in the field of constitutional law. These complications are compounded by *extra-disciplinary* challenges from the fields of international and transnational law, which – in addition to echoing the critiques offered by intra-disciplinary detractors of constitutional TWAIL – also (implicitly) challenge the political wisdom of expending intellectual energy in pursuing it. For example, in addition to arguing that north and south depend on 'where you stand',[34] David Kennedy suggested that critically-minded scholars abandon their faith in the emancipatory promise of constitutionalism, and instead focus on the ways in which the interplay between international political economy, law and politics structures contingent patterns of political and socioeconomic domination.[35] Similarly, Peer Zumbansen has asked critically-minded scholars to resist the 'constitutional itch'[36] and instead devote attention to 'captur[ing] the theoretical and conceptual challenges arising in a context … very different from that of a (Western) nation state, marked by evolving conceptions of the state, the rule of law, notions of the separation of powers and a system of normative hierarchy, with some form of constitutional text or order at the pinnacle of the pyramid'.[37]

When approached together, the challenges to Southern constitutionalism that come from intra-, supra- and extra- disciplinary perspectives cluster around four more substantive objections. The first concerns the credibility of its geographical positioning. The second questions its under-argued political commitments. The third doubts its theoretical distinctness, and the fourth is suspicious about its practical productivity. In the following sections I will answer them in turn, and in the process sharpen my initial understanding of Southern constitutionalism.

III. From placing to gazing: the ex-centric 'South' and its politics

Attempts to sharply delineate the location of the South in the map of the world are problematic not only for those who don't think that the label of the south is theoretically or politically productive, but also for those who think that it is. As Jean and John Comaroff argued, 'a number of nation-states of the South, far from being marginal to the global economy, are central to it'.[38] Within such global economy, 'the working classes of Euro-America, [are] situated ever more at southern margins', and 'southern capital buttresses, even owns, many signature Euro-American businesses'.[39] Similarly, as B. S. Chimni argued, the location of the 'Third World' does not need to be 'dogmatically affirmed'[40] to usefully bring into conversation 'a plurality of practices of collective resistance' that struggle for 'a modicum of welfare to long suffering peoples of the third and first worlds'[41] and pursue 'a set of strategies directed towards creating a world order based on social justice'.[42] Finally, Siba Grovogui has argued that Global South

> is not a directional designation or a point due south from a fixed north. It is a symbolic designation meant to capture the semblance of cohesion that emerged when former colonial entities engaged in political projects of decolonization and moved toward the realization of a postcolonial international order.[43]

As 'symbolic designation with political implications', it captures 'the objectives of equality, freedom, and mutuality in the form of a new ethos of power, … subjectivity … and responsibility to self and others in an international order free of the institutional legacies of colonialism'.[44] Finally, the idea of Global South entails:

contingent and evolving agendas that are internally consistent. These agendas include the pursuit of new social, cultural, and economic orders as well as norms of universality, international morality, law, and ethics that markedly differ from those emerging from colonial rule.[45]

In following Chimni and Grovogui, we might be tempted to simply imagine 'the South' as rhetorical shorthand for a particular set of political preoccupations, which are in principle divorced from any stable spatial referent. Doing so, however, would be problematic for two reasons. First, we would lose an opportunity to articulate the theoretical, and not only the political distinctness of the project of Southern constitutionalism. In order not to lose that opportunity, we must redefine the meaning of 'South': away from the name for the result of an empirical observation ('Look at the South over there!'), and towards understanding it as a name for a particular form of gazing at constitutional phenomena. As Comaroff and Comaroff argued, the importance of South lies in its 'ex-centricity: in the angle of vision it provides us, from which to estrange our world in order better to make sense of its present and future'.[46] As a result, Southern constitutionalism, like any other '*[t]heory from the South*' is not necessarily 'about the theories of people who may be wholly or partially of the south', but rather 'about the effect of the south *itself* on theory'.[47]

The second problem that would come with following Chimni's and Grovogui's approach to the relationship between spatial referents and political aspirations is that it neglects the fact that a wider meta-political frame provides the meaning to them both. What enables the critical valorisation of constitutional experiences in the polities neglected by comparative constitutional law is not simply a sensitivity to 'legacies of colonialism' (Grovogui) or commitment to a 'modicum of welfare' (Chimni). As a theoretically self-aware project that engages in an ex-centric gaze at the multiplicity of neglected constitutional experiences world-wide, Southern constitutionalism would also have to negotiate its relationship with the background meta-political assumption that sustains that multiplicity, which is the object of its gaze: the frame of global political pluralism.

IV. What kind of pluralism? Between three worlds and two cardinal points

This brings us to the second challenge to the project of Southern constitutionalism: the under-determined content of its political commitments, which in turn demands two specific answers. First, how *thick* should Southern constitutionalism's understanding of the pluralist meta-frame be? Second, how *strong* should its commitment to it be?

The first question presents itself as the result of the fact that global political pluralism has different normative registers which are not necessarily compatible. Constitutional orders of nation-states may reflect an underlying commitment to an organising frame of national pluralism. However, there are a number of constitutional projects – both territorial and non-territorial – whose aim is not national, but *socioeconomic* emancipation. When the two collide, which one should Southern constitutionalism privilege as a matter of its baseline ethical commitment? Without a normative theory to come to its rescue, and without a built-in visual zoom telling it which national and sociopolitical demands to privilege in concrete cases, Southern constitutionalism would perforce remain agnostic about the demands of Maoist rebels in India, Zapatista insurgents in Mexico, Miskito Indians in Nicaragua, or rich Santa Cruz secessionists in Bolivia.

In Grovogui's account, the question of normative dissonance among different pluralist registers is concealed under an optimistic vision where '[t]he Global South is ... characterised by contingent and evolving agendas that are internally consistent'.[48] Not all have been this optimistic. For Hardt and Negri, for example, attempts to achieve constitutional emancipation through the vocabulary of popular sovereignty have today 'become all but incommunicable'.[49] The absence of agreement on the specific normative content of global political pluralism will, as Gayatri Chakravorty Spivak argued, make 'nationalist-left ... and globalist nationalist ... compute "good" and "bad" differently'.[50] While the answer to the question how to order registers of pluralism might be productively pursued in normative theory,[51] in this article I leave this question open. As an imagined 'school of thought', a meta-politically self-aware Southern constitutionalism should leave enough space for 'creative internal contestations' about desirable or possible constellations of global political pluralism.[52]

This brings us to the second question. If Southern constitutionalism must rely on a certain commitment to the meta-political frame of global pluralism, how strong should that commitment be? On the one hand, the very fact that there are three worlds and two, politically salient, cardinal points suggests the world's (or globe's) irreducible plurality. On the other hand, nothing in those names implicates the perpetuation of global political pluralism that would *maintain* the identity of either the Third World or Global South. Rather than dignifying the political experiences of under-developed, oppressed or peripheral countries as co-equal members of the international community, both concepts can dignify the imaginations of radical political agency whose aim is to politically *remake* the entire world and *transcend* the perpetuation of (semi-)peripheral political subjectivities.

One of the best examples of this radical open-endedness is the text that introduced the concept of the Third World into the sphere of political ideas. Proposed by French geographer Alfred Sauvy in his 1952 article, 'Three Worlds, One Planet', the Third World denoted not only the aggregate of under-developed countries fighting for decolonisation, but was also described by Sauvy as a neglected political reality that complicates the political competition between the worlds of Western capitalism and Eastern communism.[53] More importantly, in choosing the name 'Third World', Sauvy explicitly gestures to the canonical text of constitutional theory, the revolutionary pamphlet of Emmanuel Joseph Sieyès, 'What is the Third Estate?', which, at the turn of 1788–1789, provided intellectual justification for the French revolution.[54] Paraphrasing Sieyès, Sauvy concluded his adaptation of the vocabulary of the Third Estate with an ominous prediction: 'For after it has been ignored Third World, exploited, scorned as the Third Estate, wants, too, to be something'.[55]

A more radical interpretation of Sauvy's gesture reveals itself, however, by going back to Sieyes's original text. In *What is the Third Estate*?, the Third Estate was already 'everything' for Sieyès; its ambition to become 'something' could not – and was not – interpreted modestly, as a demand by the Third Estate for mere political *equality*. Rather, that 'something' was much more radical: the existence of the Third Estate, as the embodiment of the entire Nation, as the manifestation of its constituent power. Transposed to the vocabulary of Third *World*, this conclusion would remain equally radical: the term Third World would denote not a demand for political equality – among existing states – but rather the recognition of the constituent power of those most numerous, downtrodden and excluded – the global plebs, if you will – to reconstitute the world *in its totality*, unconstrained by any particular template of global political pluralism. As a result, the hidden rhetorical implications of Sauvy's programmatic text should guide us to an the answer to our second question. The immanent political *surpassability* of the promise of Third World (or Global South) prevents Southern constitutionalism from committing too strongly to a vision of a world organised around co-equal sovereign units. While political plurality will remain an irreducible fact of any political organisation of the world, global political *pluralism* – as a particular form of its ethico-political affirmation – will only partially and contingently overlap with the project of Southern constitutionalism.

V. Material constitutionalism, constitutional imagination and the anthropologies of sovereignty

The third charge that looms over Southern constitutionalism is the absence of its theoretical distinctness. Between the small-N doctrinal and normative approach of comparative constitutional *law*, and large-N empirical approach of comparative constitutional studies, it is not immediately clear what distinct methodology or theoretical approach could be embraced by Southern constitutionalism in order to escape Hirschl's charge of being 'essentially the global constitutional "non-north"', and nothing else.[56] The answer to that charge was already implicitly offered by Baxi, who, more than a decade and half ago, argued that a counter-hegemonic 'comparative constitutionalism needs to transform itself into constitutional ethnography, or the anthropology of power-fields'.[57] For Baxi, in reaching out to ethnography and anthropology, Southern constitutionalism would be able to ask new questions:

> [W]hat patterns of play(competitive politics) and war (violent social annihilation) stand combined as codeterminants of lived histories of power and the received notions of constitutionalism? ... [H]ow does one relate the operations of markets ... to constitutional development, and changing notions of constitutionalism underlying it ... given the dominance/hegemony of a solitary superpower? ... [H]ow do we fashion narratives of social suffering from a subaltern perspective on constitutionalism?[58]

At the moment, none of these questions can be posed from within either a more normatively inflected comparative constitutional *law* or a more empirically oriented comparative constitutional *studies*. However, beyond setting the stage for a project that we could tentatively call comparative constitutional emancipation, Southern constitutionalism's engagement with ethnography and anthropology would enable it to offer a contextual intervention in the register of constitutional *theory*.

For example, is it really the case, as Western constitutional theorists argue, that we cannot imagine struggles for political emancipation without couching them in the vocabulary of a constituent 'we', the first person plural?[59] In contrast to nearly all contemporary debates about the meaning of constituent power of the people in the West, Danilyn Rutherford's ethnographic work on Papuans' struggle for independence has shown that Papuans have no trouble demanding a radical change in their political status by invoking the *third person singular*, not the first person plural. Instead of asserting their demands as 'we, the people of Papua', they simply claim that 'Papua deserves independence'.[60] By showing how the political project can be defended, demanded and performed at an imaginative distance from oneself, Rutherford's work opens new possibilities of thinking about the relationship between nationhood and popular sovereignty.

Equally, as David Graeber argued, the Schmittian distinction between friend and enemy, which otherwise continues to fascinate much of Western constitutional theory, has no purchase in the regions of Africa where there is 'no fundamental difference in the relation between a sovereign and his people, and a sovereign and his enemies'.[61] Sovereign power emerges not as the result of war, nor from an alienation of the original freedom as Western social contract theorists liked to imagine, but through an unending 'constitutive war'.[62] As

Graeber reports, very often 'raids or rain random gunfire on "enemy villages" … actually turned out to be inhabited by the king's own subjects, [so] there is no fundamental difference in the relation between a sovereign and his people, and a sovereign and his enemies'.[63] In contrast to the attempts of Western constitutional imagination to sharply delineate between the inside and the outside, 'there is almost never a clear line between what we'd now call "war" and what we'd now call "banditry," "terrorism," "raids," "massacres," "duels," "insurrections," or "police actions"'.[64] Unlike Western constitutional imagination, which does its best to suppress awareness of the fragility and tenuousness of the inside/outside binary and seeks to reduce the 'credibility gap' generated by the governors' claim to authority, Nilotic constitutional imagination acts as a reminder of that fragility.[65]

The work in anthropology of state and sovereignty usefully estranges us from the ways in which we think about the foundational conceptual building blocks of Western constitutional theory in the abstract. It also compels us to question their correspondence with constitutional reality. Both in the notional 'North' and 'South', nation-states are increasingly unwilling or unsuccessful in suppressing political challenges to the paradigm of popular sovereignty, on which they notionally rely. In a number of European countries, religious communities, are 'closing themselves off to the world and its interventions, settling disputes, enacting sociality, managing their public finances and negotiating their own moral economies', with little or no influence from the wider state.[66] In Latin America, a state's power is oftentimes privatised and 'show[s] up completely unannounced … embodied in highly unorthodox forms'.[67] Instead of being reliant on the symbolical forms of popular sovereignty, the authority of the private statal substitutes is the result of 'of a continual enactment of very concrete techniques of rule'.[68]

Given the hollowing out of the idea of popular sovereignty both in the North and in the South, the ex-centric approach to constitutional imagination allows us to ask questions that otherwise don't appear on the radar of Western constitutional imagination. In addition to Baxi's questions, we could pose new ones: Who are the intended beneficiaries of a narrative construction of political authority? Who are its potential and actual losers? How are they distributed spatiotemporally? The point, I hasten to add, is not simply to deflate the universalistic aspirations of Western constitutionalism, or simply to record the political technologies and imaginaries that exist at variance from it. To exist as a theoretical gesture distinct both from current approaches to constitutionalism in the juridical field, *and* from the anthropologies of state and sovereignty, Southern constitutionalism's emphasis on the diversity of political technologies of rule and the variety of constitutional imaginaries must be implicated in a purposive project.

VI. Southern constitutionalism and experiments in emancipation

This brings us to the final suspicion looming over the project of Southern constitutionalism: its allegedly dubious political productivity. As we saw earlier in the article, these charges come both from within the field of constitutional law, as well as from without. What unites them is an overarching view of the task of critically-minded legal scholars: to *demask* and to *describe* the larger legal, economic and political structures that frustrate projects of socio-political emancipation, rather than perpetuate a futile hope that political emancipation can be facilitated through a new constitutional imagination, or institutional design.

The first problem with these views is that they neglect the fact that Western constitutional imagination – even if one believed that it lost its grip on constitutional reality – continues to exist as a political resource. One which can be mobilised by powerful states to shame, cajole, seduce, or disenchant the actors who wish to pursue radical political change at variance from the templates of Western constitutionalism. In confronting Western constitutional imagination with ex-centric constitutional experiences both from the notional 'North' and the 'South', Southern constitutionalism would contribute to the counter-hegemonic pluralisation of the idea of constitutionalism in general. At the very least, as Mark Tushnet suggested, such a pluralised account of constitutionalism 'may contribute to analytic clarity in law as it did in political science'.[69] In doing so, Western constitutionalists may discover that there are some 'normative attractions [to it], at least in nations where the alternative of authoritarianism is more likely than that of liberal democracy'.[70] Furthermore, as Michael Rustin and Doreen Massey argued:

> [f]orms of government that may not be democratic according to the norms and procedures of western constitutionalism, may nevertheless have their own means of taking account of the wishes and interests of their citizens, and may be more responsible, for example in regard to the crisis of global warming, than some capitalist nations.[71]

More radically than Tushnet, then, the ex-centric gaze of Southern constitutionalism might also undermine the sharp differences between liberal-democracy/authoritarianism, and democratic/technocratic government. By divorcing constitutionalism from Western constitutional imagination, strong CGS might productively estrange believers in constitutionalism from their Western constitutionalist assumptions, pressing them to ask new questions hidden behind the vocabulary of popular sovereignty, the separation of powers and the rule of law. To do so productively would also require us also move past the 'adjectival' constitutionalisms I mentioned in the introduction, which, in mounting *limited* spatio-ideological challenges to Western constitutionalism, actually help perpetuate its hegemony. Beyond the adjective 'Chinese' or 'socialist', there is a larger question of meritocracy, the selection of political talent, the vigour of government, and the quality control of political decisions. Beyond the adjective 'Bolivarian' there is the question of the distribution of democratic responsiveness across space and time. Both adjectival qualifiers conceal deeper conceptual challenges to Western ideas of constitutional self-government.[72]

Irrespective of the recent turn of fortune for the Bolivarian revolution in Venezuela, the contrast between the ways in which the American and Venezuelan constitutions deal with the questions local self-government is highly instructive. Under the US Constitution, local governments are little more than 'convenient agencies for exercising … such powers as may be entrusted to them' by the state. As a result, 'the state may modify or withdraw all such power, may take without compensation such property, hold it for itself, or vest it with other agencies, expand or contract the territorial area, unite the whole or part of it with another municipality, repeal the charter and destroy the corporation … with or without the consent of the citizens, or even against their protest'.[73] In contrast, the Venezuelan constitution exhibits a high degree of spatial responsiveness to grassroots demands, guaranteeing 'citizen participation into the process of defining and managing public affairs and monitoring and evaluating the results achieved' at the municipal level (Art 168.) At that level of government, individual municipalities can be reconfigured based on 'neighbourhood or community initiative', with an aim of providing 'for the decentralisation of the administration of the Municipality, citizen participation and the providing of better public services' (Art 173). If we stayed within the parameters of Western constitutional imagination, which conjoins the exercise of popular sovereignty with representative democracy and multiparty elections, we wouldn't be able to chart a richer morphology of *formal* democratic responsiveness that emerges once we estrange ourselves from the hegemony of the framing devices of Western constitutionalism. Nor would we be able to contrast it with the abomination of humanitarian crises that 'financial martial laws' inflicted on some American municipalities, all under the aegis of liberal-democratic, popular self-government.[74]

By the same token, the ex-centric perspective of Southern constitutionalism also contributes to the accentuation of real life socioeconomic scandals that Western constitutional thought keeps suppressed. Beyond skewing our glance at the pockets of democratic commitments in non-liberal democratic constitutional orders, Western constitutionalism also suppresses the factual irresponsiveness of Western liberal democracies to the notional 'will of the people'. In the context of the world's largest democracy, the United States, these claims are not new in *political science*. As Elmer Schattschneider famously argued, the people is not sovereign, but semi-sovereign. Behind the unitary *vox populi* there is a 'heavenly chorus', which, irrespective of its diversity, nonetheless sings with 'an upper class accent'.[75] More recent empirical research demonstrates an even more dramatic and systematic disregard for the political preferences of ordinary people. According to Martin Gilens and Benjamin Page, 'the preferences of the average American appear to have only a minuscule, near-zero, statistically non-significant impact upon public policy'.[76] For Gilens and Page:

> [w]hen a majority of citizens disagrees with economic elites or with organized interests, they generally lose. Moreover, because of the strong status quo bias built into the U.S. political system, even when fairly large majorities of Americans favor policy change, they generally do not get it.[77]

Neither the project of transnational law (Zumbansen) nor a polit-economic approach to international law (Kennedy) can fulfil this task. In being focused on the empirical comparison of constitutions around the world, the project of comparative constitutional studies cannot do that either, irrespective of its sympathies for the perspective of the global south. As a result, calling us to resist the 'constitutional itch' in spite of the complementarity of those projects should then be justified not on the alleged analytical superiority of non-constitutionalist lenses, but rather on the *political return on intellectual investment* on behalf of the approaches that aspire to supplant it. In other words, calls to rebalance theoretical energies away from constitutional templates need to be backed up: how was, does, or will, the diversity of struggles for emancipation in practice *be aided* by the shift in focus, away from the constitutionalist analytic, and towards the study of the crumbling public-private divide, global value chains, hybrid legal regimes or the legal frames of international political economy?

Was the constitutional struggle for socioeconomic emancipation in Bolivia, Ecuador or Venezuela usefully aided by the theoretical articulation of a new brand of non-liberal democratic *Bolivarian* constitutionalism? Would that struggle have been more successful had it relied on the insights of critical international or transnational legal studies? Is it even possible to make such judgments? While critically-minded international and transnational legal scholars have been right to undermine the hegemony of constitutionalism in the study of the contemporary legal and political conjuncture of the early twenty-first century, heeding their demand to *further* demote the constitutionalist frame would call for proof of the comparative effectiveness of the anti-constitutionalist agenda in legal scholarship.

VII. Excursus: metamodernism as the cultural frame of Southern constitutionalism

Aware of the historical defeats of projects which sought to design large-scale territorial spaces for sociopolitical emancipation in the second half of the XXth century, Southern constitutionalism is inescapably marked by a particular cultural sensitivity. In dignifying the projects that would seek to echo this gesture in a new political conjuncture, it would work in the shadow not only of the *moral* anxieties of liberal democrats, but also the matching *strategic* anxieties of post-Marxists and radical democrats. For Hardt and Negri, as the most influential among the latter, emancipatory politics based on the idea of popular sovereignty within a discrete constitutional order 'misidentifies and thus masks the enemy'.[78] For both, '(re)establish[ing] local identities that are in some sense outside and protected against the global flows of capital and Empire' is as pointless as it is historically discredited.[79]

The tectonic changes in international finance in the 1970s and 1980s contributed not only to the 'tendential destruction of "progressive constitutionalism" in the Western 'core',[80] but also to the catastrophic implosions of what were once seen as alternatives to Western constitutionalism. In then-Yugoslavia, IMF-imposed austerity policies in the early 1980s undermined not only the ideological alternative to liberal democratic constitutionalism (socialist self-management), but also contributed to the large-scale political violence that followed.[81] With this in mind, one might argue that it is simply too hopeful (if not naïve) to think that the resilience of, say, a Venezuelan 'new geometry of power', its local deliberative democracy and its Bolivarian constitutionalism in the early twenty-first century, could ever critically depend on the ingeniousness of these ideas, and not on the structural, external constraints of international economy, or the will of powerful states. In other words, while Southern constitutionalism has its own dignity vis-à-vis projects of demasking, its resilience as a project would depend on its keen awareness of the emotive nuances that animate it in its refusal to capitulate before the projects that reframe legal and political phenomena through the lens of transnational law or international political economy.

Such affective disposition is best captured by a cultural frame that is neither modernist nor post-modernist, but *metamodernist*. While it shares the 'hermeneutic of suspicion'[82] with TWAIL, a metamodernist, ex-centric Southern constitutionalism also transcends it. In rejecting both the 'century of modernist ideological naivety [as well as] the cynical insincerity' of post-modernism, its orientation is 'nostalgi[c] as much as [it is] futurist'.[83] In giving dignity to the discrete constitutional experiences of the countries of the global south – inspired by the limited successes of political projects in the twentieth century, with which they bear a family resemblance – a metamodernist Southern constitutionalism carries a residual optimism about the potential contribution of a more self-aware constitutional design to a variety of projects of political emancipation. In paying more attention to external sociopolitical conjuncture, such Southern constitutionalism would exhibit 'pragmatic romanticism unhindered by ideological anchorage' of the overarching ideologies of liberalism, communism, or nationalism. Its metamodernism would be marked by a spirit of oscillation, 'the mercurial condition between and beyond irony and sincerity, naivety and knowingness, relativism and truth, optimism and doubt, in pursuit of a plurality of disparate and elusive horizons' of political emancipation.[84] In pursuing those horizons, CGS would continue to oscillate around its meta-political gravity centre: global political pluralism.

Conclusion

To meet the charges of geographical naivety, disciplinary sterility and self-defeating political partisanship – this ex-centricity had to be defined not in relation to the physical location of 'the West', but rather in relation to the disciplinary topography of contemporary constitutionalism and its adjacent disciplines. From the perspective of *that* map, Southern constitutionalism's ex-centricity is further defined by three sets of relations. First, it would be ex-centric in relation to the contemporary ways of doing comparative constitutional law, which are either doctrinal and normative (comparative constitutional law) or empirical and quantitative (comparative constitutional studies) in their orientation. Second, Southern constitutionalism is ex-centric in its qualitative focus on political phenomena, which have so far eluded the label 'constitutional', either because of disciplinary, ethical, or geographical considerations. Rather than exploring the formal manifestations of constitutionalism in practice (constitutional texts and constitutional jurisprudence) Southern constitutionalism is more interested in *material* constitutionalism, understood as the sum of political technologies that enable a large-scale, territorially-based political project to endure over time. Third, Southern constitutionalism is also ex-centric in relation to Western constitutional imagination. Rather than taking for granted the diffusion of its central building blocks, such as popular sovereignty, self-determination and constituent power, it is more interested in the local mutations of Western constitutional imagination. Consequently – fourth – Southern constitutionalism is ex-centric in relation to the absence of explicit political aspiration in existing approaches to constitutionalism. Rather than being seen as an (implicit) vehicle for dignifying the ideology of liberal-democratic constitutionalism (comparative constitutional law), or as a vehicle for the augmentation of constitutional *knowledge* as such (comparative constitutional studies), Southern constitutionalism is a project whose aspiration is to contribute to a wider study of *comparative constitutional emancipation*.

Disclosure statement

No potential conflict of interest was reported by the author.

Notes

1. For the discussion of how best to describe TWAIL see Okafor, "Critical Third World Approaches to International Law."
2. Bonilla-Maldonaldo, *Constitutionalism of the Global South*.
3. Robinson, *Blue Mars*, 433.
4. Bussani, "Comparative Law Beyond the Trap of Western Positivism."
5. Robinson, *Blue Mars.*, 433.

6. Spivak, "Constitutions and Culture Studies." 144. For an example of such catachrestic constitutionalism, see Chatterjee, "Introduction: Postcolonial legalism."
7. Franck, "The Emerging Right to Democratic Governance."
8. Weiler, *The Constitution of Europe*.
9. Walker, "The Idea of Constitutional Pluralism."
10. Oklopcic, "Three Arenas of Struggle."
11. Tushnet, "Authoritarian Constitutionalism."
12. Hirschl, *Comparative Matters.*
13. Ibid., 16.
14. Ibid., 282.
15. Ibid., 223.
16. Ibid.
17. Bonilla-Maldonaldo, *Constitutionalism of the Global South*.
18. Walker, "The Idea of Nonliberal Constitutionalism."
19. Graeber, "The Divine Kingship of the Shilluk."
20. Anderson, "Societal Constitutionalism, Social Movements".
21. De Sousa Santos, "Transformative."
22. Baxi, "Constitutionalism as a Site of State-Formative Practices," 1209.
23. Ibid., 1210.
24. Ibid.
25. Anderson, "Societal Constitutionalism, Social Movements."
26. Bonilla-Maldonaldo, *Constitutionalism of the Global South*, 12.
27. Hirschl, *Comparative Matters*, 17.
28. Ibid., 219.
29. Dobner and Loughlin, *The Twilight of Constitutionalism*.
30. Krisch, *Beyond Constitutionalism*.
31. Barber, *The Constitutional State*, 2.
32. Loughlin, "Constitutional Theory," 183.
33. Loughlin, "The Constitutional Imagination," 18.
34. Kennedy, "Law and the Political Economy of the World," 7.
35. Kennedy, "The Mystery of Global Governance."
36. Zumbansen, "The Incurable Constitutional Itch."
37. Zumbansen, "Law and Society and the Politics of Relevance," 4.
38. Chimni, "Third World Approaches to International Law," 5.
39. Ibid.
40. Ibid.
41. Ibid., 6.
42. Ibid., 27.
43. Grovogui, "A Revolution Nevertheless," 176.
44. Ibid.
45. Ibid.
46. Comaroff and Comaroff, "Theory from the South: Or, how Euro-America is evolving toward Africa," 127.
47. Comaroff and Comaroff, "Theory from the South: A Rejoinder."
48. Grovogui, "A Revolution Nevertheless," 177.
49. Hardt and Negri, *Empire*, 54.
50. Spivak, "Nationalism and the Imagination," 87.
51. Isiksel, "Global Legal Pluralism as Fact and Norm."
52. Okafor, "Critical Third World Approaches to International Law."
53. Sauvy, "Trois Mondes, Une Planète."
54. Ibid.
55. Ibid.
56. Hirschl, *Comparative Matters*, 219.
57. Baxi, "Constitutionalism as a Site of State-Formative Practices," 1209.

58. Ibid.
59. Lindahl, "Possibility, Actuality, Rupture."
60. Rutherford, "Why Papua Wants Freedom," 361.
61. Graeber, "The Divine Kingship of the Shilluk," 55.
62. Ibid., 54.
63. Ibid., 55.
64. Ibid., 54.
65. For the role of constitutional imagination in narrowing down 'credibility gap' see Loughlin, "The Constitutional Imagination."
66. Comaroff J. and Comaroff J. 2009, 52.
67. Krupa, "State by Proxy: Privatised Government in the Andes."
68. Ibid.
69. Tushnet, "Authoritarian Constitutionalism," 396.
70. Ibid., 397.
71. Rustin and Massey, "Rethinking the Neoliberal World Order,"127.
72. Weiwei, *China Wave*, 61.
73. *Hunter v. Pittsburgh*, 207 U.S. 161, 179 (1907).
74. Chad Selweski, "Michigan Senate Passes Emergency Manager Bills," *Macomb Daily Tribune*, 10 March 2011. http://www.dailytribune.com/article/2011/03/10/news/303099968/michigan-senate-passes-emergency-manager-bills
75. Schattschneider, *The Semisovereign People*, 34.
76. Gilens and Page, "Testing Theories of American Politics," 576.
77. Ibid.
78. Hardt and Negri, *Empire*, 47.
79. Ibid., 45.
80. Brenner et al., "New Constitutionalism and Variegated Neo-liberalisation," 135.
81. Orford, *Reading Humanitarian Intervention*, 13.
82. Sunter, "TWAIL."
83. Metamodernist Manifesto http://www.metamodernism.org/
84. Ibid.

Bibliography

Anderson, G. "Societal Constitutionalism, Social Movements, and Constitutionalism from Below." *Indiana Journal of Global Legal Studies* 20, no. 2 (2013): 881–906.

Barber, N. *The Constitutional State*. Oxford: Oxford University Press, 2012.

Baxi, U. "Constitutionalism as a Site of State-Formative Practices." *Cardozo Law Review* 21, no. 4 (2000): 1183–1210.

Bonilla-Maldonaldo, D. *Constitutionalism of the Global South*. Cambridge: Cambridge University Press, 2013.

Brenner, N., J. Peck, and N. Theodore. "New constitutionalism and variegated neo-liberalization." In *New Constitutionalism and World Order*, edited by S. Gill and C. Cutler, 126–142. Cambridge: Cambridge University Press, 2014.

Bussani, M. "Comparative Law Beyond the Trap of Western Positivism." In *New Frontiers of Comparative Law*, edited by Cheng Tong-lo and Salvatore Mancuso. Hong Kong. Lexis-Nexis, 2013.

Chatterjee, P. "Introduction: Postcolonial Legalism." *Comparative Studies of South Asia, Africa and the Middle East* 34, no. 2 (2014): 224–227.

Chimni, B. S. "Third World Approaches to International Law: A Manifesto." *International Community Law Review* 8 (2006): 3–27.

Comaroff, J., and J. Comaroff. "Reflections on the Anthropology of Law, Governance and Sovereignty." In *Rules of Law and Laws of Ruling: On the Governance of Law*, edited by Franz von Benda-Beckman, Kebeet von Benda-Beckman and Julia Eckert. Farnham: Ashgate, 2009.

Comaroff, J., and J. Comaroff. "Theory from the South: Or, how Euro-America is evolving toward Africa." *Anthropological Forum*.22, no. 2 (2012): 113–131. 127.

Comaroff, J., and J. Comaroff.'Theory from the South: A Rejoinder." *Cultural Anthropology* (2012).http://www.culanth.org/fieldsights/273-theory-from-the-south-arejoinder.

De Sousa Santos, B. "Why Has Cuba Become a Difficult Problem for the Left?." *Latin American Studies* 36, no. 3 (2009): 43–53.

Dobner, P., and M. Loughlin. *The Twilight of Constitutionalism*. Oxford: Oxford University Press, 2010.

Franck, T. "The Emerging Right to Democratic Governance." *American Journal of International Law* 86, no.1 (1992): 46–91.

Gilens, M., and B. Page. "Testing Theories of American Politics: Elites, Interest Groups, and Average Citizens." *Perspectives on Politics* 12, no 3 (2014): 564–581. 576.

Gill, S., and D. Graeber. "The divine kingship of the Shilluk: On violence, utopia, and the human condition, or, elements for an archaeology of sovereignty." *Journal of Ethnographic Theory* 1, no. 1 (2011): 1–62.

Grovogui, S. "A Revolution Nevertheless: Global South in International Relations." *The Global South* 5, no. 1 (2011): 175–190.

Hardt, M., and A. Negri. *Empire*. Cambridge: Harvard University Press, 2001.

Hirschl, R. *Comparative Matters: The Renaissance of Comparative Constitutional Law*. Oxford: Oxford University Press, 2014.

Isiksel, T. "Global legal pluralism as fact and norm." *Global Constitutionalism* 2, no. 02 (2013): 160–195.

Kennedy, D. "Law and the Political Economy of the World." *Leiden Journal of International Law* 26 (2013): 1–43.

Kennedy, D. "The Mystery of Global Governance." *Ohio Northern University Law Review* 34 (2008): 827.

Krisch, N. *Beyond Constitutionalism: The Pluralist Structure of Postnational Law*. Oxford: Oxford University Press, 2010.

Krupa, C. "State by Proxy: Privatized Government in the Andes." *Comparative Studies in Society and History* 52, no. 02 (2010): 319–350.

Lindahl, H. "Possibility, Actuality, Rupture: Constituent Power and the Ontology of Change." *Constellations* 22, no. 2 (2015): 163–174.

Loughlin, M. "Constitutional Theory: A 25th Anniversary Essay." *Oxford Journal of Legal Studies* 25, no. 2 (2005): 183–202.

Loughlin, M. "The Constitutional Imagination." *Modern Law Review* 78, no. 1 (2015): 1–25.

"Metamodernist Manifesto" (2011).http://www.metamodernism.org/.

Okafor, O. "Critical Third World Approaches to International Law (TWAIL): Theory, Methodology, or Both?" *International Community Law Review* 10 (2008): 371–378.

Oklopcic, Z. "Three arenas of struggle: A contextual approach to the constituent power of 'the people'." *Global Constitutionalism* 3, no. 02 (2014): 200–235.

Orford, A. *Reading Humanitarian Intervention: Human Rights and the Use of Force in International Law*. Cambridge: Cambridge University Press, 2003.

Robinson, K. S. *Blue Mars*. New York: Bantam Books, 1997.

Rustin, M., and D. Massey. "Rethinking the Neoliberal World Order: How neoliberalism disorganises the world." *58 Soundings: A journal of politics and culture* 20, no. 2 (2014): 116–135.

Rutherford, D. "Why Papua Wants Freedom: The Third Person in Contemporary Nationalism." *Public Culture* 20, no. 2 (2008): 345–373.

Sauvy, A. "Trois Mondes, Une Planète." Accessed January 10, 2016. http://www.homme-moderne.org/societe/demo/sauvy/3mondes.html

Schattschneider, E. E. *The Semisovereign People: A Realist's View of Democracy in America*. Boston: Wadsworth Publishing, 1975.

Spivak, G. C. "Constitutions and Culture Studies." *Yale Journal of Law and Humanities* 2, no. 1 (1990): 133–147.

Spivak, G. C. "Nationalism and the Imagination." *Lectora* 15 (2009): 75–88.

Sunter, A. "TWAIL: Naturalized Epistemological Inquiry." *Canadian Journal of Law and Jurisprudence* 20, no. 2 (2007): 475–507.

Tushnet, M. "Authoritarian Constitutionalism." *Cornell Law Review* 100, no. 2 (2015): 391–462.

Walker, G. "The Idea of Nonliberal Constitutionalism." In *Ethnicity and Group Rights*, edited by Ian Schapiro and Will Kymlicka, 154–186. New York: NYU Press, 1997.

Walker, N. "The Idea of Constitutional Pluralism." *The Modern Law Review* 65, no. 3 (2002): 317–359.

Weiler, J. H. H. *The Constitution of Europe: 'Do the New Clothes Have an Emperor?' and Other Essays on European Integration*. Cambridge: Cambridge University Press, 1999.

Weiwei, Z. *China Wave: Rise of a Civilizational State*. Hackensack: World Century Publishing, 2012.

Zumbansen, P. "Law and Society and the Politics of Relevance: Facts and Field Boundaries in 'Transnational Legal Theory in Context'." *No Foundations* 11 (2014): 1–37.

Zumbansen, P. "The Incurable Constitutional Itch: Transnational Private Regulatory Governance and the Woes of Legitimacy." *Osgoode Hall Law School Research Paper* 10, no. 6 (2014): 1–18.

Disrupting civility: amateur intellectuals, international lawyers and TWAIL as praxis

John Reynolds

ABSTRACT

This paper is a reflection on the role of intellectuals in engaging with Palestinian solidarity movements and liberation discourses, and on the place of international lawyers specifically within that context. The paper considers 'the question of Palestine' as a rigorous test for intellectuals in the Global North today, and examines particular debates over free speech, civility and balance that unfolded in the wake of Israel's 2014 war on Gaza. It considers the interventions of international lawyers in these debates with reference to Edward Said's 'amateur' and 'professional' intellectuals, and explores ways in which anti-colonial international lawyers (as amateur intellectuals) can transcend prevailing professional orthodoxies to deploy language, arguments or tactics that rupture liberal legal processes and narratives on Palestine.

Introduction

> It is a spirit in opposition, rather than in accommodation, that grips me because the romance, the interest, the challenge of intellectual life is to be found in dissent against the status quo at a time when the struggle on behalf of underrepresented and disadvantaged groups seems so unfairly weighted against them. (Edward Said)[1]

> The @IDFSpokesperson is a lying motherfucker. (Stephen Salaita)[2]

This paper is a reflection on the role of intellectuals in engaging with Palestinian solidarity movements and liberation discourses, and on the place of international lawyers specifically within that context. My point of departure is Edward Said's *Representations of the Intellectual*, and the particular distinction Said draws between professional and amateur intellectuals (his twist on Gramsci's traditional and organic intellectuals or, from a more explicitly Third World perspective, on Fanon's colonial and native intellectuals). The paper considers 'the question of Palestine' as a rigorous test for intellectuals in the Global North today, and examines debates over free speech, political expression, academic freedom, civility and balance. It does so in the context of two particular 'affairs' that unfolded in the wake of Israel's 2014 war on Gaza, and that are indicative of broader restrictions on the intellectual space to critique such colonial violence. I present these examples as the Salaita affair (regarding Steven

Salaita's loss of a tenured appointment at the University of Illinois over positions he expressed publicly during the Israeli bombardment), and the Schabas affair (regarding the campaign against William Schabas serving as chair of the UN Commission of Inquiry on the Gaza war).

The next section begins by elaborating Said's framing of the amateur intellectual in relation to contemporary debates on Palestine. The following two sections then use the Salaita and Schabas affairs to deconstruct the figure of the professional, conformist intellectual. The prevailing conventionalism ensured that mainstream international lawyers (as professional intellectuals) for the most part maintained conservative positions during these affairs and deferred to the presumed legitimacy of Israel's use of force. I interrogate and contest the paradigms of civility and balance that are imposed in this context. The fifth section moves to rehabilitate the partisan, subversive intellectual as a counterpoint. In doing so, I seek to build on Said's conception of the amateur intellectual by instilling a particular sense of partisanship that draws on Walter Rodney's notion of the 'guerrilla intellectual'. Following on from this, the sixth section begins to think normatively and prescriptively against prevailing professional orthodoxies, considering international law as a space of social movements as well as of elite institutions. I explore some of the ways in which anti-colonial international lawyers (as amateur intellectuals) can deploy language, arguments or tactics that subvert or rupture liberal legal processes and narratives on Palestine, and that may allow us to think about Third World Approaches to International Law (TWAIL) as praxis.

Amateur intellectuals

Given that the badge of professionalism is something that most lawyers will wear with pride, it must be emphasised at the outset that Said uses the term pejoratively, to unveil the depoliticised expert figure whose professional intellectualism is self-serving and deferential to established, and establishment, structures. For Said himself, by contrast, it is a spirit of opposition rather than accommodation that grips him. While his homage to the 'romance' of intellectual life may connote a somewhat idealised self-representation of a critic who nonetheless had his own dalliance with the PLO hierarchy, his emphasis on dissent – against a status quo that is so unfairly weighted against subjugated groups – resonates today as sharply as ever in the Palestinian context. Israeli domination and segregation throughout historic Palestine continue to become both socially and legally more entrenched by the day, the colonisation of the West Bank carries on apace and the bombardments of Gaza become more brutal and ruthless in their mechanised violence. And while this hot violence of Israel's periodic wars on Gaza dominates our news feeds at sporadic intervals, the slow, cold violence of the state's legal armoury serves to entrench other particular forms of control in Israel and East Jerusalem.[3]

Where Said characterises the Dreyfus affair and the first world war as 'rigorous tests for intellectuals' in the early 20 century,[4] the nature of Zionism and the situation in Palestine presents a comparably rigorous test for intellectuals in the early twenty-first century. It is by no means the only such test presented from that region of the world, but it remains arguably more significant than ever. The positions that we in the Global North take or fail to take on Israel/Palestine define our politics in relation to state power, to imperialism, to resistance, to the international donor industry. For Richard Falk, Palestine stands among the three pre-eminent issues for progressive emancipatory politics today. He places 'support for the Palestinian Solidarity Movement, including its BDS campaign as…a creative form of resistance to oppressive circumstances' at the centre of the agenda, alongside the struggle against unjust and unsustainable forms of globalised neoliberalism, and the need to urgently address the ecological and existential threats of climate change.[5] How we situate ourselves on Palestine is as revealing of our thinking as our positions on the commodification of social services or the destruction of the planet. Palestine functions very much as a frontier for imperialism and a testing-ground for its technologies of war. It functions equally, therefore, as a magnet and metaphor for anti-imperial analysis and activism.[6]

Said's portrayals of the intellectual are universal in their outlook but very much shaped by his own positioning as a Palestinian intellectual in physical and metaphysical exile. As such, his description of the 'public role of the intellectual' as being one of perpetual 'outsider, "amateur," and disturber of the status quo' is auto-biographical in many respects.[7] Said's amateur intellectual is defined by an 'unquenchable interest in the larger picture, in making connections across lines and barriers, in refusing to be tied down to a specialty, in caring for ideas and values despite the restrictions of a profession'.[8] He contrasts such pursuit of truth with 'the insiders, experts, coteries, professionals' and with conformists who fail to question corporate thinking, and class, racial or gender privilege, who fixate instead on 'what is considered to be proper, professional behaviour – not rocking the boat, not straying outside the accepted paradigms or limits, making yourself marketable and above all presentable, hence uncontroversial and unpolitical and "objective"'.[9] Such professionalism is marked by an attitude that views scholarship as a nine-to-five pursuit in atomised spaces of niche research, in which the cult of the expert proliferates and intellectual work puts itself in the service of power. In a Western context Said saw this corruption of the role of the intellectual as bound up in depoliticisation, writing in 1988 that 'among the left the use of the word intellectual has fallen into disrepute and disuse. And what instead has appeared are words like professional and scholar and academic ... I think it's partly because of the refusal of American Left intellectuals to accept their political role.'[10]

The realm of public international law is heavily professionalised, institutionalised and depoliticised. Whether it is human rights or international criminal justice, world trade rules or foreign investment law, the mainstreams of these fields are populated by professional lawyers, academics and advocates who take pride in being part of projects that they see as progressive – advancing rights, combating impunity, facilitating commerce and enterprise. But when it comes to Israel/Palestine these fields are marked by a fundamentally conservative streak. The need to be seen as balanced and to hold both sides of the (uneven) conflict to account – as the international human rights organisations and UN fact-finding missions reporting on Palestine typically oblige themselves to do – obfuscates the structural dynamics of dispossession, exclusion and domination that have long been at play. It is notable that Said specifically cites the international lawyer, along with the military strategist, as exemplifying the type of professional intellectual who speaks and deals in a language that has become highly specialised but largely detached from the material realities over which it is layered. That specialised language masks the brutality of war and occupation, sanitises state violence and terror, barbarises resistance. There is perhaps something in the balancing and equivalencing tendencies of law and legal structures that feeds in to the attitudes of lawyers and helps explain why legal scholars have been particularly reactionary in their engagement on Palestine. Thus we hear the constant refrain of the empty phraseology of 'both sides', 'balance' and 'proportionality'; the internalising of Israel's self-executing right to self-defence; and the incorporation of the insidious euphemisms of 'collateral damage', 'surgical strikes', 'moderate physical pressure', 'knocks on the roof', and so on.

The vocabulary of coloniser and colonised, on the other hand, is largely absent from the lexicon of professional international law when it comes to Palestine, while so many human rights lawyers (both in practice and the academy) are still unwilling to talk about Israeli apartheid or to engage with the Boycott, Divestment and Sanctions (BDS) movement,[11] for fear of a perceived loss of objectivity. At a time when Israel is ramping up its internal and external efforts to prohibit boycotts by law, when Western governments are signing agreements with Israel that commit themselves to clamping down on BDS activities,[12] and when US legislators are seeking to use the Transatlantic Trade and Investment Partnership agreement as a vehicle for that same end in Europe,[13] challenging this orthodoxy remains essential. Principled action does not come without complication, however. Being an intellectual who pursues a 'vocation for the art of representing…involves both commitment and risk'.[14] A stated commitment to Palestinian liberation in much of the Western academy and institutional political life bears risks of professional marginalisation as well as the stigma of being branded anti-semitic – as many who speak critically of Israeli state policy (including Jews and Jewish Israelis) regularly are, despite all available evidence and logic.

The Salaita affair

Some of the limitations that typify professional intellectual thinking can be seen in the debates over freedom of expression that followed the University of Illinois at Urbana-Champaign's (UIUC) termination of the tenured appointment of a Palestinian-American scholar of Native American studies in 2014. Steven Salaita lost his job, essentially, over the positions he took publicly during Israel's summer war on Gaza that year, primarily through the medium of Twitter. From the beginning of the Israeli bombing campaign in early July, Salaita was relatively prolific in his tweets on the situation as it evolved, covering a range of aspects including: updates on the number of children killed by Israeli forces in Gaza; criticism of US support for Israel; mockery of what he characterised as the Zionist propensity to blame Hamas for everything that is wrong throughout the world; emphasis on the importance of BDS as a tactical response to Israeli aggression; and gratitude for what he saw as growing solidarity with Palestinians from around the globe. Some of his posts were marked by a rawness, anger and language that are the product of watching atrocities, injustices and misrepresentations unfold in real time: 'Fuck you, #Israel. And while I'm at it, fuck you, too, PA, Sisi, Arab monarchs, Obama, UK, EU, Canada, US Senate, corporate media, and ISIS'.[15]

It was because of such utterances that Salaita's contract was revoked, on grounds of 'incivility'. Significantly many of his tweets had engaged the very themes of civilisation and civility, in the context of race and colonialism:

> I hope #Israel's brutality in #Gaza compels people to think about the violence inherent to Western notions (and practices) of modernity.[16]
>
> #Israel has often tested weapons in #Gaza. That's what most colonizers do to entrapped native populations. They like to call it 'progress.'[17]
>
> #Israel's bombardment of #Gaza provides a necessary impetus to reflect on the genocides that accompanied the formation of the United States.[18]
>
> The technology of colonialism changes, but in every era the colonizer's great advantage was restricting the geography of the native. #Gaza.[19]

It is worth noting that such conceptually grounded statements outweigh the more visceral formulations in Salaita's Twitter feed that were presented in complaints to UIUC as 'vile', 'vulgar', or 'anti-semitic', and as evidence that Salaita would be better placed in a 'loony bin'.[20] Salaita explains that he uses Twitter to 'put forward a decolonial perspective that draws from certain influences, among them Indigenous thought, critical theory, and literary analysis. Most of my tweets distill decolonial theory into workaday language.'[21] This, like Salaita's expressions of gratitude for 'our Jewish brothers and sisters around the world deploring #Israel's brutality in #Gaza',[22] is not acknowledged in the reactionary complaints over his less 'civil' critiques of that brutality. The broader point, however, is that characterisations of the incivility of a racialised voice in a settler-colonial state cannot be viewed in isolation from the historical and ongoing contexts of the 'civilising mission'. The legitimacy of despotic rule over the 'uncivilised' barbarians, and the denial of liberties to them – for their own improvement – is of course central to classic Millsian liberal imperial thought.[23] Civility is bound up with exclusionary processes designed to construct barriers and keep the ruling classes in the ascendancy. John Locke's political subjects, for example, are defined by their Christianity, their respect for English law and property, and the 'civility in their language'.[24] This serves a very particular function in colonial projects, with civility of discourse and comport used as a marker of the level (or absence) of humanity and sovereignty in the colonised, and thus implicated in their conquest and extermination.

In a settler-colonial society such as the USA, then, civility does not exist in a historical or ideological vacuum and does not operate as a neutral concept. It is a term with particular imperial and violent sensibilities; it is 'the discourse of educated racism…the sanctimony of the authoritarian…the pretext of the oppressor'.[25] It is not insignificant that Salaita's scholarship is concerned with comparative settler-coloniality and that his position in Illinois was in an American Indian and Indigenous Studies department. His experience is symptomatic of a broader marginalisation of decolonial pedagogy in US higher education, which extends from Native American to Palestine studies. In the use of the idiom of civility by university administrators engaged in such marginalisation, the echoes of coloniality are stark. In response, Salaita is unapologetic:

> Insofar as 'civil' is profoundly racialized and has a long history of demanding conformity to the ethos of imperialism and colonization, I frequently choose incivility as a form of communication. (Or it is chosen for me.) This choice is both moral and rhetorical. Anybody familiar with age-old colonial discourses about the suitability of natives for self-governance understands that the language of civilization is profoundly compromised. Those who decry my 'incivility,' then, implicate the cultures and histories from which my rhetoric and morality emerge.[26]

The very purpose of progressive politics is to disrupt accepted orders of power, and to reconstitute what is civil and desirable in society. This is what Palestine solidarity politics does. Conscious of this, invocations of 'incivility' are central to the work of pro-Israel groups in combatting Palestine solidarity organising. Support for Palestinian liberation is invariably dismissed as uncivil, regardless of how respectfully it is articulated. In the face of remorseless state violence against a besieged population, it would appear that Salaita (understandably) prioritises moral clarity over meek platitudes of civility, and language that cuts through the imposed constraints of balance to unmask the gravity of atrocity: 'After all, there is nothing civil about dead children in an ice cream freezer'.[27] Through his 'incivility manifesto', Salaita embraces the charge of incivility as the amateur intellectual's modus operandi – that of opposition to militarism and institutional discrimination, antagonism towards the commercialisation of the academy and agitation to democratise academic spaces.

For Joan Scott, who served as chair of the American Association of University Professors' Committee on Academic Freedom and Tenure from 1999 to 2005, civility is now 'a synonym for orthodoxy', a framing for the contempt for unorthodox ideas or behaviour which – with its distinctly European Christian bourgeois heritage – 'has become a watch word for academic administrators'.[28] Thus it was that Phyllis Wise, the Chancellor of UIUC who oversaw Salaita's dismissal, justified the decision on grounds that tenure 'brings with it a heavy responsibility to continue the traditions of scholarship and *civility* upon which our university is built'.[29] The utility of civility as a silencing mechanism is clear, and in this sense it functions in a similar manner to the charge of anti-semitism when it is spuriously invoked to muffle criticism of Israeli state practice.[30] We can also discern here the type of 'background repression' that preconditions societal norms and mindsets, vitiates objectivity and renders critical voices unacceptable, even where there are no formal restrictions on academic freedom.[31] Judith Butler explains that the conservative seizure of academic freedom in the USA has emphasised an orthodoxy of 'balance' – with the consequence that state legislatures are empowered to enforce this balance, necessitating surveillance and interference. Academic freedom as such is 'restrictively liberal'; 'if the conservative seizure of academic freedom is to fail, there must be more robust and substantive ways to relate academic freedom to ideals of democracy that include not only right of free expression but opposition to forms of surveillance that target political viewpoints'.[32]

In this context it seems clear that there are *particular* political viewpoints that are targeted. UIUC itself provides a number of recent examples that highlight the selectivity of Salaita's punishment: 'Tellingly, in 2012, UIUC took no action when a professor made racist comments at a gathering of white supremacists, and in 2010, UIUC reinstated a lecturer who had been terminated for making homophobic comments in an email to a student'.[33] And just six months before she presided over Salaita's sacking for his tweets, Chancellor Wise had herself been subjected to a torrent of misogynistic and racist invective by students using a '#FuckPhyliss' hashtag on Twitter, after she decided not to cancel classes during extreme weather. Despite the vitriolic nature of the tweets, Wise refused to discipline the students, stating: 'The negative comments, as offensive as they were, are protected speech'.[34] This appears as the tolerance of an authority fully convinced by the sanctity and robustness of its own liberalism, in much the same way that decisions permitting neo-Nazis to parade through a predominantly Jewish suburb (home to many Holocaust survivors),[35] or allowing homophobes to picket military funerals, are held up as evidence of the unshakeable American commitment to free speech.[36] These liberal values come undone, however, when it comes to criticism of Israel, such that the Center for Constitutional Rights now speaks of the 'Palestine exception' to free speech in the USA.[37]

As such, the Salaita affair raises important questions of political speech, freedom of expression and modes of engagement for public intellectuals, for whom media such as Twitter have become important sites of intervention and intellectual production. The apparently successful interference of private donors with the staff profile of a public university in this case is a chilling turn. While the Committee on Academic Freedom and Tenure that reviewed the case – in response to a complaint by the Department of American Indian Studies against the decision of the University's Chancellor and Board of Trustees – found that the supposed 'incivility' of a candidate's utterances were not acceptable grounds for the termination of her contract, the spectre of professionalism instead surfaces as an alternative justification:

> extramural utterances – political speech – 'rarely bear upon a faculty member's fitness for office'. The Chancellor elided the distinction between the two. They should be disaggregated. We do not believe that Dr Salaita's political speech renders him unfit for office. Further, we find that civility does not constitute a legitimate criterion for rejecting his appointment...We do believe, however, that the Chancellor has raised a legitimate question of whether his professional fitness adheres to professional standards.[38]

The question then arises as to how such professional standards are defined or interpreted. One of Salaita's own tweets, just days before his firing, was somewhat prescient in this regard: 'In the United States, academic, corporate, or political respectability is available merely by ignoring Israeli ethnic cleansing. #Gaza.'[39] University of Illinois emails relating to the Salaita affair that were released under a court order in August 2015 provide a telling insight into the thinking of university management on this question of what constitutes professional fitness, standards and values:

> A related policy might address the question of 'controversial' hires – this is murkier, because people's ideas of what is controversial will differ. But a crude rule of thumb is, if you think someone's name is going to end up on the front page of the newspaper as a U of I employee, you can't make that decision on your own say so. You need to get some higher level review and approval...We welcome the widest possible range of viewpoints and positions, but not all positions. And that [sic] there are some things that are not consistent with our values.[40]

> The University, as the state's public university, needs to, in many ways, reflect the values of the state. [41]

This resembles Said's very definition of the professional intellectual – the duty of an academic intellectual is to conform to the official position; in essence, 'at the University of Illinois at Urbana-Champaign, academic freedom is the freedom to pursue the widest possible range of viewpoints and positions, except for those that are not consistent with our values, which must reflect the values of the state'.[42] The particular invocation of professionalism in this case finds echoes in the firing of Angela Davis from the University of California, Los Angeles. That university's board of regents had ordered the firing of Davis in 1969 on the basis of her Communist Party membership, but a California Superior Court overturned this. Governor Ronald Reagan continued his crusade to fire Davis, and successfully obtained a decision from the board of regents to do so in 1970, which he said was based 'on her *unprofessional* conduct as shown by speaking around various campuses already troubled by dissension'.[43] Her conduct was unprofessional and her rhetoric (in speeches made off-campus) was uncivil – 'inflammatory'.[44] Davis was resolute in her (amateur intellectualist) tirade against institutionalised racism and sexism: 'When people start saying that we are out to subvert, that we are subversive, we should say Hell yes, we are subversive. Hell yes, and we're going to continue to be subversive until we have subverted this whole damn system of oppression'.[45]

More than 40 years later, in railing against the dogma of civility, Salaita is conscious of 'how something that sounds so innocuous, even desirable, is in fact repressive'.[46] In international law, in many ways, it has been ever thus. The language of 'civilisation' was deployed through foundational international legal doctrines and texts to exclude indigenous and Third World peoples from sovereignty, to rationalise the coloniality of the League of Nations mandates, and to retain a superior standing for 'civilised nations' in the United Nations era, through Article 38(1)(c) of the Statute of the International Court of Justice. For much of international law's history, and to this day, the civilised/uncivilised binary has been a central narrative feature. We can look at one international lawyer's intervention in the Salaita debate as illustrative of a broader mindset within the discipline. Dov Jacobs is a legal academic, practitioner and self-described 'expert blogger' on issues of international criminal law and human rights.[47] In July–August of 2014, while the situation in Gaza was raising numerous questions around the laws of armed conflict and the possible jurisdiction of the International Criminal Court, and while fellow international criminal law bloggers were intensively debating the situation, Jacobs stayed silent on his blog. When he did choose to intervene on events relating to Gaza, it was with a piece not on the war itself but on the Salaita affair, challenging the idea that any principles of academic freedom of expression were at stake in Salaita's case.[48] Viewed through the lens of Palestine as a litmus test of sorts for intellectuals, the politics of this are not insignificant. Jacobs took particular issue with the tweet in which Salaita referred to the Israeli Defence Forces (IDF) spokesperson as a 'lying motherfucker'. A statement like this, Jacobs said, cannot stem from any academic thinking; it is just a crude insult. Jacobs contrasted this to his own approach, whereby he 'always provides detailed reasoning' for any 'strong feelings' he might have on the tribunals, prosecutors or judges in The Hague. If he were to use a profanity to describe the Prosecutor of the International Criminal Court, he would not see it as unjustified for his employers to fire him.[49]

Part of the problem with Jacobs' response is that his discussion of Salaita's tweet as 'generally insulting' and 'simply being very rude' (which itself, as I have noted above, is not fully representative of the larger collection of Salaita's tweets) is based on a de-contextualised and apolitical understanding of the term 'motherfucker'. This is a professional intellectual perception which elides the distinct social and historical trajectories of the word in the USA as it emerged from the slave plantations, was carried on though jazz culture, given a revitalised political content by black power movements in the 1960s and 1970s, and continues to enjoy widespread and often politicised usage in contemporary hip-hop culture. As Michael Kearney points out, Salaita, as a person of colour in the USA, is situated firmly in this tradition of minority dissent and resistance.[50] And as a postcolonial scholar of Palestinian origin, Salaita is doubtless well-versed in Said's contention that: 'Knowing how to use language well and knowing when to intervene in language are two essential features of intellectual action'. [51] Salaita could have chosen any number of words to describe the IDF spokesperson, but he chose a term that has a particular identification with opposition to establishment racism or violence and is widely understood in that context: at least for certain communities but 'perhaps not for white academics'.[52] As Earl Washington explains:

> The white majority culture tends to put what the black minority culture says into its own (white) frame of reference. Consequently, whites would define 'motherfucker' as a very negative and slang term – literally incest. That definition, however, is only one intended by those who use the word.[53]

Calling the Israeli army spokesperson a lying motherfucker should be understood not as a mindless insult, but as a challenge to the political language used to defend the massacre of Palestinians and as an assertion of the falsehood upon which that defence rests. Political language deployed by the state apparatus is, of course, often an exercise in defending the indefensible, 'designed to make lies sound truthful and murder respectable'.[54] This essentially is one of the functions of the military spokesperson when Israeli forces engage in the bombardment of Gaza. The objection of the professional intellectual in this case, however, appears to be based on the perception of personalised insult, rather than on the allegation of institutional dishonesty. The effect of such an objection is to deflect from the underlying issue of an atrocity being perpetrated. The appearance of reasonableness and civility becomes more important than truth itself; the concern is with the 'motherfucker', not the 'lying'. It is this aspect of professionalism – deflection rather than reflection – that we must vigorously contest. C. Wright Mills reminds us of the imperative of heeding the intimate relationship between personal morals, intellect and political stand: 'If the thinker does not relate himself to the value of truth in political struggle, he cannot responsibly cope with the whole of live experience'.[55] Resistance to official narratives is essential to smashing the stereotypes with which we are swamped. For Said this necessitates 'unmaskings or alternative versions in which to the best of one's ability the intellectual tries to tell the truth'.[56]

Since the 2014 war on Gaza we have seen powerful usages of the term 'motherfucker' continuing in public discourse in other situations of structural and racial injustice, most notably in the context of racist police violence in the USA. After the announcement of the grand jury decision not to indict the police officer who killed Michael Brown in Ferguson, Missouri, the Atlanta hip-hop artist and social activist Killer Mike made an eloquent and impassioned speech, telling the agents of power that 'you motherfuckers got me today, but you motherfuckers will not own tomorrow', and telling his audience that 'it's about poverty, it's about greed, and it's about a war machine…the one thing I want you to know is that it's us against the motherfucking machine'.[57] Similarly, in a globalisation context, Third World resistance to Western-dominated financial institutions is epitomised in Seun Kuti's characterisation of the IMF as 'international motherfuckers'. The critical awareness among oppressed communities of the role of law and institutional structures in their oppression is crucial here if local resistance and global solidarity is to be able to take root and shape alternative horizons – whether for Palestinians, black communities in the USA or subjugated groups elsewhere. The organic intellectuals in the Black Lives Matter movement are very much aware of this; hence the significance of their visit to Palestine in January 2015 and the ongoing deepening of Black–Palestinian solidarity.[58] This echoes the ethos of previous generations of African American intellectuals, who saw themselves 'become a Palestinian',[59] or the thrust of a Black Panther party that situated itself in 'radical kinship' with the Palestinians.[60] Freedom remains a constant struggle in Ferguson and Palestine alike,[61] where communities continue to be confronted with the physical machine of militarised violence. Intellectuals who challenge the security state justifications for such, meanwhile, are susceptible to different forms of silencing in their own fields.

The Schabas affair

William Schabas was met by such attempts at silencing upon his appointment as chair of the UN Independent Commission of Inquiry on the 2014 Gaza Conflict. Schabas, like Richard Goldstone before him, would not be considered a radical by any means. He is seen, rather, as an international lawyer with 'perfect professional credentials…a distinguished and justly influential scholar in the field',[62] a progressive but mainstream authority on international human rights law and international criminal law. As such, he might have been assumed a relatively uncontroversial choice for a UN post charged with investigation and documentation of international legal questions in Gaza in comparison to a more critical legal scholar like Richard Falk, whose appointment in 2008 as UN Special Rapporteur on human rights in occupied Palestine incensed Israel and its supporters. Despite this, Schabas faced vehement opposition from the outset. Denunciation from Israel's apologists in UN advocacy circles (such as Hillel Neuer and Gerald Steinberg) and in legal academia (Alan Dershowitz and Oren Gross) is perhaps par for the course. But some observers may not have expected to find liberal international lawyers – like Phillipe Sands and Robert Howse – collectively pontificating online about Schabas's purported bias, and the need instead for impartiality and 'the highest standards of judicial integrity'.[63] These demands that judicial standards be applied, it must be noted, are made in the context of a fact-finding process with no judicial mandate. Some international lawyers went as far as to argue that the specific criteria applied to judges under the Code of Ethics of the International Criminal Court should be applied to Schabas, in a manner that constructs an indefensible lack of impartiality on his part.[64] Such expectations are far removed from the human and material realities of people living through conflict and occupation, but are indicative of the type of thinking that is coloured by a perennial need for artificial balance and ostensible professionalism.

As a result of pressure on the UN process from a broad church of pro-Israel campaign groups, think-tanks, political actors and professional intellectuals that threatened to derail the Commission of Inquiry's work, Schabas was ultimately left with little choice but to resign. The primary impetus for the campaign against him was based on a public statement he had made previously (but which was recycled and presented out of context) criticising Israeli military practices and suggesting that Prime Minister Netanyahu may have a case to answer, as well as a legal opinion he had provided to the PLO (regarding technical aspects of accession to the Rome Statute of the International Criminal Court). Although his was not a judicial appointment, supposed standards of judicial independence were applied – liberally constructed not as independence and impartiality in conducting the inquiry itself (which Schabas had fully committed himself to exercising), but as retroactive independence of any opinion on any question relating to the region being investigated. It bears noting that such high thresholds have not traditionally been applied even to international judges themselves. Hersch Lauterpacht, who had furnished legal advice to the state of Israel over the years and had helped draft its declaration of independence, sat as a judge in the *Israel v. Bulgaria* case in the International Court of Justice. Israel's application was ultimately declared inadmissible in that case, but not without Lauterpacht dissenting.

In Schabas' case, however, because he had expressed opinions on Palestine in the past, he was not deemed an appropriate choice to lead an inquiry on Palestine. This is reflective of an emerging pattern when it comes to international institutional appointments on contested terrain such as this, where relevant experience and prior expressions of opinion or interest can count against an applicant or nominee. Regarding the choice of his own successor as UN Special Rapporteur, Falk points out that Makarim Wibisono 'was explicitly chosen in 2014 to be Special Rapporteur for Palestine on the perverse rationale that he was more qualified than other candidates *because* he had no expert knowledge of the subject-matter'.[65] Professional human rights intellectuals and international criminal lawyers are expected not to care about Greece or Syria in 2016 any more than they cared about Yugolsavia or Somalia in 1993. There is a professional stigma attached to being overly 'passionate' about a particular issue or conflict. International legal historians or researchers who identify with a cause are rebuked on the basis that their work 'fails to provide objectivity'.[66] Herbert Marcuse warns of the pitfalls of such fetishisation of nominal objectivity: 'in a democracy with totalitarian organization, objectivity may…foster a mental attitude which tends to obliterate the difference between true and false, information and indoctrination, right and wrong'.

> The result is a *neutralization* of opposites, a neutralization, however, which takes place on the firm grounds of the structural limitation of tolerance and within a preformed mentality. When a magazine prints side by side a negative and a positive report on the FBI, it fulfills honestly the requirements of objectivity: however, the chances are that the positive wins because the image of the institution is deeply engraved in the mind of the people. Or, if a newscaster reports the torture and murder of civil rights workers in the same unemotional tone he uses to describe the stockmarket or the weather, or with the same great emotion with which he says his commercials, then such objectivity is spurious – more, it offends against humanity and truth by being calm where one should be enraged, by refraining from accusation where accusation is in the facts themselves. The tolerance expressed in such impartiality serves to minimize or even absolve prevailing intolerance and suppression.[67]

Said himself recounts how he 'was accused of being active in the battle for Palestinian rights, and thus disqualified for any sober or respectable platform at all'. In contrast to so-called 'universal intellectuals' such as Jean-Paul Sartre or Michel Foucault, those who have been personally involved in any way with a specific cause are cast as biased. For Said, such aspersions amount to 'plainly anti-intellectual and antirational arguments'.[68] Hamid Dabashi picks up on this distinction: 'Sartre and Foucault cared widely about the entirety of the colonial and colonizing world, while Fanon and Said cared deeply about Algeria and Palestine, and from these two sites of contestation they extrapolated their politics and ethics of responsibility towards the rest of the world'.[69] While Fanon's commitment to Algeria was on the basis of a broader anti-colonial sensibility rather than national identity, and while Sartre and Foucault certainly did not refrain from taking positions on specific sites of contestation, there is something to the suggestion that the European intellectual's engagement is often seen in the West as less 'emotive' than that of the Third World intellectual. The subtext of racialisation is difficult to escape. Indigenous and minority communities in settler-colonial societies are similarly often cast as irrational, to the point that their language may be criminalised on the basis of state claims of violence, whether in the context of anti-segregation activism during the Jim Crow era or hip-hop lyricism today.[70] For Palestinians, African-Americans and other racialised voices to be seen as professional, they need to appear as devoid of race politics as possible. Such distortions of the 'all lives matter' variety must be exposed and discredited.

International institutional life is not simply a world of insiders and professionals but one of conformists. While there clearly are questions of race at play, when it comes to Palestine it is not only a question of race. Even insiders like Schabas and Goldstone, if they make the mistake of straying beyond the circle or opting not to conform by engaging in 'politicised' processes, will be cast out for behaving in 'unwise and counterproductive' manners that compromise hegemonic conceptions of justice.[71] Such deviations are framed as individual aberrations (and, for those of Jewish origin, as evidence of 'self-hating' character flaws) and as such are qualitatively different from the constructed cultural deficiencies that exclude Palestinians en masse from the ambit of professional credibility. Both forms must be challenged robustly, however. Said is again instructive here, underlining the importance of the intellectual's role in the 'sense of being unwilling to accept easy formulas, or ready-made cliches, or the smooth, ever-so-accommodating confirmations of what the powerful or conventional have to say, and what they do. Not just passively unwillingly [sic], but actively willing to say so in public.'[72]

Partisanship and the guerrilla intellectual

For all of the value that Said's thinking on the representations and affiliations of the intellectual brings in unpacking the dynamics of institutionalised power and opening up spaces of dissent and disruption, his amateur intellectual nonetheless appears at times a somewhat idealised and elite figure. This section thus seeks to home in on a particular sense of partisanship or militancy, so as to distinguish from the kind of liberal advocates who may have similarly romantic ideas of themselves speaking on behalf of the disadvantaged as those which Said ascribes to his truth-seeking intellectual. It also seeks to stretch Said's sometimes narrow conceptualisation of the intellectual as the university intellectual, and to extend his analysis to non-campus spaces.

An academy-centric theory of the intellectual risks side-lining the knowledge production of movement activists and the representative function of working class organic intellectuals, as well as obscuring portraits of the artist as intellectual. Against Said's privileging of the writer-intellectual over the artist-intellectual (painters, film-makers, photographers, hip-hop lyricists, folk troubadours) or the social movement intellectual (political leaders, union activists, grassroots campaigners), Sean Scalmer argues that a 'contemporary sociology of intellectuals needs to encompass diversity'.[73] This is essential to reflect the reality that so many of those who 'represent' as socio-political thinkers diverge in expectation, context and priorities from the carefully sculpted image of the book-writing intellectual. This is significant in the context of our discussion of hip-hop above, for instance. How might Said have related to the street culture representations of Black Lives Matter? On one hand, as Scalmer notes, Said's narrow depiction of the intellectual to the exclusion of musical artists, in particular, is surprising given his 'musicological passions'. On the other hand, his own aesthetic sensibilities may have meant that the protest missions of hip-hop or folk music were 'not to Said's forbiddingly classical tastes'.[74] This sense of a certain aloofness or elitism also speaks to Said's lack of emphasis on 'activist wisdom' ('practically oriented and contextually bound...painfully acquired and artfully deployed') in his vision of intellectual achievement.[75]

To build on and bolster Said's idea of the virtuous amateur intellectual, then, we can inject it with a more active sense of partisanship and draw on Walter Rodney's notion of the 'guerrilla intellectual'. During his time at the Institute of the Black World in the USA in 1974, Rodney spoke of the 'intellectual struggle' within (and against) an institutional architecture that represents the power of the ruling class.

> I use the term 'guerrilla intellectual' to come to grips with the initial imbalance of power in the context of academic learning...the books, the references, the theoretical assumptions, and the entire ideological underpinnings of what we have to learn in every single discipline. Once you understand the power that all this represents, then you have to recognize that your struggle must be based on an honest awareness of the initial disparity. And that's how the guerrilla operates. The guerrilla starts out by saying, the enemy has all and we have nothing in terms of weapons, but we have a lot of other things.[76]

It is in response to such pre-existing imbalances of power that Marcuse calls for pursuit of 'a partisan goal, a subversive liberating notice and practice' as a counterpoint to the entrenched aversion to partisanship in liberal work.[77] The imperative is to transcend the limitations of liberal freedoms and tolerance, given that their value is premised on an equality that is typically illusory. Where institutionalised inequality, class structures, socio-political privilege and legalised state violence predominate, the conditions of tolerance are inherently loaded. Critical or dissenting speech is subject to background limitations that precede the explicit limitations on speech defined by courts and institutions. The freedom of expression that is formally granted in equal measures to all protagonists – whether they advocate hate or humanity – is a form of 'non-partisan tolerance' that is '"abstract" or "pure" inasmuch as it refrains from taking sides – but in doing so it actually protects the already established machinery of discrimination'.[78] As such, there is no neutral position, even in the 'freest' of existing societies. Struggles for freedom are always partisan – intolerant of the repressive establishment and antagonistic to societal structures in which the game is rigged.

Hence Rodney's articulation of the guerrilla intellectual, whose mission is to sabotage the power disparity. Jean Genet saw his support for and engagement with the Palestinian liberation movement (as well as the Black Panthers) as a similar enactment of 'the intellectual as guerrilla'. Genet was, at the same time, careful to emphasise the distinctly anti-colonial contours and qualifications of his partisanship: 'The day the Palestinians become a nation like any other nation, I'll no longer be a part of it'.[79] Rodney's argument also speaks clearly to Global North–South dynamics, where his metaphor of guerrilla tactics finds echo in Georges Abi-Saab's reflection of 'operating behind enemy lines' as a Third World jurist in Western-dominated international legal institutions.[80] Given the inequality of arms in these contexts and beyond, for Rodney the task of the guerrilla is to wage a struggle on her own terms, not by confronting the dominant power directly but by occupying the terrain, entering the institutions and setting free the entire structure.[81]

With this in mind, the 'major and first responsibility of the intellectual is to struggle over ideas…in his own sphere of operation'.[82] For many intellectuals this is the sphere of the academy, and requires transformation of their own academic institutions. The Salaita affair reinforces this imperative. The burdens of professionalism and civility arguably weigh more heavily on the university intellectual because of her position in an institutional context. A broader conceptualisation of the intellectual's role challenges the university intellectual to discard those burdens and get her hands dirtier but, as we have seen at UIUC and beyond, this is dis-incentivised by the very nature of the system in which the university intellectual operates. As such, the first point of engagement for the university intellectual is her own sphere of operation. But Rodney's struggle over ideas also entails engaging beyond the university and transcending the distinctions between different forms of labour. The task of intellectuals and educators is that of 'relating ideas to the movement of the masses', both by 'expropriating bourgeois knowledge' and by cultivating alternative and subversive sites of knowledge production.[83] Rodney's own life and praxis very much straddled academic, activist and community spaces: 'Walter did not confine his activities to the cloisters and lecture rooms at the university, but shared his knowledge and exchanged ideas with the most despised and rejected elements of Jamaican society – the Rastafari brethren'.[84] In this sense he embodies the role of the institutionally embedded but liminal and oppositional scholar, oriented to the South and struggling against (Northern) hegemonic thought, institutions and learning. Rodney's life and work embodied a richness of intersecting contributions from his multiple standpoints as Marxist and Pan-Africanist, university academic and community educator, social critic and political activist. The synthesis of these various ways of being – as enacted across continents – and Rodney's insights on the dynamics of black and Third World political and social development, are of continued value in thinking about praxis of the South. Rodney's admiration for figures like CLR James and Lenin is based on their capacity for intellectualising and doing at the same time; 'for surely there was no real reason why one should remain in the academic world – that is, remain an intellectual – and at the same time not be revolutionary'.[85] This vista of praxis helps us to incorporate some of the practical and tactical aspects of activism into Said's framing of the amateur intellectual.

Amateur international lawyers?

International law is a space of elite institutions but also a space of social movements. One of the significant contributions of TWAIL scholarship has been to show the possibilities (and importance) of reshaping the field of international law from outside or below, and of imagining counter-hegemonic international law at least coexisting with and destabilising imperial international law,[86] even if unable to supplant it in the present conjuncture. International legal advocacy from and for Palestine has traditionally deployed quite orthodox legal arguments grounded primarily in international humanitarian law. It has tended for the most part to focus on the need for better institutional enforcement of international law, rather than highlighting law's role in structural oppression. In recent years, however, Palestinian grassroots activism and international solidarity campaigns have begun to use international law, through the BDS movement and other initiatives, in more expansive ways than professional international lawyers and institutions themselves are comfortable with. The task as I see it for anti-colonial or Third Worldist international lawyers (as amateur intellectuals) in thinking about a type of TWAIL praxis in this context is to support and serve such movements where possible and appropriate (with technical contributions), as well as to go beyond the language of law and to continue exposing the biases and blindnesses of the profession (with conceptual contributions and critiques) where necessary.

One crucial role of the intellectual, Said argues, is to dismantle the restrictions that we artificially construct and impose on our thinking and communication. He notes, by way of example, that 'the international lawyer speaks and deals in a language that has become specialized and usable by other members of the same field, specialized experts addressing other specialized experts in a lingua franca largely unintelligible to unspecialized people'.[87] As I have emphasised above, this specialised language that international lawyers speak often serves to obscure the violence of war and occupation and the asymmetries of power relations, or to mask the usurping of popular sovereignty by corporatist ideology. Demystifying the impenetrable language of international trade and investment treaties; problematising the reductive assumptions and classifications of international humanitarian law; challenging and transcending the prevailing orthodoxies in the discourse and landscape of international law; deploying legal language, arguments or tactics with a distinct anti-colonial bent: these can be the contributions of the international lawyer-as-intellectual that offer potential antidotes to outright disenchantment with the law.

Attempts to pursue such antidotes in the Palestinian context may be roughly grouped into three categories. I present these as illustrative of some of the tactics being employed, and do not intend to suggest that what follows is an exhaustive exegesis of the work being done. First, legal processes relating to Palestine can be subverted by activists invoking the prevention of war crimes as their defence against charges of interfering with the property of weapons manufacturers or settlement produce retailers,[88] by legal representation of the boycott campaigns of unions, associations and solidarity movements who are targeted by Zionism's own reactionary lawfare,[89] or by the utilisation of quintessentially liberal legal institutions to articulate more radical anti-colonial arguments. Much of this work is essentially about 'being political lawyers and using the appropriate doctrinal hooks as they become available'.[90] Here, advocates for justice for Palestine can take further insights from the work of Jacques Vergès, Third Worldist and internationalist legal practitioner, whose rupture defences went some way to exposing and exploiting the contradictions inbuilt in the French colonial state's use of criminal law against Algerian liberation fighters. Notably it has been said of Vergès that in the *professional* sense, 'his tactics are anything but lawyerly, but they've succeeded again and again [and] undoubtedly wreak havoc on hyprocrisy'.[91]

Both Steven Salaita's case and the 'Southampton affair' (regarding the cancellation of an international law conference on Israel by University of Southampton management in April 2015 on dubious 'security' grounds) ended up engaging professional sites of law in the form of domestic courts, with somewhat diverging implications for the notion of academic freedom. In August 2015 a United States District Court in Illinois held that Salaita did have a valid case to be answered for breach of contract and violation of his constitutional free speech rights. In November 2015 UIUC settled with Salaita to avoid proceeding to trial, and agreed to pay him damages to the tune of 10 years of his contracted salary. While this amounted to a formal acknowledgment that Salaita had been wronged, he was not reinstated. The 'decimation of the American Indian Studies Program at UIUC [as] an additional price tag paid by the university's capitulation to internal and external forces' is the lingering legacy.[92] The litigation had secondary impacts in the form of the resignation of Phyllis Wise as UIUC Chancellor (albeit with the cushion of a $400,000 severance payment and a $300,000 faculty position) and the court-ordered release of university correspondence that exposed management practice. Overall it may be seen as at least a partially successful outcome in terms of protecting free expression rights on Palestine, and as illustrative of the benefits of engaging professional legal institutions in certain circumstances. The English High Court's endorsement of the cancellation of the Southampton conference, by contrast, demonstrates the limitations involved in accessing such conservative spaces.

Second is the move of opening up what we might call alternative 'amateur' arenas of political–legal struggle beyond the courts and the professional institutions. Civil society-led 'people's tribunals' have come to occupy an important space in international affairs in filling certain vacuums left by formal international legal institutions and providing what Falk calls a 'jurisprudence of conscience'.[93] The Russell Tribunal on Palestine can be understood as a kind of amateur international law process which confronts questions that the professional legal institutions in Geneva and The Hague shirk – the arms trade with Israel, European Union complicity in Palestinian suffering, Israel's citizenship, nationality and residency laws as constitutive of apartheid, and corporate profiteering in conjunction with military occupation. The Russell Tribunal has displayed a reach beyond its own proceedings and findings, its multifaceted identity seeing, for example, one jury member (Michael Mansfield) advocating before a UN committee in Geneva one week, another (Roger Waters) discussing Palestinian rights in *Rolling Stone* magazine the next. Notably, following the findings of the 2011 Russell Tribunal Cape Town session on the apartheid nature of Israeli legal systems and concerted research and activism on the issue by Palestinian social movements and international lawyers, in 2012 the UN Committee on the Elimination of Racial Discrimination was pushed along the unprecedented path of censuring Israel under the rubric of apartheid and segregation.[94] This evokes the idea of international legal jurisprudence emanating from below. The special session of the Russell Tribunal convened in the wake of Israel's 2014 assault on Gaza was notable for the urgency and efficiency with which it was convened, while so many international institutions dallied, and for going beyond the standard war crimes analysis to tackle difficult questions around the proliferation of racist discourse and incitement to violence in Israeli public and political life.[95] The Hessel Tribunal, a localised version of the Russell Tribunal (named after French second-world war partisan and patron of the Russell Tribunal on Palestine, Stéphane Hessel) hosted by the grassroots Bil'in Popular Committee against the Wall and Settlements in 2013, is another striking demonstration of social movement usage of international law.

While aimed at fundamentally reshaping international law from below, TWAIL scholarship has, however, also shown how this transformative project has been unsuccessful for the most part. The mimicking of classic courtroom structures in these popular tribunal interventions is certainly not without its limitations but at least does hold some value in exposing the structural imbalances in the coloniser/colonised relationship. While it may not be immediately and quantifiably 'effective' in the professional legal sense of delivering a binding and enforceable judgment, the very idea of this type of guerrilla tactic matters – as a disruption of official processes and narratives, as an intervention in the ongoing ideational 'legitimacy war' playing out over Palestine/Israel,[96] and as a bridge to activism happening outside of legal spaces.

Third, and most importantly perhaps, it is vital for international lawyers to feed into broader political mobilisation and solidarity movements, and for legal actions and BDS activism to complement and reinforce one another. International lawyers are well-placed to support the important work of Palestinian social movements and global solidarity campaigns through, for instance, continued research and analysis of the apartheid features of Israel's population control regime, on the legal intricacies and impacts of settlement colonies, on the nefarious role played by corporate actors that aid and abet Israeli policy, and on any other forms of legal intervention that feed into concrete substantiations of BDS. While the demands of the Palestinian BDS call stem from the language and normative claims of international law, and cannot completely avoid the baggage that this entails, BDS nonetheless provides a blueprint for using international law without being overly hamstrung by the law's internal contradictions and biases.

It is worth contrasting the BDS campaign, as an amateur or organic intellectual movement for Palestinian liberation, with the professional articulation of the PLO's quest for statehood and UN membership. Whereas the statehood initiative collapses the larger Palestinian self-determination claim into one limited element, and has at times reduced the liberation struggle into a question of who to lobby on the Security Council, BDS has provided a mode of praxis for people around the world to respond – in many different and expansive and creative ways – to the call to express material solidarity with Palestine. This is slowly but very surely bearing fruit,[97] and in this sense the amateur grassroots tactic is proving more successful than the elite professional one. The other key point to emphasise here is that of a given tactic being not only about the concrete result that it achieves in the short term but the platform it lays for the longer-term strategic horizon, and the ways in which organising now shapes the conditions that materialise later. If we think about what the Palestinian liberation project might look like the day after decolonisation, for instance, tactics centred around BDS elicit a vision which avoids simply mirroring failed nationalist state structures that are hierarchical, exclusionary and patriarchal, and imagines instead the possibility of a mode of popular sovereignty that is more open, horizontal and inclusive.

In a piece on the engagement of international legal scholars with Palestine, Jean d'Aspremont characterises the partisan deployment of international law in pursuit of justice as the intellectual equivalent to hurling stones at an illicit occupying force.[98] Edward Said of course famously did physically hurl a stone at the edifice of an illicit occupying force. And through this powerfully symbolic act he reminds us of the importance of remaining militant in the pursuit of our political projects, if not in our conviction in the law itself as an end. The challenges before TWAILers and anti-colonial lawyers as amateur or partisan intellectuals, then, involve engaging the law tactically where appropriate, moving beyond the landscape of law where necessary, and exposing the suffocating tendencies of blinkered professional thinking always.

Disclosure statement

No potential conflict of interest was reported by the author.

Acknowledgments

Many thanks to the participants in the September 2015 TWAIL/Third World Quarterly writing workshop at the National University of Ireland, Maynooth for their valuable comments on an earlier draft of this article - in particular to Robert Knox and Mazen Masri for their close reading and incisive comments. Thanks also to the anonymous reviewers for their generous and constructive feedback. All errors of style and substance remain mine alone.

Notes

1. Said, *Representations of the Intellectual*, xvii.
2. Steven Salaita, twitter.com/stevesalaita/status/489022495392301057, July 15, 2014.
3. Cole, "Bad Laws."
4. Said, *Representations of the Intellectual*, 8.
5. Richard Falk, "A Few Notes on What is Left (or Toward a Manifesto for Revolutionary Emancipation)," *Global Justice in the 21st Century*, https://richardfalk.wordpress.com/2011/06/19/a-few-notes-on-what-is-left-or-toward-a-manifesto-for-revolutionary-emancipation, June 19, 2011.
6. Tawil-Souri and Matar, *Gaza as Metaphor*.
7. Said, *Representations of the Intellectual*, x. See also Said, *Out of Place*.
8. Said, *Representations of the Intellectual*, 76.
9. Said, *Representations of the Intellectual*, xiii, 74.
10. Said, "American Intellectuals," 44–45.
11. The Palestinian call for boycott, divestment and sanctions (BDS) against Israeli state institutions and agents was issued in 2005 by a broad collective of Palestinian political parties, unions and civil society organisations. It is modelled to a certain extent on the South African

precedent, and calls for international solidarity in the form of consumer boycotts, commercial divestments and economic sanctions until Israel ends it occupation of Palestinian territory and its systems of racial domination over the Palestinian people. See Palestinian BDS National Committee, "Palestinian Civil Society call for Boycott, Divestment and Sanctions," https://bdsmovement.net/call, July 9, 2005.

12. See, for example, "Memorandum of Understanding between the Department of Foreign Affairs, Trade and Development Canada and the Ministry of Foreign Affairs of the State of Israel regarding Public Diplomacy Cooperation," signed January 18, 2015.
13. "US Trade Bill with EU includes Landmark anti-BDS Provisions," *Ha'aretz*, June 30, 2015.
14. Said, *Representations of the Intellectual*, 13.
15. Steven Salaita, https://twitter.com/stevesalaita/status/490871788638072833, July 20, 2014.
16. Steven Salaita, https://twitter.com/stevesalaita/status/495219022607446017, August 1, 2014.
17. Steven Salaita, https://twitter.com/stevesalaita/status/490697281344397312, July 22, 2014.
18. Steven Salaita, https://twitter.com/stevesalaita/status/490862112957530112, July 20, 2014.
19. Steven Salaita, https://twitter.com/stevesalaita/status/491397701054267393, July 22, 2014.
20. Complaints annexed to: Committee on Academic Freedom and Tenure (CAFT) of the University of Illinois at Urbana-Champaign, "Report on the Investigation into the Matter of Steven Salaita," December 23, 2014.
21. Salaita, *Uncivil Rites*, 6.
22. Steven Salaita, https://twitter.com/stevesalaita/status/490186075022049280, July 18, 2014.
23. Mill, *On Liberty*, 24.
24. Locke, *Some Thoughts concerning Education*, 102.
25. Salaita, *Uncivil Rites*, 105.
26. Salaita, *Uncivil Rites*, 42.
27. Salaita, *Uncivil Rites*, 184.
28. Joan Scott, "The New Thought Police," *The Nation*, May 4, 2015.
29. Phyllis Wise, "The Principles on which we Stand," https://illinois.edu/blog/view/1109/115906, August 22, 2014 (emphasis added).
30. See, for example, the 'Principles against Intolerance' adopted by the regents of the University of California in March 2016, which conflate anti-Zionism with anti-Semitism, and which Saree Makdisi and Judith Butler describe as 'the latest manifestation of a well-funded and increasingly desperate – even panicky – political campaign to eradicate criticism of Israeli policy from American campuses…a thinly disguised attempt to suppress academic freedom and stifle open debate on our campuses.' Saree Makdisi and Judith Butler, "Suppressing Criticism of Zionism on Campus is Catastrophic Censorship," *Los Angeles Times*, March 23, 2016.
31. Marcuse, "Repressive Tolerance."
32. Butler, "Israel/Palestine," 16–17.
33. Center for Constitutional Rights, "The Firing of Steven Salaita: Palestine Solidarity and Academic Freedom," http://ccrjustice.635elmp01.blackmesh.com/sites/default/files/attach/2015/02/Salaita_Factsheet_1-29-15.pdf, January 2015.
34. Phyllis Wise, "Moving past Digital Hate," https://www.insidehighered.com/views/2014/01/30/chancellor-u-illinois-responds-twitter-incident, January 30, 2014.
35. *National Socialist Party of America v. Village of Skokie*, 432 US 43 (1977).
36. *Snyder v. Phelps*, 562 US 443 (2011).
37. Center for Constitutional Rights and Palestine Legal, "The Palestine Exception to Free Speech: A Movement under Attack in the US," http://ccrjustice.org/the-palestine-exception, September 2015.
38. Committee on Academic Freedom and Tenure (CAFT) of the University of Illinois at Urbana-Champaign, "Report on the Investigation into the Matter of Steven Salaita," December 23, 2014.
39. Steven Salaita, https://twitter.com/stevesalaita/status/490672699631742976, July 20, 2014.
40. Email from Nick Burbules (UIUC Professor of Education Policy) to Chancellor Phyllis Wise, February 11, 2014.
41. Email from Christopher Kennedy (Chairman of the UIUC Board of Trustees) to Robert Easter, February 10, 2014.

42. Corey Robin, "Academic Freedom at UIUC: Freedom to Pursue Viewpoints and Positions that reflect the Values of the State," *Crooked Timber*, August 10, 2015.
43. Quoted in "Commie Angela Davis is booted from Teaching: Regents finally able to kick Red Afro from Campus, Classes," *Desert Sun*, June 20, 1970 (emphasis added).
44. Wallace Turner, "California Regents drop Communist from Faculty," *New York Times*, June 20, 1970.
45. Ibid.
46. Salaita, *Uncivil Rites*, 60.
47. Jacobs' blog, 'Spreading the Jam', is listed on his CV under the heading 'Expert Blogging'. Said, incidentally, is somewhat scathing of 'expertise and the cult of the certified expert... For "expertise" in the end has rather little, strictly speaking, to do with knowledge.' Said, *Representations of the Intellectual*, 77, 79.
48. Dov Jacobs, "Is the Salaita Situation really about 'Academic Freedom'?", Spreading the Jam, https://dovjacobs.com/2014/09/13/is-the-salaita-situation-really-about-academic-freedom, September 13, 2014.
49. Ibid.
50. Michael Kearney, Response to Jacobs, "Is the Salaita Situation really about 'Academic Freedom'?", Spreading the Jam, September 26, 2014.
51. Said, *Representations of the Intellectual*, 20.
52. Kearney, Response to Jacobs.
53. Washington, "Black Interpretation," 210.
54. Orwell, "Politics," 265.
55. Wright Mills, *The Politics of Truth*, 19.
56. Said, *Representations of the Intellectual*, 22.
57. Alex Young, "Killer Mike gives Emotional Speech in Wake of Ferguson Verdict," *Consequence of Sound*, November 25, 2014.
58. Kristian Davis Bailey, "Dream Defenders, Black Lives Matter & Ferguson Reps take Historic Trip to Palestine," *Ebony*, January 9, 2015.
59. Jordan, *Moving towards Home*.
60. The influence of the Palestinian struggle on George Jackson's thought and writings in prison, for example, is vividly detailed in an exhibition entitled 'George Jackson in the Sun of Palestine', curated by Greg Thomas of Tufts University and on display indefinitely at the Al-Quds University prisoners' museum in Abu Dis, Jerusalem from October 2015.
61. Davis, *Freedom is a Constant Struggle*.
62. Joseph Weiler, "After Gaza 2014: Schabas," *EJIL: Talk!*, November 4, 2014.
63. See https://twitter.com/philippesands/status/562737869719339011.
64. Weiler, "After Gaza 2014."
65. Falk, "Weakening and discrediting the UN: The Mission of Israeli QGOs," *Global Justice in the 21st Century*, https://richardfalk.wordpress.com/2015/04/17/weakening-and-discrediting-the-un-the-mission-of-israeli-qgos, April 17, 2015. Without sufficient prior knowledge of the region, Wibisono was unprepared for the level of obstruction he would meet from Israel; he resigned as a result after just over a year.
66. Allain, "On Coming to Terms," 155.
67. Marcuse, "Repressive Tolerance" (emphasis added).
68. Said, *Representations of the Intellectual*, x.
69. Dabashi, "The Discreet Charm," 7.
70. See, for example, Kubrin and Nielson, "Rap on Trial"; and Tanovich, "R v. Campbell."
71. Weiler, "After Gaza 2014."
72. Said, *Representations of the Intellectual*, 23.
73. Scalmer, "Edward Said," 46, 49.
74. Scalmer, "Edward Said," 45.
75. Scalmer, "Edward Said," 48.
76. Rodney, *Walter Rodney Speaks*, 111.
77. Marcuse, "Repressive Tolerance."

78. Ibid.
79. Genet et al., "Jean Genet," 45–46. Genet spent time in Palestinian camps and PLO training bases on the Syrian–Jordanian border in the early 1970s, and was in Beirut at the time of the Sabra and Shatilla massacre in September 1982. See Genet, "Quatre heures à Chatila."
80. Abi-Saab, "The Third World Intellectual in Praxis."
81. Rodney, *Walter Rodney Speaks*, 112.
82. Rodney, *Walter Rodney Speaks*, 113.
83. Rodney, *Walter Rodney Speaks*, 110, 113.
84. "Walter Rodney Memorial Programme," Kensington Town Hall, July 25, 1980.
85. Rodney, *Walter Rodney Speaks*, 16, 19.
86. Rajagopal, *International Law from Below*; and Rajagopal, "Counter-hegemonic International Law."
87. Said, *Representations of the Intellectual*, 9.
88. *Richardson v. Director of Public Prosecutions* [2014] UKSC 8.
89. *R. Fraser v. University & College Union*, 2203390/2011, Judgment of March 22, 2013.
90. Reynolds, "Anti-colonial Legalities," 38. See also Knox, "Strategy and Tactics."
91. Sash Lewis, "The Luminous Bastard," http://sashlewis.blogspot.com/2009/07/luminous-bastard.html, July 10, 2009.
92. "Statement: Over 80 Academics respond to Steven Salaita Lawsuit Settlement," http://mondoweiss.net/2015/11/academics-settlement-university.
93. Richard Falk, "A Jurisprudence of Conscience," Al-Jazeera, November 23, 2011.
94. Committee on the Elimination of Racial Discrimination, "Concluding Observations: Israel," UN Doc. CERD/C/ISR/CO/14–16, March 9, 2012, para 24. See also Dugard and Reynolds, "Apartheid."
95. The Russell Tribunal on Palestine, "Extraordinary Session on Gaza: Summary of Findings," Brussels, September 25, 2014.
96. Richard Falk, "The Palestinian 'Legitimacy War'," Al-Jazeera, December 24, 2010.
97. On the successes of the BDS movement, see, for example, Ben White, "Game Changer: 10 Years of BDS," Al-Jazeera, July 9, 2015; and "BDS Victories," https://bdsmovement.net/victories.
98. d'Aspremont, "The International Legal Scholar."

Bibliography

Abi-Saab, Georges. "The Third World Intellectual in Praxis: Confrontation, Participation or Operation behind Enemy Lines?." *Third World Quarterly* 2016. doi:10.1080/01436597.2016.1212653

Allain, Jean. "On Coming to Terms with the Israeli Palestinian Conflict: *From Coexistence to Conquest – International Law and the Origins of the Arab–Israeli Conflict, 1891–1949*, Victor Kattan." Book review. *Journal of the History of International Law* 12 (2010): 155–160.

Butler, Judith. "Israel/Palestine and the Paradoxes of Academic Freedom." *Radical Philosophy* 135 (2006): 8–17.

Cole, Teju. "Bad Laws." In *Letters to Palestine: Writers Respond to War and Occupation*, edited by Vijay Prashad, 19–24. London: Verso, 2014.

Dabashi, Hamid. "The Discreet Charm of European Intellectuals." *International Journal of Zizek Studies* 3, no. 4 (2009): 1–8.

d'Aspremont, Jean. "The International Legal Scholar in Palestine: Hurling Stones under the Guise of Legal Forms?." *Melbourne Journal of International Law* 14 (2013): 1–17.

Davis, Angela Y. *Freedom is a Constant Struggle: Ferguson, Palestine, and the Foundations of a Movement*. Chicago, IL: Haymarket, 2016.

Dugard, John, and John Reynolds. "Apartheid, International Law, and the Occupied Palestinian Territory." *European Journal of International Law* 24 (2013): 867–913.

Genet, Jean, Ruediger Wischenbart, and Gitta Honegger. "Jean Genet: The Intellectual as Guerrilla." *Performing Arts Journal* 9 (1985): 38–46.

Genet, Jean. "Quatre heures à Chatila." *La Revue d'études Palestiniennes* 6 (1983): 3–19.

Jordan, June. *Moving towards Home*. London: Virago, 1989.

Knox, Robert. "Strategy and Tactics." *Finnish Yearbook of International Law* 21 (2010): 193–229.

Kubrin, Charis E., and Erik Nielson. "Rap on Trial." *Race & Justice* 4, no. 3 (2014): 185–211.

Marcuse, Herbert. "Repressive Tolerance." In *A Critique of Pure Reason*, edited by Herbert Marcuse, Barrington Moore Jr. and Robert Paul Wolff, 95–137. Boston, MA: Beacon Press, 1969.

Locke, John. *Some Thoughts concerning Education*, 1693. Reprint, Cambridge: Cambridge University Press, 1934.

Mill, John Stuart. *On Liberty*. Boston, MA: Ticknor & Fields, 1863.

Orwell, George. "Politics and the English Language." *Horizon* 13, no. 76 (1946): 252–265.

Rajagopal, Balakrishnan. *International Law from Below: Development, Social Movements and Third World Resistance*. Cambridge: Cambridge University Press, 2003.

Rajagopal, Balakrishnan. "Counter-hegemonic International Law: Rethinking Human Rights and Development as a Third World Strategy." *Third World Quarterly* 27, no. 5 (2006): 767–783.

Reynolds, John. "Anti-colonial Legalities: Paradigms, Tactics & Strategy." *Palestine Yearbook of International Law* 18 (2015): 8–52.

Rodney, Walter. *Walter Rodney Speaks: The Making of an African Intellectual*. Trenton, NJ: Africa World Press, 1990.

Said, Edward W. "American Intellectuals and Middle East Politics." *Social Text*, no. 19–20 (1988): 37–53.

Said, Edward W. *Out of Place: A Memoir*. New York: Alfred A. Knopf, 1999.

Said, Edward W. *Representations of the Intellectual: The 1993 Reith Lectures*. New York: Vintage, 1996.

Salaita, Steven. *Uncivil Rites: Palestine and the Limits of Academic Freedom*. Chicago, IL: Haymarket, 2015.

Scalmer, Sean. "Edward Said and the Sociology of Intellectuals." In *Edward Said: The Legacy of a Public Intellectual*, edited by Ned Curthoys and Ganguly Debjani, 36–56. Melbourne: Melbourne University Press, 2007.

Tanovich, David M. "R v. Campbell: Rethinking the Admissibility of Rap Lyrics in Criminal Cases." *Criminal Reports (7th)* 24 (2016): 27–43.

Tawil-Souri, Helga, and Dina Matar (eds.). *Gaza as Metaphor*. London: Hurst, 2016.

Washington, Earl M. "Black Interpretation, Black American Literature, and Grey Audiences." *Communication Education* 30, no. 3 (1981): 209–216.

Wright Mills, C. *The Politics of Truth: Selected Writings of C. Wright Mills*. Oxford: Oxford University Press, 2008.

Migration, development and security within racialised global capitalism: refusing the balance game

Adrian A. Smith

ABSTRACT
Within international labour migration, received wisdom holds that the migration-development and migration-security couplings co-exist in discord. The migration-development-security relationship is perceived to swing like a pendulum. In this article I reject the simple pendulum formulation which suggests security stands at odds with development. I examine the ways in which migration controls occur through and reproduce racialised global capitalism. Capitalist development and security work together to undermine the resistance struggles of those designated migrant labour. Students of labour migration must refuse the game of balance and instead entrench our analytical efforts within the creative self-activities of ordinary working people.

Introduction

Considerable interest surrounds the relationship between international migration, development and security in the contemporary moment. While the interplay of these sets of ideas and policy spheres is widely accepted, received wisdom holds that the migration-development and migration-security couplings co-exist in tension. In the case of the former, scholarly and policy commentators now celebrate the power of 'low-skilled' temporary labour migration and financial remittances to produce economic development or growth in the Global South.[1] Yet, in the context of 'migration management', security is taken as a new mode of governance deployed to mediate the disruptive threat posed by migration in the Global North. Whereas migration's linkage with development is now understood in positive terms, its linkage with security is presented as negative or anomalous, and the migration-development-security relationship is perceived as discordant or contradictory. The resulting claim is one of policy incoherence framed in terms of pendulum swings, between development and security or between competing conceptions of development.

Ongoing scholarly entanglements do not appear to question certain presuppositions underlying this received wisdom. In deep disagreement with the simple pendulum formulation, it seems fitting to invoke the cheeky refrain of Terry Eagleton (following Raymond Williams) that 'when in doubt, the Englishman thinks of a pendulum';[2] so too, it would appear, does the migration scholar. But its 'simple harmonic motion'[3] cannot possibly capture the rich texture of temporary labour migration. Operating as a facile metaphor to convey complex relations and dynamics, it reinforces a series of problematic and dangerous understandings. The simple pendulum suggests that, in descriptive terms, security and development stand in tension with each other and that, in prescriptive terms, achieving balance or equilibrium is the best way forward. It also promulgates a linear conception of social change. All of this masks the state-rooted regulation of temporary labour migration – especially pertaining to the unfolding logic of racialised capitalism.

If there is any pendulum that speaks to the dynamics of temporary labour migration, it is that of the torture instrument – the pendulum blade, as depicted in Edgar Allan Poe's macabre short story about the Spanish Inquisition, The Pit and the Pendulum.[4] Through a first-person stylised account documenting the horrors of the plight of a mythical prisoner, we are led through the inner reflections of this unidentified narrator as they navigate from inquisitorial trial and auto-da-fé to imprisonment in the 'condemned cells at Toledo', a 'subterrene world of darkness'.[5] All that swings are the moods of the narrator – between fearfulness and "insensibility"[6] or 'slumber' as they attempt to traverse the perimeter of the darkened prison in search of an escape – and, as the terror unfolds, the pendulum blade. In line with Poe's reflections, I propose an inquisition of a different sort. Calling into question the prevailing orthodoxy surrounding temporary labour migration, I take a seemingly heretical stance in rejecting security and development as contradictory. Instead, I illustrate the ways in which state-managed temporary labour migration requires the production of racialised, unfree and migrant, labouring bodies through processes of pacification. These processes service both security and development and, in turn, are contingent upon and reproduce racialised global capitalism.

The article opens with a review of prominent articulations of the pendulum formulation. The second section addresses the dominant paradigm of security as it is employed in the study of international migration, attending to critical revisions of the national security focus of migration orthodoxy. These approaches seek not to contest security as an organising concept but to supplement it with accounts of 'human security' or 'securitisation'. The task here is to problematise the adoption of security-indebted approaches beginning with – but not limited to – the discursive affixing of the concept of security to the migration policy agenda. Next, I address the emergent idea of migration as development and, in the fourth section, the way in which it is entrenched within global governance. The final section addresses how the tandem of security and development feed and are fed by pacification and, specifically, processes and relations of racialisation, unfreedom and migration. It is from these dire prospects that Third World approaches to international law (TWAIL) accounts must emerge.

On migration and pendulum swings

An emergent analysis addresses the international scholarly and policy discourse surrounding the migration-development-security 'complex' or 'nexus'.[8] Succinctly characterising prevailing accounts, migration scholar Ninna Nyberg Sørensen remarks that:

> Migration, development and security are integrally linked but habitually studied in 'pairs' related to the geopolitical concern at hand: migration–security when concerned with national and regional policy agendas of the Global North; migration–development when concerned with the problems (and possible solutions) for the migrant-producing Global South...[9]

Given the Global North's institutional dominance in driving 'asymmetrical debates' and agenda-setting, Sorenson calls for revised analytical frameworks that account for the intersection between migration industries and markets for control. While Sørenson sees development potential turning on policies enabling migrant participation in societal transformation, they also warn that 'the pendulum soon will swing back the other way' in the face of 'powerful actors' in international security and private surveillance.[10]

Likewise, scholar Hein de Haas deploys the metaphor of the pendulum swing to characterise the debate on the migration-development relationship.[11] Focused on postwar Europe, de Haas contends that 'the [research] debate on migration and development has swung back and forth like a pendulum between optimistic and pessimistic views'[12] driven by ideological shifts in development theory. De Haas recounts the 'sudden mood swings' in the historical record: 'from optimism in the 1950s and 1960s, to pessimism, scepticism and relative neglect since the early 1970s, and towards more optimistic views since 2000'.[13] These swings mirror the respective rise and fall of neoclassical and developmentalist-modernisation accounts of migration versus structuralist theoretical accounts.[14] In the most recent period, de Haas identifies an emergent 'disappointment' or 'pessimism' in European countries and warns of the 'huge danger of naïve optimism'.[15]

Disciplined by the need to present 'sensible and realistic policy responses',[16] these accounts adopt similar claims. Framed as swings in the pendulum, Sørensen, de Haas and others identify incoherence in the scholarly and policy spheres of migration, security and development.[17] The pendulum metaphor signifies the core claim that security and development stand in tension with each other, and that the solution for migration policy rests with recalibration and balance. In contrast, the account offered here contests the formulation in two interconnected ways. First, the formulation diverts attention away from addressing a fundamental challenge of emancipatory praxis, that of setting the relationship between 'strategy and tactics'.[18] The production of 'policy-relevant' and analytically pertinent knowledge becomes a stand-in for allowing tactical considerations, conceived of in a short-term and reactionary way, to drive if not undermine long-term strategic political agendas of emancipation. The policy and analytical dilemmas of our time cannot be divorced from emancipatory agendas and praxis.

Second, 'security discourse' is precisely one of the dominant framings through which governing elites undermine challenges to status quo relations. Security forms an integral part of efforts to subsume questions and challenges of labour migration into a framework of liberalism. In this respect, the basic pendulum formulation appears to explain away what we might term 'productive tensions', especially as they relate to the role of national states in mediating capitalist relations. The danger of such a formulation rests in the promulgation of what one scholar has termed 'the classic liberal balance between security and liberty'.[19] It appears to insist on (western) liberal-capitalist conceptions of balance and the resolution of tensions without consideration of their utility for states and capitalist accumulation. Taken together, these interconnected claims motivate the ensuing analysis.

Security as critical analytical paradigm

A growing preoccupation with the influence of security on international migration stems from the now well-entrenched belief that im/migration represents a burden and threat to the wealthy national states of the Global North. Migration is construed as a challenge to state sovereignty and autonomy and its national territorial borders. Northern states increasingly respond through the intensification of restrictive migration and border controls. Meanwhile, an emergent set of critical scholarly interventions re-evaluates the presuppositions of migration regulatory controls especially in relation to state-centric conceptions of security. Questioning wealthy states' singular focus on national security and the control of territorial borders, critical scholarly approaches seek to revise understandings of state sovereignty and citizen security. These approaches, while continuing to operate on the contested – and ultimately fraught – terrain of security, typically adopt 'human security' and 'securitisation' framings and deploy the idea of 'insecurity'.[20]

Armed with the understanding of security for some at the expense of insecurity for others, the human security approach advocates a people-centred agenda which takes the human being as the '"end" of development, not only as a "means" to increased economic productivity or legal coherence'.[21] Certain proponents are especially attentive to the linkages between human security and migration and, in particular, the human security of non-citizens.[22] In contesting state-centrism, the human security approach revises the normative claim that national security should serve as the sole impetus behind migration regulatory policies.[23] If the security-seeking state legitimately adopts restrictive migration controls, then cross-border mobility represents a modus operandi for the security-seeking individual striving for resolution of their 'immediate security needs'.[24] In this way, 'human security sketches out how national governments can reorient their own security policies', and that of international peace and security, around 'all human lives'.[25] The aim of human security, then, is not to 'obviate state security' nor to 'encompass all of the security agenda' including 'territorial integrity and the distribution of power among nations'.[26] Instead, the human security approach to migration strives for the enlargement of security and analogous policies to account for the insecurity of non-citizens such as migrants.[27]

Proponents of human security typically pair their approach with international human rights and human development or capabilities approaches. Ultimately, however, human security is construed not as a panacea but rather as a way to supplement or 'plug some of the gaps' in the international human rights regime as it pertains to non-citizens or 'aliens'.[28]

For its part, the securitisation approach addresses the pervasive extension of security into policy spheres and onto political issues that, as a rule, are otherwise deemed unrelated.[29] Analytically, securitisation regards security as a 'discursive process' or 'speech act' through which 'new security threats' are socially constructed by moving issues from 'the realm of typical politics' to 'the realm of exception' and existential threat.[30] The discursive construction of migration as existential threat in turn justifies the use of urgent and extraordinary counter-measures (read: 'states of exception' or 'rule-breaking behaviour'). Principally, the securitisation of migration functions to circumvent democratic processes, placing migration policies effectively above or outside of the regular course of politics. In other words, the discursive process of securitisation functions in the name of protecting 'fundamental values of society and the State' by suspending the application of those values. This 'drive' for securitization and the state's 'will' to master it,[31] are perceived as the impetus behind the deepening restrictions imposed on migration.

Seeking to identify and disrupt these discursive moves, the securitisation approach draws a sharp distinction between exception and normality. In addition, proponents of the approach, like those of the human security approach, also have sought to present human rights as a meaningful 'counter-weight' to security.[32] In this respect, liberty and security are held out as binary and dichotomous distinctions. Herein lie the limits of the securitisation approach, which I reject on the basis of my anti-racist Marxist approach to the regulation of temporary labour migration. Thus, I stand firmly against the adoption of a security-entrenched account or defence of labour migration.

Following Anti-security interventions, exception and normality as well as liberty and security constitute 'false binaries' erected within the diverse liberal tradition.[33] Whereas the former claims the disruptions and intrusions done in the name of security mark a state of exception,[34] the latter claims that 'liberty is security and security is liberty'. Both pairings 'obfuscate and reify the security problematic' in the service of status quo relations.[35] The obfuscation is rooted in a commitment to a foundational myth of modern western political theory: that of the sharp 'clash' between supposedly diametrically opposed logics of sovereignty (Hobbesian security versus Lockean liberty).[36] In contrast, I echo Mark Neocleous's call for a 'critique of security' forged on a politics not merely critical of security but in fact altogether 'against' it.[37] Following Neocleous, I find 'misleading' the claim that liberalism emerged out of 'some kind of shift in balance away from security and towards liberty'.[38] By at least the close of the eighteenth century, most liberal adherents saw – and continue to perceive – security as the formative if not 'necessary' object of government.[39] The commonplace refrain of balancing or trading off 'a certain amount of liberty in our desire for security' during the 'war on terror' both substitutes for real argument and stifles political contestation.[40] A critique of security, forged on the understanding that the concept of security is irredeemably flawed, constitutes a refusal to play the balance game.[41]

A crucial aspect of the critique of security turns on an interrogation of the role of the state in governing civil society. Affixing the idea of security to a given issue or field provides the state with justification 'to tighten its grip on civil society and ratchet-up its restrictions on human freedoms'.[42] Beyond constituting hegemonic discourse, Anti-security accounts refer to these processes (and practices) of fabricating 'a social order' as pacification.[43] The essential work of pacification is to fabricate a liberal-capitalist order through the rendering of productive labour. Pacification is thus rooted in primitive accumulation and extended through ongoing accumulation by dispossession, including the emergence and spread of capitalist relations through the colonial enterprises of competing European powers.[44] Migration processes serve as response and outcome to the inter-related forces of primitive and dispossessive accumulation and colonialism-imperialism.[45]

The concept of pacification provides a supremely useful analytic around which to organise our understandings of temporary labour migration regulation.[46] Pacification connotes the general means by which labour is rendered productive within capitalist social relations, owing to class dynamics and struggles.[47] But attentiveness to migration and class cannot occur without considering racialisation, understood as the process of ascribing significance and value to bodies through perceived physical traits or stereotypes. Racialisation occurs by virtue of its perpetuation through and effects on migration processes and relations leading to the production of migrant labouring bodies, Global South-North relations and the impacts of capitalist accumulation on a global scale. The imposition of the 'dangerous South' on the 'pristine' North is a dominant narrative within the paradigm of security that neither critical human security and securitisation approaches nor Anti-security accounts have taken up yet. The dangerous-pristine, South-North distinctions envelop states and peoples and are more than mere discursive constructions. Indeed, they develop out of longstanding socio-historical-legal processes and practices of which racialisation and racism assume crucial roles.

From 'migration and development' to 'migration as development'

Thus far, I have argued that it is not favourable to adopt the paradigm of security because both security and liberty are central to the problem at hand: the ongoing role of national states in the racialised pacification of unfree migrant labouring bodies. I shift now to address migration and development. Just as migration is perceived as a threat to national security of the Global North, it too is held out as a means of enhancing or bolstering economic growth in the Global South. Temporary labour migration, as I discuss below, has been posed as a response to restrictive migration and border controls, one which is said to produce positive developmental benefits and outcomes. Temporary migration as development shuns the curtailment of migration by enforcing the differentiation between 'desirable' and 'undesirable' forms.

International migration has long represented a strategy of resistance and mitigation for poverty in the absence of socioeconomic development in a given locale.[48] While clearly not a new consideration, the contemporary perspective holds that migration positively impacts economic development when it works as a 'on tool and engine' to facilitate development. It not only takes migration and development as intersecting policies and processes but also assumes migration, if properly directed or 'managed', can serve as a pivotal driver of development.

Within the 'migration as development' perspective, a great deal turns on claims about the meaningful contribution of remittances to sending country development.[49] While many of these claims are highly disputed, remittances are said to lessen the pressure on national accounts, providing a reliable, stable and relatively substantial source of foreign exchange earnings; enhance public finances leading to investment in infrastructure and employment creation; and supplement or even replace foreign direct investment and development aid. Alongside remittances,[50] circular or temporary labour migration marks a pivotal feature of the perspective. Temporary labour migration not only works in service of poverty mitigation and reduction by addressing chronic shortages of paid employment and formal opportunities in the labour market, but also offers ongoing or recurring opportunities for remittance-driven development.

The migration-as-development perspective has drawn considerable attention within the global political and development dialogue and agenda. Within the United Nations system, there are a dizzying array of groups, agencies, inter-agencies, commissions and other institutional bodies pursing the migration-as-development agenda, addressing issues ranging from how to leverage the benefits of remittances to how to deepen migrant labour market integration, expand migrant capabilities, build migrant skills and formal training opportunities, and harness diaspora networks.[51] That said, despite garnering considerable interest, international migration is noticeably absent from key documents of the global development agenda. The eight Millennium Development Goals (MDGs) failed to mention migration, an exclusion supported by commentators such as Ronald Skeldon given its highly contentious political nature, even though 'it is virtually impossible to envisage progress towards achieving the existing MDGs without some kind of migration'.[52]

The global development dialogue incorporates migration as development. A popular version of the underlying logic of migration as development is that 'a combination of population growth in the South and greater awareness of the (better) living conditions offered in the North presents the international community with a development challenge'.[53] Proper or effective migration management, as the logic goes, can assist countries and peoples with meeting this challenge. But what is meant by 'proper' or 'effective'?

Global governance of migration: a national state affair

Embedded within the global development dialogue rests a concern with the management of migration.[54] As a central focus of global policy in the contemporary period, migration management is understood in terms of global governance and security.[55] It represents 'a global governmental response'[56] aimed at transforming disorderly migratory flows into orderly ones. But, notwithstanding ongoing calls,[57] there is little in the way of formal international cooperation on migration: 'There is no global regime to regulate migration',[58] nor a 'World Migration Organisation within the UN system'.[59]

Contemporary policy remains organised around 'nationalised governance of migration'[60] affirming, in the face of a range of claims to the contrary, the ongoing importance of national states in the regulation of labour migration. Now, the existence of international labour and human rights might be identified as the (emerging) basis of global coordination on migration. In addition to protections afforded through International Labour Organisation conventions, the International Convention on the Protection of the Rights of All Migrant Workers and Members of Their Families, which was signed in 1990 and entered into force in July 2003, forms the centrepiece of international human rights of migrant workers. Despite calls for greater attention to the Convention, and to the 'counter-hegemonic' practices of human rights activism,[61] there not only remain 'convergences and divergences' in international legal rights regime pertaining to migrant labour, but in fact a fundamental 'paradox': its organisation around and through state sovereignty.[62]

The modern national state functions within a global system of national states said to be driven by growing interdependence.[63] In contrast, the national state is characterised by independence and non-encroachment. The equality of national states in international law underwrites migration management. Central to national state equality are the principles of sovereign authority and territorial integrity which, within the modern international system, intersect to define the parameters of the nation state. That is to say, sovereign authority of the state is of a more or less fixed territorial scope. Deriving legitimacy from efforts to preserve this scope, the state seeks to enforce national territorial borders under the guise of representing the aspirations of its citizenry and maintaining internal order, fundamentally through the provision of national security.[64] Security captures the protection of the national territorial state against external imposition or aggression and the grouping of sovereignty and territoriality with citizenship.

Within the contemporary national state system, sovereign territorial states regulate the trans-border movement of people. The principles of sovereignty and territoriality structure labour mobility which lends credence to the core assumption that, as articulated by Martin, receiving states determine 'how many, from where, and in what status' migrants enter the country based on the,achieve[ment of] national goals, such as maximising economic growth, maintaining public finances, and ensuring social cohesion and national security'.[65] In affirming the equality and authority of states, migration management through global governance rests on a presupposition of national security and the securitisation of migration. The implementation of restrictive migration policies is articulated in terms of the preservation of national sovereignty and security. Security, as 'the main modality of governance',[66] performs a crucial function in the justification of neoliberal migration management.

It is important to see that migration management depends on, and in turn perpetuates, myths of equality and non-encroachment of states. Migration as development (or, as some prefer, migration-for-development) stems from the im/migration control agenda of receiving states. But we would be remiss not to acknowledge that regulation of the trans-border movement of people relies upon the global system of national states. The existence and perpetuation of territorial borders serve to enforce national difference in the form of corresponding behaviours and subjectivities.[67] Sending states assume pivotal roles in imposing capitalist market dependence on their respective labouring populations.

Temporary labour migration amounts to a 'proper' and 'effective' form of contemporary migration management. It has been posed as a response to restrictive migration and border controls, one which produces positive developmental benefits and outcomes. As development, temporary migration shuns the curtailment of migration by enforcing a crucial differentiation. Against concerns of illegal or undocumented migration as a threat to national security, intensifying claims of territorial border porosity, and deepening desires to heavily curtail permanent settlement, temporary labour migration is constructed as a policy of deterrence to a range of unwanted or undesirable migratory flows. In this way, temporary labour migration enforces the production of 'desirable' and 'undesirable' migration and migrants providing a process through which it can be determined who belongs and does not belong within the national states of the Global North.

While a recounting of the history of the migration-development relationship shows a longstanding appreciation of the linkage, the emergence of migration as development is important as a rejection of certain traditional assumptions. Namely, migration as development does away with the belief that development aid or assistance will end the need for migration. Indeed, the growing emphasis on temporary labour migration by receiving and sending states, the World Bank and others represents acceptance or acknowledgement that continued migration is a necessary if not indispensable feature of human existence. That said, its reliance upon restrictive migration controls through the denial of permanent settlement and citizenship, and its imposition of precarious migration status, ensures migrants and their respective states cannot gain the upper hand through these processes.

Navigating the pendulum blade of temporary labour migration

In the face of persistent claims that the security paradigm runs counter to the development agenda or paradigm, I argue that security informs development and, in turn, the idea of development is inescapably caught within the logic of securitised migration. The co-constitution of these paradigms owes to the logic and practices of global capitalist relations – as both take on liberal meanings to function in service of capitalist accumulation. Rather than identifying the security paradigm or the development paradigm as separate and distinct spheres, it is more apt to refer to the ‚development/security paradigm'" of migration management under contemporary global capitalism. As that dominant paradigm makes clear, 'securing populations in the Global North'[69] proves integral to pacifying labouring populations in the Global South. But those Northern populations are secure insofar as they themselves are pacified, a dynamic that goes to the essence of contemporary liberal-democratic capitalism. The ‚global interconnectivity of pacification'[70] functions through a number of means including state-managed temporary labour migration and the complex transnational regulatory dynamic of im/mobilisation which, as argued elsewhere, relies upon and reproduces global apartheid.[71] With the aim of deepening understanding of the racialised class dimensions of the global interconnection of pacification, this final section addresses the pacification of temporary labour migration as the rendering of racialised capitalist order.

The prevailing accounts of the migration-development-security nexus not only fail to reckon with the understanding that temporary labour migration demands and justifies pacification, both in terms of liberal capitalist security and development. The limits of the existing critical accounts are even more apparent in the face of an interrogation of racialised capitalist order. A stubborn unwillingness to contemplate racialisation and racism pervades the respective studies of development and security and, albeit to a far lesser extent, migration. In development studies, the absence of an accounting of racialisation and racism has led to a 'profound silence'.[72] A pivotal insight is that many of these critiques focus on the migration-as-development agenda as a policy discourse and as such operate at the level of critical discourse analysis. These approaches occur at the expense of meaningful consideration of ongoing material practices, relations and effects.[73] They appear to divorce discourse from embodiment and labouring bodies from discourse in ways that prove ahistorical, anti-materialist and overly problematic for consideration of the ways in which temporary labour migration is produced and migrant labour is incorporated into labour markets and wider social life in the Global North.[74] Set within the material practices and context of migration management, regulatory practices have crucial racialised effects and are themselves the product of racialised practices of 'differentiated belonging'.[75]

In security studies, racialisation and racism are similarly absent from core accounts. Where racialisation and racism receive limited deployment, they operate to enforce the newness of the discourse of securitisation of migration, which is said to represent a modern form of racism.[76] In migration studies, where accounts of xenophobia and racism have enjoyed wider appeal, there are attempts that seek to identify the hateful vitriolic flung at migrants by reactionary groups of the Global North, but far too few accounts address the ongoing and systemic racist nature of labour migration policies. But, as Wilson rightly suggests, racism is not merely reflected in prevailing security, development and migration policies; it is not simply an exceptional way through which to smooth out the rough edges of the supposedly contradictory relationship between migration-security and migration-development. Rather, racism is mobilised[77] as a key basis for the very linkage between migration, development and security within global capitalism. Pacification lies at the heart of the explanation.

The pacification of migrant labour represents a key process dependent upon the existing process of racialisation of global capitalism and, at the same time, working to deepen racialised global capitalism. The development/security paradigm of contemporary migration management is indebted to pacification to render labour racialised, unfree and migrant. As specific processes of pacification, racialisation and racism function to characterise and ultimately impose a hierarchical process of valuation of labouring bodies and of national states in Global South-North relations. In other words, unfree migrant labour is a racialised form of productive labour utilised within contemporary global capitalism. In addressing the racialised pacification of unfree migrant labour we see that, as Wilson astutely notes, 'capitalism is productive of difference'.[78] It is in this context that migrant labour is characterised as both existential threat to the national security of receiving states and agent of development for sending states. These characterisations are put to *productive* use for the purposes of capitalist accumulation in the Global North and South.[79]

Extending the application of Anti-security, two interventions bolster an account of the pacification of migrant labour.

Temporary labour migration pacifies through the production of unfree, migrant and racialised labouring bodies

States, on behalf of capitalist classes, deploy temporary labour migration regimes to render labour productive in unfree, migrant *and* racialised terms. I (and others) have discussed unfreedom and migration elsewhere.[80] Accounting for racialisation and racism requires attention to the role of law and the national state system in the production of labouring bodies. These laws and states police racialised national belonging (including citizenship) at the same time as they produce racialised migrant labouring bodies.

Pacification is structured through unequal and hierarchical South-North relations

The pacification of temporary labour migration occurs through the hierarchical global system of national states. In the current 'empire of capital',[81] a 'postcolonial' geopolitical context in which sovereign territorial states orchestrate capitalist internationalisation, dominant states of the Global North have sought to integrate states of the Global South into global capitalism through trade and financial liberalisation[82] and cross-border population movements. Stemming from 'the reconfiguring of imperialism after formal colonialism',[83] the universalising spread of national sovereignty throughout the Global South solidified the myth of the equality of states. And while the emergence of postcolonial states posed a not-unimportant challenge to the persistent rejection of non-white self-governance, and to a geopolitical rule of order bathed in white supremacy, it did so on complex terms.[84] The rise of near-universal sovereignty did not release newly independent states from the dictates of capitalist market dependence. Uneven capitalist development left the former colonial states with the considerable burden of ensuring the survival of vast and often disparately situated swaths of people.

The mechanism of indebtedness, whether in the form of aid, trade, finance or all of these, ensured a certain continuity of inequality and hierarchy between peoples and states along the South-North divide. Other measures deployed include temporary labour migration through which the enforcement of differentiated belonging ensured the depletion of human resources in the form of labour power from the Global South within the North. In the context of temporary labour migration programmes, capitalist imperialism signifies that migrant-receiving states garner their power by harnessing universal sovereignty and unevenness of global capital accumulation, relying upon relative economic and political dominance over sending states. However, these programmes also rest on the core myth of sovereignty as non-encroachment in the internal affairs of the state, a conceit that denies overwhelming evidence demonstrating otherwise in ongoing Global South-North relations. Quite crucially, labour-sending states perform the dirty work of labour exportation or 'brokerage'.[85] This produces a complex interplay of receiving and sending states in the transnational regulation of labour migration.[86]

Within capitalist imperialism, the national state system tethers migrant workers to their sending states giving those states a pivotal disciplinary role.[87] Capitalist imperialism, thus, definitively shapes the 'new' political economy of development. In this we see that the security-development dichotomy intervenes to mask ongoing efforts towards 'population control'.[88] Temporary labour migration represents a continuation of 'Malthusian-eugenist' population control of the 'wretched of the earth'. It marks the ongoing 'forcible incorporation' of the wretched into global capitalism, presenting the practices through which 'poverty and destitution' were 'naturalised and racialized' between peoples and states of the Global South and North.[89]

Racialised labour production and TWAIL

Coupled with the absence of meaningful anti-racist accounts within the prevailing orthodoxy surrounding the migration-development-security nexus, one cannot help but detect an unwillingness to venture into what Marx termed a critique of political economy. There exists utter disregard for labour – conceptually and ontologically; in terms of production and social reproduction – lending to, following Samir Amin, its 'disappearance … from the scope of bourgeois social thought'.[90] The omission, although deeply troubling, is not unexpected given the now well-entrenched retreat from class analytical frameworks and certain forms of class struggle in certain parts of the world.[91] Adding to these troubles is the absence of meaningful engagement taking up the mantle of anti-racist class indebted analysis. Where, for instance, is TWAIL on the racialised pacification of unfree migrant labour within global capitalism? While TWAIL scholars undoubtedly have produced crucial insights on colonialism, imperialism and the constitution of the international legal system;[92] while TWAIL's lineage certainly includes currents of 'critical race theory' and state formation, Third World resistance struggles and even a brand of Third World Marxism found almost exclusively in the work of B.S. Chimni;[93] and while there are emergent signs of scholars in and around TWAIL deepening engagements with open-ended Marxist and 'Fourth World' orientations;[94] it seems quite odd that processes of pacification – especially racialisation, unfreedom and migration – have yet to receive sustained treatment by adherents. If it would be myopic to place responsibility squarely on TWAIL – and it would – it would also be remiss not to acknowledge that the absence of robust accounts of racialised labour production in global capitalism aligns TWAIL with bourgeois social thinking.

That said, what is needed to remedy racialised labour's absence and disappearance is not 'empty and false chatter' but 'concrete analyses'.[95] If nothing else, TWAIL is well positioned to extend the concrete analysis of the nationalised governance of temporary labour migration and state territoriality. But its adherents must attend more forcefully to racialised global capitalist social relations of which the pacification of labour assumes a crucial role. The claim is not that we must return to outmoded (and, frankly, tired) conceptions of 'labour' that apply to an all-too-specific and narrow subset of social life – the industrialised, male worker within heteronormative family units, blanketed by the privilege of whiteness. To deeply appreciate the ways in which global capitalism produces labour and the commodity of labour power, we would do well to utilise the concept of pacification and its effects on labouring bodies, and to draw on materialist and indigenous ontologies to contest the dissociation of labouring bodies and their relations to each other and their natural(ised) surroundings.

If within contemporary global capitalism racialised unfree migrant labour lives in fear of the pendulum blade of the capitalist development/security paradigm, the task is not to further abstract labouring bodies from consideration. The prevailing orthodoxy surrounding migration management 'provide[s] no window into understanding the lives, standpoints, and self-activity of transnational migrants themselves, including their role as political actors or organisers'.[96] To identify temporary labour migration regimes as projects of pacification designed to quell worker resistance and political struggles is to appreciate that pacification necessarily presupposes worker resistance struggles. This amounts to a reading or accounting of resistance as a defining feature of ordinary peoples' lives. The development/security paradigm strives to undermine the kernels of resistance found within the self-activities of those designated migrant labour.

In this respect, we might then strive to re-envision development not as a paradigm or project invested in furthering capitalist accumulation and Global South-North hierarchies and inequalities, but by 'incorporating the whole complex of unequal material relationships and processes which structure engagement between the Global South and the Global North',[97] as 'a creative social process' nourished by 'the matrix' of 'the way[s] of life of the ordinary people'.[98]

Conclusion

In this article I explore the role of migration regulatory controls within scholarly accounts concerned with migration, development and security, placing particular emphasis on temporary labour migration. The ways in which security and development discourses shape migration policies form a pressing consideration of contemporary scholarly and policy debates. Heightened awareness of two sets of linkages, on one side migration and security and on the other migration and development, drives these contestations. Critical security-indebted accounts, which have their origins within critical international relations theory, include calls to incorporate human security and securitisation approaches. These seek to address the insecurity of non-citizens, the 'insecuritised migrant' or 'crimmigrant' rendered 'rightless'.[99] For its part, much of the recent enthusiasm for the migration and development linkage – termed by some migration *as* development – stems from the deployment of temporary labour migration and a deep reliance on financial remittances. Received wisdom holds that while temporary labour migration fosters economic growth, the securitisation of migration leads to intensification of restrictive migration at the expense of this growth potential. Thus, the migration-development-security nexus is perceived as a discordant or contradictory relationship.

In contrast to received wisdom, I work against the adoption of an analytical framework grounded on a mythical contradiction. The relationship is far from contradictory in its productive effects and, as such, neither capitalist development nor security can provide the necessary foundation for an emancipatory praxis for migrant labour – because, as central organising practices of national states within global capitalism, both work in service of capitalist accumulation and the preservation of hierarchy, unevenness and inequality. Crucially, the prevailing orthodoxy refrains from disrupting certain core presuppositions about the pacification of temporary labour migration, embedded within the racialised inequalities and hierarchies of Global South-North relations which persist within contemporary global capitalist order. Temporary labour migration amounts to the pacification of migration through the ongoing production of racialised, unfree and migrant labouring bodies. If we are to bring an end to pacification, we must confront head-on the racist dynamics of global capitalist relations. But even as the prospects appear dim, all is not lost. Contestation is found in the creative resistance struggles of ordinary people. The task, therefore, is to work towards the articulation of analytical frameworks that deepen, link and consolidate struggles to contest the balancing game of the capitalist development/security framing.

Disclosure statement

No potential conflict of interest was reported by the author.

Acknowledgements

I wish to acknowledge the supremely helpful engagements with participants in the Maynooth workshop, along with written feedback from Clíodhna Murphy, two anonymous reviewers and the special issue editors. Incisive commentary from Amar Bhatia led me to revisit the initial framing of the argument, revamp the alternative framing, and ultimately lift the article (and its author) out of the 'pit' of despair – for this, I am immensely grateful.

Notes

1. My discussion of temporary labour migration throughout is meant as a reference to Canada's Temporary Foreign Worker Programme (TFWP). As I have noted elsewhere, Canada's Seasonal Agricultural Worker Programme (SAWP), Live-In Caregiver Programme and Low-skilled Pilot Project (known formally as the Pilot Project for Hiring Foreign Workers in Occupations that Require Lower Levels of Formal Training) all form the core components of the early twenty-first century TFWP (see Satzewich 1991; Stasiulis & Bakan 2005; Sharma 2006; Choudry et al. 2009; Fudge & McPhail 2009). The TFWP turns on the deployment of unfree migrant labour whereby dull economic compulsion is sharpened through politico-legal compulsion. Although the use of migrant workers through the TFWP relies on economic compulsion generally, migratory status is the fundamental politico-legal mechanism of labour unfreedom. The pivotal instrument is the temporary work permit or authorisation which subjects non-citizens to the constant threat of repatriation (Sharma 2006; Goldring, Berinstein & Bernhard 2009; see also Walia 2010).
2. Eagleton, After Theory, 136.
3. Matthews et al., "The Pendulum", 262. While I reject the metaphorical utility of the 'simple pendulum' here, I reserve judgment on whether we should do away with the pendulum metaphor altogether in social sciences, as complex pendulums, which convey a sense of multiple moving parts, may apprehend behaviour in more nuanced and sophisticated ways.
4. Poe, "The Pit and the Pendulum," 747.
5. Ibid., 748.
6. Ibid., 747, 748, 753.
7. Ibid., 746, 751.
8. Sørensen, "Revisiting the Migration-Development Nexus," 62.

9. Ibid., 62. Sørensen goes on to add: 'security–development when concerned with complex policy problems in countries emerging from violent conflict', which I have excluded given the focus of the current analysis on migration. That said, it is through this pairing that the security paradigm is applied to address emergent issues in the Global South. My argument below works against the logic of extending security because, as I argue, the problem rests with the security paradigm itself.
10. Ibid., 72.
11. De Haas, "Migration and Development Pendulum."
12. Ibid., 10.
13. Ibid., 11.
14. Ibid., 12.
15. Ibid., 10.
16. Ibid., 12.
17. Sørensen, "Revisiting the Migration-Development Nexus," 71.
18. Knox, "Strategy and Tactics".
19. Dauvergne, "Security and Migration Law," 540.
20. On migrant 'insecurity', see Castles and Miller, *Age of Migration*. On migrant insecurity in the Canadian context, see Faraday, "Made in Canada."
21. Alkire, *Conceptual Framework*, 3–4.
22. See Edwards and Ferstman, *Human Security and Non-Citizens*, especially Cholewinski's chapter; Dauvergne, *Making People Illegal*; Truong and Des Gasper, *Transnational Migration and Human Security*; Bach, "Global Mobility, Inequality and Security."
23. Weber et al., "Migration Control and Human Security," 334.
24. Juss,"Human Security and Migration Control," conclusion.
25. Alkire, *A Conceptual Framework*, 4.
26. Ibid.
27. This understanding is partially consistent with the critique of human security levelled by David Chandler, a controversial intervention which spawned a mini-spat in the field. See Chandler, "Human Security"; Ambrosetti, *Human Security as Political Resource*; Owen, "Critique that Doesn't Bite"; Wibben, "Human Security: Toward an Opening"; Chandler, "Human Security II."
28. Edwards and Ferstman, *Human Security and Non-Citizens*, 46; United Nations, *Rights of Non-Citizens*; Lillich, *Human Rights of Aliens*.
29. The securitisation approach is attributed to the Copenhagen school of international relations and its constructivist framework of analysis; see Buzan et al., "Security: A New Framework for Analysis"; Wæver, "Securitization and Desecuritization"; Krause and Williams, "Broadening the Agenda of Security Studies?" See also Huysmans, "Migrants as a Security Problem"; "The Securitization of Asylum" ; Bourbeau, *Securitization of Migration*; Ibrahim, *Securitization of Migration*; Russo, "Security, Securitization and Human Capital."
30. Canadian Association for Refugee and Forced Migration Studies, "Securitization of Migration"; Themistocleous, "Securitizing Migration: Aspects and Critiques."
31. Munck, 1231.
32. For a discussion of securitisation of migration in the Canadian context, see Crépeau and Nakache, "Controlling Irregular Migration in Canada."
33. Neocleous and Rigakos, *Anti-Security*; Neocleous, "The Problem with Normality."
34. Neocleous and Rigakos, *Anti-Security*, 19.
35. Ibid., 16.
36. Neocleous, *Contemporary Political Theory*, 134.
37. For an elaboration, see Neocleous, "Against security"; Neocleous, *Critique of Security*.
38. Neocleous, *Contemporary Political Theory*, 142 (emphasis removed).
39. The historical alignment of liberalism with limited government is 'an idea which seems to presuppose that the state is always already likely to trample on civil society in general and liberty in particular. But the suspicion that there is always a risk of too much governing is always tied to the question: why is it necessary to govern at all? And with this question liberalism not

only finds itself unable to escape the politics of security, but actually reasserts security as the fundamental aim of government'; Neocleous, *Contemporary Political Theory*, 142.

40. Neocleous, *Contemporary Political Theory*, 131–2.
41. Ibid., 134. Derived from Marx's intervention in *On the Jewish Question*, 'To Marx's comment that security is the supreme concept of bourgeois society, we might add that this is so because security is the supreme concept of liberal ideology' (142). For Neocleous, the provocative call is to 'eschew the language of security altogether' – including, quite pivotally, in its contemporary incarnation as 'state of emergency' – and deem the concept of security 'part of the problem' (134). The task, therefore, is to build 'real alternatives to the authoritarian tendencies in contemporary politics' (147).
42. Ibid., 146.
43. Neocleous, *Fabrication of Social Order*; Neocleous, *Critique of Security*.
44. Accumulation by dispossession is a concept developed by geographer David Harvey. For a slightly different take on accumulation by dispossession see Phillips, "Migration as Development Strategy?"
45. Pacification proved the handmaiden of European colonialism, standing for confrontation with the 'recalcitrant and rebellious'; Captain Bernardo de Vargas Machuca cited in Özcan & Rigakos, "Pacification" 1.
46. Neocleous and Rigakos, *Anti-Security*; Özcan and Rigakos, "Pacification."
47. Van Hear, "Reconsidering Migration and Class"; Milanovic, "Global Inequality."
48. Beginning with the early work of cartographer Ernst Ravenstein, one of the forebears of migration studies, a positive correlation has been identified between migration and development. Ravenstein identified the growth of industry, commerce and transportation as a central driving force behind the movement of people. Ravenstein, "Laws of Migration." Working in the classical tradition of political economy in the 1950s, and contesting emergent neoclassical and Keynesian economic formulations, Saint Lucian economist Arthur Lewis provided the clearest articulation of the classical economic coupling of migration and development understood as economic growth. Lewis posited that colonial locales experiencing labour surpluses due to the lack of productivity within the subsistence agricultural or traditional sector enjoyed 'unlimited supplies of [cheap] labour' which, through migration, could be put to productive use in the industrial sector. See e.g. Lewis, *Economic Development*. Lewis's colonial 'dual economy' model, a body of ideas for which he shared the Nobel Prize, and which was later revised by the likes of Michael Todaro and John Harris, provided an economic rationale for harnessing international migration for economic development. Harris and Todaro, *Migration, Unemployment and Development*; Todaro, *Model of Labour Migration*.

    Commencing in the 1970s, the classical and neoclassical perspectives faced intense scrutiny from Marxist-inspired critiques of development and appeared to drop out of favour by the 1980s, especially with respect to the migration-development coupling – but not in terms of the primacy of economic growth. Castles and Miller, *Age of Migration*, 75. However, nearing the end of the twentieth century, and continuing on into the early twenty-first, a proliferation of scholarly and policy interest re-emerged on the international migration-development nexus.
49. Lindley, "Remittances"; Kapur, "Remittances"; Mundaca, "Remittances, Financial Market Development"; Taylor, "New Economics of Labour Migration"; De Haas, "International Migration, Remittances and Development."
50. De Haas, "Migration and Development"; Taylor, "New Economics of Labour Migration"; Kunz, "'Remittances are Beautiful'?"
51. Nurse, "Diaspora, Migration and Development."
52. Skeldon, "Migration Policies," 2. The inclusion of migration and human mobility in four of 17 Sustainable Development Goals is said to correct their absence from the MDGs. International Organisation For Migration, "Inclusion of Migration in UN Sustainable Development Goals, a Milestone," (25 September 2015), https://www.iom.int/news/inclusion-migration-un-sustainable-development-goals-milestone.
53. Sørensen, "Revisiting the Migration-Development Nexus," 65.
54. Gamlen, "New Migration and Development Optimism."

55. Munck, 1238. Chamie and Dall'Oglio, "Overview"; Newland, "Governance of International Migration".
56. Munck, 1238.
57. Wickramasekara, "Globalisation, International Labour Migration."
58. Martin, *International Labour Migration*, 201.
59. Koslowski, *Global Mobility*, 9.
60. Phillips, "Migration as Development Strategy?", 246.
61. Basok, "Counter-hegemonic Human Rights Discourses."
62. Thomas, "Convergences and Divergences"; Fudge, "Precarious Migrant Status."
63. Commission on Human Security, *Human Security Now*, 10–1.
64. Castles and Miller, *Age of Migration*, 41.
65. Martin, *International Labour Migration*, 204–5.
66. Munck, 1231.
67. Rodriguez, *Migrants For Export*.
68. Wilson, *Race, Racism and Development*.
69. Ibid., 3.
70. Rigakos, 64.
71. Smith, "Pacifying."
72. Wilson, *Race, Racism and Development*, 3.
73. Gagnon and Khoudour-Castéras, *Tackling the Policy Challenges*.
74. See Smith, "Bunk House Rules." For the roots of this argument see McNally, *Bodies of Meaning*. See also materialist feminist accounts, e.g. Hennessey and Ingraham, *Materialist Feminism*.
75. See e.g. Smith, "Troubling 'Project Canada.'" This appears to sideline analytical interventions on migrant incorporation or treatment, including ongoing practices of constructing migrant illegality/legality.
76. Ibrahim, "Securitization of Migration."
77. Wilson, *Race, Racism and Development*, 2; see also White, *Thinking Race, Thinking Development*.
78. Wilson, *Race, Racism and Development*, 11.
79. Smith, "Pacifying"; Smith "Troubling 'Project Canada'"; Smith, "Bunk House Rules."
80. e.g. Smith, "Bunk House Rules."
81. Wood, *Empire of Capital*.
82. Kiely, *Spatial Hierarchy*.
83. Wilson, *Race, Racism and Development*, 69.
84. Smith, "Troubling 'Project Canada.'"
85. Rodriguez, *Migrants For Export*.
86. Smith, "Troubling 'Project Canada.'"
87. Rodriguez, *Migrants For Export*.
88. See the discussion in Wilson, *Race, Racism and Development*, chapter 3.
89. Ibid., 76.
90. Amin, *Three Essays on Marx's Value*, 13. While I find Amin's formulation here quite instructive in framing my core interjection I am attempting to pose to TWAIL, I do not necessarily share all of his presuppositions.
91. See Wood, *Democracy Against Capitalism*.
92. Anghie, *Imperialism, Sovereignty*.
93. e.g. Chimni, "Marxism and International Law."
94. Knox, "Critical Examination"; Bhatia, "South of the North."
95. Amin, *Three Essays on Marx's Value*, 14
96. Wright, "Challenging States of Illegality," 198.
97. Ibid., 4.
98. Veltmeyer, *Bringing History Back In*, 13.
99. See Juss, "Human Security and Migration Control."

Bibliography

Alkire, Sabina. A Conceptual Framework for Human Security, Centre for Research on Inequality, Human Security and Ethnicity, CRISE, Queen Elizabeth House, University of Oxford, 2003 at 3-4. http://www3.qeh.ox.ac.uk/pdf/crisewps/workingpaper2.pdf.

Ambrosetti, David. "Human Security as Political Resource: A Response to David Chandler's `Human Security: The Dog That Didn't Bark." *Security Dialogue* 39, no. 4 (2008): 439–444.

Amin, Samir. *Three Essays on Marx's Value Theory*. Monthly Review, 2013.

Anghie, Antony. *Imperialism, Sovereignty, and the Making of International Law*. Cambridge; New York: Cambridge University Press, 2005.

Atak, I., and F. Crepeau. "The Securitization of Asylum and Human Rights in Canada and the European Union." In *Contemporary Issues in Refugee Law*, edited by S. Juss and C. Harvey, 227–256. Cheltenham: Edward Elgar Publishing, 2013.

Basok, Tanya. "Counter-hegemonic Human Rights Discourses and Migrant Rights Activism in the US and Canada." *International Journal of Comparative Sociology* 50, no. 2 (2009): 183–205. doi:10.1177/0020715208100970.

Bhatia, Amar. "The South of the North: Building on Critical Approaches to International Law with Lessons from the Fourth World." *Oregon Review of International Law* 14, no. 1 (2012): 131–175.

Bourbeau, P. *The Securitization of Migration: A Study of Movement and Order*. New York: Routledge, 2011.

Buzan, Barry Ole Wæver, and J. De Wilde. *Security: A New Framework for Analysis*. London: Lynne Rienner, 1998.

Canadian Association for Refugee and Forced Migration Studies. *Online Research and Teaching Tools – "Securitization of Migration"*. http://rfmsot.apps01.yorku.ca/glossary-of-terms/securitization-of-migration/.

Castles, Stephen, and Mark J. Miller. *The Age of Migration: International Population Movements in the Modern World*. 4th ed. New York: Guilford, 2009.

Chandler, David. "Human Security: The Dog That Didn't Bark." *Security Dialogue* 39, no. 4 (2008): 427–438.

Chandler, David. "Human Security II: Waiting for the Tail to Wag the Dog – A Rejoinder to Ambrosetti, Owen and Wibben." *Security Dialogue* 39, no. 4 (2008): 463–469. doi:10.1177/0967010608094041.

Chimni, B. S. "Marxism and International Law: A Contemporary Analysis." *Economic and Political Weekly* 34, no. 6 (1999): 337–349.

Choudry, Aziz, Jill Hanley, Steve Jordan, Eric Shragge, and Martha Stiegman. *Fight Back: Workplace Justice for Immigrants*. Halifax: Fernwood, 2009.

Commission on Human Security. *Human Security Now: Final Report*. New York: CHS, 2003.

Crépeau, François, and Delphine Nakache. "Controlling Irregular Migration in Canada: Reconciling Security Concerns with Human Rights Protection." *IRPP Choices* 12, no. 1 (2006): 3–42.

Dauvergne, Catherine. "Security and Migration Law in the Less Brave New World." *Social & Legal Studies* 16, no. 4 (2007): 533–549.

Eagleton, Terry. *After Theory*. London: Penguin, 2004.

Edwards, Alice, and Carla Ferstman. *Human Security and Non-Citizens: Law, Policy and International Affairs*. Cambridge: Cambridge University Press, 2010.

Faraday, Fay. *Made In Canada: How the Law Constructs Migrant Workers' Insecurity*. Metcalfe Foundation, 2012.

Fudge, Judy. "Precarious Migrant Status and Precarious Employment: The Paradox of International Rights For Migrant Workers." *Comparative Labour Law & Policy Journal* 31, no. 1 (2012–2013): 95–132.

Fudge, Judy, and Fiona McPhail. "The Temporary Foreign Worker Program in Canada: Low-skilled Workers as an Extreme Form of Flexible Labour." *Comparative Labour Law and Policy Journal* 31, no. 5 (2009): 5–45.

Gagnon, J., and D. Khoudour-Castéras. *Tackling the Policy Challenges of Migration: Regulation, Integration, Development*. Paris: OECD Publishing, 2011.

Gamlen, A. "The New Migration and Development Optimism: A Review of the 2009 Human Development Report." *Global Governance* 16, no. 3 (2010): 415–422.

Goldring, Luin, Carolina Berinstein, and Judith Bernhard. "Institutionalizing Precarious Migratory Status In Canada." *Citizenship Studies* 13, no. 3 (2009): 239–265.

Harris, J., and M. Todaro. "Migration, Unemployment and Development: A Two-Sector Analysis." *American Economic Review* 60 (1970): 126–142.

Hein de Haas. "International Migration, Remittances and Development: Myths and Facts." *Third World Quarterly* 26, no. 8 (2005): 1269–1284.

Hein de Haas. "Migration and Development: A Theoretical Perspective." *International Migration Review* 44, no. 1 (2010): 227–264.

Hein de Haas. "The Migration and Development Pendulum: A Critical View on Research and Policy." *International Migration* 50, no. 3 (2012): 8–25.

Hennessey, Rosemary, and Chrys Ingraham, eds. *Materialist Feminism: A Reader in Class, Difference, and Women's Lives*. New York: Routledge, 1997.

Huysmans, Jef. "Migrants as a Security Problem: Dangers of 'Securitizing' Societal Issues." In *Migration and European Integration: The Dynamics of Inclusion and Exclusion*, edited by Robert Miles and Dietrich Thränhardt. Madison, N. J.: Farleigh Dickinson University Press, 1995.

Ibrahim, M. "The Securitization of Migration: A Racial Discourse." *International Migration* 43, no. 5 (2005): 163–187.

International Organization For Migration. "Inclusion of Migration in UN Sustainable Development Goals, a Milestone." September 25, 2015. https://www.iom.int/news/inclusion-migration-un-sustainable-development-goals-milestone.

Juss, Satvinder S., ed. *"Human Security and Migration Control" in The Ashgate Research Companion to Migration Law, Theory and Policy*. Farnham and Burlington: Ashgate, 2013.

Kapur, D. "Remittances: The New Development Mantra?" United Nations Conference on Trade and Development G-24 Discussion Paper Series No. 29, May 2004.

Kiely, Ray. "Spatial Hierarchy and/or Contemporary Geopolitics: What Can and Can't Uneven and Combined Development Explain?" *Cambridge Review of International Affairs* 25, no. 2 (2012): 231–248.

Knox, Robert. "A Critical Examination of the Concept of Imperialism in Marxist and Third World Approaches to International Law" A thesis submitted to the Department of Law of the London School of Economics for the degree of Doctor of Philosophy, London, April 2014.

Knox, Robert. "Strategy and Tactics." *The Finnish Yearbook of International Law* 21 (2012): 193–229.

Koslowski, Rey, ed. *Global Mobility Regimes*. New York: Palgrave Macmillan, 2011.

Krause, Karl, and M. C. Williams. "Broadening the Agenda of Security Studies? Politics and Methods." *Mershton International Studies Review* 40, no. 2 (1996): 229–254.

Kunz, R. "'Remittances are beautiful'? Gender Implications of the New Global Remittances Trend." *Third World Quarterly* 29, no. 7 (2008): 1389–1409.

Lewis, W. A. "Economic Development with Unlimited Supplies of Labour." *Manchester School of Economic and Social Studies* 22, no. 2 (1954): 139–191.

Lillich, Richard B. *The Human Rights of Aliens in Contemporary International Law*. Manchester: Manchester University Press, 1984.

Lindley, A. "Remittances." In *Global Migration Governance*, edited by A. Betts, 242–265. Oxford: Oxford University Press, 2011.

Martin, Philip. *International Labour Migration: The Numbers-Rights Dilemma" in Global Mobility Regimes, edited by Rey Koslowski, 201*. New York: Palgrave Macmillan, 2011.

Matthews, Michael, R. Colin Gauld, and Arthur Stinner. "The Pendulum: Its Place in Science, Culture and Pedagogy." *Science & Education* 13 (2004): 261–277.

McNally, David. *Bodies of Meaning: Studies on Language, Labor, and Liberation*. Albany, NY: State University of New York Press, 2001.

Milanovic, B. "Global Inequality: From Class to Location, from Proletarians to Migrants." *Global Policy* 3, no. 2 (2012): 125–134.

Munck, Ronaldo. "Globalisation, Governance and Migration: An Introduction." *Third World Quarterly* 29, no. 7 (2008): 1227–1246.

Mundaca, B. "Remittances, Financial Market Development, and Economic Growth: The Case of Latin America and the Caribbean." *Review of Development Economics* 13, no. 2 (2009): 288–303.

Neocleous, Mark. "Against Security." *Radical Philosophy* 100 (2000): 7–15.

Neocleous, Mark. *Critique of Security*. Montreal and Ithaca: McGill-Queen's, 2008.

Neocleous, Mark. "Security, Liberty and the Myth of Balance: Towards a Critique of Security Politics." *Contemporary Political Theory* 6, no. 2 (2007): 131–149.

Neocleous, Mark. *The Fabrication of Social Order: A Critical Theory of Police Power*. Sterling, VA: Pluto Press, 2000.

Neocleous, Mark. "'The Problem with Normality: Taking Exception to 'Permanent Emergency'." *Alternatives: Global, Local, Political* 31, no. 2 (2006): 191–213.

Neocleous, Mark, and George Rigakos, eds. *Anti-Security*. Ottawa: Red Quill Books, 2011.

Newland, Kathleen. "The Governance of International Migration: Mechanisms, Processes, and Institutions." *Global Governance* 16 (2010): 331–343.

Nurse, K. "Diaspora, Migration and Development in the Caribbean." Canadian Foundation for the Americas [FOCAL] Policy Paper, 2004.

Owen, Taylor. "The Critique that Doesn't Bite: A Response to David Chandler's 'Human Security: The Dog that Didn't Bark'." *Security Dialogue* 39, no. 4 (2008): 445–453. doi:10.1177/0967010608094038.

Özcan, G., and G. Rigakos. *"Pacification" in The Wiley-Blackwell Encyclopedia of Globalization edited by George Ritzer*. Malden, MA: Wiley-Blackwell, 2012.

Phillips, Nicola. "Migration as Development Strategy? The New Political Economy of Dispossession and Inequality in the Americas." *Review of International Political Economy* 16, no. 2 (2009): 231–259.

Poe, Edgar Allan. *The Pit and the Pendulum*. Charlottesville, Va: Generic NL Freebook Publisher, 1993. eBook Collection (EBSCOhost), EBSCOhost. Accessed November 9, 2015.

Ravenstein, Ernst. "The Laws of Migration." *Journal of the Statistical Society of London* 48, no. 2 (1885): 167–235.

Ravenstein, Ernst. "The Laws of Migration." *Journal of the Statistical Society of London* 52, no. 2 (1889): 241–305.

Rigakos, George. ""To extend the scope of productive labour": Pacification as a Police Project." In *Anti-Security*, edited by Mark Neoceleous and George Rigakos, 57–83. Ottawa: Red Quill Books, 2011.

Rodriguez, Robyn Magalit. *Migrants for Export: How the Philippine State Brokers Labour to the World*. Minneapolis, MN: University of Minnesota Press, 2010.

Russo, R. "Security, Securitization and Human Capital: The new wave of Canadian Immigration Laws." *International Journal of Human and Social Sciences* 296, no. 3 (2008): 587–596.

Satzewich, Vic. *Racism and the Incorporation of Foreign Labour: Farm Labour Migration to Canada since 1945*. London: Routledge, 1991.

Sharma, Nandita. *Home Economics: Nationalism and the Making of 'Migrant Workers' in Canada*. Toronto: University of Toronto, 2006.

Skeldon, R. *Migration Policies and the Millennium Development Goals*. Policy Network Progressive Governance Paper, London, 2008.

Smith, Adrian A. "The Bunk House Rules: A Materialist Approach to Legal Consciousness in the Context of Migrant Workers' Housing in Ontario." *Osgoode Hall Law Journal* 52, no. 3 (2016): 863.

Smith, Adrian A. "Pacifying the 'Armies of Offshore Labour." *Socialist Studies* 9, no. 2 (2013): 78.

Smith, Adrian A. "Troubling 'Project Canada': The Caribbean and the Making of 'Unfree Migrant Labour'." *Canadian Journal of Latin American & Caribbean Studies* 40, no. 2 (2015): 274.

Sørensen, N. N. "Revisiting the Migration-Development Nexus: From Social Networks and Remittances to Markets for Migration Control." *International Migration* 50, no. 3 (2012): 61–76.

Stasiulis, Daiva K., and Abigail Bakan. *Negotiating Citizenship: Migrant Women in Canada and the Global System*. Toronto: University of Toronto, 2005.

Taylor, J. E. "The New Economics of Labour Migration and the Role of Remittances in the Migration Process." *International Migration* 37, no. 1 (1999): 63–88.

Themistocleous, Andreas. "Securitizing Migration: Aspects and Critiques." *The Globalized World Post*, 2013. http://thegwpost.com/2013/05/16/securitizing-migration-aspects-and-critiques/.

Thomas, C. "Convergences and Divergences in International Legal Norms on Migrant Labor." *Comparative Labor Law & Policy Journal* 32, no. 2 (2011): 405.

Todaro, M. "A Model of Labor Migration and Urban Unemployment in Less Developed Countries." *American Economic Review* 59 (1969): 138–148.

United Nations. *Office of the High Commissioner for Human Rights. The Rights of Non-Citizens*. Geneva; New York: United Nations, 2006.

Van Hear, N. "Reconsidering Migration and Class." *International Migration Review* 48 (2014): S100–S121.

Veltmeyer, Henry, ed. *"Bringing History Back In" in The Critical Development Studies Handbook: Tools for Change*. Halifax: Fernwood, 2011.

Walia, Harsha. "Transient Servitude: Migrant Labour in Canada and the Apartheid of Citizenship." *Race & Class* 52, no. 1 (2010): 71–84.

Wæver, Ole. "Securitization and Desecuritization." In *On Security*, edited by Ronnie Lipschutz, 1–3. New York: Columbia University Press, 1998.

Weber, Leanne, et al. "Migration Control and Human Security." In *The Ashgate Research Companion to Migration Law, Theory and Policy*, edited by Satvinder Juss, 535–562. Ashgate.

White, Sarah. "Thinking Race, Thinking Development." *Third World Quarterly* 23, no. 3 (2002): 407–419.

Wibben, Annick. "Human Security: Toward an Opening." *Security Dialogue* 39, no. 4 (2008): 455–462. doi:10.1177/0967010608094039.

Wickramasekara, Piyasiri. "Globalisation, International Labour Migration and the Rights of Migrant Workers." *Third World Quarterly* 29, no. 7 (2008): 1247–1264.

Wilson, Kalpana. *Race, Racism and Development*. London and New York: Zed Books, 2012.

Wood, Ellen. *Democracy Against Capitalism*. Cambridge: Cambridge University Press, 2003.

Wood, Ellen. *Empire of Capital*. London and New York: Verso, 2005.

Wright, Cynthia. "Challenging States of Illegality: From 'Managed Migration' to a Politics of No Borders." *Labour/Le Travail* 62 (Fall 2008): 185.

Index